Discrimination in Organizations

Using Social Indicators to Manage Social Change

Rodolfo Alvarez
Kenneth G. Lutterman
and Associates

Discrimination in Organizations

Jossey-Bass Publishers
San Francisco • Washington • London • 1979

DISCRIMINATION IN ORGANIZATIONS
Using Social Indicators to Manage Social Change
by Rodolfo Alvarez, Kenneth G. Lutterman, and Associates

Copyright © 1979 by: Jossey-Bass Inc., Publishers
433 California Street
San Francisco, California 94104
&
Jossey-Bass Limited
28 Banner Street
London EC1Y 8QE

Library of Congress Cataloging in Publication Data

Main entry under title:

Discrimination in organizations.

    (The Jossey-Bass social and behavioral science
series)
    Bibliography: p.
    Includes index.
    1. Racism—United States. 2. Sexism—United States.
3. Social indicators—United States. 4. Organiza-
tional behavior. 5. Organizational change.
I. Alvarez, Rodolfo, 1936–   II. Lutterman,
Kenneth G.
HN65.D496   301.18'32   78–62567
ISBN 0–87589–429–1

Manufactured in the United States of America

JACKET DESIGN BY WILLI BAUM

FIRST EDITION
Code 7931

The Jossey-Bass
Social and Behavioral Science Series

Dedication

To the Mexican American Legal Defense and Educational Fund (MALDEF) for its pioneering legal work for protection of the civil rights of Mexican Americans against all forms of institutional discrimination. MALDEF's national offices are located at 28 Geary Street, San Francisco, Calif., 94108.

Preface

Racism has been described by Dr. Bertram Brown, director of the National Institute of Mental Health, as "the nation's number one mental health problem." However, systematic research on racism has yet to produce a body of knowledge upon which practical solutions on a mass scale can be based. For example, during the 1930s and 1940s social scientists, notably social psychologists, focused a great deal of attention on racial prejudice—how to identify the prejudiced individual, how that individual learns prejudicial attitudes, and how these can be changed. That research probably received most of its impetus from the general study of the authoritarian personality and other such studies stemming from the activities of Nazi Germany against Jews. Later the same style of research on personal attitudes was applied to the condition of black people in the United States. But in contrast to this individualistic attitudinal approach, relatively little systematic research on the identification, perpetuation, and modification of institutional discrimination has been done. A formal definition of institutional discrimination is presented in the first chapter of this volume. In essence, the term refers to those institutional arrangements whereby certain categories of people are either excluded from or disadvantaged in the distribution of power, property, and satisfaction. In a sense, institutional discrimination is the obverse of distributive justice. The very concept of institutional discrimination is relatively new, having come into general use in the late 1960s and early 1970s. Perhaps before that time the overwhelming extent of institutional discrimination in, for example, education, housing, transportation, employment, and recreation precluded systematic research. The freedom rides, lunch counter sit-ins, and school desegregation efforts led to a greater public awareness of the pervasive institutional character of discrimination against blacks. The first decade the concept of institutional discrimination was in general use was characterized by imprecision and mere assertion that the phenomenon exists.

By 1974, however, the concept had been sufficiently developed and sharpened that institutional discrimination was accepted as a general phenomenon in society: some authors focused their attention on institutionalized racism and others on institutionalized sexism. Application of this conceptual approach would thereafter spread rapidly to study of the treatment of the handicapped and the aged. Nevertheless, in 1974, invoking the study of institutional discrimination was still more an invocation of a conceptual frame of mind than of a systematic approach to analyzing empirical data. This meant that discussion of institutional discrimination could be characterized in two ways. First, it was being conducted almost exclusively at a very abstract conceptual level. Whole institutional sectors of society at large were considered. For example, in the case of housing, all types in all areas of the country were treated as a unitary phenomenon and the discussion might encompass the role played by many other institutional sectors, such as the financial community and government regulatory agencies. Second, the abstract character of the referents meant that data consisted mainly of examples selected because they were convenient to a particular author's argument. Systematic data produced by rigorous measurement was all but nonexistent.

Discrimination in Organizations began in 1974 in our discussions on the steps necessary to analyze and act on claims and counterclaims concerning the existence of institutional racism. We quickly agreed the abstractness of the discussion must be reduced by focusing on empirical research on specific organizations rather than attempting to deal with such complex sectors of society as "transportation" or "education." Our concern was to deal with concrete organizations. They might be in the field of transportation or education, but they could be readily encompassed by a relatively small research project. We next agreed to focus on *measuring* institutional discrimination. This turned our attention to the work of the social indicators movement.

While the concept of institutional discrimination was being formulated, another set of social scientists was independently discussing how to measure social change as a phenomenon in society at large. This group was composed primarily of demographers and others oriented toward quantitative analysis and the use of mathematical techniques. They focused on developing a set of "social indicators" (somewhat equivalent to the well-known economic indicators) to describe and evaluate the general quality of life in society at any given time. Although still a relatively new development in social science, the social indicators movement had by 1974 made considerable technological progress. But social indicator models were still being used to describe the general state of society, that is, the attempt was to create "models" of society viewed as a social system and to understand how specific indicators of the quality of life (for example, rate of disease, amount of crime, and percentage voting in elections) were correlated to each other and to other aspects of social structure.

The idea from which this book was ultimately to emerge was to develop a small conference to bring together three principal groups of people to develop a new direction in the study of institutional discrimination, a direction that might have more explicit relevant policy results than the abstract analyses by which it was previously characterized. Thus we conceived of a "working conference" to which we would invite social scientists interested in applying social indicator models to the study of institutional discrimination within formal organizations. It appeared eminently reasonable to call attention to the potential application of technological advances in social indicator models to the study of structure and process within all kinds of formal organizations by focusing on the phenomenon of institutional discrimination. We sought by this conference to accelerate the construction of measurement and analytic tools (social indicator models). We limited the research conference to issues of sexism and racism within organizations. Although the issues of *personal* racism and sexism are basic to our society, systematic research on *institutional* racism and sexism has developed extremely slowly. But two recent studies of employment and pay have shown how institutional racism/sexism can be measured and studied across time. Phyllis A. Wallace and others discuss the court decision in the AT&T case in *Equal Opportunity and the AT&T Case* (1976). A methodology was developed to determine the presence or absence of discrimination in hiring, promotion, and pay and resulted in a consent decree that dramatically altered hiring, promotion, and payment of minorities and women. In 1973, AT&T agreed to pay $38 million in back wages and other adjustments, a figure later increased to $80 million. The use, or misuse, of psychological and "intelligence" test scores by AT&T was also drastically changed.

Somewhat similarly, Peter Nordlie and others of Human Sciences Research, Inc., developed a set of measures of institutional racism for the U.S. Armed Forces. Their measures provided a way for the army and other organizations to assess the extent recruitment and promotion were conditioned by race in contrast to education, time in grade, and so forth. Their methods enabled the army to look at actual changes—or nonchanges—within the army as a whole as well as within the various branches and units. Using the same measures across time, one could assess what progress was being made and examine, for instance, what was effective and where problems continued to exist.

What is unique about both of these studies is that they focus on the organization in which the discrimination occurs. In contrast to general demographic or census studies, which document the existence of discrimination against women or minorities but provide little leverage for change, these studies of particular organizations allow managers, citizens, or courts to hold the organization accountable for their discriminatory or non-discriminatory actions. In contrast to social-psychological studies of attitudes or good intentions or of executive orders, they enable one to assess performance and to monitor change. But these kinds of studies of an organization across time are relatively rare. This conference was designed to encourage researchers to examine institutional discrimination in its various forms and settings and to encourage them to develop better ways of measuring institutional discrimination in employment, in the provision of services, and so forth.

National Institute of Mental Health Grant No. USPHS MH14242 subsidized a symposium to explore ways of making the transition from applying social indicator models, which were being used primarily for labor force analyses, to organizational analysis. The Symposium on Social Indicators of Institutional Racism/Sexism, held on April 29–30, 1977, at the University of California, Los Angeles, was widely publicized within the social science community. An announcement of the symposium was sent to each member of the Section on Occupations and Organizations of the American Sociological Association. The Social Science Research Council graciously made available their list of scholars interested in social indicators research. Announcements were placed in various newsletters and other communications media of social science professional associations whose members might have a particular interest in the project. The response was most encouraging. Over two hundred papers and abstracts of potential papers were received; thirty-six were selected for presentation at the symposium and from among those, sixteen were selected for this volume.

The sixteen chapters reflect the current state of the art in the application of social indicator models to the study of institutional discrimination within organizations. It may be idealistic to say that the measurement devices presented in this book are tools that can be used to direct sociocultural change in the areas of racism and sexism, but we would not have embarked on this enterprise were we not somewhat idealistic. Better tools will surely be created as the technology of social measurement and public policy analysis develops. The chapters in this book were selected because each provides a special insight into some aspect of the effort to explore new ways of measuring racism and sexism within formal organizations. They should be viewed as a confident first step toward developing tools to open a new era in organizational analyses. These chapters provide only some broad vistas of the task ahead. They heighten rather than satiate the need for measurement tools that are valid both for research purposes and for monitoring progress toward managerial objectives.

A clear definition of the objectives toward which organizational effort and resources are to be committed is extremely important. Even very large and very rich organizations have limited resources; it simply is not possible to be all things to all people without endangering the organization's existence. Cultural values play an important role in defining managerial objectives. Neither the use of social indicator models nor the application of scientific analysis to the study of organizational performance can make value decisions for people. However, the understanding social science provides can help clarify existing alternatives and their reasonably predictable outcomes, given specifiable conditions. Social science does not provide final answers. Rather, as described in the first chapter, social science can be an important element in obtaining clearer understanding of existing alternatives and their reasonably predictable outcomes, given specifiable conditions. This process may require people both inside and outside of a particular organization to give priorities to their values, indeed, to choose between increased accomplishment on one or more values at the expense of compromise or abandonment of other values.

Social indicators thus contribute to increased rationality in the unfolding of social change—but not necessarily in the advancement of one set of values over another. Rather, social indicator models can help raise the level of collective consciousness with which other people choose the direction of their social and cultural evolution. As organizations face increasingly politicized special interest groups, they must present evidence of the internal state of affairs and of plans to change the state of affairs in desired directions. Among the most exciting contributions social science can currently make is evidence of the kind and degree of organizational participation by people traditionally excluded from organizational power and resources: the very poor; the very young or old; the physically or mentally handicapped; those with unusual sexual, religious, or political orientation; women; and racial-ethnic minorities. This volume focuses on the measurement of institutional discrimination against women and minorities. Clearly, however, the social indicators and the analytical perspectives discussed here can be readily used to analyze the quality of life experienced by other groups of people in their interactions with organizations.

Thus, this volume raises questions of distributive justice and its measurement that are of central concern to a wide variety of audiences: professional managers interested in improving production and commitment of personnel in their organizations, advocates of civil rights and civil liberties interested in safeguarding the rights of disadvantaged classes, social scientists interested in a deeper understanding of functional processes of organizations, and proponents of the increased use of social indicators for obtaining more precise measurement and monitoring the quality of life in the world around us.

September 1979   RODOLFO ALVAREZ
                                                    Los Angeles, California

                                                    KENNETH G. LUTTERMAN
                                                    Rockville, Maryland

Acknowledgments

Discrimination in Organizations represents an effort to demonstrate the utility of social science for formulation and implementation of public policy. Nowhere is the cooperative nature of social science more explicit than in this type of work. The editors are indebted to a wide range of individuals working in academic institutions, government agencies, and private organizations for their encouragement, support, and varied contributions that ensured the success of both the Symposium on Social Indicators of Institutional Racism-Sexism as well as in bringing this volume to fruition.

Because of the positions they held, members of the advisory committee to the symposium were particularly helpful: Carlos Alcala, civil rights officer for the California Department of Health; Edgar F. Borgatta, professor of sociology at Queens College; John Coffey, management consultant in Washington, D.C.; David A. Copus, acting director of special investigations for the Equal Employment Opportunity Commission; Martin H. Gerry, director of the Office of Civil Rights at the Department of Health, Education, and Welfare; Jose Hernandez, professor of sociology at the University of Wisconsin, Milwaukee; William Hastie, attorney with Public Advocates in San Francisco; John Koehler, assistant director for national security and international affairs at the Congressional Budget Office; James Morishima, director of Asian American studies at the University of Washington; Laura Nader, professor of anthropology at the University of California, Berkeley; James Ralph, chief of the Center for Minority Group Mental Health at the National Institute of Mental Health (NIMH); Sanford Jay Rosen, director of litigation at the Mexican American Legal Defense and Educational Fund; Richard Shapiro, of the section on racism and mental health, Center for Minority Group Mental Health at NIMH; James E. Teele, professor of sociology at Boston University; and Walter Wallace, professor of sociology at Princeton University.

During the symposium, April 29–30, 1977, the assembled scholars learned from three speakers who had been active in different public arenas about past battles in the field of public policy formation and the utility of social research in the courts. Although their speeches are not included in this volume, the thoughts they shared with us strengthened our resolve to produce a work as useful to managers as to researchers. For their insights and inspiration on the fight for social justice we thank: Ramona Ripston, executive director of the American Civil Liberties Union of Southern California; Stanley Pottinger, former assistant Attorney General, Civil Rights Division, of the U.S. Department of Justice; and Carlos Alcala, civil rights officer for the California Department of Health.

Special thanks for their distinguished work as research assistants and in reviewing early drafts of chapters in this volume are due to Carol W. Telesky and Gary Rhoades. Neither the symposium nor the preparation of the manuscript for this volume could have taken place without the cheerful and timely secretarial help of Wanetta Jones, Jackie Rosin, and Miriam Stein, as well as the wonderful staff of the UCLA Central Stenographic Bureau under the direction of Ellen Cole. Special mention must also be made of the cooperation and patience exhibited by authors of chapters in the preparation of this volume.

Finally, for their steadfast encouragement and support, without which our work could have never seen the light of day, we express our profound appreciation to our wives: Edna R. S. Alvarez and Jean C. Lutterman.

RODOLFO ALVAREZ
KENNETH G. LUTTERMAN

Contents

~~~~~~

xix

Contents xxi

The Authors

RODOLFO ALVAREZ is associate professor of sociology at the University of California at Los Angeles. He received his Ph.D. degree in sociology from the University of Washington in 1966. From 1966 to 1972 he served as assistant professor of sociology at Yale University and as visiting lecturer at Wesleyan University in 1971. While at UCLA he has acted as director of the Chicano Studies Center (1972–74) and was the founding director of the Spanish-Speaking Mental Health Research Center (1973 to 1975). Alvarez was president of Alpha Kappa Delta, the International Sociology Honor Society, from 1976 to 1978. He is a member of the board of directors of the Mexican American Legal Defense and Educational Fund and first vice-president of the American Civil Liberties Union of Southern California.

KENNETH G. LUTTERMAN is chief, Social Sciences Section, Behavioral Sciences Training Branch, Division of Manpower and Training Programs, at the National Institute of Mental Health. He received his Ph.D. degree in sociology from the University of Wisconsin at Madison in 1962. From 1953 to 1962 he was instructor, assistant professor, and acting chairperson of the Department of Sociology at St. Olaf College. Lutterman did his postdoctoral studies in psychometrics and econometrics at the University of Wisconsin from 1962 to 1963, where he served as assistant professor until 1968. He was visiting professor at Stanford University from 1974 to 1976.

DANIEL MENDOZA DE ARCE is professor of sociology in the College of Cultural Studies at Governors State University. He received his Ph.D. degree in sociology from the University of Uruguay in 1970.

ILENE NAGEL BERNSTEIN is associate professor of law and sociology at Indiana University. She received her Ph.D. degree in sociology from New York University in 1974.

BENJAMIN P. BOWSER is assistant dean of the Graduate School and lecturer in sociology at Cornell University. He received his Ph.D. degree in sociology from Cornell University in 1975.

WILLIAM P. BRIDGES is assistant professor of sociology at the University of Illinois, Chicago. He received his Ph.D. degree in sociology from Northwestern University in 1975.

SHIRLEY VINING BROWN is assistant professor and director of continuing education at the University of Maryland, Baltimore. She received her Ph.D. degree in sociology and social work from the University of Michigan in 1975.

JOHN CARDASCIA is a doctoral candidate in sociology at the University of Wisconsin, Madison.

PAULA J. DUBECK is assistant professor of sociology at the University of Cincinnati. She received her Ph.D. degree in sociology from Northwestern University in 1973.

PAULA ENGLAND is assistant professor of sociology and political economy at the University of Texas, Dallas. She received her Ph.D. degree in sociology from the University of Chicago in 1975.

JOHN P. FERNANDEZ is division operations manager, Customer Services, North Division, Bell Telephone Company of Pennsylvania. He received his Ph.D. degree in sociology from the University of California, Berkeley, in 1974.

LOWELL L. HARGENS, JR. is associate professor of sociology at Indiana University. He received his Ph.D. degree in sociology from the University of Wisconsin in 1971.

ANTHONY HAUSNER is a health statistician for the Office of Health Resources Opportunity, U.S. Public Health Service. He received his Ph.D. degree in social psychology from the University of Kentucky in 1975.

ROSABETH MOSS KANTER is professor of sociology and professor of organization and management at Yale University. She received her Ph.D. degree in sociology from the University of Michigan in 1967.

JOYCE P. KAUFMAN is employed by the U.S. Department of Defense. She received her Ph.D. degree in political science from the University of Maryland in 1978.

PETER MCDONOUGH is senior study director at the Center for Political Studies, Institute for Social Research, at the University of Michigan. He received his Ph.D. degree in political science from the University of Michigan in 1969.

STEVEN D. MCLAUGHLIN is a research scientist with the Battelle Human Affairs Research Centers in Seattle, Washington. He received his Ph.D. degree in sociology from Washington State University in 1975.

DAVID NASATIR is professor of behavioral science and chair of the behavioral science graduate program at California State University, Dominguez Hills. He received his Ph.D. degree in sociology from the University of California, Berkeley, in 1966.

PETER G. NORDLIE is president of Human Sciences Research, Inc. He received his Ph.D. degree in social psychology from the University of Michigan in 1958.

JAMES M. O'REILLY is a doctoral candidate in sociology at Duke University.

OMAR L. PERAZA is an executive with the planning and development department of Encyclopaedia Britannica.

BARBARA F. RESKIN is associate professor of sociology at Indiana University. She received her Ph.D. degree in sociology from the University of Washington in 1973.

JAMES E. ROSENBAUM is associate professor of sociology at Northwestern University. He received his Ph.D. degree from Harvard University in 1973.

CATHERINE E. ROSS is a doctoral candidate in sociology at
Yale University.

JORGE REINA SCHEMENT is assistant professor of radio-
television-film at the University of Texas, Austin.
He received his Ph.D. degree in communication from
Stanford University in 1976.

ROBERT SNIDER is a senior statistical analyst for Marketing
and Research Counselors of Dallas, Texas.

Discrimination in Organizations

Using Social Indicators to Manage Social Change

Part One

Overview

≈≈≈≈≈≈≈≈≈≈≈≈≈≈≈≈≈≈≈≈≈≈≈≈≈≈

The first chapter in this volume presents a theoretical overview that accomplishes two major objectives. First, it provides several new contributions to the growing literature on institutional discrimination. Moreover, it does so within a much broader conceptual framework than the subject is normally treated in, by noting the central role that *sponsorship* and *ascription* play in the allocative process as opposed to the traditional social science focus on *achievement* as the sole legitimate basis for societal rewards. The chapter makes the point that the study of institutional discrimination can be substantially advanced by focusing on the study of specific organizations as relatively smaller social systems than whole societies and thus more readily comprehended by smaller teams of social scientists with fewer resources. Additionally, the computer-assisted use of social indicator models allows for continuous monitoring of the allocative process and, thus, for guided social change. The second major objective of this chapter is to provide a conceptual context for the relevance and value of the more highly specialized investigations presented in Chapters Two through Seventeen.

1

1

Institutional Discrimination in Organizations and Their Environments

Rodolfo Alvarez

Measuring institutional discrimination within and between organizations with social indicators is the central theme of this volume. *Institutional discrimination* is a set of social processes through which organizational decision making, either implicitly or explicitly, results in a clearly identifiable population receiving fewer psychic, social, or material rewards per quantitative and/or qualitative unit of performance than a clearly identifiable comparison population within the same organizational constraints. This definition is equally applicable to larger social systems, such as whole societies; however, in this volume, it is used to

Note: I am deeply grateful to the many people who directly or indirectly assisted me in the preparation of this chapter. For their comments on early drafts, special thanks go to my six undergraduate students in a special seminar on institutional discrimination: Lynn Cadwalader, Percy Cerff, Chrissanthia Hillman, Felicia Jackson, Craig Koester, and Raymond Ramming. Valuable comments were also made by Edna Alvarez, Kenneth Lutterman, Shelley Mercer, and Walda Fishman.

guide research on specific organizations. The multiplicity of empirical referents in this formal definition and the complex interrelationships among them require the use of social indicators and sophisticated methods of statistical analysis. In many ways it is not possible to separate these technological measurement capabilities from the substantive issues in the study of institutional discrimination. This chapter attempts to provide an overall conceptual context within which most studies of institutinal discrimination can be understood. It also attempts to provide a novel conceptual approach that will stimulate new avenues for empirical research into the multifaceted phenomenon that is institutional discrimination.

Development of Social Indicators

Social Indicators generally refers to statistical indexes by which demographers, population analysts, and social policy analysts estimate the state-of-being of a given population, at a given time, with respect to a particular set of characteristics previously determined (or thought) to be relevant to the state-of-being in question (Bauer, 1966). Institutional sectors previously considered essentially independent of each other have been discovered to be intimately interdependent. This awareness has given rise to strong demands for careful consideration of the "environmental impact" of proposed changes in one sector on those sectors with which it is interdependent. The need for rational articulation between institutional sectors has focused the attention of a much broader range of social scientists on the value of social indicators for the production of information that can be used to assess the results and implications of given policies. This realization has in turn extended the range and character of indicators used and of population characteristics measured. Technological advances in computer design and increased availability of computers along with development of highly sophisticated methods of statistical analysis have made it possible to develop highly useful "social indicator models" of whole institutional sectors of our society (Land and Spilerman, 1975). These advances make it possible to obtain relatively realistic simulations of highly complex institutional sectors and continuously to monitor the implications of changes in one aspect upon a variety of other interdependent characteristics.

One limitation of the social indicators movement has been that the usual data base for such studies has been the general population of some territorial location—the country, a region, state, or city. This means that only social scientists with access to very large resources, such as computer facilities and U.S. Bureau of the Census data, are able to work with such large data sets.

A second, and perhaps more serious, limitation has been that the data employed by demographers and population analysts within the social indicators movement have pertained almost exclusively to characteristics of individuals. The individual person becomes the statistical unit of analysis. The analytical dimensions of which social indicator models are normally composed are therefore those characteristic of individuals. Although the distinguished accomplishments of the social indicators movement can easily be applied, they have not been brought to bear fully upon such issues as the analysis of institutional discrimination *within* specific *organizations*. Such application would do much to develop a more decidedly "social systems" perspective among social scientists concerned with the development of social indicator models. Moveover, it would further advance the application of social indicator models to interactions *between organizations* as an extension of the analysis of interactions between various internal parts of a single organization. Although such an effort has begun, it has not yet demonstrated its full potential, and most social scientists working in this area are still treating the individual as the fundamental statistical unit, rather than focusing on the organization.

The social indicators movement clearly has much to contribute to both inter- and intraorganizational analysis. The purpose of the conference of which this book is a product was to encourage and focus the attention of social scientists within the social indicators movement on the study of institutional discrimination as it occurs within and between specific organizations in order to move the discussion away from broad, and difficult to assess empirically, generalizations about society, a situation in which neither individuals nor organizations are accountable.

The chapters in this book are among the first concrete demonstrations of how this can be achieved and of how social indicator models can improve our knowledge about institutional discrimination. Moreover, accountability of what and how things are done in organizations is the quintessential managerial function. To adequately discharge that responsibility, managers need increasingly more precise and more frequent assessments of organizational processes within their purview. With computer assisted use of social indicator models, the modern manager in a modern large complex organization might be able to obtain an almost continuous monitoring of personnel and reward allocation processes. Continuous monitoring can facilitate greater control over the rate and direction of social change that an organization will undergo at any given time in response to specific pressures from specific constituencies, as will be discussed throughout this chapter.

Institutional Discrimination Versus Personal Prejudice

There are two kinds of institutional discrimination: primary and secondary. The distinction is important to the researcher and needs to be briefly discussed. *Primary* institutional discrimination refers to the establishment of *new* patterns of action within an organization. *Secondary* institutional discrimination refers to the *maintenance* of established patterns of action that impact negatively upon a given population.

The study of personal prejudice has a long history of significant accomplishments in social science. A great deal is known, for example, about conditions under which individuals of one racial or religious group develop attitudes and values harmful to the well-being of another group. The existence of personal prejudice among members of an organization, however, may be neither a necessary nor a sufficient condition for institutional discrimination to result from that organization's decision-making processes. Future research may produce empirical findings that require this analytical assertion to be altered, however. For example, it does seem reasonable to expect that the greater the prevalence of personal prejudice among members of an organization, the more likely the occurrence of institutional discrimination resulting from "purely" functional organizational decisions affecting the population against whom prejudicial attitudes are held.

Most organizational problems can be solved in several ways. The option chosen is usually justified in terms of its functional contribution to organizational effectiveness and efficiency. Needless to say, persons participating in decision-making processes may exercise their own personal prejudice against a particular population even to the point of selecting costlier and less effective options for the organization. However, even if none of the participants is personally prejudiced against a particular population, the option selected might still create a new primary pattern of institutional discrimination against that population. For example, the decision not to recruit from colleges more than five hundred miles from a corporate headquarters might be justified strictly on the basis of the extra costs involved, without any conscious thought that this new policy might preclude consideration of women or minority applicants.

The case of secondary institutional discrimination can be similarly independent of personal prejudice. Regardless of whether the original practice was consciously prejudicial to a given population, subsequent members of the organization may continue to carry it out without being personally prejudiced against the group in question. Secondary institutional discrimination may thus consist of simply carrying out traditional organizational practices without regard to, or even awareness of, how these practices impact upon particular populations. Organizations often have neither interest in nor knowledge of how their practices affect any given population; particular organizational goals narrowly conceived are pursued without regard for anything else. Another possible connection between personal and institutional discrimination is that unexamined traditional practices within an organization can provide the social context within which organizational participants learn values and attitudes prejudicial to particular populations. Observation that people of a particular race or that women are systematically excluded in the decision-making process may lead those who otherwise have the organization's well-being at heart to conclude that these populations are innately unsuited to participate

in the organization or to receive its benefits. These newly culti-
vated values of personal prejudice may subsequently figure significantly in both the failure to change existing practices and
the establishment of new institutional patterns in the same organization or elsewhere. For the time being, however, in the
absence of systematic evidence, it is important to proceed on
the assumption that personal prejudice is neither a necessary
nor a sufficient condition for even the creation of primary institutional discrimination. Seldom, if ever, are *totally* new organizational procedures invented. Rather, relatively new organizational procedures evolve out of old procedures as an organization
adjusts to changes in its internal and external environment. New
decisions are most frequently made by selecting options that are
most compatible with existing organizational practice. Thus if
established institutional practices already discriminate against
a particular population, it is likely that instances of primary institutional discrimination will occur as new procedures are
implemented so as to be compatible with the old. This aspect of
organizational growth and renewal *can* take place without personal prejudice playing any significant role.

The analysis of institutional discrimination can take place
at a level involving only organizational variables. The remainder
of this chapter constitutes an attempt to clarify some of the
conceptual and measurement issues that emerge in the study of
institutional discrimination and the conditions under which it
might be found.

Distributional Analysis Within Organizations

The definition of institutional discrimination used in this
analysis gives central importance to the idea of *distribution*. The
centrally important characteristic of distribution is not that it
occurs, or that some get more and some less, but rather that it
is *justified* in particular ways. The analysis of distributive justice
deals with questions of how it comes to pass that everyone in
a given social system, in this case an organization, comes to participate in the allocative process in such a manner that the share
they receive is normatively viewed as equitable or not. The obverse of that is that institutional discrimination deals with the

question of how it comes to pass that some populations get less than their normatively expected share in the allocative process. In either case the variable to be explained is justifiability; that is, on what basis can a particular distribution pattern be justified. Distribution may be considered the independent variable in this analysis; it is going to occur no matter what else takes place. The outcome of the allocative process is justified or not depending upon the normative interpretations of the *manner* in which the process operates even if by no more sophisticated an explanation than "might makes right." Thus we may view justifiability as the dependent variable in this analysis. The central and exciting part of the analysis takes place in the identification and articulation of antecedent and intervening variables by which to characterize normatively the process as eventually justifiable or not.

Justifiability is a phenomenon that needs considerably more scholarly and research attention than it has thus far received. Justifiability for allocation of rewards rests on the degree to which the contributions an individual makes are related to some aspect of organizational functioning. That is, the sole justifiable defense for a particular distribution pattern is that it is more or less required in order to obtain the quantity and quality of contributions needed for the organization to *do* and *be* what it purports. Presumably, degree and quality of task accomplishment will decrease to the extent that the organization departs from that pattern of reward distribution. Said differently: If an organization attempts to be something other than what it has been in the past, basic patterns in the allocative process must change so the same or new populations of participants are rewarded for the new amounts or types of accomplishments desired.

Past sociological analysis of the allocative process focused almost exclusively upon *achieved* characteristics of individuals thought to determine the quality and quantity of their contributions to organizational functioning. Levels of expert knowledge or degree of performance skill achieved are examples of these. Ideally, *ascribed* characteristics such as race, sex, kinship relationships, and other such "fixed" attributes of individuals were not deemed to have any legitimate role in organizational

functioning outside of very small personally owned and controlled organizations, such as the mom and pop store. When
found to play a significant role in other organizational settings,
such findings were deemed unusual and, implicitly, inappropriate. However, as Turner's (1960) analysis of sponsored versus
contest mobility among schoolchildren indicates, such factors
often come into play. The introduction of sponsorship into the
analysis of reward allocation has increased our understanding of
the process; but the implication remained that both sponsorship
and ascribed characteristics, upon which sponsorship was presumably based, are viewed as an illegitimate basis for reward still.
This analysis, by contrast, proceeds on the notion that all three
types of characteristics (ascription, achievement, and sponsorship) can contribute directly to task accomplishment within
organizations. It is the *level of contribution to task accomplishment* that determines the degree of justifiability in the allocative process. The hypothesis is that contributions to organizational task accomplishment based on sponsorship and ascribed
characteristics may account for such findings as recently reported (Long, 1978) that reaching the rank of full professor is
not related to the quantity or quality of microbiologists' research contributions. We may further hypothesize that sociologists have labored under the influence of a theoretically induced
blind spot in the assumption that only achieved characteristics
have a legitimate role to play in the allocation of rewards to
organizational participants. Those who manage organizations, as
opposed to those who merely study them, may have known all
along that sponsorship and ascribed characteristics make their
own extremely valuable contributions to the health and welfare
of an organization.

   Sponsorship refers to the fact that one or more persons
have an active interest and take concerted action to ensure the
allocation of rewards to a particular individual. Two major characteristics of sponsorship are the sponsors' reasons for acting as
sponsor and the location of sponsors inside or outside the organization above or below the sponsor. The sponsor's reason for
acting as sponsor may or may not include the achieved or ascribed characteristics of the person being sponsored. Most
likely, sponsorship occurs when the sponsor conceives of the

act of sponsorship as having some benefit to the conduct of his or her organizational function and at the cost of relatively little or no threat to the sponsor's own status and reward structure. The conditions under which acts of sponsorship occur is an important area for the future research on institutional discrimination. Another such topic is the relative effectiveness of sponsorship based on the location of sponsors. Six locations may be identified with reference to the location within the organization of the person being sponsored. Sponsors may be inside or outside the same organization and they may be at the same organizational level (peer) as that of the person being sponsored; they also may be above or below that level. This sixfold classification of sponsorship location may later turn out to be important in terms of the number of sponsors required to exercise a given amount of power or influence on behalf of candidates for organizational rewards. The visibility and the effectiveness of acts of sponsorship may vary considerably depending on the sponsor's location.

As noted earlier, one of the principal differences between traditional sociological analysis of the allocative process and that proposed here is that this analysis explicitly admits the contributions to task accomplishment that can be made by both ascribed and sponsorship attributes of populations that play functional roles within organizations. Traditional sociological analyses place disproportional, if not exclusive, emphasis on achievement characteristics. It is for subsequent researchers to determine whether the perspective advocated here can withstand the test of empirical evidence. This analysis views *justifiablity* as an outcome, that is, as the dependent variable, and distribution of rewards as the independent variable. Achievement, ascription, and sponsorship attributes of those who receive the rewards are viewed as either intervening or antecedent variables. By giving priorities to these three types of attributes, it should be possible to construct a Guttman-like scale (Edwards, 1957) of justifiability as in Figure 1. Another way of saying this is that the issue is not whether rewards are distributed to different kinds of people in different ways. Distribution occurs even if on no more equitable a basis than that might makes right. But that is precisely the point: On what bases can rewards be distributed

Figure 1. Justifiability Scale

	Task-Related Sponsorship		Non-Task-Related Sponsorship	
	Ascribed Characteristics		*Ascribed Characteristics*	
Achievement Characteristics	Task-Related	Non-Task-Related	Task-Related	Non-Task-Related
Task-Related	a	b	m	n
Non-Task-Related	c	d	o	p

Justifiability Scale

Highest	a	3	S/Achieve
	b	2	S/Ascribed
	c		Ach/Ascrib
	m		
	d	1	S
	n		Achieved
	o		Ascribed
Lowest	p	0	

in order to maintain a socially stable society in which the over-whelming proportion of participants believe themselves rewarded according to their contribution to accomplishment of the organizational mission and therefore attribute legitimacy to the allocative process? The threefold answer given in this analysis suggests the creation of a Guttman scale by which to measure the degree of justifiability of reward distribution within any given organization.

Figure 1 suggests the basis on which to construct such a scale. Cell *a* describes a very high level of justifiability for rewards allocated by an organization; all three types of characteristics (achieved, ascribed, and sponsorship) of organizational participants are directly related to the task they perform within and for the organization. It might be hypothesized that cell *a* describes the organizationally ideal extreme with an atmosphere of high morale and commitment to the organization and its purposes. Cell *p* constitutes what may be the least justifiable description of the allocative system within an organization, when organizational rewards are distributed completely independent of any strong direct relationship between the organizational task performed and the achieved, ascribed, or sponsorship attributes of those receiving the organizational rewards. Such wholly unjustified allocative conditions are probably rare in a statistical sense. An organization thus described might be viewed as sociologically pathological; low morale among those who actually do the work and high potential for disorganization through internal revolt or external takeover might be expected to result from such a corrupt allocative system. Perhaps the two extremes described by cells *a* and *p* are statistically rare. Perhaps organizational life in modern society is normally lived in the conditions described by cells *b* through *o* in the following Guttman-scale-like order: *b*, *c*, *m*, *d*, *n*, *o*. Higher justifiability for the allocative process is obtained when two types of task-related characteristics are present than when only one determines the distribution of rewards; and within that frame, sponsorship is what ties the allocative process to the distribution of power. It may be obvious, but worth stating explicitly, that stability within any social system is not likely to be obtained, and if momentarily obtained certainly not long maintained, unless the allocative process is in consonance with the distribution of power. Power is a potentially fluid phenomenon that can change location depending on a wide variety of circumstances. But it should be clear that without the sponsorship of powerful individuals or groups either inside or outside the organization, participants would have a very difficult time performing their duties; indeed, their duties are defined by the confluence of circumstances created by the demands of powerful elements. When a participant knows that his or her performance is sanctioned by some powerful element, it is not only psychologically rewarding in the sense of protection to self, but it is existentially meaningful in the sense that one's work product is useful to some compelling purpose outside the self.

Sponsorship creates the context within which achievement characteristics can become meaningful; what I have become and what I have the potential of becoming takes meaning within what is perceived to be existentially possible under the currently operative, or probably operative, power arrangements. The capacity to achieve in new areas is a way of bringing new participants into the organization and maintaining adaptability to the environment. But if the protection of powerful elements in the social system can be expected to be forthcoming only by excelling at skills that others can also achieve, the fear of vulnerability, should performance or achieved skills become increasingly difficult or unobtainable, will dictate that morale and high commitment might not be maintainable in the long run. Perhaps morale and commitment to the organization are best maintained in the long run by the widespread belief among participants that what they *are* also makes a valued contribution to their performance. Because ascribed attributes are viewed as "permanent," whatever contribution these characteristics are perceived to make to organizational performance produces the psychic assurance that the participant is not likely suddenly to lose his or her usefulness. This may explain why some elite groups go to such lengths to ensure that others do not aquire their attributes; by keeping themselves distinct they maintain their assured role in the social system. In summary, the proposed Guttman scale of justifiability gives primacy to sponsorship, followed by achieved and ascribed characteristics, in that order, under normal conditions. Under various conditions of crisis the exigencies of the situation may require a temporary alteration of this order so as to meet the crisis.

Some hypothetical examples may serve to illustrate some of the issues raised by the proposed formulation of the problem. Such an example might be the case of a female historian being considered for promotion at a major research-oriented university. Many aspects of her ascribed characteristics (woman) may be significantly related to her role in the organization were she a historian of some subject having to do with women. Her own personal experiences might be more likely to give her insight into a historical treatment of women than if the same work were to be done by a male historian. Obviously, she might take some things for granted and thus overlook some elements a male historian would question. However, traditionally, most historians have been male, so the influx of women into the discipline may be more likely to produce new insights based on task-related attributes of women. In any case the contrast in perspectives will surely enrich the discipline. The point is that ascribed characteristics frequently help to predispose people for entry into certain organizational roles; indeed, their ability to contribute to the organizational task may be to some extent significantly based on ascribed characterstics. This may be as true in the social and pscyhological disciplines where the researcher is part of the phenomenon being investigated (blacks studying black community norms) as in many other areas of science. For example, not only might Jewish scientists have a particular interest in Tay-Sachs disease, but their own personal experience might provide insights and clues that could influence the formulation of hypotheses and research strategies. Similarly, black scientists might have a particular role to play in the study of sickle cell anemia. The point is *not* that only people with certain ascribed characteristics can do certain jobs in an organization, but rather that *both* ascribed and achieved characteristics can be directly task related.

Similarly, sponsorship of a particular candidate for receipt of organizational rewards can be related to some specific organizational task or to the overall organizational mission. Sponsorship is a phenomenon that deserves much more attention from the sociological community than it has received. Perhaps the researcher's bias toward treatment of so-called achieved characteristics of candidates for organizational rewards has masked the impact of sponsorship on the allocative process. Perhaps also the procedure by which degree of achievement is determined in the allocative process may tend to make sponsorship behavior appear not as sponsorship but rather as merely an objective evaluation of the relative merits of candidates. For example, in the case of the hypothetical historian, letters of recommendation from other historians at the same or different universities as the candidate in effect "sponsor" the allocation of rewards in the form of determining whether that person's actual or potential achievements as a historian merit promotion. Such presumably objective evaluations may obscure such facts as personal friendships; a sense of commonality based on former prep school, college, or graduate school affiliation; common religion, social class, race, or sex; or a host of other possible characteristics of the candidate and sponsor that may or may not be related to the quality of the candidate's purely task-related contributions to the organization. It has already been noted that sponsorship will most likely occur when the sponsor obtains some benefit in the conduct of his or her organizational function at relatively little cost to the sponsor's own ration of rewards to performance. Assuming, hypothetically, that in the past the overwhelming majority of "distinguished" historians were white male graduates of private preparatory schools, ivy league colleges, and a handful of graduate schools at private universities, then a certain sense of threat to their own status might lower their evaluation of the achievements of nonwhite female graduates of public high schools and colleges and a wide variety of graduate schools at public universities. There may be a conscious or unconscious vested interest in helping people *like* ourselves succeed as a device to reinforce the validity of our own success. This interest may realistically vary considerably from those person's actual or potential contributions to the specific organizational task or to the overall organizational mission. Such sponsorship patterns may, however, be organizationally functional in an interorganizational system, such as the one that determines the value and prestige of history departments among research universities. If those whose opinions about the quality of academic departments are sought are themselves characterized almost exclusively by similar achievement, ascribed, and sponsorship criteria, then the candidates, the work, and the departments they rank highly are most likely also to be similar. We may sponsor people like ourselves elsewhere in the hope that normative reciprocity will ultimately produce an increase, or at least the prevention of a decrease, in our own standing. The increased confidence in a secure future that pattern of behavior produces may itself produce both organizational stability and higher individual productivity. For a host of reasons those who have sponsorship may in fact be better able to carry out their assigned tasks within the organization. Thus also the circle may be closed in a sufficiently large number of cases that the self-fulfilling prophecy obscures a considerable proportion of acts of sponsorship that may in fact be non–task related.

The obscurity of sponsorship may be dramatically destroyed when new populations (for example, women, minorities, public school graduates, or people of lower-class origins) begin to compete for higher-level positions. It may be that in stable organizations, as in a stable society, evaluations of what constitutes achievement meritorious of rewards is normally determined by those of higher social rank than that of the candidate. The boss determines which employee will be promoted. Except in rare circumstances full professors disproportionately determine who among their many junior colleagues will be elevated to the limited number of senior positions. Those in higher rank within the candidate's organization may consult their similarly high-placed counterparts in other organizations for "objective" performance assessment. But as already suggested, such objectivity may be more apparent than real, the sponsors acting more under "enlightened" self-interest than in accord with subordinates' performance. Organizational instability may be created as new populations expose traditionally obscured sponsorship patterns to new sponsorship patterns from peers as well as from persons of lower social rank both within and outside the candidate's organization. The fact that other women or minorities may act as sponsors for a candidate may be viewed as illegitimate or unjustified, not because sponsorship was not a critically important factor in the past but because it comes from a new sector of society, a sector that may not be perceived as at least maintaining, if not increasing, the prerogatives of those already in more powerful positions within the organization considering evaluation of a candidate for organizational rewards.

Sponsorship *of* and *by* populations that have not previously been able to compete for high-level organizational rewards may be continually called into question until, at least, either of two events occur. Sponsorship by new populations may begin to be viewed as legitimate when those already in power are satisfied that their power and prerogatives are not made vulnerable by the influx of the new populations. That can occur if they perceive that sponsorship is reserved for those whose achieved characteristics are truly task related to either or both their specific organizational function or to the overall mission of the organization and that such "new" participants have a stake in maintaining the organization's essential character. It may be hypothesized that when only the truly accomplished, by traditional achievement criteria, are sponsored by new groups, the truly accomplished among "traditional" organizational participants already in higher ranks will have no sense of threat; indeed, they may act as cosponsors for new candidates as a way of improving the quality of the organization. Less distinguished traditionals may be very threatened and react negatively. It may also be hypothesized that highly accomplished members of new populations who do not personally enjoy the sponsorship of organized groups among these new populations are more likely to be sponsored by highly accomplished traditionals because that reinforces the myth that only those who make the most and the best contributions succeed as well as because of the lack of potential threat of connections to groups that might make demands on other grounds. Later in this chapter the issue will again be raised in a discussion of representativeness versus representation of new populations. The sense of threat and thus greatest opposition to new candidates may come from traditionals who fear the modesty of their own actual or potential contributions might be revealed by comparison to the new candidates. A second condition under which sponsorship of and by new populations may come to be viewed as legitimate (institutionalized) is when sponsoring groups outside the organization of the candidate in question become sufficiently powerful to be capable of creating severe costs to the organization. The fact that organized groups of women sponsor a particular person for a position within an organization such as a university or business can directly affect both that person's and the organization's performance capacity. Women's organizations both outside and inside the university can generate a variety of obstacles or opportunities that impede or facilitate the university's functioning. The fact of sponsorship based on otherwise non-task-relevant characteristics of the candidate can thus become centrally task related. Under such conditions even persons of very modest actual or potential task-related achievement by traditional criteria may be hired and highly rewarded by the organization merely because they have the requisite ascribed characteristics and sponsorship by powerful new groups in the organizational environment. In the short run this tactic may be cost effective for the organization because it is thus allowed to continue operation until such time as more traditionally "acceptable" members of the new population can be found or until the balance of power changes and the organization can simply let these people go without fear of retaliation by sponsoring groups. Depending on the amount and kinds of organizational resources available, the organization may resist such pressures for a greater or lesser length of time. Moreover, whether the power of such groups is perceived as temporary or permanent and whether it is declining, holding steady, or increasing will enter into the organizational decision either to move competitively to defeat the efforts of sponsoring groups or to bargain, co-opt, or cooperate with them (Thompson and McEwen, 1958).

The institutionalization of new populations at higher levels within organizations than ever before (that is, the acceptance of their participation as normal and appropriate) most likely cannot be enacted outright or even in a short period of time. Rather, institutionalization is a crescive process. It is evolutionary. It requires the working out of compromises based on realistic assessments of self-interests and of relative amounts of power on the part of contending individuals and groups. Established groups may seek to protect their prerogatives by insisting that new sponsoring groups wish their candidates to be hired by the organization in question solely because of their "in-group" affinity and not by virtue of their achieved qualifications. Established groups are, at least initially, not likely to accept the argument that ascribed characteristics and/or sponsorship can have highly beneficial consequences for the organization, partly perhaps because acceptance of that argument undermines their claim that their rewards were based not on sponsorship or their own particular ascribed characteristics but on achievement alone. This argument will probably be used most strongly when sponsoring groups either inside or outside the organization are "below" the status level of the person(s) being sponsored. By contrast, new sponsoring groups may be hypothesized to seek greater participation of their own candidates in the allocative process by insisting that only persons equally or more highly qualified than competing traditional candidates are sponsored, thus pointing out that the only reason for exclusion appears to be either their ascribed characteristics or the fact of their being sponsored by new groups.

Moreover, new sponsoring groups may be able to articulate a case for the contribution that both ascribed characteristics and sponsorship contribute to specific role performances as well as to the organization's overall mission. In any case, once having hired and rewarded people with new ascribed characteristics, the organization may discover that these people can make extremely valuable contributions in unexpected ways. A woman historian may have particular insights a male historian might not; a black police officer might be better able than a white officer to function in certain social situations. The point is that whether ascribed characteristics, sponsorship, or achieved characteristics are viewed as actually or potentially making a valued contribution to the performance of specific organizational tasks or to the organization's overall mission is normatively determined. The accumulation of practical experience and systematic research as well as the evolution of cultural values determines what is normatively prescribed and proscribed in social mores no less than in legal regulations. These evolutionary interrelationships may not occur in any particular sequence. Thus women or blacks originally hired for reasons of sponsorship and/or because of legal regulations may later be discovered to be able to make outstanding contributions to organizational effectiveness precisely because of their ascribed characteristics and the fact of being sponsored. Note that some such job- or task-related contributions from ascribed characteristics and from sponsorship could not be discovered until *after* women and blacks were admitted to (that is, rewarded with) the position of police officer, for example. Hypothetically, then, institutional discrimination may have implicit severe costs for organizational functioning by preventing the discovery of adaptations that may increase organizational efficiency and effectiveness.

Justifiability in the Empirical Study of Institutional Discrimination

The study of institutional discrimination can proceed in either of two principal ways. The researcher may simply conduct a thorough textual analysis of policy statements that guide organizational activity in various sectors and at various hierarchical levels. Such studies can reveal how formal policy and procedures either implicitly or explicitly place disproportional burdens on a given population such that the ratio of rewards to performance that population experiences is less than that of a comparison population.

A different approach to the study of institutional discrimination, the approach employed by the vast majority of the chapters in this volume, proceeds by the conduct of empirical investigation of organizational activity. This approach may in fact be more appropriate because in our society most forms of institutional discrimination of the kind that concerns most of the researchers represented in this volume is legally prohibited. The fact that it is formally prohibited may prevent the explicit statement of discriminatory intent in policy statements. However, it does not prevent its existence through informal agreements, implicit understandings, or practices, the consequences of which were never previously questioned. The results of such agreements, understandings, and practices can be discovered through empirical analysis of the actual activities that transpire within and between organizations in the conduct of their mission. When such study is conducted at frequent enough intervals, it can have the effect of putting that organization under continuous monitoring. This kind of analysis is now possible through the use of social indicator models (Land and Spilerman, 1975). The use of such models is an important addition to the repertoire of analytical tools available to the student of organizations. Perhaps its most important research consequence is that it allows field experiments. When a large set of interrelated variables by which the organization is modeled is continuously monitored and a change in one variable is introduced and observed, it is then possible to observe directly how a multiplicity of other variables do or do not covary.

The empirical study of institutional discrimination begins with the comparison of the allocative experiences of two or more populations within a given social system; for all practical purposes in this book the social system is a formal organization of some kind. Institutional discrimination is *unjustified* disproportionate distribution. Disproportionate allocation is unjustified when it is based on characteristics (ascription, achievement, or sponsorship) that are irrelevant for accomplishing the organization's mission in which the population in question participates. Thus the initial finding of proportionate or disproportionate distribution among comparison populations does not of itself establish the existence of institutional discrimination. The issue immediately becomes whether the distributional patterns found to exist are *justifiable*, and if so on what bases. The level of justifiability for existing allocative patterns is established by the number of task-related factors (see Figure 1). In a just world, organizations would distribute the most rewards to those participants who can be best described by cell *a* of Figure 1; the next most to those in cells *b*, *c*, and *m*; followed by those in *n*, *o*, and *d*; and the least rewards would go to people described by cell *p*. The order of reward allocation would be determined by the number of task-related factors listed, within that number giving stronger weight to achieved attributes, ascribed attributes, and sponsorship, in that order. The critical element in the determination of justifiability is whether or not rewards are distributed according to the task relatedness of the contributions of candidates for rewards. Task relatedness refers to either the specific

organizational role a person plays or that person's contributions
to the organization's overall mission. It is unjust to distribute rewards on any other basis.

A Scientific Caveat

The empirical search for institutional discrimination is the
analysis of data in the attempt to identify unjustified distribution
patterns. Lack of justifiability is determined by the finding that
the populations compared are "identical" in every task-related
respect save for the critical difference of some non-task-relevant
characteristic or set of characteristics. In other words, given
identical task-related contributions, the comparison populations
are statistically expected to receive approximately equal reward
levels under the null hypothesis that institutional discrimination
does not exist.

Science does not proceed by finding that a relationship
among a set of variables is empirically valid or true. Rather, the
strength of a scientific explanation lies in the fact that it has *not
yet* been empirically disproven or invalidated. Thus scientific
explanation is held tentatively, in recognition that introduction
of another additional empirically measurable concept into the
analysis might generate observations that disprove the truth
claims of the explanation. Moreover, with each advance in
measurement technology, including the creation of new social
indicators, it is possible to introduce into the analysis other variables related to the criterion variable (distribution of rewards)
in such a way as to invalidate the truth claims of the original
proposition. Those propositions that fail to be invalidated by
evidence collected in a variety of instances, in a variety of ways,
from a variety of places, at a variety of points in time, among
a variety of people, and so on come to be regarded as scientific
laws simply because the continued failure of attempts to disprove them increases confidence in them. The point, however, is
that even so-called scientific laws are explanatory propositions
that are held tentatively until evidence to the contrary is found.
So it is with empirical analyses of the allocative process within
and between organizations. If distribution is consistent with the
task relatedness of contributions participants make to the social
system in question, we say it is justified. If not, we look for

"corruption" of that relationship by some non-task-relevant attribute; indeed, we say institutional discrimination has occurred. That corruption could be due to theft, mismanagement, or some other socially and/or legally inappropriate activity. When that corruption can be said to be based on the sex or race of participant populations, we call it institutional discrimination in the usual narrower sense. In its broader meaning institutional discrimination refers to social processes by which organizational rewards are distributed according to other than task-related contributions that are legally sanctioned by the given society. Criteria such as race and religion have by constitutional mandate been viewed in our society as inappropriate bases upon which to discriminate in the allocation of rewards beyond those areas in which these attributes are directly relevant to the task. For example, it is directly task relevant, and therefore appropriate, to discriminate against Southern Baptist ministers when hiring a rabbi for a Jewish synagogue. Discrimination on the basis of race is legal and constitutional for some purposes because it is an attribute directly relevant to the task. Other criteria such as sex and national origin can be determined by constitutional amendment or statutory mandate to be inappropriate bases on which to discriminate. However, the point must be emphatically made that what is viewed as task related, and therefore a justifiable basis for disproportionate distribution, clearly varies over time, place, and cultural context. Moreover, there is frequently a time lag between a cultural value acquiring saliency among a large constituency and that value being implemented into law. Thus until recent legislation, *age* was viewed as a justifiable basis on which to discriminate in distributional decisions, but it is no longer. Currently being disputed in our society, for example, is the issue of whether sexual orientation (homosexuality) is a justifiable basis for discrimination in distributional questions.

During a period of "cultural transition" much of the controversy revolves around whether there exists an empirical relationship between the characteristic in question and the task to be performed; and if there is, what is the nature of the relationship and its constraints on the task. Examples of current controversies for which more systematic empirical evidence is needed are homosexual teachers of young children and female

news reporters in male athletes' locker rooms. Those who fear
the potential loss of their own status or even of their jobs may
be most likely to call attention to the "unusual" features characterizing the new population rather than to their capacity to
perform the task independent of such an identification. Tolerance toward subgroups with distinctive values may vary according to the degree to which such "deviants" are perceived as
a threat to the rest of society, or for our purposes the organization in question. The greater the perceived threat, the greater
the intolerance toward those labeled "deviant" (Alvarez, 1968).

For all these reasons it is critically important that the nature of scientific explanation and the basis on which confidence
in it is built be clearly understood. In our society the charge of
institutional discrimination has serious legal and economic consequences and should not be lightly made. When charges and
countercharges are made and "scientific" evidence is presented
to defend such assertions, it is important to realize that decisions
made at every stage of the research process might have yielded
different results in any particular study. Confidence in scientific
explanation derives from the weight of cumulative evidence and
not from the results of any one study.

A Procedural Example

For illustrative purposes we may start with the lay observation that women are less frequently promoted to the position
of president in business corporations. The research process begins with the null hypothesis that there is no institutional discrimination (that corporate presidencies are evenly distributed
between men and women). The studies on the subject might
produce evidence that the distribution of corporate presidencies
is disproportionately biased in favor of men to a statistically significant extent. Legal charges might be made. Women's groups
might bring strong political pressure to bear on public policymakers to take action to improve the situation, for example, to
change social practices so the evidence will not invalidate the
null hypothesis. The business community might respond that no
action is required because they hire for and promote into the
position of corporate president only from among people with
relevant managerial experience. Studies could be initiated to

determine whether institutional discrimination impedes a proportionate share of women from acquiring the managerial experiences deemed important for eventual selection to high office. Other studies might inquire as to the actual relevance of
such experiences for performance of the job of corporate president. Assuming the task relevance of these experiences, still
other studies might compare men and women grouped by various categories of managerial experience. They might find wom-
en do get selected for corporate presidencies with greater frequency with increasing levels of experience but that at every
level, even the highest, of comparable experience men are more
frequently selected for corporate president to a statistically
significant extent. Thus we have "explained away" *some* of the
outcome variation on the criterion variable, but we have not
failed to disprove the null hypothesis.

If the process were to stop here, the weight of scientific
evidence would be in favor of the assertion that institutional
discrimination exists in the selection of corporate presidents.
In many situations the social and political pressure for change
of presumably unjustified patterns in the allocative process
grow more rapidly than the rate of increase in the cumulation
of scientific evidence that has public policy relevance. Such
pressures can and sometimes do result in costly precipitous action that subsequently is demonstrated as unnecessary by increasingly cumulative evidence. However, a certain amount of social
and political pressure is useful in raising public awareness of the
potential problem, with the result that alternative suggestions
are made as to reasons for the finding. These suggestions can in
turn be systematized and used in the next wave of studies. For
example, it might be argued that managerial experience alone is
not sufficient for successful discharge of the duties of corporate
president. Other achieved skills are also important. Moreover,
success in the presidency may be due only partially to what the
person has *become* (achieved attributes). Much of success in
that position may be due to what the person *is* (ascribed attributes). The fact that a person is tall or was a distinguished ath-
lete might inspire confidence in others. Motivating and inspiring
confidence in others may be a major function of the task of
being president. Similarly, success in the position of president

may to a very significant extent depend on "who is for you" (sponsorship attributes). The fact that a person has held office in a professional or trade association or is a member of a major country club or church or in some other way can be thought to have one or more constituencies of support that can play a role in achievement of corporate goals may be important in the selection process because providing leadership toward corporate goals is a major function of the task of being president.

The point is that public debate can bring out the fact that successful performance of the duties of corporate president requires a multitude of attributes, some achieved, some ascribed, and some based on sponsorship. Often persons who score maximally or highly on one attribute or set of attributes score minimally on the other two. The choice may then come down to that between a potential president who scores only satisfactorily (that is, minimally acceptable) on all three types of attributes *required* for the position of president versus another candidate who scores maximally on one or more attributes within a set or even two sets but is seriously lacking in one or more attributes within another of the three sets. In any case public debate heightens awareness of the multidimensional character of the problem.

The next wave of scientific studies would have as their objective the systematic analysis of data on each of the attributes (within each of the three sets: achieved, ascribed, and sponsorship) said to be directly related to the presidential task. The point is that the research process proceeds by continuing to introduce variables into the analysis until all possible task-related attributes have been taken into account systematically. At the end of the research process it may be found that there is no difference in the rates of women and men hired or promoted into the position of corporate president. It might be that when all known legally and socially task-related criteria are taken into account in the analysis, two things result. First, the proportion of promotions is much higher in those categories described as "justified" in Figure 1 than in the "unjustified." Second, the proportion of men and women does not differ to a statistically significant extent within any level of justifiability. In that event we have failed to disprove the null hypothesis and can with specifiable confidence assert that there is no institutional discrimination in the hiring and promotion of persons into the office of corporate president. In this case we have explained away all the originally observed variation between men and women.

If a statistically significant difference between the proportions of men and women continues to be evident even after systematically taking into account such a large number of task-related attributes, then we may assert the existence of institutional discrimination precisely because we have failed to explain away the originally observed variation. Notice, however, that failure to explain away the variation may be a result of the analysis not yet having incorporated all the key variables relevant to selection as corporate president rather than to the existence of institutional discrimination. Thus the explanation of the variation as due to institutional discrimination is held tentatively until further empirically based theoretical analysis can better account for the variation in results either by the identification of some key variable not included or on some other basis. At this point the question for the policymaker is how much evidence is *enough* before action can reasonably be taken? Certainly the time for action arrives when the cumulative weight of investigations tends to point in a given direction especially, so when, cumulatively, studies have systematically included nearly all known attributes making for success in the role of corporate president. At that point the difference in rates for men and women can be said to be unjustified and action should be taken. If studies have been properly done, they will clearly identify potential points of intervention on key attributes. If men and women appear to be fairly distributed on several key attributes, but not so on others, then changes in social policy can be focused on those attributes to produce the desired results.

For example, if persons who have been athletes or who are of large physical stature have been traditionally considered good prospects as corporate presidents because they inspire confidence, such assumptions may need further investigation. It may be that women and men are approximately evenly distributed on attributes other than physical stature. Women of large stature, although numerically few, might get promoted at a statistical rate comparable to that of men of similar stature. If women and men have approximately equal frequency of appointment within each descending size category, then the null hypothesis fails to be disproven and we must conclude that institutional discrimination does not occur on the basis of sex. However, there still remains the question of whether large physical stature is a pertinent task-related criterion for promotion to the position of corporate president. Indeed, because women become increasingly rare in ascending categories of physical stature and increasingly frequent in descending categories, it may be argued that physical stature acts as a *masking variable* to obscure the intention to discriminate against women. Research then turns to the issue of the degree to which physical stature is task related. Does it, for example, demonstrably improve the quantity and quality of presidential behavior for the president of a business corporation to be of large physical stature? Do large presidents inspire greater confidence than shorter ones? Do companies with large presidents show more profit over time than those with shorter ones? If it can be evidently demonstrated that these and similar questions must be answered negatively, then it can be argued that physical stature may be an explicit or implicit device by which to obscure discrimination against women or racial minorities whose average height is much below that of those normally chosen for the position of corporate president. Systematic research must demonstrate that a variable such as physical stature is clearly related to task performance for it to be a justifiable explanation for variation in promotion rates between men and women or between one racial group and another. Notice, however, that the analysis has contributed to the introduction of increased rationality into the selection process. Indeed, greater control is achieved not only over the selection of able presidents but also over the kinds of characteristics of presidents that may actually contribute to corporate organizational performance. Not only is personal prejudice put to severe evidenciary test, but so too are general cultural myths and corporate traditions that may have been unknown impediments to improved corporate efficiency and effectiveness. This control emerges from the resulting systematic knowledge of variables functionally related to promotion, which allows us then to make the substantive decisions whether to intervene in favor of other criteria.

The preceding example demonstrates the tentativeness with which research results must be held. Corporate traditions and cultural myths that in fact detract from corporate efficiency and effectiveness may be built into the research process in some obvious and some not so obvious ways. Depending on where the research process is truncated prior to implementing results for policy formulation, its findings either challenge or reify such myths. If the research process is truncated after the findings of no difference between candidates of either sex or between racial groups so long as comparisons are made within particular categories of physical size (that is, holding size statistically constant), then the myth of size inspiring confidence might well take on the halo of scientific support. If the research process is not truncated until it is determined whether size or some other factor inspires confidence and produces greater corporate efficiency, then a very different policy alternative might be chosen. Institutional discrimination may be consciously or unconsciously hidden behind such masking variables. The search for justifiability can thus be an integral and welcomed aspect of the search for improved efficiency and effectiveness in corporate performance.

There is still another side to the issue of justifiability of the criterion variables used to make distributional decision. Institutional discrimination may frequently be hidden under the myth of excellence. By using an unnecessarily high degree of what are otherwise task-related criteria, it is possible to achieve the same ultimate outcome as if the distributional decision has been based on criteria totally unrelated to the task. *The issue is how good is good enough for the task.* It is possible to "hide" intention to discriminate against a certain race or sex by setting the standard for decision unjustifiably high given the requirements of the task for which the distributional decision is to be made, even though all the criteria invoked can be empirically demonstrated to be task related. An analogy to efficient manufacturing may be instructive. In fulfilling their responsibilities to stockholders, a corporate board of directors may be viewed as fully justified in firing an executive who insisted on producing a machined product that, while good enough in terms of serviceability and marketability by being within 1 centimeter of specifications, was instead machined within .000001 centimeter of specification. Imagine the higher costs involved: higher-quality stock required to sustain the more exact milling; higher-quality milling equipment to operate at such high tolerances; stricter, higher-quality maintenance procedures and equipment to maintain operation of the milling equipment; perhaps higher-quality housing for the milling equipment; more highly skilled and experienced personnel capable of such esoteric work; and so on for a wide variety of other associated costs. A competing company could easily produce and market a product within 1 centimeter of specifications at such a substantially reduced cost as to take over the market for the product.

Institutional discrimination of this character is most likely to occur in institutional settings whose traditional ideologies and corporate myths set excellence as a goal. Research-oriented universities may be particularly susceptible to this aspect of institutional discrimination. For example, in hiring a professor at a major research-oriented university, the corporate myth that calls for hiring only the "best" could be used as the basis on which not to hire a black faculty member. If that person has published a book, the choice could go to the candidate who published two or three; if the black candidate is known to be a good teacher, the choice could go to someone who has won a national teaching award. The criteria are all task relevant, but the degree to which they are exemplified can be *beyond* task relevance, the defense being that the decision was based on excellence, not race. Another variation of this phenomenon consists of giving extraordinarily high importance to one criterion within a set of relevant criteria. In the case of the hypothetical professor, insisting the candidate have published a book in spite of other comparable work, such as professional articles or excellence in teaching or in community service, could be used to mask racial or sexual discrimination as an institutional policy when such a narrow standard is neither necessary nor useful for performance of the professorial role. Indeed, requiring such a high degree of professional excellence on such a narrow dimension of all its professors might be excessively costly for the university in a wide variety of ways analogous to the wastefulness of producing a machined product of much greater precision than either the task or the market requires. Institutions that have a generalized goal of excellence, such as universities generally but also professional schools and professional associations, may be particularly susceptible to this type of institutional discrimination. To be sure, excellence is a highly desirable goal. However, not every professor needs to have won a Nobel prize in order to be an excellent faculty member; it is impractical to set that as an institutional goal.

Moreover, the criteria for excellence in the pursuit of one goal need not be the same as the criteria for excellence in the pursuit of other goals. Universities, like most large complex organizations in which most of the work of modern society is performed, has a multiplicity of goals, each of which is differentially pursued within various sectors of the organization and within levels of each sector. A university may espouse affirmative action among faculty as a way of being responsive to the needs of nontraditional populations, for example, an ethnic minority community that traditionally is not well represented among students or for whose needs traditional academic research is relatively irrelevant. However, the hiring and promotion of faculty with nontraditional research interests, styles of work, and extrauniversity involvements may be brought to a standstill through institutionalized decision-making processes wherein traditionally oriented faculty anonymously apply criteria that, although perhaps relevant to traditional subjects and areas of academic work, might be much less or not at all relevant to the type of work the university may in fact need done by new nontraditional faculty. Faculty, after all, like high-level corporate officers, participate in the overall success of the organization both in terms of the specific role they play in particular positions as well as through a wide variety of nonroutine, highly particularized contributions to the accomplishment of the organization's overall mission in society.

In short, the organizations through which most of the work of modern society is done are complex; they simultaneously have to accomplish a great multiplicity of goals. Some of these goals may be or appear to be contradictory to a greater or lesser extent. The degree to which various constituencies inside and outside the organization are aware of their own capacity to influence organizational behavior affects their willingness to grant or withhold their approval of what and how things are done by the organization. Conflicting demands by countervailing interests normally lead to a series of temporary standoffs whereby each interest group obtains the minimum rewards sufficient to satisfy it and obtain its willing approval of organizational practices consistent with the similar satisfaction of all other actively contending interest groups. No contending interest can maximize the types and amounts of rewards it seeks without dangerously reducing the satisfaction of others and thereby threatening the organization's viability. These standoffs are temporary because of constantly changing conditions that momentarily make one group, in a sense, more essential than others. Moreover, as obviously important contending groups learn to coordinate their activities to mutually improve the benefits they obtain from the organization, the consciousness of other, previously satisfied groups is aroused regarding their decreasing relative share of organizationally available rewards. Consciousness may lead to effective mobilization, which can lead to a new accommodation that seeks the minimum satisfaction of each of the now actively contending groups in order to preserve the system for the mutual benefit of all.

The preceding discussions may be summarized by two major points. The search for justifiability of the decision to discriminate in the allocative process leads to the empirical verification (1) that the criteria on which the discriminative decision is made are actually related to task performance and (2) that the level of performance required on those criteria is appropriate to the particular corporate objectives for which the decision is made. Justifiability, then, is a question of applying proper criteria, at proper times, to proper personnel, for proper objectives. It remains to be seen whether instruments (social indicators) can be developed to assess empirically the degree to which this fine-tuned matching of criteria to performance level to personnel to corporate goal actually takes place in organizations of various kinds in our society.

Organizationally Distributed Rewards

Depending on the organizational task in question and the level of performance required for that task, some types of organizationally distributed rewards are more pertinent than others. Moreover, rewards are devices by which to elicit and sustain the kind of performance desired. Thus because the desired performance may be the result of some combination of achieved, ascribed, or sponsorship factors, the usual organizationally distributed rewards may vary widely over the following major types: participation, opportunity (access), wealth, nonmaterial rewards and punishments, and power.

Participation

Perhaps the single most important reward organizations in modern society can bestow on individuals is *participation*. The sheer fact of how a population is distributed within an organization is differentiable from subsequent "opportunity" that may be available to incumbents of certain positions. Opportunity as an organizational reward will be discussed later. Participation is basic in that *whether* it occurs and, if it does, *how* it occurs may in fact set the basis for distribution of all other organizational rewards. Participation is discussed here as the distribution of populations to positions, which can be of two kinds: physical and social.

Physical Distribution. The physical distribution of populations of interest (women and racial minorities) to positions within organizations can be conceptualized in at least four major ways: horizontal, vertical, sectorial, and locational. Horizontal distribution refers to the proportional distribution of persons at the same organizational level within a given organizational hierarchy (for example, supervisors within a marketing division). In this case the questions asked would center around issues such as the proportion of women or minority persons in supervisory positions. The universe to which reference would be made in this case would be that particular horizontal slice of the organization. By contrast, vertical distribution refers to the comparative proportions of either minority persons or women employed at the various hierarchical levels of the organization within that particular hierarchy. The basic issue would be whether proportional representativeness at each level of the hierarchy were equal for each population. Thus entry into this area of investigation might begin by asking whether the proportion of women at the department head level within the marketing division of a large corporation were equal to the proportion of women at lower levels, such as supervisor, salesperson, secretary, or clerk.

The third major area of comparison is that of whole operational *sectors* of the organization with one another. In this case the comparison might be between the entire marketing division and each other division within the organization as whole entities (for example, divisions of engineering, security, maintenance, planning, and research). The guiding question would be whether the population in question (women) is comparatively distributed in equal proportions within the set of organizational sectors. It might be, for example, that in an automobile manufacturing organization women constitute 50 percent of the marketing division but less than 1 percent of the engineering and design divisions. In that hypothetical organization it would be conceivable for women to be distributed in equal proportions (1 percent) at every level of the hierarchy within the engineering and design divisions. Thus representativeness on a vertical dimension might be viewed as more evenly distributed than in the marketing division, where women might constitute 100 percent of the secretaries and nearly that proportion of salespersons but none at any other levels such that an overall distribution of 50 percent within the division would be highly skewed toward the bottom end.

Analysis of distribution of populations by organizational sectors is very similar to analysis by the fourth area, location. A corporation may achieve complete representativeness of minority personnel vertically, horizontally, and sectorially at its branch location in Georgia but fail to do so at its branch location in Oregon (in the case of multinational corporations the comparison might be between the United States and South Africa). Thus interesting issues in the study of equality can be generated by these hypothetical examples. Without prematurely entering the discussion of other distributional dimensions, it is important to note that achievement of proportional distribution on one dimension of analysis can be far from satisfactory from another analytical perspective. One hypothetical case might be viewed as more equitable than another because of what will be discussed later as the distribution of power. That is, overall, women might be viewed as better off if they held 1 percent of the positions at each hierarchical level (including the vice-presidential level) than if they held 100 percent of the positions at a substantially lower level and none of the power-exercising positions above. A similar example is that of having *some* positions at all organizational locations as compared to having many positions in one location but none in all the others.

Horizontal, vertical, sectorial, and locational distributional issues are conceptually independent of each other; but in any concrete situation these issues might objectively not be separable. However, the researcher is constrained to separate them analytically in order to be able to collect relevant information for empirical analysis and to point to the precise junctures at which interventions can be introduced. Statistically the critical issue is twofold: The population in question (minorities or women) must be distributed "comparatively equally" *within* each of these four major aspects of organizational structure as well as *between* them. It can be asserted that without comparatively equal physical distribution of populations all other questions of social distribution go begging. The following discussion of representation versus representativeness demonstrates the critical nature of physical distribution as the base on which subsequent questions of social distribution are built.

Social Distribution. Independent of questions dealing with representativeness along vertical, horizontal, sectorial, or locational dimensions of the organization is the issue of fundamental consequence that has to be addressed in the study of institutional discrimination. That thorny subject is the issue of *representation* versus *representativeness.* This is a question of what social meaning is given to the distribution of people and the ideological perspectives they hold. Although it is a fundamental subject, representation is a phenomenon that is both elusive and difficult to measure in empirical terms. *Representation* refers to advocacy for the interests of a particular popula-

tion whether or not the advocate is a member of that population. *Representativeness* refers to the distribution of members
of a particular population within vertical, horizontal, sectorial,
and locational dimensions of an organization whether or not
any of the distributed persons actually engage in representation
(advocacy) for the interests of the given population.

Militant activists for a given cause frequently are heard
to make charges of "opportunism," "sell out," and "assimila-
tionist" against persons who by some objective sexual or racial
criterion have to be included as members of the population in
question but who nevertheless do not advocate or even espouse
values that population presumably holds. Instead, these persons,
who may well have been distributed within the organization to
achieve an organizational defense against the charge of nonrep-
resentativeness, take on the organization's prevailing values.
Thus it is conceivable, at least in a hypothetical sense, that
a black community that believes itself exploited by the institutional practices of a supermarket would continue to believe itself exploited even after a change in hiring practices resulted in
representative proportions of black people at all vertical, horizontal, and sectorial dimensions of the market. New people
hired might be viewed as believing in and subscribing to the
same institutional practices previously considered detrimental
to the interests of the black community. The question of representation, unlike that of representativeness, invokes ideas of
loyalty to and advocacy for given values and objectives. Given
a measure of regard and security for themselves, representatives
of a given population could possibly prefer to engage in representation of the organization's interests over or against the collectively self-perceived interests of the population from which
the representative originated. It is difficult enough for social
scientists to develop measurement tools to measure representativeness; it is many times more difficult, if indeed it is possible
at all, to develop tools that systematically measure representation (its quantity and quality).

The contraposition between representativeness and representation raises still another measurement dilemma. The dilemma of how to achieve *legitimacy* may well be more properly
discussed in the section on the distribution of power, but it

should at least be mentioned here. It remains for future researchers to determine whether it is empirically the case that
representation is more likely to be achieved through representativeness. Even if most blacks in an organization give primacy to
traditional organizational values rather than to distinctively
black community values, some may still find ways of introducing black community values so as to modify institutional practices and achieve more favorable outcomes for the black population. Perhaps the probability of black community representation
is much higher among black participants than it would be among
even the most well-intentioned organizational participants of
other racial and ethnic backgrounds. That is an empirical question that remains to be answered.

Another empirical question, the answer to which appears
much more obvious, although systematic evidence is lacking, is
the question of satiation of protests. Protest is much less likely
to be satiated when a population is told to view a nonmember
as representative of that population's best interests. It appears
that most communities whose consciousness-of-kind has been
raised to the point of taking action against a particular organization become satiated as to their perception of legitimate action
on the part of the organization when they are convinced of substantial representativeness of their own group within the organization's ranks. Perhaps representativeness serves to reduce fear
and the perception of threat, thus increasing perception by
a population of legitimate action on the part of organization.
Even if the perception of threat is not reduced and the observing population fears wrongful action by the organization (perhaps representativeness is perceived to be achieved by coopta-
tion of traitors or "sellouts"), it may still be more difficult
to attack an organization characterized by representativeness
than one that is not. There remains, for example, the doubt
that those accused of selling out the popular interests may in fact
be falsely accused and should be given time to prove their loyalty. It is in this sense that some organizations may engage in the
manipulation of legitimacy. An organization may in fact make
it patently clear to its personnel that their own *personal* interests
require a particular organizational stance and thus have these
"ethnic" representatives act as advocates of organizational poli-

cy to the "ethnic" population, rather than the reverse. Hypothetically, organizational policy might be more believable and
less threatening when enunciated by representatives of a particular population even though it remains essentially unchanged
with regard to its impact on that population's interests.

The issue of the legitimacy of organizational policy is
inextricably intertwined with the tension between representation and representativeness in ways that need a considerable
amount of empirical research. That kind of research question
will require much work to develop empirical measurement instruments to determine levels of legitimacy attributed to organizational policy by given populations under given conditions of
representation and representativeness. Moreover, the issue of
power, which will be raised later, is also intricately intertwined
with that of representation and representativeness. Different
population groups are able to amass and wield different kinds of
power (normative, utilitarian, coercive). Their location within
a broadly conceived social system allows certain population
groups to provide varying amounts of sponsorship to individuals
and to groups.

From a certain perspective, sponsorship can be viewed as
the willingness to exercise power on behalf of a given individual
or category of individuals. Many members of a given population
acting in concert can successfully sponsor the greater allocation
of rewards to an individual even though they are located below
that person in the organization's stratificaton system. They may
even be more effective if they act from outside the organization,
where they may be freer from the threat of reprisals. One or
a few well-placed sponsors *above* the individual being sponsored
might be just as or even more efficient in accomplishing the task.
The point is that the sponsor's power is in part independent and
in part dependent upon the sponsor's social system location: inside or outside the organization and above, at the same level, or
below that of the person being sponsored. A second point is
that the amount of manifest power a sponsoring group is able to
muster will determine the manner in which the organization is
likely to deal with their acts of sponsorship. Weak groups are
likely to be dealt with by competitive strategies. As was the
case with the Bureau of Indian Affairs for many decades,

a weak group is likely to be told that their representativeness within the organization is unimportant and that their peculiar interests and perspectives can be better represented by a non-Indian.

The potential for exploitation is obvious. Organizations deal with stronger groups according to a variety of strategies selected first on the basis of whether their power is viewed as increasing, decreasing, or holding steady and second on whether their power is viewed as short term, of moderate duration, or potentially of very long duration. Bargaining, co-optation, and cooperation with such sponsoring groups are strategies that will ultimately result in varying degrees of representation and representativeness of the given population within the organization. The degree of *legitimacy* attributed by the sponsoring population to the degree of its representativeness or representation within the organization will surely depend on whether its own consciousness-of-kind and its power are increasing or decreasing.

Distribution of Material and Nonmaterial Rewards and Punishments

Each of the chapters in this book touches to some extent on four types of rewards and punishments that can be said to be distributed to populations within organizations. Some of these rewards or punishments are more easily measurable than others. Consequently, some are merely mentioned as elements for which it would be desirable to develop social indicators. Others can actually be taken into account. Each type of reward/punishment will be discussed very briefly, starting with the most tangible, therefore the most measurable, and moving toward the least tangible.

Financial Distribution. Distribution of finances can be of two kinds: pay and organizational wealth. The issue of distribution of pay to populations within organizations has received considerable research attention and has been the basis for some lawsuits. The issue is most simply summarized as: "Equal pay for equal work." The research question is not merely whether all members of the criterion population (women) in an organization receive an average rate of pay less than the average received by all men in the organization. That is a useful overall statistic;

but generally fewer women have traditionally been appointed at the higher organizational levels, so that average would reflect gross differences in the vertical, sectorial, or locational distribution of that population. The research question thus quickly becomes whether differential rates of pay for men and women exist under the same organizational constraints. Although some researchers are willing to stop at that, clearly there is a need to introduce into the analysis such variables as time in grade, prior professional experience, pertinent educational experience and training, and other related factors. Not only can introduction of these variables provide an explanation for differential rates of pay, it also provides knowledge of intervention points for effective management. This type of anlaysis must proceed cautiously because racial minorities and women may possibly not be given the same organizational job title as their white or male counterparts when in fact they perform the same function. Thus the researcher has to exercise care and ingenuity in ensuring comparability of function and not merely similarity of job title.

The issue of differential distribution of organizational wealth is perhaps more difficult to grasp than that of equal pay for equal work. Institutional discrimination may exist in the manner in which perquisites of office are distributed to people at the same organizational rank. People at the same organizational level may receive equal pay; but because of the particular job assignment or official position, some may have access to and use of organizational resources not available to others of the same rank. The assistant to the vice-president for public relations may have an expense account; the assistant to the vice-president for plant maintenance might earn approximately the same salary, but that role might not be deemed to merit an expense account, or at least not one of the same size. To the extent that racial minorities or women are differentially distributed to various types of positions, even within the same organizational level and at equal pay rates, there may still exist differential distribution of organizational wealth.

Promotion in rank has not only material implications in that it is normally associated with higher pay, but frequently it is associated with the right to greater *use* of organizational wealth as well. Moreover, as will be discussed in subsequent sections, it also has implications for greater exercise of organizational power as well as being a psychic reward in that it is tangible evidence that the individual is valued by and valuable to the organization. Thus development of social indicators by which to measure not only the very act of promotion but a broad variety of its attendant characteristics is of considerable importance to the study of institutional discrimination. Some of the chapters in this volume attempt to investigate the problem of differential promotion rates by sex and by race. These chapters reveal that a great deal of empirical research and theoretical development remains to be done around the concept of promotion. What is the negative psychic impact, for example, of nearly assured failure to be promoted upon women and minorities in some organizations as contrasted to the positive psychic impact upon nonminority males of knowing they have a realistic opportunity for advancement without fear of arbitrary exclusion? That touches on the perception of opportunity, which will be discussed later but needs to be mentioned here as an aspect of how organizational wealth is distributed. Systematic empirical analyses of promotion may eventually turn out to be among the most fruitful by-products of using social indicators to study institutional discrimination.

Power Distribution. Distribution of *power* within organizations is perhaps even more difficult to measure than the distribution of organizational wealth. Power, whether viewed as the capacity to get things done, as Rosabeth Kanter defines it in Chapter Two, or defined in traditional Weberian terms, is among the most crucial organizational elements. Yet it is also among the most difficult to measure. It is a commonplace observation that organizational charts do not necessarily reveal the real location of organizational power. One of the consequences of the study of institutional discrimination is that it is focusing research attention once again on this critical variable in the study of organizations.

Theoretical analyses based on Max Weber's classic description of normative, remunerative, and coercive forms of power are numerous in the research literature on organizations (see Etzioni, 1961). However, I know of no social indicators that permit quantitative measurement of these three aspects of power.

Such measurement requires the existence of a generally accept-able definition of power. A useful definition may be the follow-ing: Power is the ability of party A to obtain compliance from party B, with or without regard to either party B's or C's wishes, where party C refers to the majority of all other parties who to-gether with A and B constitute the social system in question. Authority or legitimized power is the ability of party A to secure compliance from party B *with* the consent of either or both party B and C. Thus even though party B might not consent to A's exercise of power over B, it may still carry the weight of authority because others (that is, C) believe that exercise of power to be proper. Thus others in the institutionalized net-work of relationships would participate in securing compliance from B. Similarly, party B may willingly comply with A, but C may not approve it as being in the general interest of the social system. Thus, party B may be in violation of C's normative stan-dards (some of which may be informal while others may be formalized into rules or even laws) by complying with A. The point is that A's power is legitimized and thus takes on the spe-cial character of authority by virtue of the willingly given ap-proval of B and C. The source of A's power comes from either normative, remunerative, or coercive means. In most situations, some combination of all three types of power is operative, which makes it very complicated to determine whether the granting or withholding of rewards is justified (as previously discussed in the procedural example).

The attempt to measure power and authority within or-ganizations through the use of social indicators thus becomes a matter of measuring the ability of various constituencies to obtain their objectives. As previously suggested, strategies (com-petition, cooperation, co-optation, and bargaining) by which parties in a variety of situations obtain their objectives might be an important avenue for further research in the development of social indicators of power. Another possible fruitful avenue for development of social indicators of power might be the condi-tions under which *representation* of their interests is accepted by various constituencies under varying degrees of their own population *representativeness* within the four major dimensions (vertical, horizontal, sectorial, and locational) of organizational structure. Each organization has many constituencies both inside and outside the organization. These constituencies are distinguished on the basis of at least two sets of criteria. One is visibility; some constituencies are manifest while others are latent. The second is the degree of priority the constituency has in the eyes of the organization. Thus some constituencies are targeted for organizational response when they demand resources controlled by the organization, and others are untargeted, that is, ignored or even hurt by it. In effect the model is a four-celled matrix. One of several possible focuses for future research is the question of how groups get to be targeted and manifest as well as how some are untargeted and yet manifest. It would prove valuable to investigate how groups move from one condition to another in terms of how the organization orients to its constituencies. This, of course, is largely a political research question concerning the degree of consciousness-of-kind a constituency has about itself and how that constituency can impact on an organization to become both manifestly present and worthy of being targeted for organizational response.

An empirical question worth pursuing is whether and under what conditions a latent constituency might be targeted for organizational resources without any active demand on its own behalf. This touches on how corporations "create" new markets. Relationships with new constituencies outside the organization may give their counterparts inside the organization added power under certain circumstances; at a minimum it may create pressures for representative distribution of that population within the organization. Thus the development of social indicators of physical representativeness and of social representation may provide a key to research linking the distribution of power to that of types of constituencies in ways that will increase our knowledge of power processes in social systems. Which populations have *representation* inside an organization may have a significant effect on how those populations are treated externally by the organization. For example, banks are known to engage in "red lining" and thereby severely restricting or totally eliminating loans to certain geographical areas where some populations are known to concentrate. It is not likely that if those populations were *represented* among bank policymakers

the bank as an organization would subsequently institutionally discriminate against those populations. The practice of
"steering" among real estate firms is another example where
representation within the organization to protect the interests
of an external constituency (patients, clients, customers, students, and so forth) would most likely produce more equitable
behavior *between* organizations. This, of course, presumes that
patients, clients, customers, students, and the like are able to
form organizations of their own in order to focus pressure and
create an effective response by the correspondent hospital, bank,
university, or whatever.

   Opportunity Distribution. A very much less measurable
multidimensional phenomenon within the study of institutional
discrimination in organizations is that of *opportunity*. Not only
is opportunity itself difficult to measure, but any analysis of its
distribution would surely have to include the *perception* of opportunity as well. The perception of opportunity is at least as
important as the actual amount of opportunity for minorities
and women to participate fully in the life of any given organization.

   Indeed, if people perceive themselves not to have any
opportunity for promotion, then that perception itself may become more significant in determining their *morale* and subsequent behavior than the actual amount of opportunity available.
The degree of opportunity members of different populations
(men, women, or minorities) perceive depends considerably upon the proportion of people like themselves they actually see in
different organizational levels and sectors. Paula Dubeck, in her
analysis of opportunity structures in Chapter Four, argues that
the proportion of women at a given level of an organization in
effect determines the perception of others, both women and
men, as to what opportunities exist for women in that organization. If there has never been a female chief executive officer in
an organization, then future generations of women and men will
not perceive that position as one potentially to be filled by
women. Ironically, it might be argued that the fewer women in
high positions within an organization, the more likely a woman
is to see an opportunity for herself. However, the contrary ef-

fect seems to be the more standard response. That is, if they do not have women in a particular function within an organization, that is because they discriminate against women for that position and therefore there is no opportunity for one to be hired. Thus some independent measure of opportunity is necessary in order to assess the degree to which it is accurately perceived. The degree of inaccuracy in the perception of opportunity may itself be disproportionately distributed among various populations within organizations. Undoubtedly, development of social indicators of opportunity as well as of the perception of opportunity will have to be based on some empirically measurable criterion, the degree of which is an indication of the available opportunity. Among these might be recruitment practices; this would require an analysis of whether and what kinds of networks organizations use to recruit personnel for various kinds and levels of positions. Ways applications for positions are processed may offer a basis on which to develop some measures of differential allocation of opportunity. Network analysis is an important new area of sociological investigation. It would probably be beneficial to find ways of applying those techniques within the context of organizational analysis.

There remains much to be done by way of conceptualizing the study of opportunity within organizations. Hiring and promotion are perhaps as good a starting point as any for the analysis of opportunity. But there are innumerable questions that may be raised about many different facets of opportunity that need systematic empirical analysis. The one aspect of opportunity that has received some systematic sociological attention is that concerning the development of careers within organizations (Glaser, 1968). However, this line of work has been handicapped by a lack of measurement instruments to generate reliable data on differential promotion rates for specific populations in specific types of organizational structures. Most analyses of organizational careers are not data based and to the extent that they are they usually rely on ad hoc cases cited merely as a convenience to illustrate the analyst's generalizations. Social indicators for study of institutional discrimination may begin to systematically fill this gap in the data base for the study of careers. For example, some chapters in this volume indicate that careers of women and minority organizational participants may be truncated by too rapid a series of early promotions or by promotion into dead-end positions from which no further career mobility is likely. Thus early opportunity for experiences that provide a foundation on which to build for an extended chain of promotions may be much more advantageous in the long run than an early promotion to a seemingly high position from which further upward movement is virtually precluded. Too quick a research focus on comparative promotion statistics between traditional personnel and populations only recently included in particular organizations may erroneously indicate high opportunity and conceal the long-term lack of it.

Psychic Reward and Punishment Distribution. Perhaps the most difficult to measure of all the different rewards/ punishments that can be distributed to incumbents of various organizational positions are those clearly intangible phenomena such as prestige, camaraderie, and respect for past achievements, and for future development potential. Among the intangibles mentioned, *respect* could be the most important. It is perhaps out of respect for actual and potential accomplishments of personnel over whose careers they can exercise influence that incumbents of powerful positions engage in the phenomenon of *sponsorship*. Earlier I noted that sponsorship may come from six major areas. Each source yields certain psychic rewards. Sponsorship is extremely difficult to measure. Perhaps more often than not both those who sponsor and those who are sponsored would prefer not to have it be known, perhaps prudently so. Indeed, in some cases the sponsored may not even be aware that they are being sponsored. Even if no attempt to obscure is made, it is still difficult to know when an act is an act of sponsorship and when it is merely the performance of duty. For example, when a group of vice-presidents discusses who among lower-level executives might be ideal candidates for a given position, they may suggest names due to sponsorship or they may suggest them merely because they are qualified without intent to make a special case for anyone. The development of social indicators for measurement of the degree and kind of sponsorship in organizations would advance substantially the study of institutional discrimination in particular and the study of career development within organizations in general. Turner (1960), for example, has suggested that vertical social mobility based strictly on prior meritorious performance is probably as rare (indeed perhaps impossible) as that based strictly on sponsorship without regard to merit. Among those qualified for a position based on meritorious prior performance, the person selected for appointment is most likely to be the one who has the most extensive degree of sponsorship by those able to influence (whether appropriately or not) the selection process. Strong sponsorship may further a career that lacks some merit as much as high merit (based on either achieved or ascribed factors) may further a career that lacks some sponsorship. However, it is very unlikely that much career advancement is possible without a fairly good balance between merit and sponsorship.

The question remains, sponsorship by whom? In some situations sponsorship for appointment to high-level organizational positions may come from below, that is, from those in positions under the position to be filled. In other situations sponsorship might be exercised by constituencies outside the organization in which the appointment is to be made. Customers, clients, suppliers, competitors, and others in the community within which the appointing organization operates may be in a position to influence the appointment. The most likely source of sponsorship, however, especially in large organizations, is incumbents of higher positions within the same organization. These persons are in a position to give advice in career management, to look out for and forewarn about potential difficulties, to recommend experiences that may later be deemed desirable for promotion, and so forth. In short, the sponsor may act as a guardian angel. The question for the study of sponsorship is how to measure guardian angel activity by objective standardized instrumentation that can be utilized in different organizational settings. Without unobtrusive yet systematic social indicators of sponsorship (as well as a number of other similarly important but intangible forms of reward/punishment activity), it is impossible to determine whether women and members of minority populations are differentially sponsored for career mobility within organizations. It is clear, however, that such phenomena as sponsorship greatly affect the distribution of these populations throughout the structure of organizations. Moreover, the success that it assures provides tremendous psychic rewards to recipients; their increased self-assurance may enable them to perform beyond a level and quality than they might otherwise. A self-fulfilling cycle may thus be set in motion. Their improved performance is an indication of merit for further sponsorship, which in turn further assures success.

Another area of study, therefore, is the psychological impact upon the person being sponsored of knowing sponsors' identities and their potential reasons for acting as sponsors. For example, assuming approximately equal numbers and quality of publications, a white assistant professor may remain unaware of having been the beneficiary of sponsorship by a senior professor in the promotion to tenure. The net result could be a more self-confident person even more able to be productive due to the belief that past achievement alone produced the promotion. A comparatively qualified black person without "hidden" sponsors among senior professors might have to resort to requests for sponsorship from nontraditional locations inside and outside the organization: black scholars elsewhere, junior faculty, and students, for example. This person might also ultimately obtain tenure. But the question remains as to the psychological impact of having such tangible evidence that sponsorship and not personal achievement was the decisive element in obtaining promotion. Just as the person in the first example might be forever confident of the merit of his or her own work and the justifiability of the promotion, the second person might forever have self-doubts due to unmasked sponsorship. Thus whether sponsorship is hidden or overt, offered or requested, has psychological implications for the sponsored as well as for the sponsor.

Conclusion

An organization is a complex social system composed of many functionally varied and interdependent elements, somewhat akin to an intricate fabric woven from a variety of strands and threads. The tightness or looseness of the weave in the fabric, let alone the different types of weave, is reflected by the statistical interrelationships among social indicators by which the elements that compose the system are measured. Distribution of six major types of rewards (participation or distribution of populations within organizational structure may be the major reward, followed by the distribution of wealth, power, opportunity, and psychic rewards/punishments) may be viewed as the independent variables. Antecendent and intervening variables that set conditions for distribution were seen to be of three types: sponsorship, achievement, and ascription (in that order of importance in a stable society). The degree to which performance by organizational participants is directly related to the organizational task was viewed as the criterion for justifiability, which is the dependent variable. It was proposed that eight levels of justifiability may be described by dichotomous cross classification of task relatedness and non–task relatedness of these three conditional variables. To the extent that the six major types of rewards are proportionately distributed to comparison populations (men-women, majority-minority, and so forth) within each level of justifiability, institutional discrimination does not exist within organizations under investigation. Indeed, the research procedure suggested is to expect equal distribution; otherwise stated, this is the null hypothesis. Institutional discrimination is said to exist when the evidence reveals a statistically significant departure from the null hypothesis after all variables known to be potentially relevant to the criterion variable (task performance) have been taken into account in the analysis.

A perspective espoused here is that organizational analysis will be enriched, both theoretically and empirically, by the results of research on issues pertinent to the study of institutional discrimination within organizations. In short, it is not possible to study institutional discrimination within organizations without studying the very nature of organizational phenomena. The remainder of this book amply demonstrates this thesis. Each chapter makes a contribution as much to the study of organizations generally as to the study of institutional discrimination in particular.

Part Two

Examining Opportunity and Power in Organizations

~~~~~~

Access to power and opportunity is the central theme of the two chapters in this part. Each chapter attempts to provide a set of conceptual tools, measurement possibilities, and analytical contingencies with which to understand better the issues of access to power and opportunity. Both Rosabeth Moss Kanter and James Rosenbaum advocate an approach that promises to bring opportunity structures for sexual and racial populations into the mainstream of research on organizations.

In her chapter Kanter urges consideration of more than simple questions of equal pay for equal work or of equity in recruitment practices. She suggests that advancement prospects and accessibility to organizational power by particular groups within the organization be examined and that attempts be made to identify the major problems of measuring opportunity and power distributions. Her major objective is to identify fertile areas for future investigation, including such issues as the psychic effect of given opportunity structures on individual attitudes and behavior, the differential difficulty of moving through various mobility chains within an organization, and the variety of ways to determine who has organizational "clout."

James Rosenbaum provides specific technical research suggestions on the study of opportunity structures, mapping out the implications of viewing opportunity as embedded in organizational structure. He advocates the analysis of labor markets from the "demand" side as well as from the "supply" side, as traditionally done, at the same time that structural features of the organization are taken into consideration in determining the degree of opportunity available to sexual and racial populations. This approach has extensive implications, not all of them positive, for the affirmative action movement.

Kanter and Rosenbaum do not consider questions of how to determine whether discrimination actually exists and whether it is institutional or personal. However, they do delineate some of the social indicators needed to obtain systematic data on particular organizational structures, and they do present some models by which the resulting data may be analyzed.

2

Differential Access to Opportunity and Power

Rosabeth Moss Kanter

This chapter examines indicators of differential access to opportunity and power inside organizations and offers an approach to measurement. It provides a set of analytic tools and measurement possibilities for deciding how to compare the situations of people inside organizations in order to determine whether there is systematic disadvantage by race and sex. As Thurow (1975, p. 163) points out in criticizing wage competition models of discrimination and suggesting that his job competition model has greater explanatory power, "Discrimination can exist even when equal wages can be paid for equal work if individuals are not allowed to perform (or acquire the characteristics necessary to perform) equal work. These other types of discrimination stand outside of the standard competitive model of wage or price discrimination."

Like many social scientists, Thurow views occupational discrimination (one of seven types of discrimination he identifies) chiefly in terms of proportional representation of women, blacks, or other racial-ethnic minorities in preferred or less preferred occupations—in other words, as defined by numbers of people currently occupying various statuses (with controls for the numbers available to occupy them). There is certainly some merit to beginning with numerical distributions. I have argued elsewhere that proportional representation of one social type in a group numerically dominated by another social type is not only a convenient shorthand measure of less than equal access to that group but also represents a handicap that members of the minority social type bear in trying to be full-fledged, competent, and rewarded members of that group, occupation, or job category (Kanter, 1977a, pp. 206–242; 1977b; see also Hughes, 1944).

But complete understanding of *institutional* racism or sexism requires much more than such simple numerical counts (and comparison with labor supply), for a variety of reasons having to do with the nature of organizations and the nature of individual careers. First, individuals do not remain fixed in present statuses; they move. But access to movement is itself differentially distributed and defined by the organization as a system as well as the characteristics of individuals. Second, organizations are also decision-making bodies, and various interests have differential likelihood of being reflected in organizational decisions. Individuals' capacities to be *effective* in their jobs, and thus to be given access to greater rewards, is also affected by a number of organizational factors. Thus in addition to examining the representation of minorities and women across hierarchical levels and vertical divisions, we must also ask questions such as: Are people of different race/sex status represented in the leadership coalition? Do they have advancement prospects? Are they so situated to have the chance to develop organizational "clout"? Are their views likely to be represented in organizational policies? Do they have equal organizational capacity to be effective leaders? Regardless of the degree of equality in present statuses, is there equal opportunity to move into more desirable jobs, to increase in skill and reward?

I propose that conceptualization and measurement of *opportunity* and *power* will provide data to answer these questions. Both the variables and their measurement are based on a theory

of the structural determinants of organizational behavior derived
from extensive fieldwork in large organizations (Kanter, 1977a).
The theory suggests that, taken together, the structure of opportunity, the structure of power, and relative numbers (proportions and social composition) form the central explanatory dimensions of an integrated structural model of human behavior
in organizations and that it is the relationship between opportunity, power, and relative numbers that indicates the presence
of institutional racism/sexism.

Opportunity

Opportunity refers to the advancement, movement, or
skills-growth prospects stemming from the present job. Jobs are
important not only in and of themselves but also in terms of
their relative access to other, future jobs:

Positions in organizations are located in an opportunity
structure that tends to affect such matters as how many occupants of such positions move, at what time intervals, in what
direction, and with how many further moves likely. The opportunity structure in which a person's present job is located has
both direct and indirect effects on mobility and is thus significant for examining discrimination in several ways. Directly, of
course, it shapes real prospects, what the objective chances are
for people in some positions to move to what kinds of other
positions. In this sense it is comparable to what economists call
"internal labor markets" (Doeringer and Piore, 1971).

Opportunity also has an indirect effect on future mobility
through its effects on the attitudes and behavior of jobholders.
People low in opportunity tend to lower their aspirations, become less engaged with or committed to work, and behave in
ways that usually make others regard them as unsuitable for promotion; high opportunity has the opposite effect, encouraging
people to adopt attitudes and behaviors that further their initial advantage (Kanter, 1976; 1977a, pp. 129–163, 246–247).
Tannenbaum and others (1974, p. 8) were picking up part of
these indirect effects of opportunity when they wrote, "Hierarchy, in American plants at least, represents to many organization members the path of achievement; movement along the

hierarchy implies personal success or failure. Thus, hierarchy, which is a basic *organizational* characteristic, has profound *psychological* implications for members" (emphasis added). Miller and Rissman (1961) also argue that structure (job conditions) and cognitive factors (such as evaluation of opportunities and risks) are the source of worker behavior and attitudes often labeled "intrapsychic" motivational or affective tendencies. Thus sometimes institutional racism/sexism impacts on people's opportunity in a way that makes them appear to deserve their lack of mobility, but this is instead a function of limited situations.

Opportunity is also important in a third way for those concerned with ameliorating institutional racism or sexism. Affirmative action is aimed not only at distributing people more fairly through existing positions in the present but also at ensuring an equitable future distribution. Thus to get women or minorities into apparently equal present jobs that contain unequal degrees of opportunity would eliminate apparent *present* discrimination but not eradicate *future* discrimination.

The importance of measuring opportunity is an idea shared by a growing number of social scientists. Rosenbaum (1976a, 1977) has independently developed a number of concepts and measures similar to those proposed here, and he is testing those concepts and refining the measures in an analysis of personnel records from a subsidiary of a major corporation. In addition, excellent mathematical models of opportunity chains have been developed (Schinnar and Stewman, 1976; White, 1970) that tie individual mobility prospects to such systematic variables as vacancies in existing jobs, creation of new jobs, or disappearance of old jobs. But such mathematical models often make assumptions that are not compatible with the empirical realities Rosenbaum and I have encountered in organizations (such as the complexity and nonregularity of career pathways); and they do not address themselves to differential degrees of opportunity created by the structure of tracks, career paths, and internal labor markets. Furthermore, the focus on vacancies turns attention away from what is critical in measuring institutional racism or sexism: how the organization distributes opportunity to individuals in different career lines by shaping the nature of mobility pathways. Both Rosenbaum and I, then, have chosen to emphasize the empirical measurement of opportunity in real organizations in terms of the location of jobs in opportunity structures, with relatively little attention to patterns of openings, though recognizing that the existence of vacancies places an absolute limit on the extent to which individuals' opportunity is actualized in mobility

Issues in Measuring Opportunity

Before I suggest some approaches to measuring opportunity, it is important to keep several issues in mind. Both jobs and individuals are located in opportunity structures. Jobs carry with them high or low amounts of opportunity for occupants as a class, but the pyramidal nature of most organizations (and/or a scarcity of openings) also generates competition among those same job occupants for whatever mobility might exist. Thus it is important to measure structural characteristics of jobs and to make some comparisons among individuals in those jobs of structural features that account for relative opportunity even within jobs with the same objective opportunity. To put it another and simpler way, individuals can have their opportunity to advance limited in at least three ways: (1) by being in a low-ceiling, low-opportunity, dead-end job (from which relatively few people advance and not very far); (2) by losing out in competition for scarce mobility, as a function of random events or individual characterstics; or (3) by coming to a job that usually contains opportunity by a "wrong route," which precludes further advancement because of a lack of appropriate prior experience (Kanter, 1977a, pp. 136–139). (The third way often happens to minorities and women who are brought into a job by an unusual path as a result of affirmative action, as I found in my fieldwork.) Thus measurement must attend to both job and individual analysis.

Another issue in measuring opportunity is lack of relevant knowledge of career paths by organizations themselves. Rosenbaum is fortunate in having access to personnel records over a large number of years so that he is able to document actual movements individuals made within a specific organization and thus to describe the opportunity structure in practice rather than in theory. Many of the measures I propose assume some access to personnel records, even though I am aware that such access is usually very limited, short of lawsuits, which allow records to be subpoenaed (but which may preclude the researcher from gaining other kinds of access to the organization). Most large organizations, even in their human resource planning departments, otherwise have only a vague sense of what constitute career pathways except in terms of very short ladders describing the hierarchy within a specific function—such as Billing Clerk I, BC II, BC III—and even there the hierarchy defines relative status but *not necessarily the path by which individuals move.* (See Kanter, 1977a, p. 132, for further examples of the lack of clarity about mobility in a large corporation.)

Second, job ladders and the number of steps associated with them also may not be comparable across functions or positions. Number of ladder steps opening up from a job has often been taken as an indicator of opportunity (Grinker, Cooke, and Kirsch, 1970), but the amount of advancement reflected in what is formally defined as a "step" may vary greatly. The division of job classifications into a large number of steps may still not mean much opportunity for the people in them if the distance between bottom and top (in status, pay, work conditions, and so forth) remains the same. So many indicators are very tricky, and many weights and adjustments have to be made, just as they do for lateral (as opposed to vertical) moves.

Finally, the measurement picture is further complicated by the fact that organizations have multiple indicators of status, all of which may vary independently. Grade designation of the job, wages and rank of the individual in it, and status of those to whom the job reports may differentially correlate, depending on a variety of organizational circumstances. In practice this means that opportunity might also contain a variety of relatively independent dimensions. The question, for example, of what constitutes a "promotion" cannot always be answered easily, even though the commonsense view thinks of promotions as obvious matters.

I propose that in general all three issues present the greatest measurement problems at the middle and upper levels of organizations and for those organizations where career paths are not as self-consciously designed as in a civil service system. The clarity of pathways, the straightforward designation of ladder steps, and the correlation between job grade, wages, and status of contiguous or linked positions would probably be greatest at the lower levels.

These complex issues must be addressed in a complete examination of opportunity. They should be kept in mind as I propose some specific indicators of opportunity.

Opportunity in the Job Category

The most appropriate measures are relative, that is, used to compare jobs in the same organization. Opportunity in the job itself can be measured using indicators such as the following:

1. Number of steps possible from job
   a. The number of levels above ever attained by job occupants over the last ten to fifteen years: the largest number of moves ever made and the percentage of job occupants who have ever made the most moves (larger absolute numbers and larger ratios indicate greater opportunity)
   b. The official progression for job classification: the number of official ladder steps (larger number of official steps indicates greater opportunity)
   c. The modal progression for job occupants over the last ten to fifteen years: the number of steps attained for people who held job at each past year
   d. The modal progression for past job occupants: the percentage who have moved up at least one level, two levels, three levels, or four or more levels
   e. Top managers', current supervisors', and job occupants' ratings of likelihood of job occupants ever attaining one more level, two more levels, three more levels, four or more levels
2. Promotion rates
   a. The percentage of job occupants promoted per year over the past ten to fifteen years
   b. Supervisors'/superiors' ratings of the percentage of job occupants expected to be promoted in the next two years
   c. Current job occupants' perception of the likelihood of a promotion within the next two years

3. Prospects and possibilities, including lateral moves
   a. The number of different positions open to job occupants
      and their relative likelihood (by retrospective analysis of
      previous occupants and by prospective opinions of top
      managers, supervisors, and occupants)
   b. Qualitative analysis of the kinds of positions into which
      occupants move and their relative status and reward
   c. The average tenure of occupants in that position over the
      past ten to fifteen years and whether tenure ended by
      promotion, resignation, or termination (longer tenures
      indicate less opportunity, unless shorter tenures derive
      from leaving the organization)

   With all such indicators the specific nature of any particular organization needs to be taken into account: how it differen-
tiates levels, how rewards are distributed across levels, job classification systems, and so forth. It is difficult to suggest measures
in the abstract; instead, the development of instruments and
analytical tools would best be preceded by fieldwork and informant interviewing. The *absolute* level of the job also needs to be
taken into account (for example, closer to the top, the number
of levels possible begins to decline even though there might
be a great deal of opportunity as measured by qualitive indicator 3b).

Individual Opportunity

   These sets of indicators are useful for comparison within
a job classification of the relative opportunity of job occupants.

1. Relative age and tenure
   a. The number of standard deviations above or below mean
      age of all current job occupants (much older indicates less
      opportunity)
   b. The number of standard deviations above or below mean
      length of stay in job of all job occupants (much longer in-
      dicates less opportunity)
2. Promotion probabilities
   a. The individuals' own rating of likelihood of promotion and
      of going how high, to what kinds of jobs

     b. Superiors'/supervisors' ratings of likelihood that individuals
       will be promoted in the next two to five years, and to what
       kinds of jobs
3. Route to present job
     People who come to a job via an unusual route often get
stuck, even in theoretically high-opportunity jobs, because
they lack requisite job-related or interpersonal background; so
the person's job *history* often shapes job *future*. This indicator
requires two steps:
     a. Identification of the prior positions and perhaps organiza-
       tional locations held by job occupants (for entry-level jobs
       this might be an educational position) and ranking of these
       paths in terms of the frequency of their use
     b. Analysis of individuals' routes, points of origins, in terms
       of whether they represent common (what ranking or route)
       or unusual routes to the job
     In general, more common pathways tend to be associated
with more opportunity. The exception is instances in which an
individual's career is being controlled directly by top officials of
the organizations, such as a person being groomed for higher
positions who is being moved around the organization in unusual ways in order to gain wide experience.
4. Cohort effects
     In all individual opportunity comparisons it may be
important to test wider cohort effects: individuals' standing vis-
à-vis all those who entered the organization at the same time,
whether certain cohorts *as a whole* tend to be characterized by
greater opportunity. Stevenson (1977) has suggested some methodological techniques based on labor market theory. Such
cohort effects would serve as backdrop for conclusions about
individual opportunity to any given job category.
5. Qualitative informant reports
     Organization members also may have perceptions of who
seems to be on a "fast track," groomed for the top, helped
to move along quickly. They also often know who is considered to have "reached his or her level." Informant reports
can be used to identify the extremes of high- or low-opportunity individuals, which then can be compared with other
sources of data.

Organizational Power

Power refers to influence and resource access in the organization in conjunction with or in addition to whatever formal authority (that is, accountability for tasks or the actions of
others) is contained in the official definition of a job. That is,
power is the capacity to mobilize resources, human or material.
This is a broader and less value-laden definition than those that
see power as people's ability to impose their wills over others.
Here power is viewed as efficacy and therefore as a primary factor in the capability of those in positions of accountability as
well as those with a stake in an organization's decisions. Relative degrees of power account for who is most likely to be influential in defining and shaping organizational policies and
decisions. Relative power also accounts for who can behave
most effectively in leadership roles—that is, mobilize subordinates or colleagues in the interests of task accomplishment in
such a way that morale as well as output is maximized. A careful review of the organizational behavior literature on leader
effectiveness indicates that power in the larger organization
(power *outside* the immediate work group) often accounts for
a large part of a leader's effectiveness as well as style *inside* the
immediate work group for which he or she is accountable (Kanter 1976, 1977a). Thus power is defined in organizational terms
as an issue of systemic connections and not as an attribute of
the person.

With respect to institutional discrimination, relative organizational power or powerlessness is significant in two ways. First,
it impacts directly on the question of which people are in the
best position to influence or shape organizational goals, policies,
and decision. (*Institutional* racism or sexism is, of course, indicated not merely by examining and aggregating individuals' situations inside an organization but also by examining an organization's overall policies and their effects.) Second, to the extent
that degrees of power contribute to leader style and capacity
and follower morale, power differences determine who becomes
and is seen as effective and thus is given the chance to accumulate more power. The notion of cycles of advantage and disadvantage is as relevant to power as to opportunity.

Determining Clout

Power is *not* equivalent to hierarchical position or to such measures of formal authority as numbers of subordinates. It is a much more subtle and elusive concept, referring to something often masked or hidden in organizations, and is thus a concept that is difficult to measure. Measurement critically depends on definition of the concept.

Organizational power can be measured directly in terms of what organization members call "clout" or "credibility." For example, relative power could be determined by self and other ratings of an individual's ability to intercede favorably on behalf of a subordinate (or peer) in trouble with the organization; get a desirable placement for a talented subordinate; get approval for expenditures beyond the budget; get above average salary increases for subordinates; get items on the agenda at policy meetings; get fast, regular, or frequent access to top decision makers; or get early information about decisions and policy shifts. Note that "clout" is less a function of influence *downward* (over subordinates) than of influence *upward* and *outward*.

Clout is likely to be developed by people who participate on committees and functions outside their own home base, department, or unit. An overall institutional indicator, then, of the representation of kinds of individuals in organizational policy is very straightforward: who participates, in which activities, of what importance to the organization and to career advancement, and how frequently.

Organizational power also comes from an individual's location in the system. Analysis of individual power potential can determine whether an institution systematically places individuals of different race or sex statuses in unfavorable power situations. My own theoretical and empirical work has led to differentiating two global ways power can be accumulated in organizations: through *formal position attributes* (job characteristics) and through *informal network connections* (alliances throughout the organization). Approaches to the measurement of each can be suggested. Note that these indicators are proposed for comparison of pepole in leadership roles, such as managerial, administrative, or professional jobs.

Power Access Through Formal Position Attributes

I have argued elsewhere that job activities contribute to power when they are *extraordinary* (pioneering, nonroutine, discretionary), *visible* to others, and *relevant* to current organizational problems (Kanter, 1977a). Relevance in an institutional sense has more to do with broad features of a job (its field, for example, finance or marketing or heart surgery) and the historical and environmental situation of an organization than with the latitude available to individuals (though individuals can also be perceived as acting in more or less "relevant" ways within their field). Thus measures of the positional side of power will focus primarily on the discretion-routinization dimension and the visibility dimension.

The positional or formal structural-locational side of power can be viewed in terms of the capacities jobs provide for individuals. These capacities would be examined in terms of the *relative* standing of individual jobholders within the same organization in order to determine whether people are consistently clustered by race or sex on the power measures. These are within-organization comparisons.

Analysis centers around indicators whose component parts vary from rather objective items to those that depend upon the ratings of informants from inside the organization. (The issue of how to gather the data to make the appropriate determinations for an index will not be dealt with here, although in general a combination of methods is likely to be the most appropriate: surveys of job characteristics that rely on individual responses, examination of official job description, informant interviews, direct observation, and judgments or ratings by panels of "experts.")

Job analysis of positional contributions to potential for organizational power can involve the following indicators:

1. Degree of routination (the greater the routinization, the lower the organizational power)
   a. The number of activities specified by formal rules (more rule specification indicates greater routinization)
   b. The number of prior occupants of the job (the fewer the

predecessors, the less the routinization, with the *first* incumbent—no predecessors—having the greatest power potential)

c. The variety of activities the occupant engages in (greater variety indicates less routinization)

d. The reward structure for job occupants, what higher-level people look for and reward in their performance: reliable subordinate behavior (greater routinization) or outstanding subordinate behavior (less routinization); smooth handling of everyday events (greater routinization) or unusual performance, innovative outputs (less routinization)

e. The number of quantitative measures of performance (more concrete and quantitative measures indicate greater routinization)

2. Amount of discretion occupant may exercise

a. The range of independent decisions that can be made without checking with higher (or other) authorities (greater range indicates greater discretion). (This is also part of measuring the degree of centralization/decentralization in an organization. More decentralized organizations show larger numbers of people relatively higher on the power indicators and thus are more generally empowering systems, even though the *absolute* power of the most central people might decline. See Bachman, Smith, and Slesinger, 1966; Blau and Schoenherr, 1971; Kanter, 1977a, pp. 275–279; Leavitt, 1951; and Tannenbaum and others, 1974, for supportive evidence.) A decision-making index consisting of a number of areas and a scale of authority within the areas can be constructed. For example, areas include hire personnel, fire personnel, promote personnel, determine salary level, department/unit expenditures within budget, department/unit expenditures outside budget, and policies about daily activities, such as lunch breaks or time of meetings. Within each area an authority scale can include: Does leader (and/or work unit) (1) have the final say (that is, is department autonomous?), (2) make recommendations that are usually accepted by higher authorities, (3) make recommendations with no guarantee of their reception, or (4)

have no say? The four points can be considered with re-
pect to peers or colleagues, immediate subordinates, people more than one level below immediate subordinates in
same department, or secretaries and support staff.
   b. The number of channels outside the work unit decisions in
those areas must pass through and the number of people
who have some say over each (more channels, more people
indicate less discretion). (This is also related to degree of
bureaucratization in an organization.)
3. Visibility
   a. The location of a position: completely inside a functional
or product area, straddling the boundaries, a link or inter-
face with other departments or units (more outside unit
formal affiliations indicate more visibility; more formal
interfaces indicate greater visibility)
   b. The amount of information about activities in the unit
known to other units (more information indicates greater
visibility)
   c. The amount of publicity given to unit's or position's activities—for example, the amount of space in organization
publications (more publicity indicates more visibility)
   d. The amount of interest others in the organization have in
the unit's or position's activities (more interest indicates
more visibility)

Power Through Alliances

   The informal side of power is even more hidden and elusive than the formal side because it is not an official part of an
organization's operations and may even be masked in the interests of presenting a nondiscriminatory face. In addition, the
matter of alliances shades off into friendships. Friendships are
considered private and voluntary, not something the organization controls, and therefore not something for which it *institutionally* can be held accountable. Is the fact that cliques form in
part on the basis of social similarity a result of "natural human
preference" or a sign of discriminatory intent? It is also hard in
this domain to show that alliances have any job-related or official relevance at all, regardless of commonsense observations

that they do. Do private men's clubs really handicap women executives? Do they handicap women enough to hurt them in their jobs? What is the evidence? And even if the private clubs are opened, what is to prevent the "old boy network" from retreating and closing another door?

Despite the obvious problems with examining the informal, alliance-based side of power, it is still important to attempt measurement and analysis. It can be shown that organizations, through their policies and job placements, can do some things to put individuals into more favorable or less favorable positions with respect to power-generating alliances. (See Kanter, 1977a, pp. ·278–281, for examples of empowering strategies that work through creating the conditions for alliances.) And it is around alliances that one of the negative effects of low proportional representation of race or sex group (that is, tokenism) has its effects. People in the "token" status (numerically rare) may have more difficulty being accepted as a part of the colleague group and thus making alliances essential to organizational power (Hughes, 1945; Kanter, 1977a, 1977b). Alliances with three groups contribute to organizational power: subordinates, peers, and sponsors.

Subordinate Alliances. Because people move through organizational careers at different rates, through different pathways, and with position changes representing different amounts of organizational distance, present subordinates do not always remain in that position vis-à-vis any individual leader; they may turn out to be peers or superiors some day. But even in addition to the effects of variations in career patterns and the fact that organizations do not move members of cohorts in uniform ways, subordinate mobility in general also means that subordinates represent one source of future power alliances throughout the organization. Thus the mobility-linked and power-linked characteristics of any leader's subordinates can be identified and differentiated in terms of their potential contribution to powerful alliances.

The relevant characteristics of subordinates include *opportunity*, the advancement prospects of their job category (high-opportunity subordinates indicate greater potential alliance power) and *routinization* and *discretion* in subordinates' jobs, measured by routinization and discretion indicators such as those already proposed (high routinization and low discretion indicate less potential alliance power).

Peer Alliances. It is clearer here why peer alliances can contribute to power; this is the classical source of organizational politics. Well-known sociometric and network measures could uncover the peer groupings in an organization, and the clustering or exclusion of people by race or sex could be taken as signs of institutional racism/sexism—if there were also a way of identifying the more powerful peer networks.

But in keeping with the other measures proposed here, indicators of *potential* alliance power through *organizational situation* can also be developed. Formal organization policies can facilitate or hinder the development of peer networks and individuals' access to peer alliances: (1) the extent of participation in formal training programs, workshops, or orientations with others at the same approximate level and organizational age (more participation indicates greater potential alliance power); (2) the frequency of cross-department or cross-unit meetings of approximate peers (greater frequency indicates greater potential alliance power); (3) the extent of "matrix" or "project" or "task force" management, which routinely brings together approximate peers (jobs organized in this way indicate greater potential alliance power); (4) the extent to which the job is intradepartmentally or extradepartmentally focused (more intraunit focus indicates less potential alliance power); and (5) the extent to which the job involves relative isolation (more isolation indicates less potential power).

Sponsor Alliances. The importance of sponsors (also known, somewhat inappropriately, as "mentors") for organizational careers is well known; I have analyzed their contribution to power elsewhere (Kanter, 1977a). The question of who has sponsors in any organization is tricky because, as my own field research has shown, the sponsor-protégé relationship is a subtle one, often not overtly and explicitly acknowledged by either party. In this area the analyst might have to rely on impressionistic, qualitative, and observational data, such as organization members' reports of where the ties seem to be and who appears to be "sponsored" by whom. Again, organizational policies can also facilitate the development of sponsorship relationships in ways similar to those discussed as facilitators of peer alliances: by providing access to interaction with potential sponsors at higher levels in the organization through training programs and workshops, extradepartment meetings, flexible task structures, and less isolated jobs or ones that may report up several levels.

Respondents' self-reports can also be used to compare relative access to organizational superiors and thus to potential sponsorship, with items such as the following: more senior people seem interested in the person's career and express interest in what the person is doing; more senior people have offered help in career discussions, career decisions, job information, or job placement; more senior people have helped the person learn about his or her present job and about the organization; more senior people are available for advice about the present job; more senior people are available to the person for inside information on what is happening in the organization, what decisions are in the wind; rank/title of highest-ranking person in the organization the individual in question would feel free to call to ask about career advice, for explanation of a policy decision, for a lunch date, for an organizational favor, or for a personal favor; and index of sociability by levels (frequency of seeing people at x, y, z, higher levels for different purposes, for example, for lunch or off-the-job sociability).

Conclusion

This chapter has outlined an approach to examining institutional racism/sexism inside organizations by focusing specifically on the distributions of opportunity and power. Concepts have been clarified, indicators proposed, and measurement problems discussed. I hope this analysis will help delineate social indicators that are organizationally relevant—that consider not only the distribution of people across positions at any one time but also how those positions constrain future prospects and access to influence through their location in structures of opportunity and power.

3

Career Paths and Advancement Opportunities

James E. Rosenbaum

The movement for affirmative action is entering a new era. The fact that this is happening is partially an indication of past researchers' successes, but this new era may present new and more difficult problems. Advances in social science permitted new analyses, which showed the role of discrimination and showed that it existed in spite of performance and ability (Oaxaca, 1976). Moreover, despite economic theories that predicted market mechanisms would not permit discrimination to continue, new sociological-economic theories showed the kinds of mechanisms that permit the perpetuation of discrimination (Thurow, 1975).

Yet the effectiveness of these investigations has brought reform to a new phase, and in this second phase these analyses

Note: The author is grateful for comments from Edgar Borgatta, George A. Farkas, and Eric Hanushek. Support by a grant to the author by the Manpower Administration, U.S. Department of Labor, assisted in the preparation of this chapter. Of course, the material presented here does not necessarily reflect their views.

may not be so useful. Many organizations that have begun to implement affirmative action programs currently need indicators to discern whether women and minorities who have already been promoted one step higher continue to have opportunities for future promotions or whether they have been promoted to dead-end positions. Their promotions may look fine when judged by previous methods of analysis, for they reflect real gains in the present; but the question is whether these individuals will continue to have opportunities in the future. Most current analyses consider discrimination only in terms of wages (Oaxaca, 1976) or levels (Bergmann and King, 1976; Cassell and others, 1975); few consider long-term opportunities. It will take many years to see the ultimate effects of current affirmative action promotions on employees' opportunities for future advancements. However, within organizational contexts there are ways to estimate the likely effects. This chapter presents an attempt to do this by analyzing the opportunity structure in organizations.

A first step to analyzing opportunity structures in organizations is to consider simple indicators. One can consider indicators that reflect the probability of advancement to a higher level from various jobs (Kanter, 1977b; Rosenbaum 1976b). One can also consider indicators that reflect the probability of advancement for individuals with particular personal attributes (Kanter, 1977b; Rosenbaum, 1976b; Wise, 1975). But after this has been done there is still an enormous task that remains: combining these various indicators. This task is important for several reasons.

First, single indicators may fail to detect patterns of interconnected opportunities among job positions—what we may call *career tracks*. As Hughes (1963) has repeatedly noted, jobs rarely appear as isolated entities. Rather they tend to appear as interconnected jobs that constitute careers, and various careers have different promotion opportunities. Analytic procedures that permit the analysis of interconnections must be used so one can discern the opportunities inherent in a particular position and extend the analysis to consider the effects of different career histories on subsequent promotions.

Second, single indicators do not permit one to analyze the interaction between job opportunities and personal characteristics. Sociological and economic research has exhibited a penchant for studying labor market and mobility processes in a segmented fashion, on the one hand analyzing social structures, vacancy chains, or demand by employers and on the other hand analyzing personal attributes and the supply side of the labor force. The recent work of McFarland (1976), Sørensen (1975), Spilerman (1977), and Stewman (1975) suggests that they are in the initial stages of bringing these two approaches together.

Most economic and sociological research on labor markets and social mobility tends to emphasize the supply side of labor markets and the individual attributes that correlate with income and social status. Harrison White (1970) has begun to analyze the demand side of labor markets and the structural features that influence social mobility. White criticizes analyses that deal only with the supply side in that they do not "specify the actual mechanisms and processes of movement" (p. 272). He does not intend his criticism to exclude human capital approaches or sociological regression models from consideration, for each has capacities that his own approach lacks. "Vacancy models in the present form are applicable only to restricted systems of jobs for single incumbents" and cannot be used to assess the effects of "as many attributes as Duncan considers—family background, education, sex, age" (p. 282). The question that remains is how to combine the two kinds of analyses.

Third, single indicators may misestimate the magnitude of opportunity barriers if one does not first control for other attributes. In particular there is likely to be overestimation of the effects of particular job positions on opportunities if race and sex are not controlled. This will be an especially important factor if affirmative action eliminates the blatant kinds of discrimination that formerly led to these apparent opportunity rates.

This chapter does not propose complete answers to these problems, but it aims to identify the problems and provide useful directions. The first two sections describe the phenomenon of historical carry-over effects and give some examples. The next several sections consider comparable effects for individual personal attributes. The final section proposes some quantitative models for analyzing these effects and the interactions of personal and positional indicators.

The issues discussed here are substantively important and empirically testable with available data. In a previous study of official school record data I showed the way internal organization of high school curriculum tracking tends to structure students' careers within high school and afterwards in ways that give early events and selections long-term consequences (Rosenbaum, 1976a). I speculated that "career tracking" might also occur in other kinds of organizations so that early events in an individual's career may have consequences on career selections made much later.

I am currently analyzing the complete personnel records for a large corporation (13,000 employees) over a fourteen-year span. Although the analyses have not yet addressed the issues of concern here, some of the ideas that are testable with these personnel data will be presented. Because most companies compile comparable information, the kinds of analyses discussed here may be done in other companies to improve the implementaton of affirmative action policies.

Effects of Lateral Moves and Department Shifts

Before discussing quantitative issues, I shall consider some qualitative data. Schreiber and I conducted an as-yet-unpublished pilot study of men and women at lower- and middle-management levels in a large organization, asking their reactions to the company affirmative action program. Both the men and the women expressed the view that in some cases affirmative action was promoting women into positions from which they might have less opportunity. They mentioned a number of reasons for this.

One reason was that some women were promoted before being given sufficient breadth of experience. This company had customarily required a lateral move (a job change across departments at the same level) before promotion to the next level, on the grounds that it gives breadth of experience. Thus most promotions to second-level management occurred only after employees held jobs in two different departments at the first level. Respondents speculated that the affirmative action program might be hurting some women's promotion opportunities into the third level by promoting them to the second level before they had held lateral positions.

Another reason mentioned for concern about subsequent opportunity was the nature of some affirmative action promotions. Although lateral movement within a level was encouraged, promotions generally took place within departments in which the employee had recent experience. Some respondents felt the affirmative action program in some cases seemed to contradict that tradition. In an apparent effort to advance women as rapidly as possible, the company had promoted some women to whatever vacancies first appeared, even if they were in deparments very different than those in which the individual possessed experience. In particular they mentioned instances of women being promoted from nontechnical to technical departments without preparation. Respondents felt this had made it difficult for the individuals to adapt to the new job, and it might permanently limit these women's future opportunities.

The affirmative action program in this company was still quite new, so no one really knew what opportunities these women would have in the future. These respondents' views were speculations; but it is noteworthy that they were expressed by both women and men and their underlying logic is cogent. Organizations do tend to have deeply ingrained rules and practices about promotion, and it is quite possible that the affirmative action program is *only a brief exception* to these rules. Once the immediate quotas are filled and problems are perceived to be remedied, the affirmative action program may end. To the extent that this is imminent, these respondents' speculations may be realistic.

It is this kind of concern that emphasizes the importance of analyzing the opportunity structure of organizations. To the extent that an affirmative action program is promoting minorities or women into low-opportunity positions, program's successes will be limited and short-lived. Moreover, to the extent that an affirmative action program is promoting minorities or women into positions for which *these particular individuals* have not been prepared and from which they will have low advancement opportunity, the program's success will be limited. The point is that an individual's opportunity is not only a function of that individual's new position but also a function of that individual's own personal attributes and career history.

The analyses discussed here do not presume insincere motives of affirmative action officers. In particular, the situation described in the previous example could easily occur inadvertently, out of a sincere concern for quickly remedying a discriminatory situation. However, even actions taken out of sincere motives may turn out to be less beneficial than originally imagined. Indeed, that is the meaning of *"institutional* racism/ sexism"—it occurs in the institution *regardless* of individuals' motives. The kinds of analysis proposed here can be useful to an organization's affirmative action officers in analyzing the likely long-term consequences of their actions.

Relative Long-Term Effects of Lateral Moves and Promotions

The previous example calls into question customary preconceptions about the relative value of lateral moves and promotions. A lateral move may be considered less beneficial than a promotion for an individual's career. One gets more status and generally a better salary from a promotion than from a lateral move. However, in the larger context of a person's entire career the previous example suggests that a lateral move may sometimes be more valuable than a promotion.

Insofar as the value of a particular position is dependent upon the individual's previous positions, an analyst must go beyond simple indicators of the opportunity coefficients for each particular job and find a way of describing the opportunities the particular job offers as a function of that individual's previous positions. Such an analysis may find many cases where lateral moves will not have long-term effects on future promotion opportunities. However, it may find some cases where lateral moves will improve an individual's long-term future promotion opportunities, possibly even carrying over to affect selection decisions much later in an individual's career. If this is the case, lateral moves may improve an individual's opportunities to a greater extent than a quick promotion without a lateral move might.

Analysis of Carry-Over Effects of Job Histories

A hypothetical example illustrates the concept of historical carry-over effects. Assume that level-1 job occupants have a 50 percent chance of getting to level 2; level-2 job occupants have a 40 percent chance of ultimately getting to level 3 or above. Then we can infer that the averagel level-1 occupant has a 20 percent (50 percent times 40 percent) chance of ultimately getting to level 3 or above.

In addition, assume that lateral moves within level 1 might improve an individual's chances of getting to level 2 such that people without lateral moves have a 30 percent chance of getting to level 2, while people with a lateral move have a 70 percent chance (controlling for years of service and so forth). Assuming no interactions, we would infer that level-1 employees having a lateral move have a 28 percent (70 percent times 40 percent) chance of ultimately getting to level 3 or above, while those without a lateral move only have a 12 percent (30 percent times 40 percent) chance. This illustrates a case where lateral moves have an immediate effect on promotions.

Affirmative action poses the issue whether a lateral move at first level or promotion to second level helps a first-level person more in getting to third level. In this example one would be more likely to attain third level if promoted to second level (40 percent) than if given a lateral move (28 percent). Yet this assumes that a first-level lateral move is no longer taken into account after one gets to second level.

If a first-level lateral move is taken into account in the subsequent promotion decision from second to third level, then an individual may have better opportunities by choosing a lateral move over a promotion. For example, in this illustration, if half the employees with lateral moves and a third of the employees without lateral moves are promoted from second to third level, then first-level employees with lateral moves have a better chance of getting to third level than those at second level without lateral moves.

The numbers in this illustration are arbitrary and surely do not prove that lateral moves are better for one's career than promotions. But the illustration shows the way that lateral moves could offer greater opportunities than promotions. Moreover, it points out a number of mistakes that could be made if one only considers average opportunities from single positions, without taking account of possible influences from career history. The methodological point is nothing new; others discussed it decades ago. However, the substantive point is important. Simple transition matrices of job mobility in an organization tend to give only average mobility from a position and ignore historical features and the way they may totally transform career opportunities.

Of course, there are many different departments in most large companies; and it is possible that some departments may value lateral moves less than others. Consequently, in considering where to place employees who do not have a lateral move, an affirmative action officer might promote them to departments that do not penalize individuals without lateral moves.

The respondents in the pilot study suggested that some promotions to very different departments (such as from nontechnical to technical departments) might hurt an employee's ultimate opportunities. This contention can be tested. To test it one would examine the records of job moves in the company and look at the second-to-third-level promotion rates of those previously promoted into similar departments compared with those previously promoted into very different departments than they had occupied in first level.

These examples illustrate the kinds of issues that need to be considered in assessing the opportunity structure of an organization. Jobs are not isolated entities. As Everett Hughes (1963) and others have argued, jobs are interconnected in ways that define careers. Individuals whose job histories violate the rules prescribed for a normal career may find their deviant history coming back to effect negatively their subsequent career (Strauss, 1959).

Personal Attributes

The preceding has considered opportunities as a function of an individual's career. But an individual's personal attributes also have an influence. There is abundant research demonstrating that minorities and women tend to have lower opportunities and that those with less education, less training, and, after a point, greater age have less opportunity for advancement (Bergmann and King, 1976; Cassell and others, 1975; Oaxaca, 1976; Rosenbaum, 1978a, 1978b; Weisbrod and Karpoff, 1968). Although average coefficients could be estimated for each of these personal attributes, the implementation of an affirmative action policy requires a finer-grained analysis, including an analysis of personal attributes as features that may alter the promotion opportunities associated with a given position. One must break down the simple transition probabilities by examining those associated with different kinds of personal attributes.

Education

Numerous studies suggest that some career routes may require college education. Indeed, Doeringer and Piore (1971) suggest that the primary labor market may tend to exclude those who lack college education. Some qualitative research in the area, as well as some analyses of my own data (Rosenbaum, 1978b), suggest that many employees lacking a college degree can attain lower- and middle-management positions. This is more likely to be the case in some departments than in others (for example, plant operations more than accounting). Consequently, the analyses of promotion opportunities for a given position must be done separately for those who have college degrees and those who do not, and interactions must be considered.

Furthermore, more detailed analyses of the effects of education have found that grades and college quality have important influences on employees' rate of salary increase (Weisbrod and Karpoff, 1968; Wise, 1975). These effects are not always simple ones, and analyses tend to find important interaction effects. For instance, Weisbrod and Karpoff's analysis of one company finds that grades have an important influence on an employee's rate of salary increase for those graduating from above-average colleges but a minimal influence for those graduating from below-average colleges. If one ignored this interaction effect and only computed the average coefficient for grades, one would obtain a misleading result.

Previous studies have tended not to control for employees' job positions, and it may be that the apparent effects of grades and college quality are actually due to employees being channeled into high-opportunity jobs. Consequently, instead of analyzing the promotion opportunities associated with given positions and those associated with given educational attributes separately, it might be better to analyze to what extent positions and attributes are themselves correlated and to what extent they uniquely and jointly determine opportunities.

Moreover, it may be that positions and attributes have interaction effects similar to those described for career histories. For example, Freedman (1969) has shown that education is not an important influence on job selection for most nonmanagement positions, although education may be important for selections to management positions.

These studies suggest several areas where education has important interaction effects on promotion opportunities. If one interprets these findings as indicating the greater productivity of certain combinations of education and job variables, then this will effect affirmative action policies. This is the approach the human capital model encourages (Becker, 1964), and it is the interpretation that Weisbrod and Karpoff (1968) and Wise (1975) seem to be using. With this interpretation an affirmative action officer would be careful to assign minorities and women to those positions offering the greatest opportunities for people with a particular level of education. Thus in considering various second-level jobs for a person in the first level, one would look at the opportunities for further promotion each job offered and also at the opportunities each job offered for employees with a particular level of education and particular grades from particular colleges. This decision would be comparable to the previously discussed illustration of the carry-over effects of lateral moves except in this case the affirmative action officer would be concerned with choosing the second-level job in terms of the future opportunities it would offer this particular person. The discovery of interaction effects would have important implications for affirmative action placements.

Training

Training may have effects similar to those of education on promotion, and the effects of training programs may be analyzed in the same ways as education. However, one warning must be noted for the analysis of training programs. Although one aim of training programs may be to provide skill training, this may not be their only function. They may also provide newly promoted employees with contacts with one another and perhaps introduce them to their new superiors at the next higher level. In this way training programs may be a mechanism for creating the kinds of contacts shown to be so important to career mobility (Granovetter, 1974; Kanter, 1977a).

Insofar as this is the case, quantitative analysis may be misleading. Even if quantitative analyses indicate these programs have had a positive influence on employees' promotion opportunities, that may not indicate that if such programs are tailored to women and minorities, they will necessarily have the same influence. If such a program were exclusively offered to women and minorities, then it would fail to give newly promoted women and minorities important contacts with white male peers and superiors. This does not mean there should be no management development training programs for minorities and women; it means that one needs to investigate whether the race and sex composition of such programs alters their effects on opportunities.

In the past few years there have probably been many different kinds of management development programs run for minorities and women. It might be valuable to analyze their effects, including the effects of their sex and race composition on employees' performance ratings and subsequent opportunities.

Age

Age is often an important determinant of opportunities, yet its relationship with opportunity is complex. Generally, the relationship of age with promotion opportunity is curvilinear, in the shape of an inverted *U*. One's opportunities increase up to a point and decrease thereafter, and this is customarily portrayed in regression equations by considering an age-squared factor. Some evidence suggests that the turnaround point comes at different ages, depending on the level of one's job (Rosenbaum, 1978b). Formal or informal company rules might state, for example, that one has to make second level by age thirty-six, third level by age thirty-nine, fourth level by age forty-three, and so forth in order to have a good chance for promotion to the next level.

This kind of contention could easily be studied by quantitative analysis of official personnel records. The precise influence of age in different organizations may be different, so each case must be considered separately. But the analysis is straightforward, and the same questions would be investigated in each organization: What is the age range for promotions from each level? Is there a pivotal age after which opportunities decline? Do the age distributions differ for different jobs at the same level?

Interaction effects, similar to those discussed previously, may also operate for age. Age may be important in some departments and not in others. If this is the case, an affirmative action officer would want to promote an individual to a position that would offer good opportunities to someone of that age. If an individual is much older than the median age customarily required for promotion from a particular position, an individual's chances for subsequent promotions will not be very good, although perhaps another job that permitted promotions for older individuals could be found. If no such job could be found, any promotion—even one offering no future opportunities— would be an improvement for the individual concerned. But it might not help the long-term goals of the affirmative action program as much as promoting a younger minority or female employee who would be young enough to have the possibility for further promotions.

This kind of situation presents a cruel trade-off for affirmative action programs. Should affirmative action right old wrongs by promoting older women and minorities who have been passed over for a position for many years, or should it press for the promotion of young women and minorities who will have future opportunities for promotions to higher levels? The first solution may be considered more equitable for the individuals involved, and indeed older individuals are likely to be better qualified for these promotions because of their years of experience. But given the fact of subsequent age discrimination for the next higher level, these older individuals may be viewed as less qualified for the next promotion or may reach retirement age before they can be considered for it. The long-term welfare of the affirmative action program may be perceived as benefiting from the promotion of younger minorities and women. Such an emphasis will tend to given up on older women and minorities as past victims who must continue to be sacrificied. No one can be content with such a decision.

Race and Sex

One of the dangers of using raw promotion rates is that they may include the influence of correlated third factors. For example, education may appear to have a larger influence than it really has. Raw promotion rates for college-educated employees may be quite a bit larger than the rates for those without college, but this difference may be considerably reduced after controlling for race and sex because women and minorities have traditionally been less likely to go to college (Blau and Duncan, 1967; Patterson, 1973; Willie, 1973). After determining that much of the apparent effect of education is associated with race and sex, one must examine whether there is any justification for selection based on education. Given the extensiveness of discrimination in the past, analyses controlling for race and sex are likely to attentuate the opportunity rate differences associated with many other variables. To the extent that affirmative action has been effective in minimizing discrimination, these new reduced promotion rates are more likely to be the ones to consider.

Quantitative Models for Analyzing Interactions of Personal and Positional Factors

Having reviewed personal attributes and considered the complexities involved, it is clear that no simple solutions will adequately address these issues. Most analyses of complex situations require some kind of simplifying assumptions. Simplification is clearly required for the task of analyzing the opportunity structure of a large organization taking account of many historical factors and personal attributes for many different departments. However, some of the simplifications customarily made may not be appropriate for analyzing opportunity structures in organizations. One common simplification is to omit interaction terms. Most regression analyses do not include interaction terms or separate regressions for different subgroups, implicitly assuming no interaction. However, many of the examples presented here indicate that this assumption is unwarranted and that interactions may indeed reflect substantively important phenomena that are fundamental to an organization's operations. Furthermore, these interactions may have important implications for individuals' opportunities; consequently, affirmative action officers should be aware of these processes in order to be more effective.

There are several approaches that would be more sensitive to interactions. One is to conduct small cross-tabular analyses, such as those used as examples in this chapter. Such analyses will necessarily be incomplete; but if they are strategically chosen, they may be useful for detecting or corroborating the existence of the selection processes. Interviews with informants in relevant portions of the organization may provide the analyst with hypotheses about where such interactions may exist, and these hypotheses could be tested in limited sectors using a few of the most relevant variables. In this way small cross tabulations of a few simple variables could be used to understand interaction processes and the way they affect employees' opportunities.

A second approach is to use regression analyses that include interaction terms. By defining all variables in terms of dummy variables and by fully specifying the regression equation to include all possible interaction terms, one could analyze these relationships more fully. Regression analysis of five variables specifying all interactions is not simple to compute, but that is a difficulty largely reflected in computer time. The reading and interpretation of regression coefficients is fairly simple. Furthermore, unlike new tables, the regression analysis permits one to discern the magnitude of various direct effects and various interaction effects. Because it is the interaction effects that are so difficult to detect and because they can have profound influences, it is profitable to attempt such an approach.

Any regression with a large number of terms is likely to risk problems of multicollinearity. This presents a difficulty, but not an insurmountable problem. First, simplification may come because some interaction terms will have few or no entries. Second, one can restrict the particular jobs one considers. Even if there are eight departments in the organization, one may restrict the initial analysis of opportunity to just three departments. In that case the dummy variable specification makes the other five departments the standard to which the three departments are compared. Although multicollinearity may present insoluble problems for some jobs, this need not preclude the analysis of other jobs, for one can omit the multicollinear jobs from the analysis. Third, the units of analysis can be changed in order to minimize problems of multicollinearity. Highly correlated jobs and job sequences may be grouped together as units, after which they can be entered in the analysis. Although one cannot dismiss the problem of multicollinearity, there are often ways around it.

Another problem with this specification is the use of a dummy dependent variable. Although this problem should not be ignored, it does not present insurmountable problems, and there are procedures for correcting for it (Hanushek and Jackson, 1977, chap. 7).

Although there are some ways in which regression is an imperfect analog, it does provide a symbolic representation for the processes being considered. These methods are not only useful for analyzing the effects of jobs and job sequences, but personal attributes can also be introduced into the above regression in order to study the interactions of jobs and personal attributes.

It should be noted that this procedure requires very large samples, but big organizations provide just the kinds of numbers that are required. It is in large organizations that affirmative action programs are most important, and over the course of a few years these organizations have many individuals in each job type and individuals of the various acceptable personal attributes and who may have come to the job from the various acceptable career routes.

Although regression and log-linear methods do make the task of investigating interaction effects easier than would be the case from inspection of tables, analyzing the effects of six variables and including four-factor interactions is not a simple matter. Yet is is likely to reveal the kinds of phenomena that need to be examined and that are likely to be substantively important.

A third approach is to use mathematical algorithms for modeling the structure of employee careers. Block modeling techniques such as those described by White and his colleagues (Breiger, Boorman, and Arabic, 1975; White and Boorman, 1976) provide a convenient tool for finding relationships among positions. Such techniques could be used to describe patterns of mobility between positions and to find strong and weak career routes. Moreover, if pairs of job moves at a lower level were taken as units and their relationships to subsequent higher-level occupancies were analyzed, historical carry-over effects could be systematically analyzed. For instance, if various combinations of lateral and nonlateral moves were taken as units and their relationship to higher-level occupancies were analyzed, carry-over effects of lateral moves could be seen in terms of the career tracks they create in contrast to those created by nonlateral moves. Although block modeling techniques have not yet been applied to data on promotion in complex organizations, they would seem to have promise in that domain.

Conclusion

This chapter has reviewed many variables and considered the complex ways they may influence organizational opportunity structure and consequently influence the ways affirmative action policies should operate. It may be useful to list the variables considered here.

Summary of variables

Position: Positional opportunity
Lateral move within level
Promotion across departments

Personal: Education, grades, and college quality
Training programs
Age and age-squared
Race and sex

The aim has been to indicate the ways career tracking—in patterns of interconnected opportunities among jobs and between jobs and personal attributes—may influence people's careers and may influence the success of affirmative action programs. This chapter has argued that interaction effects need to be explicitly dealt with if affirmative action programs are to lead to long-term benefits for minorities and women.

Part Three

Assessing the Extent of Sexism and Racism in Organizational Settings

~~~~~~

The four chapters in this part consist of research exploring the existence of institutional discrimination (racism or sexism) within single organizations. Each chapter explores one or more descriptions of discrimination: proportional representation of various populations within the organization, recruitment to the organization, status attainment processes, and reward systems.

Paula Dubeck examines the management recruitment practices of a midwestern manufacturing concern. Her analysis presents a model of the recruitment process to account for the position of women within the organization. She also suggests ways social indicators can be developed to discern existing sexism in managerial recruitment.

Barbara Reskin and Lowell Hargens examine status attainment (reward-to-performance) processes to determine if they are equivalent in the scientific careers of men and women. This chapter is an excellent model of the kind of research needed to understand better the mobility of men and women (or of blacks and whites) within particular organizations. Rather than looking simply at the outcome (number or proportion of male versus female scientists), they investigate the *processes* through which success is achieved by each of the groups in question.

McDonough, Snider, and Kaufman offer an insightful conceptualization of the major issues in the study of institutional racism/sexism: job grading; the problems of "in-out," "up-down," and "equal pay"; and other problematic characteristics of formal structure within organizations. The overall purpose of the chapter is to apply a human capital model to the structure of wages within an organization. The empirical issue with which they are concerned is whether "equal pay for equal work" adequately describes organizational reality.

Peter Nordlie invokes the notion of a base standard against which can be statistically compared the proportion of black officers in command positions in the U.S. Army. Nordlie seeks to develop social indicators that can be used to monitor institutional discrimination on a continuous basis, tools that can later be used to monitor the results of programs to ensure equal opportunity in the army. Herein lies a major difficulty with the approach used by Nordlie and by others in similar circumstances: The approach is to measure *results*. This is certainly a necessary consideration. However, it needs to be applied to monitor *points of entry* into a given system and not just *points of exit*. Nordlie's approach is to establish what is the "eligible population" of officers (what others have called the availability pool) and from that to determine the "expected number" of officers for some particular purpose. Thus if a particular proportion of officers is black, that same proportion is "expected" to exist among those officers promoted to command positions. If figures are radically different, it is assumed that some degree of institutional discrimination has taken place. However, the paper does not explore the extent to which blacks have participated in experiences that systematically prepare them to assume command positions. Thus although Nordlie does not do it himself in his chapter, the technique can be applied, in a sense, further back in the promotional process to determine at what precise point blacks are kept from entering the chain of steps that ultimately leads to a command position.

4

Sexism in Recruiting Management Personnel for a Manufacturing Firm

Paula J. Dubeck

The status of women in private industry increasingly and more forcefully has been addressed through federal policies requiring affirmative action by defense contractors and by the response of the Equal Employment Opportunity Commission (EEOC) to complaints on hiring, mobility, and dismissal. Industrial management in particular has come under fire because of the limited number of women in managerial ranks and/or their not being moved within the corporate hierarchy. My research attempts to develop indicators sensitive to managerial recruitment practices and in doing so to evaluate the impact of sexism on one's gaining access to an industrial organization. The data used are limited to a sample of college graduates recruited for industrial manufacturing management positions at a midwestern manufacturing concern.

An Accounting of Women in Industry

Schwartz (1971) reviewed nationally based statistics reflecting the occupational status of women in business and their limited progress in gaining access to managerial positions. Drawing on the EEO-1 report of female employment in retail trade in nine metropolitan areas, Schwartz showed that in seven cities women represented over 40 percent of white-collar workers in retail trade. When clerical workers were excluded from computation, their representation dropped drastically, in some cases to half the original proportion. In Atlanta, for example, the percentage dropped from 47.2 percent to 25.1 percent (Schwartz, 1971, pp. 3–4). Census data on managerial employment showed that in 1940, 1950, and 1965, women made up 11.7 percent, 14.8 percent, and 14.8 percent, respectively, of those classified as "managers, officials, and proprietors." The lack of employment gains is further emphasized by the fact that at the above times women accounted for 24.4 percent, 28.8 percent, and 38.8 percent, respectively, of the work force. Schwartz also notes that in 1965 women composed only 2.5 percent of those in that occupational category earning $10,000 annually.

A number of explanations have been offered to account for the heretofore limited number of women in the managerial ranks of organizations. The accounts may be categorized roughly as those having to do with commitment to a career, skills or training, and personality characteristics. With the first it is argued that women generally do not have the commitment to long-term career goals that is required of managerial personnel; that is, women will leave their jobs to marry or to have children. Explanations based on skill or training emphasize skills of a "good manager," usually gained through business school degrees. In cases where job demands are technical, as in engineering, a technical background is also desired of managers. Because few women have business or engineering backgrounds, few are available to fill the positions. The third explanation focuses on personality characteristics associated with successful managers. Managers, for example, are assertive, aggressive, and able to make reasoned decisions. Men are considered more likely to have these attributes than women and thus are more likely to attain management positions.

Yet research does not support these arguments. It has been shown, for example, that no single set of characteristics defines a "good manager" (Fiedler, 1969; Mitchell and others, 1970), that assertiveness and the ability to make reasoned decisions are not gender-based characteristics (Moses and Boehm, 1975), and that the question of career commitment may be more a response to blocked occupational opportunities than marriage and family options attributed to women (Kanter, 1977a). The research suggests that each argument is limited to the extent of its dependence on intangible, qualitative criteria for employee selection and/or evalution. These factors in particular are likely to be subject to the bias introduced by sex stereotyping.

The presence and impact of sex stereotyping in organizations has been the focus of much recent research. Schein (1973), using male managers to define images of males, females, and successful managers, obtained a high correlation between images of male and manager but no such relationship between images of female and manager. A repeat of this research using only female managers showed the same strong relationship between male and manager but also a low, significant relationship between images of female and manager. This latter relationship, however, was very much weaker than the former (Schein, 1975). Additional evidence of sex stereotyping is found in Rosen and Jerdee's (1974) study of personnel decisions concerning promotion, development, and supervision. Male superiors were less likely to trust the judgment of female than male supervisors in questions of employee performance, were less likely to promote females than males, and were less enthusiastic about sending a young promotable female than a young promotable male to a professional training conference. Finally, there is research evidence to show that when certain traditionally positive male characteristics are used to describe females, they are given a negative assessment (Broverman and others, 1972). The characteristics include aggressiveness, independence, and assertiveness. Thus sex stereotyping not only affects the distribution of characteristics but also may result in an opposite value being assigned to those characteristics for males and females.

The implications of these findings for an organization's recruitment procedure suggest that for those firms previously recruiting only males for managerial positions, their traditional recruitment model would not apply to females. Specifically, to the extent that an organization's recruitment depends on qualitative factors, one can also expect sex stereotyping to enter into selection. In this light the seeming inapplicability of the model may derive from two sources: different criteria being used to judge male and female recruits or the same criteria being differentially applied to male and female recruits. The research on sex stereotyping suggests the first is more likely, although not to the exclusion of the second. Organizational recruitment practices must be more systematically examined in order to explore these possibilities.

Industrial Management Recruits

I examined management recruitment patterns of a large midwestern industrial manufacturing concern in which women are employed in both hourly and salaried positions. Women held approximately 40 percent of the hourly and 25 percent of the salaried positions. In the salaried ranks, however, less than 7 percent of the management positions were filled by women and no woman held a management position above entry level.

The recruitment of new managers from college graduate ranks generally followed a process in which screening took place on campuses and at the factory. Approximately 15 percent of those interviewed on campus were invited for a plant visit. A second source of college graduate recruits was "walk-in" candidates (those from local or nearby communities, who made up approximately 15 percent of the recruit population). People were interviewed at the plant by middle management as well as those under whose immediate supervision they might work as trainees. At a later date some recruits were offered positions as management trainees. During the research period persons were hired into a "trainee pool." The firm anticipated the number of managerial positions it would need to fill during the coming year and expected to fill them from the trainee ranks. The trainees were to circulate among four subunits to determine the area of their preference and best performance. Ideally, this was to determine their first placement as a nontrainee.

Data

I collected information on a sample of 290 college graduate recruits given on-site interviews for managerial positions. These recruits had been interviewed over a three-and-a-half-year period from January 1973 through May 1976, and the sample includes 116 who were interviewed but not offered a position. Because the firm kept interview files for only a limited period, usually a year unless a person is hired, I used cluster sampling to select the final sample of recruits. I used lists of persons entering managerial training since January 1973 and recruit interview files from January 1975 through May 1976. I included only college graduates in the sample and the majority had been interviewed from January 1975 through May 1976. Because there was no reason to believe recruitment patterns had changed during the period covered by my research, I consider the sample representative of all recruits. There were limitations to the sample. One was the availability of lists of trainees; persons entered the corporation at varying times over the year, so some would have individualized training and would not be included on the trainee lists. Additionally, I excluded recruits on whom there was considerable incomplete information from the final sample.

Background information gathered about the recruits included the following: sex, race, age, area of degree concentration, marital status, cumulative grade point percentage (GPA was converted to percentage possible), and leadership experience. Qualitative evaluations of the recruits included interviewer ratings about their apparent interest in the job, whether the interviewer considered the recruit qualified for the position, and whether the interviewer recommended the recruit for hire. With respect to job interest, recruits were evaluated as enthusiastic, interested, or so-so. These were assigned scores of 1, 2, and 3, respectively, and averaged across the interviews; each person received an average "job interest" score. As to their perceived qualifications, 65.8 percent were considered qualified by all interviewers; so recruits were categorized as "qualified" (receiving unanimous support) or "other" (not receiving unanimous support). On the recommendation for hire, just over half, 50.6 percent, received a unanimous recommendation, 18.7 percent received two recommendations, and 30.7 percent received one or none. Responses were categorized accordingly.

Recruit Profile

Of the 290 recruits interviewed, 28.6 percent were female; 25.2 percent were nonwhite; the median age was twenty-three years; and the majority (52.8 percent) were single at the time of their interview. The largest proportion (44.8 percent) had degrees in technical areas, such as engineering, and the second most frequent degree area was nontechnical, nonbusiness (32.8 percent), such as liberal arts or education; 22.4 percent had degrees in business; the median grade point was 2.9 (on 4.0 scale) and almost half had leadership experience in campus organizations, work, or military experience.

Female recruits differed from males in a number of ways. They were significantly younger (23.8 and 25.4 years, respectively), were more likely to be single, and performed significantly better academically. Over half the female recruits held degrees in nontechnical, nonbusiness fields; males were drawn primarily from technical degree fields. There was no difference in their leadership activity. Finally, there was no statistically significant difference in the proportion of males and females judged qualified by interviewers, but there were differences in the extent to which they received recommendations for hire. Over half the males (53.1 percent) and 43.2 percent of the females received a unanimous recommendation; 14.9 percent of the males and 28.4 percent of the females received two. This latter finding suggests a differential evaluation of female and male recruits takes place during the recruitment process. For further clarification, characteristics of those offered a position and those not are examined.

Differential Characteristics

Those offered a position in the firm differed from those not offered one in leadership experience, academic performance, and interviewer evaluations. Those offered a position were more likely to have leadership experience (56.4 percent versus 40.4 percent) and to have significantly better academic records (84.2 percent versus 42.1 percent). They were more likely to have been evaluated as qualified and to have received a unanimous recommendation for hire (74.3 percent versus 19.0 percent). The two groups did not differ on the basis of sex, race, marital status, or degree area. As to a basic set of characteristics by which the firm selects its future managers, the above results show them to be (1) leadership experience, (2) academic performance, (3) perceived qualification by interviewers, and (4) recommendation for hire.

I gave additional consideration to the interrelationship between variables, particularly where there were differences between males and females. A unanimous recommendation for a job offer was highly related to perceived qualification. Although there was no difference between the distribution of males and females considered qualified, there was a significant difference in their being recommended for a job offer. This suggests that the concept of "qualified" is interpreted differently for males and females. Second, there was no relationship between the degree area and academic performance of recruits, but controlling for sex showed this held only for females. Females in all degree areas were concentrated in the upper third of the grade distribution, whereas the better performing males held degrees in technical areas and those with business or other degrees tended to be concentrated in the lower third of the grade distribution (Table 1). This suggests a differential assessment of the academic performance of female and male recruits.

Some evidence suggests a priority ranking among variables taken into consideration. Specifically, the relative importance of leadership compared to academic performance for all recruits may be gleaned in part from the above analysis. If academic performance were as important as or more important than leadership, one would expect job offers to favor females; if leadership

Table 1. The Relationship Between Degree Area and the Academic
Performance of Management Recruits, Controlling for Sex

	Male Academic Performance			Female Academic Performance		
Degree Area	Low	Middle	High	Low	Middle	High
Technical, business related	27	25	34	4	5	10
	31.4%	29.1%	39.5%	21.1%	26.3%	52.6%
Nontechnical business	17	6	9	1	5	10
	53.1%	18.8%	28.8%	6.3%	31.3%	62.5%
Nontechnical, nonbusiness	17	15	4	7	12	13
	47.2%	41.7%	11.1%	21.9%	37.5%	40.6%
Total	61	46	47	12	22	33
	39.6%	29.9%	30.5%	17.9%	32.8%	49.2%

$\frac{2}{4df}$ =13.28   p=.01 $\frac{2}{4df}$ =3.168   p=.53

$\gamma = -.323$ $\gamma = -.170$

were more important, neither males nor females would be favored by job offers. Because the distribution of job offers does
not favor females over males, leadership seems to outweigh academic performance in the evaluation of recruits during selection.
But this conclusion must be addressed in terms of the findings
that show sex to be a major variable in analysis, particulary because some characteristics that distinguish those offered a position from those not did not prove useful when sex was taken into
account. There is some evidence to suggest that certain objective
criteria, such as academic performance, are less important in
selection decisions than are qualitative factors such as the interviewer's perception of the candidate's qualification. Because
qualitative factors are likely to be influenced by sex stereotyping, the question now becomes one of how stereotypes operate.
That is, are sex stereotypes reflected by the use of different criteria in the selection of female and male recruits or are the same
criteria being valued differently for female and male recruits?
To determine this, I examined the relative importance of selection criteria for male and female recruits.

Priorities Among Recruitment Variables

To establish ranking among the variables that would predict whether a job offer is likely to be made, I performed a stepwise discriminant function analysis using a number of the above variables, including race, degree area, leadership experience, grade point percentage, marital status, job interest, and perceived qualified (versus "other"). The recommendation to hire was omitted to allow a better clarification of the primary variables, which differentiate between those offered and those not offered a position.

I ran the initial analysis on male recruits only to establish a model assumed to have been traditionally operative and found four variables to differentiate significantly between males offered a position and those not. These are (in order of priority) (1) "qualified," (2) leadership experience, (3) job interest, and (4) academic performance. The analysis correctly categorized 76.5 percent of those not offered positions and 81.6 percent of those who were and had an overall accuracy of 79.1 percent.

When the same set of variables was used to differentiate between females offered a position and those not, the following were found to be significant discriminators (in order of priority): (1) job interest, (2) academic performance, (3) race, and (4) perceived qualified. The analysis correctly categorized 74.1 percent of those not offered a position and 77.8 percent of those offered a position; overall accuracy was 75.56 percent.

The stepwise analysis made two things apparent: (1) It is not so much the criteria as their differential application that distinguishes the recruitment of males from females. (2) Qualitative factors are significant influences in the decision process. With respect to the first, academic performance, job interest, and perceived qualified are critical differentiators between those offered a position and those not. Although perceived qualified is most important for males, job interest takes this top priority for females.

This differential priority among criteria highlights an uncertainty introduced into recruitment by gender; it may be understood by reflecting on the expressed concerns of organizations that only recently began recruiting females for management. Their questions and comments focus on the qualifications of the female recruit and whether she is "career oriented" or will leave once married. The high priority given job interest, then, suggests career orientation is a more important concern than qualifications. The lower priority for perceived qualification may also represent an uncertainty about female candidates, but in a somewhat different fashion. If the designation of "qualified" is derived from a review of a number of objective criteria (degree area, grades, and courses, for example), it is likely that the female candidate will present no ambiguity in this respect. But the meaning of qualified may be narrower when applied to females than when applied to males. That is, although females are evaluated on objective criteria, "qualified" for males may reflect an evaluation based on the combination of objective and subjective factors. One can understand the difference by using Hughes's (1945) framework for analyzing the situation of the "marginal man." Hughes notes that an individual may possess all legitimate and official criteria for holding a particular position but may be omitted from informal working networks because of a lack of trust. This trust derives in part from those characteristics associated with the type of person traditionally holding a particular position; trust in a doctor, for example, comes partly from his being white, middle-aged, and male. The individual who does not share such associated characteristics is less likely to be trusted and also is not included in informal social networks. What is operating, then, is a second set of characteristics that facilitate the establishment of a broad-based relationship, suggesting that the individual would "fit" into the organization or shares a similar set of values. Recasting this into the framework for examining recruitment, then, one can say the high priority given to perceived qualification for male candidates depicts more than a summary evaluation of objective criteria; it is more likely to reflect both objective credentials and the likelihood that the recruit will fit into the organization. For females the whole question of fitting into the organization is overlaid by uncertainty, particularly that introduced by career orientation. And if the meaning of "qualified" is narrower when applied to female recruits, this also will account for its having less influence in selection decisions.

The data analysis highlights a second set of factors that should be noted. Race was found to be important in determining which female candidates received an offer; this may be considered by the employing firm as one way to meet two affirmative action demands. A second factor, leadership, was important for males but not for females. Because leadership was an important differentiator between those offered a position and those not, one would expect it to be important in the selection of both males and females, particularly given the nature of the job. That it is not suggests recruiters have a fairly good idea about the set of credentials they believe will predict a good male supervisor but this apparently has not been established for females. So the more ambiguous concerns, which may be traced to set stereotypes, predominate.

The overall set of findings has serious implications for the long-term employment of women in management. Because leadership experience can be an employment asset, candidates beginning without it may be handicapped in their attempts to move up the organization's hierarchy over time. If, for example, it has an impact on the time it takes to gain one's first permanent position and this in turn affects one's organizational visibility, then leadership will have an impact on the opportunities available to the new managerial recruit. That it is not found to be a critical factor in the selection of female recruits suggests their mobility could be limited. Second, opportunities for female recruits will be limited because they do not share the associated characteristics of managers in general; thus it will be more difficult for them to establish trust relationships that would enhance their performance through informal contacts among peers. The combination of these two factors suggests that female managers are likely to have limited overall success in the organization in the future.

Sexism and Social Indicators

The manifestation of sexism will not be apparent in gross measures of women's employment in white-collar jobs or even necessarily in measures of managerial employment. Such indicators are less attuned to internal hierarchical differentiation than they are to summary placement levels, for instance, managers. Some indicators, however, are within reasonable reach. One can use the number of promotions or a combination of promotions plus duration of employment (similar to that of Moses and Boehm, 1975) to reflect the status of women in management; such measures may be developed for both female and male managerial employees, and over time one would expect them to converge if there is a reduction in institutional sexism. A second indicator that looks at recruitment criteria may be developed to deal with entry-level questions, identifying the proportion of women who enter an organization at different positions and how they compare to males entering at the same position. Finally, more elaborate research would generate the link between these two sets of indicators. There are some who suggest that little relationships exists between the two, but more extensive research would allow us to clarify the relationship between recruitment and long-term employment success and the consequences of sexism on each.

5

Scientific Advancement of Male and Female Chemists

Barbara F. Reskin
Lowell L. Hargens

Definitions of discrimination usually include the notion of treating individuals inequitably on the basis of their group membership (Boulding, 1976). However, the difficulty of directly observing differential treatment has often led social scientists to accept differences in outcomes as evidence of discrimination. Thus in practice discrimination is often conceived as differences between members of two or more groups in some positive or negative outcome such that the dominant group fares better than the subordinate group.

But differential outcomes need not reflect discrimination if they are consistent with relevant criteria for allocating rewards (need, merit, and so forth). For example, few would argue that giving children smaller portions of food is discriminatory. More precisely, then, discrimination occurs whenever either the criteria upon which rewards are allocated are inequitably applied (for example, when minority group members must perform exceptionally to be granted rewards that normally accrue for merely adequate performance by the dominant group) or relevant criteria are suspended for one group and replaced by irrelevant criteria (Antonovsky, 1960; Yinger, 1968), the extreme case being the use of group membership itself as the criterion. To use Merton's (1972, p. 20) terms, this is treating a functionally irrelevant characteristic as relevant. Conceptualizing discrimination as the inequitable application of criteria implies assessing it by directly examining the *links* between performance and rewards for the two groups. Even in the absence of group differences in outcomes, different rates of return to performance imply institutionalized discrimination (Althauser and Wigler, 1972). Intent is neither necessary nor sufficient for the occurrence of discrimination.

Examining the links between performance and rewards is feasible in any organizational context in which both are observable and data are available on incumbents' careers. Science represents such an institution and is a strategic sector in which to study institutionalized discrimination. Scientific norms require original research (Merton, 1957b), and published research results are visible manifestations of performance. Public sources (such as *American Men and Women of Science* or *Science Citation Index*) facilitate tracing most scientists' careers. Finally, because most scientific research is carried out in organizations whose stratification systems are well understood, ranking scientists' positions is straightforward.

Not only is there consensus that publishing is the primary basis for scientific advancement, but the process by which performance and career outcomes are related has been studied in detail (Cole and Cole, 1973; Zuckerman, 1970). It is now generally agreed that this process is one of "accumulative advantage" (Cole and Cole, 1973, pp. 119–122) in which there are feedback relationships between performance, recognition, and rewards. Briefly, collegial recognition of published work (often in the form of citations) demonstrates a scientist's merit to those who distribute rewards (promotions, grants, research assistance, and so forth), which—like recognition itself—both reinforce and thereby maintain performance and also are resources for future performance (Allison and Stewart, 1974; Reskin, 1976). But to the extent that some groups' opportunities to translate early performance or positional resources into later positional success are restricted, insititutionalized discrimination exists. The major object of this chapter is to demonstrate a technique that both provides a statistical test for such group differences in the processes of accumulative advantage—and hence for assessing institutionalized discrimination—and identifies the points where discrimination occurs. The groups we examine are female and male chemists. Thus we also address the substantive question of the extent of sex discrimination in one scientific discipline. Although we illustrate the techniques with data on scientists, they apply equally in any organizational context in which rewards depend on performance.

Evidence for Discrimination in Science

For several years both scientists and observers have debated the question of sex discrimination in science (for a review see Vetter, 1976; Zuckerman and Cole, 1975). The early empirical studies identified sex differences in outcomes but failed to consider whether returns to scientific performance differed for the sexes. Recent work bears on this issue. Cole and Cole (1973, pp. 141–143) examined the impact of sex on positional success, controlling for publications. Although the zero-order association between sex and academic rank was not destroyed, they tentatively attributed it to uncontrolled variables and concluded that there is little sex discrimination in science (1973, p. 151). Using multiple regression, Astin and Bayer (1972) also sought to estimate the impact (and in their second study to assess changes in the impact; Bayer and Astin, 1975) of sex on rank, tenure, and salary, net of relevant variables. But they omitted sex interaction terms from the regression equations, so their model implied equivalent processes linking performance and rewards for the sexes. This assumption would hold only if there were no sex discrimination in the processes of status attainment in science. The separate regression analyses for the sexes did document small sex differences in rank and larger ones in salary but provided no test of the critical assumption of equivalent processes for the sexes.

Using analyses of covariance, Reskin (1976) showed that the performance-reward processes for female and male chemists differed significantly with respect to a single but important event in the scientific career—the postdoctoral fellowship. Sex interactions occurred for both the predoctoral determinants and the positional consequences of holding a prestigious fellowship but not for the impact of the fellowship on later productivity. These results are consistent with the existence of different underlying status attainment processes for the sexes that would occur if institutionalized sex discrimination restricted the female scientists' opportunities to accumulate advantages. The competing hypothesis of lower professional commitment among the women was not ruled out entirely, but supplementary analyses reduced its plausibility.

In this chapter we apply to these same data more powerful techniques for analyzing sex differences in the accumulation of advantages. The techniques are superior because, unlike conventional analysis of covariance, which examines one dependent variable at a time, they permit systematic comparison of the entire structural equation models for two or more subpopulations. With these techniques we can thus assess the equivalence of models of the causal processes by which the sexes translate performance into positional success and use such success both for further professional advancement and to maintain their scientific productivity. Figure 1 presents the general model upon which our analysis is based. After discussing the variables in it and the methods, we report the tests of whether the parameters for the causal links differ for male and female chemists.

Data and Measures

Data Source

This study is based on data for members of several cohorts of chemists who obtained Ph.D. degrees at U.S. universities between 1955 and 1961. The names of all the female doctorates

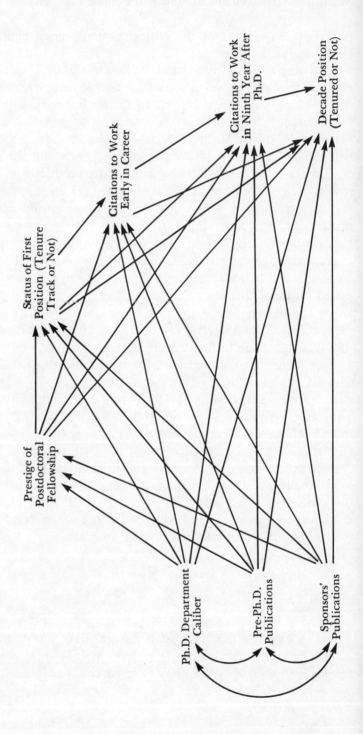

Figure 1. Process of Status Attainment in Science

(N = 231) and a systematic random sample of men (N = 221) were obtained from the American Chemical Society's biennial *Directory of Graduate Research* (*DGR*) (American Chemical Society, 1957, 1959, 1961). Information on sample members' academic sponsors' productivity was also taken from this source. Biographical data for these scientists were sought in *American Men and Women of Science* and other biographical directories and were solicited directly from the chemists not included in those sources by a mailed questionnaire. By these methods we obtained complete career histories for 86 percent of the women and 94 percent of the men.

Annual article counts were obtained from *Chemical Abstracts* (*CA*) for the period from five years before the Ph.D. through the Ph.D. year. *CA* counts all of an article's authors, regardless of order of authorship. *Science Citation Index* (*SCI*) provided data on the number of citations scientists received for publications for which they were the first authors.

Measures

In order to determine whether the sexes were equally able to accumulate advantages in the manner that theoretically occurs in science (that is, to convert performance into positional success and to utilize positional resources to maintain professional productivity and facilitate further career advancement), it was necessary to observe performance and position over time. To simplify our presentation, we included only eight variables observed over a decade. Although these are adequate for illustrative purposes and provide rather strong evidence for the nonequivalence of the processes of career advancement for the sexes, it is necessary to examine more fully specified models to identify the exact mechanisms of institutionalized discrimination.

In order to capture the process of accumulative advantage, we had to classify certain professional experiences as measures of either performance or positional rewards. Although certain features of scientists' training, for example, may reflect their own performance while also indexing access to resources that should influence later performance and position (this problem is discussed in Reskin, 1977), we arrived at the following occasionally arbitrary classification of our variables as indicators of performance or position (and hence, of positional resources): predoctoral and postdoctoral performances and predoctoral and postdoctoral positions.

Predoctoral Performance. The number of predoctoral publications provides a good measure of predoctoral performance. But predoctoral publication counts could reflect the length of time the chemist was in graduate school (and thus in which predoctoral publication could occur), so we regressed it on length of doctoral study (Ph.D. year minus B.S. year) and used the residuals from this regression as a duration-free measure of predoctoral publication.

Postdoctoral Performance. Our measures of postdoctoral scientific performance consist of citation counts, which are preferable to publication counts because they reflect both the quanitity and quality of scientists' published work (Cole and Cole, 1973, pp. 21–26). Collins (1975, p. 516), for example, claims that citations constitute the single best measure of scientific success. Although one might object that sex bias may lead to the undercitation of work written by women, the female chemists averaged more citations per published article than the males (Reskin, 1973, pp. 311–313). Thus we doubt that using citations biases our measure of women's performance.

Citations chemists received early in their careers measure their early postdoctoral performance. We obtained these data from the 1961 and 1964 editions of the *SCI*. The first volume of *SCI* was published in 1961, and a second did not appear until 1964. Thus we used 1961 citations for 1955 to 1958 Ph.D.s and 1964 citations for 1959 to 1961 Ph.D.s. Citation counts were standardized by the chemists' Ph.D. year to adjust for intercohort variation in *SCI* coverage in these early editions.

Predecade citations are the number of citations chemists received during their ninth year after the doctorate. These citations were tabulated from the volume of *SCI* corresponding to the chemists' ninth postdoctoral year.

Predoctoral Position. The caliber of the Ph.D. department reflects the quality of training available to graduate students along with a variety of resources that may facilitate their acquisition of skills and hence their productivity (Reskin, 1977). In addition, by conferring a status on new Ph.D.s, their doctoral departments influence their positional outcomes (Zuckerman, 1970, p. 246).

The productivity of the chemists' doctoral sponsors provides a second indicator of predoctoral position and resources. Like Ph.D. departments, sponsors ascribe to their students a status that affects their entry level in the scientific stratification system.

We recognize that the selection processes by which students are matched with doctoral departments or sponsors may justify viewing these two variables as measures of the chemists' promise as graduate students. But the previously cited evidence for the ascriptive effect of the Ph.D. department on scientists' positional attainments supports treating it as a measure of position and resources. Moreover, regardless of any association between these indicators of predoctoral position and the chemists' early professional performance due to selectivity, to the extent that the indicators reflect access to resources that facilitate scientists' professional development, they constitute the first stage in the process of accumulating advantages.

Postdoctoral Position. A postdoctoral fellowship—at least for male scientists (Reskin, 1976)—is the first post-Ph.D. positional reward for predoctoral achievement. In addition fellowships provide a variety of resources (free time, research resources, additional instruction, and, in some cases, considerable prestige) that facilitate scientific advancement. But because the benefits a fellowship provides should vary with its prestige (and because of the differential meaning of a fellowship per se for the sexes; Reskin, 1976), we used fellowship prestige rather than the simple fact of an award as our indicator. Fellowship prestige scores were taken from scientists' rankings of a variety of scientific awards.[1]

First postdoctoral position, like the postdoctoral fellowship, is affected by scientists' predoctoral performance, academic origins, and by having held a prestigious postdoctoral award. In turn, the first job affects scientists' subsequent careers (Hagstrom and Hargens, 1968). Graduate students generally prefer university positions (Klaw, 1968), which provide scientists maximum research autonomy (Kornhauser, 1962). But university staff who are not on a tenure track lack the resources and incentives to do research available to regular faculty. Because these aspects of university employment are critical for our purposes, we selected tenure track university employment as our measure of the first postdoctoral position.[2]

Position at the end of the first professional decade is our ultimate dependent variable. Following the previously outlined reasoning and because tenure is normally achieved in well under ten years (Bayer and Dutton, 1977, p. 264), we categorized the decade position as tenured university positions versus all others.

Method

The statistical methods we employ allow us to determine whether the status attainment processes for male and female chemists are equivalent and to locate any differences between them. To assess the overall equivalence of the sexes' status attainment processes, we first test the equivalence of the sex-specific variance-covariance matrices. The technique for locating any differences uses results from conventional multiple regression procedures to compare pairs of models of the status attainment processes. In each pair one of the models allows sex differences in parameters the other model constrains to be equal. We then determine whether the first model fits the observed data significantly better than the second by using a chi-square test. If it does, we conclude that the parameter(s) under examination differ for the sexes. By repeating this procedure for the various parameters in the status attainment process, we identify which ones differ significantly for the women and men. However, these tests do not show the direction or magnitude of the sex differences; so for each dependent variable we also estimate the parameters for the sexes separately, by means of conventional multiple regression. The regression coefficients indicate whether the sex differences are in the direction expected if the women experienced discrimination.

We begin by testing the hypothesis that differences between the observed sex-specific variance-covariance matrices can be attributed to random sampling variation (Specht and Warren, 1975, pp. 50–51), which would be the case if the sexes were subject to the same status attainment process. Thus a rejection of the hypothesis implies that the processes for the male and female chemists are not equivalent.

If this hypothesis is rejected, we proceed to determine which parameters differ for the sexes. As we indicated in the previous summary, this is accomplished through the comparison of a series of models of the process that successively permits greater numbers of parameters to vary by sex. The logic of the statistical test is as follows: The investigator specifies two models; the first, model A, allows sex differences in one or more parameters that the second, model B, constrains to be equal for the sexes.[3] Because model A is less constrained than model B, it should fit the observed data better than model B. If we can reject the null hypothesis that the improvement in fit by model A in comparison to model B cannot be attributed to sampling variation, then we may conclude that the sexes do differ in the parameters at issue.

Conventional multiple-regression analyses yield information necessary to test this null hypothesis. One obtains ordinary least-squares estimates for each equation in both models A and B (see Specht and Warren, 1975, pp. 53–60, for numerical examples) and determines the unexplained variance (mean squared residual) for every endogenous variable in each model. Then one computes the likelihood-ratio chi-square statistic, $\chi^2 = (N - d) M$, where N equals the total number of cases in the samples being studied, d equals the difference in the number of parameters estimated by the two models (that is, the number of parameters estimated for model A minus the number estimated for model B), and M equals the natural logarithm of the ratio of the products of the residual mean squares for the more constrained model to the less constrained model. The likelihood-ratio chi-square statistic has d degrees of freedom. Rejection of the null hypothesis enables the investigator to conclude that observed sex differences in the parameters freed by model A but not model B cannot be attributed to random sampling errors and therefore reflect actual sex differences.

The chi-square test will usually be done for a series of pairs of models so that all parameters in the status attainment process are examined for sex differences, either singly or in theoretically meaningful groups. However, the investigator must provide a theoretical rationale for the order in which parameters are freed by the series of models used in the analysis. For our analysis the theory of accumulative advantage provides such a rationale. Hence we begin by allowing sex differences in the impacts of earlier performance measures on later positions. It is often argued that such links are the major mechanism of accumulative advantage in science (Cole and Cole, 1973), and sex differences in their magnitudes indicate the extent to which departures from achievement (Merton, 1957b) can account for differences in the reward structures confronting male and female scientists. Next we examine the possibility that impacts of earlier positional rewards on later rewards also differ for the sexes. Because this analysis is carried out after allowing for the possibility of sex differences in the impacts of earlier performance on later rewards, it indicates the extent to which the links between earlier and later positions—net of the impact of performance on rewards—also differ by sex. In the third stage of the analysis we examine the links between earlier positional statuses and later performance by permitting these parameters to differ for the sexes. These links constitute another important mechanism for the accumulation of advantages insofar as scientists' positions do in fact differentially expose them to opportunities and reward structures and thereby lead to differential performance. Finally, we examine the links between earlier performance and later performance. This final analysis indicates the degree to which the sexes differ in the stability of their scientific performance net of differences in the extent to which earlier positional resources determine later performance.

Results

Table 1 presents the correlations and standard deviations for the eight variables. The analyses are based on the sex-specific variance-covariance matrices obtained from the correlations and standard deviations shown in Table 1.

We begin by testing the hypothesis that the overall processes of accumulative advantage are equivalent for the sexes, that is, that any differences in the sex-specific variance-covari-

Table 1. Correlations and Standard Deviations for Performance and Position Indicators (Women Above Main Diagonal, Men Below)

	1	2	3	4	5	6	7	8	Women's S.D.
1. Ph.D. caliber	–	.03	.24	.04	.01	.07	.18	-.04	98.81
2. Pre-Ph.D. publication	.00	–	.17	.18	-.03	.17	.20	.10	1.46
3. Sponsor's publication	.24	.07	–	-.04	-.08	.20	.20	-.10	.98
4. Postdoctoral prestige	.11	.04	.08	–	-.05	.06	.18	.13	2.74
5. First position	.00	-.02	-.02	.32	–	-.03	-.01	.27	.13
6. Early citations	.20	.16	.11	.22	.20	–	.48	-.03	1.02
7. Predecade citations	.23	.12	.07	.24	.23	.67	–	-.03	8.35
8. Decade position	.15	.01	.08	.26	.33	.31	.35	–	.28
Men's S.D.	102.15	1.47	1.02	2.83	.23	.98	17.65	.34	–

ance matrices are due to random sampling error. On the basis of the data we reject this hypothesis (χ^2 = 247.3, with 36 degrees of freedom) and conclude that the sexes differ in the processes by which they accumulate advantages. Now we turn to the problem of identifying which parameters in the model differ significantly by sex. By estimating the parameters in Figure 1 separately for the sexes, we determined that the sex differences were concentrated among nine of the twenty-eight possibilities.

Although one could carry out the procedures illustrated for each of the twenty-eight possible parameters, we screened the results of the sex-specific regression analyses in order to identify the parameters that appeared to vary by sex. For brevity and simplicity in this illustration we report tests for only those parameters. Most of the parameters we excluded were too small to be statistically significant for either sex. In order to learn whether examining only nine of the parameters for sex differences resulted in underestimating the sex differences in the entire status attainment process, we contrasted a model that allowed sex differences in all twenty-eight parameters with a model allowing sex differences in only nine parameters. The chi-square statistic for the test had a value close to zero. Thus the model that allows sex differences in only the nine parameters fits the data as well as the one that allows sex differences in all parameters.

Table 2 presents the results of the analysis to locate which of the nine parameters differ significantly by sex. The analysis and results are presented in four stages, successively showing the effects of (1) performance on position, (2) position on position, (3) position on performance, and (4) performance on performance.

Performance on Position

In the first step we compare the model that constrains all parameters to be equal for the sexes with a model that allows sex differences in the impacts of predoctoral publications on the prestige of the postdoctoral fellowship and predecade citations on decade positions.[4] Line 1 of Table 2 indicates that allowing sex differences in these two parameters significantly improves the fit of the model to the data. In order to determine

Table 2. Results of χ^2 Tests for Models of the Status Attainment
Processes for Male and Female Chemists

Model	Comparison with Previous Nested Model		
	χ^2	df	p
1. Model that allows sex variation in two parameters showing the impacts of performances on positions:			
Pre-Ph.D. pub.→ postdoc. prestige Predecade cit. → decade pos.	8.28	2	<.02
2. Model that allows sex variation in parameters freed in step 1 *plus* variation in two parameters showing the impacts of earlier on later positions:			
Postdoc. pres. → first position First position → decade position	18.57	2	<.001
3. Model that allows sex variation in parameters freed in step 2 *plus* variation in four parameters showing the impacts of earlier positions on later performances:			

Ph.D. caliber → early citation
    Postdoc. pres. → early citation
    First position → early citation
    First position → predecade cit.
	1.43	4	N.S.

4. Model that allows sex variation in parameters freed in step 3 *plus* variation in the impact of early citations on predecade citations	41.13	1	<.001

whether the two parameters freed in this step are larger for the men than the women (which we would expect if the accumulative-advantage processes are weaker for the women), we refer to Table 3, which provides estimates of the various parameters in the final models of our analysis.

Table 3 presents parameters for the predictors of each of the five dependent variables in the model in Figure 1. For parameters for which no significant sex difference existed we estimated a single parameter on the basis of the pooled male and female samples, which is shown in the "pooled" columns. Where the parameters differed significantly for the sexes, we

Table 3. Metric Coefficients for Regression Equations Predicting Endogenous Variables in Best-Fitting Status Attainment Model

Independent Variables	Endogenous Variables								
	Postdoctoral Fellowship Prestige			First Position Tenure Track			Early Citations		
	Men	Pooled	Women	Men	Pooled	Women	Men	Pooled	Women
Ph.D. caliber	-.082	.002			.000		.002[a]		.000
Pre-Ph.D. publication			.356[a]		.003			.102[a]	
Sponsor's publication		-.003			-.011			.103[a]	
Postdoctoral prestige	—	—	—	.026[a]		-.003	.054[a]		.014
First position	—	—	—				.627[a]		-.162
Early citations	—	—	—	—	—	—			
Predecade citations	—	—	—	—	—	—	—	—	—

Table 3 (continued)

Independent Variables	Predecade Citations			Decade Position Tenured		
	Pooled	Men	Women	Pooled	Men	Women
Ph.D. caliber	.015ᵃ			.000		
Pre-Ph.D. publication	.382			.004		
Sponsor's publication	-.023			-.002		
Postdoctoral prestige	.426ᵃ			.015ᵃ		
First position	5.506	11.021ᵃ	3.666ᵃ		.333ᵃ	.607ᵃ
Early citations				.015		
Predecade citations				—	-.004ᵃ	-.003

Note: The best-fitting model is the model that frees the five parameters found to differ by sex in Table 2.

ᵃ Metric coefficient at least twice as large as standard error under null hypothesis that population parameter equals zero.

present the separate parameters for each sex in the appropriate columns. The results for the impact of predecade citations on having a tenured position a decade after the Ph.D. are in accordance with our expectations: The coefficient for the men (.004) is significantly greater than that for the women (–.003), indicating that relatively high levels of scientific contribution yield greater rewards to the men than the women for this dependent variable. But the impact of predoctoral publications on the prestige of the postdoctoral fellowship is greater for women (.356) than men (–.082), an outcome inconsistent with our general expectation that women's accumulative-advantage processes tend to be weaker than men's. This result is an artifact of the way we coded postdoctoral fellowship prestige.[5] In a previous study of the same scientists, Reskin (1976) found that *among those who actually held postdoctoral fellowships*, this parameter was greater for the men. As previously noted, we assigned a zero to those who never held a postdoctoral fellowship and one to those who had fellowships not listed in the prestige rankings. A much smaller proportion of men than women ever had a fellowship, but the female fellows disproportionately held unranked fellowships. As a result, the correlation of pre-Ph.D. publications with this variable is larger for the women than the men. Thus rather than indicating a condition wherein women received greater payoffs for high pre-Ph.D. publication levels than men, this result is consistent with Reskin's (1976) argument that among the women postdoctoral fellowships often substituted for more permanent positions rather than being honorific awards.

Position on Position

In the second stage of the analysis we tested a model that allows for sex differences in the parameters freed in the first stage *plus* (1) the impact of postdoctoral fellowship prestige on obtaining a tenure track position for one's first job and (2) the impact of a tenure track first job on being tenured a decade after the Ph.D. We compare this model with the one examined in the first stage. Thus in this stage we are testing for sex differences in the two parameters involving the impacts of earlier on later positional attainments.

Line 2 of Table 2 indicates that allowing these two parameters to vary by sex yields a significantly better fit to the data than the previous model. Inspection of the sex-specific estimates for the impact of postdoctoral fellowship prestige on obtaining a tenure track position (see Table 3) reveals that, as expected, the parameter for the males (.026) exceeds that for the females (−.002).[6] We see that of the variables included, only postdoctoral fellowship prestige had a significant impact on this dependent variable. Given the importance of the first position on subsequent aspects of scientific careers (Cole and Cole, 1973, p. 171), this sex difference may play a major role in accounting for the divergence of the men's and women's career outcomes.

Inspecting the sex-specific estimates for the impact of a tenure track first job on being tenured a decade after the Ph.D. shows the women's coefficient (.607) is almost double the men's (.333). As a result, the small proportion of female chemists in tenured university positions a decade after the Ph.D. (Reskin, 1973) cannot be attributed to their greater difficulty in *maintaining* a positional advantage. Indeed, further analysis of this link indicates that virtually all the women who were tenured a decade after the Ph.D. began their careers in tenure track university positions. In contrast, the men often moved from first jobs that were not tenure track university positions to tenured positions in universities a decade later. Thus as far as the link between early and later positional success is concerned, the women chemists show a much stronger accumulative-advantage process than the men. However, rather than reflecting the greater emphasis on achievement norms among women, it results from their greater difficulty in obtaining a tenured university position if they did not begin their careers on a university tenure track. We have already seen that superior performance had virtually no positional payoff for the women, so it is not surprising that the impact of their early positional status was so pronounced.

Position on Performance

Sex discrimination might also prevent women from being able to take advantage of the resources certain positions usually confer to increase their scientific output. If this occurs, the men's parameters linking early position to later performance should exceed the women's. In the third stage of our analysis we compare the model shown in line 2, which permits the sexes to vary only in the impacts of selected indicators of performance on position and position on position with a model that allows the sexes to differ in (1) the impacts of the caliber of their Ph.D. department, a prestigious postdoctoral fellowship, and their first job on their early citations and (2) the impact of their first job on their predecade citations. As we see in line 3, allowing these additional parameters to vary by sex does not significantly improve the model's fit to the data. This suggests that when women obtained positions that commanded resources for productivity—either in the form of training or access to institutional resources for research—they apparently did not encounter systematic barriers to utilizing these resources to enhance their later performance.

Performance on Performance

In the final stage of the analysis we examine whether the sexes differ in the effects of earlier performance on later performance by comparing the model that allows the sexes to vary on all eight parameters considered thus far with a model that also allows them to differ in the impact of early citations on predecade citations. Before discussing the results, we must consider whether a sex difference in the impact of earlier on later performance implies institutionalized sex discrimination. According to accumulative-advantage theory (Allison and Stewart, 1974), early performance elicits a variety of rewards that facilitates later productivity. However, a strong association between early and later productivity might also reflect a stable propensity to publish (Cole and Cole, 1973, p. 114). Thus a sex difference in the impact of earlier on later performance could denote either a sex difference in the stability of scientific performance or a flaw in the system, which rewarded earlier performances with resources. Including measures of those resources in the analysis would permit us to distinguish between these two explanations, but our only measure of resources—whether the first job was on university tenure track—is too crude an indicator for this purpose. In view of this, any sex differences here need not imply discrimination. Turning to line 4, we see that the final model fits the data significantly better than the previous one, and Table 3 shows that the impact of early citations on decade citations is substantially greater for the men (11.021) than the women (3.666).

To summarize, our examination of a model of scientific status attainment suggests that the processes of accumulative advantage differed for male and female chemists in several ways. First, although the women appeared at an advantage in converting predoctoral publications to a prestigious postdoctoral fellowship, this was an artifact of our coding of the latter variable, and analyses reported elsewhere suggest that men do better than women in this respect. Second, having held a relatively prestigious fellowship aided the men—but not the women—in obtaining a tenure track position in their first jobs. Third, whether one's first job was on a tenure track was more strongly related to being tenured in a university among the women than the men; but rather than reflecting an advantage for the women, this difference appears to result from the men's greater ease in obtaining such positions regardless of where they began their careers. The implication of this result for the women's long-run occupational outcomes becomes clearer when we review the fourth difference we observed: The women did not improve their chance of ultimately obtaining a tenured university position by improving their scholarly contributions in the way that the men did. Finally, citations to their early work had a greater impact on the quality of men's later contributions than on women's. We lack the data necessary to determine the exact mechanisms by which this difference occurred, but we suspect it may be due at least partly to the inability of the majority of women to obtain positions that provide stable professional career patterns.

We should note that these five differences stand out against a fair degree of similarity in the sexes' processes of accumulative advantage. In particular, the determinants of both early and later citations in our model tended to have similar impacts for the sexes; and the impacts of the three measures of predoctoral position and performance on subsequent variables in the model also tended to be similar. Thus it appears that the ease with which the sexes attained crucial positional resources after leaving graduate school is the chief locus of the differences in their accumulative-advantage processes.

Although these findings are consistent with the existence of some institutionalized sex discrimination in science, the alternative explanation often advanced is that female scientists are less committed to their careers and may not try as hard to convert their early resources to later advancement. Although this could account for the observed differences, proponents have produced no evidence that differential commitment explains the observed sex differences.[7] Firsthand accounts by women scientists demonstrate that some sex discrimination does exist in science (Abramson, 1975; Astin, 1969; Kundsin, 1974; Roe, 1966; Weisstein, 1976). Our understanding of scientific performance suggests that commitment is not fixed for either sex by the time the Ph.D. is awarded; more plausibly, it is a function of both the opportunities for and institutionalized barriers to scientific performance.

Conclusions

Our major purpose has been to illustrate the use of techniques that provide statistical tests for the equivalence of the underlying causal processes by which members of different groups advance in careers and identify the loci of any group differences. If there is institutionalized discrimination in any organization that claims to reward workers on the basis of their performance, the processes of accumulative advantage should be weaker for one group than the other, particularly for the links between performance and positional outcomes and those between early and later positions. We found such differences among male and female chemists.

These techniques have much to offer the researcher who seeks to compare subpopulations in organizational contexts in which it is possible to specify a general model that should hold in the absence of discrimination. If the relationships in this model do not apply equally to the subgroups under study, then some process such as discrimination is at work. We must emphasize that these techniques require equally reliable and valid data for both subgroups. Differential unreliability would lead to underestimating the parameters for the groups with less reliable indicators. This would be a particular problem if that is the group against whom discrimination is hypothesized because both discrimination and measurement error would lead to weaker relationships in the processes of status attainment.

Research on discrimination has focused primarily on identifying differences in outcomes for dominant and minority groups. The availability of techniques such as the ones we illustrate direct us to move beyond searching for indicators of outcomes on which groups might differ to developing indicators of relevant organizational performance on which such outcomes theoretically depend. Whether our interest lies in the inequality of organizational reward structures or in discrimination in the application of negative sanctions, we must be able to specify and measure the relevant precursors in order to determine whether their impacts differ for different social groups.

Notes

1. Cole and Cole's (1973, pp. 270–275) sample of thirteen hundred physicists ranked ninety-eight awards, including eighteen named postdoctoral fellowships. These fellowship rankings were recoded from one for unnamed fellowships to nineteen. Scientists who had no fellowship were coded zero.

2. We coded academic institutions shown in the *DGR* as granting advanced degrees in chemistry as universities; all others are coded as colleges. We coded all positions at the assistant professor level or higher as tenure track positions.

3. More precisely, model B is "nested" in model A if all constrained parameters in model A are also constrained in model B (see Long, 1976, pp. 169–170). The statistical tests presented in this chapter require that one of the models in each pair being compared be nested in the other (Long, 1976, pp. 170–171).

4. In order to conserve space, we simultaneously tested for sex differences in more than one parameter in Table 2. In no case, however, did the results for the combinations differ from those obtained when we tested individual parameters separately.

5. This was done in order to include all available cases in the analysis rather than restricting it to the eighty-eight chemists who had held fellowships.

6. This result is not an artifact of our coding of the prestige measure; it replicates Reskin's (1976) result, which was based on more restrictive coding.

7. But see Kashket and others (1974) for data on sex differences in willingness to move to accommodate a spouse's career.

6

Male-Female and White-Minority Pay Differentials in a Research Organization

Peter McDonough
Robert Snider
Joyce P. Kaufman

Our purpose is to test three models of wage differences within a formal organization. The mixed models we elaborate detect the extent salary differences are traceable to attributes such as sex and race in balance with indicators such as education and seniority. One of the models is also designed to show how salary inequities between sex and race categories are compounded by the hierarchical career tracks built into organizational structures. The dependent variable is wages. We are thus

123

concerned with the question of equal pay for equal work. This is only one of the issues, and perhaps not the most crucial one, analyzed in the literature on sex and race discrimination. In the course of specifying and estimating models of pay differentials, we shall suggest procedures for analyzing related issues in the study of institutional sexism and racism.

Such research may address three distinct problems. The "in-out" problem is the most elemental. It concerns the number of minorities and females outside or inside a particular job market. In recent years several aggregate indicators of this problem have developed (Department of Commerce, 1973). Granovetter's (1974) study of how people get jobs introduces formal organizations and informal networks as explicit variables. This constitutes an advance over an atheoretical accounting of proportional representation by sex and race.

A second theme in research on institutional racism and sexism is mobility within organizations. The sixties and early seventies witnessed a boom in studies of occupational stratification, attainment, and mobility. Recent revisions and fresh departures have been generated by a variety of factors: the chronically modest proportions of variance explained in occupational attainment (Boudon, 1974, 1976; Hauser, 1976); an awareness that such models tend to ignore structural constraints (Hauser and others, 1975; Thurow, 1972); and the recognition that much of the previously unexplained variance in social attainment is located within occupational strata inside organizations (Sørensen, 1975; White, 1970). Scholars have also questioned the implications of treating mobility as a movement between continuous occupational and employment categories (Vanneman, 1977; Wright, 1976; Wright and Perrone, 1977).

The emphasis of most of the newer research is less on mobility as an individual or family phenomenon than on the queuing process engendered by the limited availability of openings along the occupational and job hierarchies, especially toward the top. Research is also directed at career ladders in organizational contexts rather than at indicators of educational and occupational mobility drawn from national samples or censuses. For example, Long (1976) examined differentials in employment opportunities as well as in earnings in the federal civil service, an area presumably more carefully monitored and therefore less susceptible to discrimination than the private sector. Yet the results of his analysis indicate federal hiring procedures are still biased in favor of white and male applicants and blacks and females in the federal civil service earn less than whites and males with comparable qualifications.

A third issue is that of equal pay for equal work, the main topic of this chapter. Here the dependent variable, at least, is measured on an interval metric, whereas the properties of the *explicanda* in the areas previously mentioned are usually conceptualized as nominal and ordinal. The seminal piece is Malkiel and Malkiel's (1973) study of male-female pay differentials in a formal organization.

These three areas do not exhaust the repertoire of research on institutional racism and sexism. If there is a fourth major problem area in research on institutional sexism and racism, it concerns the hierarchical structure of organizations themselves. Almost all research on institutional sexism and racism takes the job grading of formal organizations for granted. Aside from Kanter (1976), quantitative researchers have not confronted the problem. The policy implications of this line of attack are not yet clear. It seems, however, that attempts to accommodate women and minorities without modifying "normal" superior-subordinate structures may have limited value for affirmative action.

Our models focus mainly on the equal pay for equal work problem, but it will prove impossible to explain pay differentials adequately without reference to the second (mobility question) and fourth (organizational structure) issues. Thus we shall also discuss the relationships between individual mobility, individual reward, and organizational structure. Because reliable data on availability pools are hard to come by, we ignore the in-out problem altogether.

In the following section we develop the theoretical underpinnings of our empirical models. The models themselves are straightforward adaptations of regression methods. But they are modified as a function of the previously outlined conceptual issues and not vice versa. Thus we give special attention to the reasons for adjusting the quantitative tests as we turn from one issue in institutional racism and sexism to another.

Data and Models

Data were drawn from the personnel files of "Phalanstère" (Gray, 1968, pp. 169–196), a university-related research organization with 362 regular staff members as of May 1, 1976. Complete information on seven predictors was collected for 322 employees. We computed the natural log transformation of the skewed dependent variable—salary—and used antilogs to yield real dollar amounts.

Salary within Palanstère was related to several variables: seniority, educational qualification, pre-Phalanstère work experience, job classification, and the Phalanstère division where the individual works. In our general model we include sex and race as well. The objective is to determine whether pay differences between sex and race groupings remain after the effects of the other variables have been accounted for. In linear additive form the baseline model is:

$$(1)\ Salary_{log} = b_1 seniority + b_2 education + b_3 prejob\ experience + b_4 job\ classification + b_5 division + b_6 race + b_7 sex + U_{unmeasured}$$

The error term includes some important exogenous factors. One is the size of the job market in specific skills outside Phalanstère. Another is the larger institutional environment in which Phalanstère is embedded—in particular, the university community and its salary structure. But perhaps the most significant unmeasured variable is productivity itself.

Productivity is notoriously difficult to measure and compare across job categories, and modern organizations of any complexity are composed of people with formally and functionally diverse roles. To be sure, different types of organizations prize different kinds of output. A research organization values the production of knowledge; and criteria of productivity and reward can be expected to vary correspondingly in military organizations, human service organizations, profit-seeking organizations, and so on. But a major difficulty in this study and indeed in any analysis of a single complex organization is that *within* the organization the outputs associated with different tasks are to some extent noncomparable.

The point is obvious yet easy to overlook. Virtually all studies of "institutional" racism and sexism ignore specifically organizational factors and focus instead on sex and race differences in rewards for accomplishment within the same profession or occupation. For example, the fact that the scientists Malkiel and Malkiel (1973) studied happen to be employed by the same organization is quite incidental to their analysis, which excludes all personnel but scientists. Our study, by contrast, examines all employees regardless of professional or occupational status within the same organization.

The obstacles created by the absence of refined productivity measures present special problems for the assessment of institutional racism and sexism. In a rational-meritocratic system, reward is presumably keyed to "human capital" factors: education, seniority, talent—in short, to all those variables that should enhance performance as opposed to those attributes, such as sex and race, presumed to be unrelated in direct fashion to productivity. The trouble is, of course, that without firm productivity measures it becomes difficult to assign whatever variation in wages is unexplained by education, seniority, and so on either to sex and/or race discrimination or to differences in productivity. The problem is compounded by the fact that both kinds of factors may contribute, in unknown proportions, to salary discrepancies between the races and the sexes.

Thus it is important to remember we have no direct measure of productivity for the personnel in the organization under study. In practice this problem is less formidable than it might appear in principle. It turns out that we are able to explain most salary variation as a function of education, seniority, and the like. Yet some of this variation as a function cannot be explained in these terms, and much of the analysis will be devoted to the making of plausible inferences about the reasons behind such "residual" variation.

The actual predictors are measured as follows: (1) *seniority*, years on the job along an ordinal scale constructed by bracketing from more recently to less recently hired; (2) *education*, a four-category scale consisting of no college degree, B.A./B.S., M.A./M.S., and Ph.D.; (3) *prejob experience*, constructed by subtracting year of birth from year hired at Phalanstère; (4) *job classification*, a six-category indicator distinguishing between primary researchers, graduate student research assistants, administrators, nonstudent research assistants, data-processing technicians, and clericals; (5) *division*, broken up across the five operational units of Phalanstère; (6) *race*, coded as either white or minority; and (7) *sex*.

The indicator of "prejob experience" is the most problematical. Numerically, it is nothing more than age at hiring. This is a dubious indicator of experience for males with differing amounts of education and military experience; it is perhaps even more questionable for both women and minorities, who are less likely to have continuous labor force experience. Nevertheless, the correlation between age at hiring and (unmeasured) years of experience should be positive, even for females and minorities. Moreover, the fact that "age at hiring" might be a pale surrogate of experience for females and minorities is a significant datum, and the presumed discontinuity of prejob experience should be reflected for these groups in the low regression coefficients associated with the variable.

Operationalization of the other predictors is fairly straightforward. The education indicator could be further refined to reflect the quality of the graduate department, the field of the degree, and so on. But in fact Phalanstère hires uniformly from top universities, and the type of research it conducts entails specialization in areas that do not vary widely in kind. That is, Phalanstère does not house Ph.D.s in physics and Ph.D.s in English literature.

The statistical procedure used to estimate the baseline model and its variations was Multiple Classification Analysis (MCA), an algorithm equivalent to ordinary least squares when some or all the predictors do not meet interval-scale criteria (Andrews and others, 1973). According to Andrews and others

(1973, p. 47), "the beta coefficients must be interpreted with caution and are useful only for indicating the relative importance of the various predictors . . . the square of the beta coefficient is the sum of squares attributable to the predictor (after 'holding other predictors constant') relative to the total sum of squares. Thus it is tempting to interpret this beta coefficient (when squared) in terms of 'percent of variance explained.' This would be appropriate, however, *only* in the uninteresting special case when all the predictors are uncorrelated and multivariate analysis is unnecessary." It should also be noted that the coefficients themselves may vary only between zero and one; they cannot assume negative values because the predictors are assumed to be nominal scales. The betas are thus best viewed as unsigned, absolute partial regression coefficients.

Our baseline model was derived from human capital theory, which is a standard approach in the economics literature to the study of individual achievement. The theory predicts that individual attainment (in the present case, salary reward) is a function of investments, such as formal education and on-the-job training, in human resources. Human capital theory does not provide a positive model of sex-, race-, or organization-induced discrimination; such inferences must be derived from the variance in reward, which the human capital model fails to explain. Despite these drawbacks, we use human capital theory as a baseline because it is the clearest and most systematic of available models.[1] The first three indicators on the right-hand side of equation (1) are standard human capital variables. Education represents differences in skill levels, particularly relevant in a research setting. Seniority and prejob experience also represent individual resources—that is, time-dependent learning investments beyond the formal schooling. The indicators farther to the right in (1) are admixtures to the human capital model. Race, sex, and division should not, given the model, influence salary.

The role of job classification is ambiguous. On the one hand it is an indispensable variable in sociological studies of mobility; it is the organizational surrogate of occupation. On the other hand it clutters a pure human capital model, which assigns a primary role to an individual's resources—education, for example—in the determination of salary. The economist's human capital models, like the sociologist's occupational mobility models, are generally insensitive to organizational structures.

This ambiguity prompted us to test models with and without job classification. In human capital theory job classification may be superfluous but not, like sex and race, actually inimical to the workings of an efficient market. Presumably, the function of job classification is to facilitate the assignment of personnel by competence to productive activities, while the influence of sex and race may run counter to the equilibrium predicted by human capital theory.

There is still another reason for moving job classification in and out of the model. To some degree it is a proxy for the critical human capital variable of productivity. The premise is that those in higher job categories get there because they are more productive than those in lower categories, by reason of education or native endowment or both. This implies that there exist absolute differences in productivity between job categories. In particular, although variation in productivity *within* job categories may be a function of individual talent and initiative, variation *between* categories should be a function of both education and accomplishment.

Of course, it is possible to turn the argument around. Educational certification, as opposed to individual merit, is known to be a determinant of potential productivity (Wilensky, 1975). Individuals in lower job classifications may not produce more because, given their educational credentials, they are not expected to.

Job classification, then, is a two-edged indicator. It approximates productivity at the same time that productivity remains at least partially incomparable across job categories. In Phalanstère writing manuscripts and typing manuscripts for publication are both productive undertakings. The question is whether a unit change in pages published per year generates relatively the same monetary reward as a unit change in pages typed per year for publication.

With the data at hand it is extremely difficult to devise an acid test for such a proposition because productivity is confounded with job classification. Yet is is equally important to understand what is at stake. Ideally, within each job category an indicator of reward (salary) would be regressed on productivity (no direct indicator). Although the absolute mean differences between the more- and the less-productive individuals should increase between levels of the job scale, the impact of productivity on reward as estimated by the regression coefficient after controlling for seniority, education, sex, race, and so on should remain constant. If the coefficients fluctuate, then returns to productivity are not a function of individual contributions alone. Productivity is differentially weighted across layers of the organization.

In short, job classification may be thought of as an indicator of two variables: one reflecting productivity and the other institutional "lumpiness." The relative proportion of each is not known a priori; neither is the relationship between them.

We are now in a position to compare the standard model with its two principal variations. The standard model is equation (1) with and later without job classification. We expect both versions of the standard model to reduce most of the variance in wages. Furthermore, we expect that the human capital variables will do most of the "explaining." If this did not turn out to be the case, we would be looking at an organization in which sex and/or race discrimination were rampant. The baseline model provides the test for the equal pay for equal work problem.

Our first variation on the standard model was prompted by the suspicion that one of the human capital variables—seniority—behaves differentially with regard to one of the discrimination indicators—sex. This derives from an observation that is anomalous from the viewpoint of human capital theory: Many women with educational qualifications equivalent to those of men and with equal seniority stay on in formal organizations at pay scales inferior to those received by men. According to the assumptions of perfect information and unimpeded geographical mobility that are part of the human capital model, these women should move out if they do not move up.

Our suspicion that the labor market does not work this way is not wholly guesswork. In estimating model (1), we encounter a salary differential unfavorable to women. At the same time we know that Phalanstère employs many women with appreciable seniority and education. The question then becomes whether seniority and sex *jointly* influence salary, apart from education, prejob experience, division, and race.

The main reason for testing this partially interactive model has to do with the mobility problem. Possibly, women underpaid according to pure human capital criteria—that is, education, seniority, and pre-Phalanstère experience—do not leave Phalanstère because the costs associated with leaving exceed those of staying even when they have "peaked" at Phalanstère. We test this proposition by controlling for job classification, in addition to the other predictors. We do not specify an interaction between race and seniority because there are few minorities with many years of employment at Phalanstère.

The revised model is:

$$(2)\ Salary_{\log} = b_1\ (seniority * sex) + b_2\ education + b_3\ prejob\ experience + b_4\ job\ classification + b_5\ division + b_6\ race + U_{unmeasured}$$

Model (2) is an attempt to assess the differential mobility of males and females in Phalanstère. If the regression coefficient b_4 approached zero and b_1 were strong, then the mobility bias against women would be conspicuous. Again, however, because Phalanstère is a bureaucracy with formal rules we do not expect such a dramatic outcome. But some bias may exist if the salary curve for females rises less steeply than the curve for males, given identical increments in seniority as well as in job classification.

One caveat is worth noting with regard to model (2). Albeit indirectly, it addresses the "up-down" problem (mobility), an inherently dynamic phenomenon. But the data are cross-sectional. Whatever sex bias is encountered is thus evidence of the *result* of differential mobility. We cannot depict the actual *process* of differential mobility (Coleman, 1968).

Our final variation on the baseline model is aimed at what we have termed the fourth problem in research on institutional racism and sexism: the hierarchical structure of formal organizations. So far we have treated the organization of Phalanstère as a composite of a six-part job scale. This refinement is suited to the estimation of the effects of "achievement" or "productivity" on wages. We reduce the categories from six to three in order to reflect the major career trajectories at Phalanstère: academic-research, administrative-technical, and clerical. Primary researchers and graduate student research assistants go under the academic-research category; administrators, nonstudent research assistants, and data processing technicians fall into the administrative category; the third category is clerical and secretarial workers.

In one sense this modification represents a loss of information. The reduction in cut points is meant, however, to reflect qualitative distinctions in career paths. At one extreme the careers of individuals in the academic-research stratum are determined in large measure by their achievements outside Phalanstère, by their national and international reputations as scholars. This standard separates them from both the administrators and the clericals. Recognition of administrators' productivity comes almost exclusively from within Phalanstère. Yet the clericals are separated from the administrators as well as the academic-researchers. They are nonunion, hourly employees who are discouraged by university regulations from working overtime. In contrast, administrators often are expected to put in extra hours.

We are thus confronted with the difficulty of comparing productivity across job ranks. In particular we want to determine whether the structural opportunity and not just the individual ability to be productive varies systematically along career lines. As was suggested earlier, we cannot directly estimate a productivity parameter. But this does not mean the baseline model must be abandoned. It is legitimate and feasible to test the model separately for each of the three career strata, thus:

(3) $Salary_{\log} = b_1 seniority + b_2 education + b_3 prejob$
$experience + b_4 division + b_5 race\ and$
$b_6 sex\ and\ U_{unmeasured}$

Here we are interested in the variation of the beta weights across the academic-research, administrative, and clerical categories. If they do not vary, then at least one part of the baseline model is confirmed: namely, that organizational structure itself does not directly influence individual rewards. This may be true even if the regression coefficients for division, race, and sex turn out to be significant within each of the career groups. The test is not whether these coefficients, or those estimating the effects of the human capital variables themselves, diminish or increase by some constant across career groups. If this were the case, salary discrimination on the basis of race and/or sex might exist; but it would be hard to identify the peculiarly *institutional* factors in discrimination. The relevant test is whether and to what extent the betas change between career groups.

For example, it may be that for the academic researchers the human capital variables of education, seniority, and prejob experience work well in the sense of powerfully influencing their salaries and that division, sex, and race count for little. It may also happen that the human capital predictors diminish in importance among the administrators and/or the clericals and that the indicators of discrimination have an appreciable impact at least in comparison to their effect within the academic-research category. If this happens, there is putative evidence of *institutional* racism and sexism as well as of structural obstacles to reward for productivity in the subordinate career strata. That is, the human capital model would seem to work for those on top and to work less well for those near the bottom. This eventuality is of great theoretical consequence. It suggests that sex and race bias is "class" specific, operating differentially by career lines.

In the following sections we submit the baseline, the interactive, and the career line models to empirical test. The first is concerned with the equal pay for equal work question. The second is directed at the problem of mobility within organizations. The third model takes up the possibility that human capital theory applies selectively to those on top, in the middle, and at the bottom.

The Standard Model

With all seven predictors included in the MCA, we obtain an R^2 of .85. These variables combined in linear additive form explain 85 percent of the variance in the natural logarithm of monthly salary. The relative effects of the predictors are as follows:

Predictor	Beta
Job classification	.40
Seniority	.38
Education	.32
Sex	.12
Pre-Phalanstère experience	.10
Race	.04
Division	.03

Thus the determinants of salary within Phalanstère are, first, job classification, second, seniority, and, third, educational qualification. When the effects of these variables are controlled for, race and sex, as well as division and pre-Phalanstère experience, have little direct impact on variation in salaries.[2]

It is worth restating this finding in a slightly different manner. We begin with a mean monthly salary discrepancy between males and females of the following magnitude, without considering job classification, seniority, and so on:

Males	$1,580
Females	896
Difference	$ 684

The difference shrinks as each predictor is added to the model in order of importance. The raw difference falls precipitously as job classification is taken into account, for example. Figure 1 illustrates this progressive diminution.

Nevertheless, some salary discrepancy between males and females remains even after discounting the effects of the other indicators:

Males	$1,177
Females	1,046
Difference	$ 131

That is, if men and women had similar amounts of education and experience and were distributed equally across job positions and divisions, there would remain an average monthly salary difference of $131 favoring males.

Figure 1. Controlling for Sex Differences in Salary

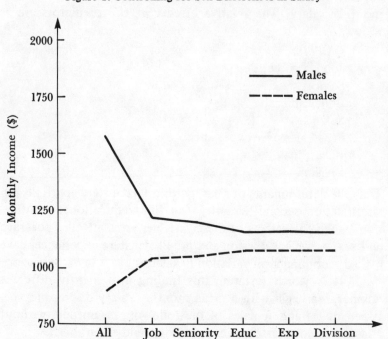

We can perform exactly the same calculations for white and minority staff members. As in the case of the male-female contrast, we start with the unadjusted salary difference:

White	$1,110
Minority	998
Difference	$ 112

Figure 2 depicts the narrowing of this differential with the successive introduction of the control indicators. The salary gap between white and minority personnel closes until, after controlling for all the other predictors, we arrive at a small differential favoring minorities:

White	$1,091
Minority	1,098
Difference	-$ 7

Figure 2. Controlling for Racial Differences in Salary

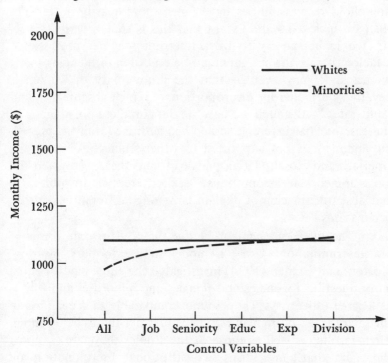

In brief, at least with regard to male-female salary differences, there remain inequalities the standard model cannot explain. The male-female gap is substantial: It amounts to $1,572 on a yearly basis.

What accounts for this gap? There are a number of possible explanations, and they are not mutually exclusive. In the first place there may not be enough detail in the job classification indicator to reflect fully the reality of work within Phalanstère. Second, it is conceivable that the surrogate indicator of pre-Phalanstère job experience (age at hiring) functions more accurately for men than for women. Women more often leave the work force to raise a family and then return to work; men tend more typically to follow uninterrupted careers.

It is also possible that the gap is due to differential rates of productivity between men and women. Men have traditionally been in a better position than women to pursue career goals; household responsibilities have fallen more heavily on females than on males. To the extent that this is true, a woman is restricted in her ability to work long hours at her profession—a factor that at the margin might be crucial in influencing merit increases. It may even be that the productivity of women is negatively affected by disproportionately high absenteeism and "quit rates." Although we have no data on these phenomena in the case of Phalanstère, it should be mentioned that the preceding argument is not supported by other studies. For example, Goldfarb and Hosek (1976, p. 106) found that, even given the most unfavorable assumptions, "sex differentials in quit rates and absenteeism cannot explain large wage differentials within occupations."

The differences might be due directly to some forms of sex discrimination. Using a model similar to ours, Gordon, Morton, and Braden (1974) investigated the equal pay for equal work question for males and females and minorities and whites at a large university. They found comparable discrepancies in the salary scales of men and women, all other things being equal. Their results (as well as those of the studies they cite) support the claim that some forms of institutional discrimination are probably common in academic and research organizations of similar size.

However, unless it can be construed as an unequivocal measure of "work"—that is, of productivity—the job classification indicator does not help to answer these questions. Eliminating job classification enables us to frame the question of salary discrimination differently. If we control for the human capital indicators of education, seniority, and pre-Phalanstère experience, there should emerge no additional difference in salaries of men and women or of white and minority staff members, the assumption being they will be granted equal *jobs* at equal pay. The elimination of job classification implies defining the indicator as one of hierarchical position and not of productivity. Strictly speaking, job classification in this sense is viewed as an arbitrary complication of the human capital model.

Thus revised, the standard model explains 78 percent of the variance in monthly salary. In order of magnitude the effects of the predictors are:

Predictor	Beta
Education	.55
Seniority	.45
Sex	.19
Pre-Phalanstère experience	.09
Division	.05
Race	.03

The adjusted mean monthly salary differences now become, by sex and by race:

Males	$1,233	White	$1,085
Females	1,020	Minority	1,172
Difference	$ 213	Difference	-$ 87

Let us first consider the increase in the mean salary difference between males and females. The $82 exacerbation of the gap ($213–$131) can be attributed to the fact that, all other things being equal, women actually do tend to enter lower job cátegories than men. Here again we must consider several possible explanations.

The gap might be a function of differential hiring patterns. It may be that women are discriminated against, either overtly or more subtly. Or it may be that aspirations are adjusted downward so that women apply for lower-ranked jobs than males with similar credentials. For example, a woman with a bachelor's degree might not be able to find a job for which her degree has supposedly prepared her; but she might be able to obtain work as a clerical. She may be overqualified for that position, but her alternatives are quite limited. Similarly, a woman might need a fairly secure job rather than one that matches her educational qualifications in order to help support her husband through school. Or she may be reentering the job market after devoting several years to raising a family and so accepts a lesser pay/job grade in the hope that it will ease her way back into the market. None of these possibilities violates the perfect information assumption of the human capital model, but they do qualify the assumption of zero costs to geographical mobility.

The results of the MCA for white and minority personnel show a reverse pattern, favoring minorities. There are few minority group members with the appropriate educational credentials for senior positions, and they are in great demand. In general, their bargaining position may be stronger than that of women. Under these conditions one way to recruit and retain minority group members is for employers to outbid the competition.

Thus when job classification is dropped from the baseline model in order to optimize the comparison between the effects of the human capital and the discrimination indicators, quite different results are obtained for women and minority staff members. For females the salary differential increases against them; for minority group members salary differences are augmented in their favor. These results may reflect a variable opportunity structure for women and minorities at Phalanstère. There appear to be somewhat different job markets for the two populations, created in large part by vast discrepancies in the numbers of "qualified applicants" by sex and race.

It bears emphasizing that the slightly privileged salary position for minorities at Phalanstère means they are not discriminated against with regard to wages. This finding should not be taken to mean that minorities are not discriminated against in recruitment and in-house mobility. We have no systematic evidence one way or the other on this point. Because minorities are few in number at Phalanstère, the remainder of the analysis will focus on male-female salary differences.

The baseline model performs quite satisfactorily by reduction-in-variance standards. Two of the three human capital indicators, education and seniority, contribute most to our understanding of pay differentials, as expected. Sex rather than race seems to be the capricious factor in salary differentials at Phalanstère. In trying to explain how the attribute of sex functions in practice to reduce the returns to women below the level predicted by the human capital model, we have suggested that women tend to be distributed in job classes beneath what their

formal education qualifies them for. In other words, we are led
to a consideration of impediments to mobility. The implications
of this are explored in the next section.

The Combinatorial Model

The female mobility problem at Phalanstère has two features. The first, to which we already referred, occurs in recruitment. At the point of entry our inference has been that women
with formal educational qualifications on a par with men are
more likely to be offered and/or to seek lower-status job grades.
Once in Phalanstère, women may continue to suffer from this
bias. For example, their career paths may be foreshortened such
that the returns on seniority for women diminish more rapidly
than for men. After a relatively short time at Phalanstère, wom-
en may have fewer places to go than men, either upward or
outward.

Two separate processes are involved here, although the
end result is the same. On the one hand women may be offered
lower-status jobs than their male counterparts, all other things
being equal. Esther (1975) found that even in such traditionally
"feminine" fields as public education, women's career ladders
tend to be truncated at the top; implicit social barriers intervene
and act to prohibit them from attaining leadership positions.

On the other hand it is conceivable that women accept
lower-status jobs at least in part because of a "fear of success"
into which they have been socialized. Although the theory itself
is controversial, results in support of it have been found to obtain more sharply for better educated, less traditional, and presumably more ambitious women. Thus if a qualified woman were
to apply for a high-status position at Phalanstère and were offered
a lower-status job, the theory predicts she would accept the job
that was offered as a way to minimize threatening conditions in
a male-dominated environment (Cabellero, Giles, and Shaver,
1975; Lockheed, 1975). Of course, a willingness on the part
of females to accept positions for which they are "overqualified"
may have structural and organizational, as well as psychological,
causes. Indeed, we suggest later that a probable factor behind

the inferior job mobility of women at Phalanstère is formed by a set of constraints on their geographical mobility—which may act independently of their supposed fear of success.

We do not have data on mobility over time within Phalanstère. However, we can estimate the degree to which seniority affects the salary levels of men and women differentially. Imagine a graph that along the abscissa measures seniority and on the ordinate measures mean monthly salary. We can plot the relationship between these variables for men and for women. This is essentially the task of model (2), which in addition to examining the combined effect of sex and seniority on salaries isolates this effect by controlling for the remaining predictors.

Our purpose is not to demonstrate that there exists an average salary difference in favor of men and against women with equal seniority. This much is deducible from the baseline model. Instead we want to determine the extent to which the *rate of change* in mean salary differs for men and women with equivalent time on the job. The task is to detect differences in the *slopes* of the male and female curves. As was done for the standard model, we shall run the combinatorial model with and without the job classification indicator.

The results of both versions of model (2) are presented in Table 1. Although the proportion of variance explained changes hardly at all, conceptualizing the effects of sex and seniority in interactive terms adds to our understanding of the determinants

Table 1. Results of the Combinatorial Model: Betas and Adjusted
Mean Salaries by Sex and Seniority

Estimated Model *Without Job Classification*		*Estimated Model* *With Job Classification*	
Predictor	*Beta*	*Predictor*	*Beta*
Seniority & sex	.53	Job classification	.43
Education	.50	Sex & senority	.42
Prejob exp.	.10	Education	.28
Race	.04	Prejob exp.	.10
Division	.04	Race	.03
$R^2 = .78$		Division	.03
		$R^2 = .86$	

**Table 1. (continued) Results of the Combinatorial Model:
Betas and Adjusted Mean Salaries by Sex and Seniority**

Seniority	*Without Job Classification: Mean Salary by Sex and Seniority*			
	Male	Female	M–F	$\frac{\text{M–F}}{\text{F}}$
1–3	$ 952	$ 822	$130	.16
4–6	1,137	940	197	.21
7–12	1,421	1,120	301	.27
13–20	1,761	1,217	544	.44
20+	2,276	1,527	749	.49

Seniority	*Job Classification Controlled: Mean Salary by Sex and Seniority*			
	Male	Female	M–F	$\frac{\text{M–F}}{\text{F}}$
1–3	$ 905	$ 896	$ 9	.01
4–6	1,038	993	45	.05
7–12	1,281	1,152	129	.11
13–20	1,628	1,211	417	.34
20+	1,943	1,477	466	.32

of salary differences at Phalanstère. The combined impact of sex and seniority on salaries turns out to be greater than that of education. Moreover, both the proportional and absolute differences in mean monthly salary between males and females increase exponentially with seniority. That is, the rate of return (as measured by salary increments) on seniority increases more rapidly for males than for females with equivalent education, pre-Phalanstère experience, and so forth. The absolute differences are portrayed in Figure 3; Figure 4 plots the proportional differences. If there were no connection between sex and seniority, the curves would run parallel to the horizontal axis. Or if we had used the male-female salaries as such rather than the summary difference between them, the separate male-female

Figure 3. Mean Monthly Male > Female Salary Differences by Years of Seniority, Adjusted for Education, Prejob Experience Race, and Administrative Division

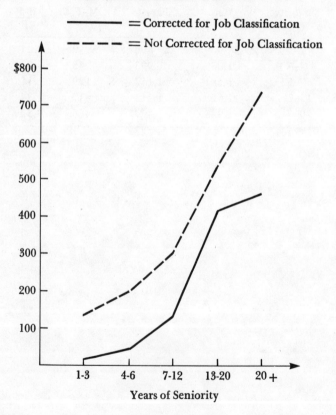

curves should rise at a constant rate with seniority, parallel to each other.[3]

The introduction of job classification softens but does not eliminate the salary bias directly attributable to the combination of sex and seniority. The proportional as well as the absolute returns to seniority are progressively greater for men than for women except at the very highest levels of seniority (twenty years or more), where the bias remains but does not actually get worse. It is clear once again from the betas in Table 1 that race is not an important determinant of salary differences in Phalanstère. If anything, there may be some slight reverse discrimination in salaries by race. Model (2) generates the following estimates, without and with job classification, respectively:

White	$1,084	White	$1,092
Minority	1,180	Minority	1,088
Difference	−$ 96	Difference	$ 4

Figure 4. Percentage Difference Between Mean Monthly Salaries (Male > Female) by Years of Seniority, Adjusted for Education, Prejob Experience, Race, and Administrative Division

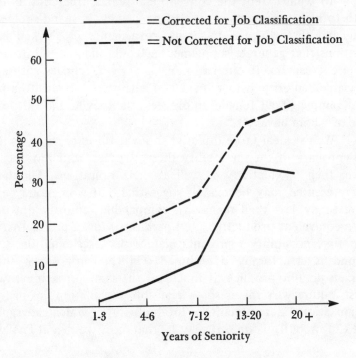

Human capital indicators help explain why males stay on at Phalanstère, but they cannot account for the continued presence of women who, relative to men, tend increasingly to be underpaid with time. Relative to males, seniority among females counts for less and less at Phalanstère.

A plausible explanation for this progressive discrepancy is that most females at Phalanstère are not mobile in the market, and the market exploits this disadvantage. Women may tend to settle for less not only because the costs of moving are high but also because they may not, by convention, need more. This characterization would ring true for married women whose incomes are supplementary to their husbands'. From a pure human capital perspective the relative immiserization of women at Phalanstère is so outrageous that they should quit or at least reduce their performance on the job.

The absence of materials on sex-specific exit patterns at Phalanstère prevents us from testing the hypothesis that turnover should be higher among females than males as a consequence, among other things, of career curtailment. We do not know to what extent the conventional female role contributes both to high turnover—because of pregnancy, husband's relocation, and so forth—*and* to virtual permanence in blocked job positions that generate supplemental family income but do not represent careers. If our reasoning is correct, females with appreciable seniority who remain at Phalanstère constitute a biased sample of all female employees, the luckier and/or more able of whom have left.[4]

We can deal more directly, though still imprecisely, with the corollary of the immobility thesis. Women who stay might lower their productivity as well as their aspirations. The data just presented may be read as suggesting that women are paid increasingly less than men with comparable seniority not *despite* equivalent productivity but *because of* lower productivity. The first possibility represents blatant sex discrimination; the second is structurally determined. On the supposition that women do not produce as much on the same job as men, we must inquire why this is so. A plausible explanation lies in the organizational determinants of productivity, of which geographical (im)mobility is one. It may be that most women at Phalanstère are presented with incentives for routine rather than con-spicuous productivity. Model (3) explores this possibility.

Model (3): Career Lines and Productivity

Organizations are held together by means of complex control mechanisms (Wright and Perrone, 1977, pp. 50–54). For those at or near the top, incentives work better than sanctions. "Creative" productivity is expected of them. Rewards are needed to prevent the best from leaving and less, perhaps, as direct goads to productivity. Toward the bottom the control structure tends to be reversed, especially in nonunion organizations. Clericals are eminently replaceable not only because their work is standardized but also to the extent that supply outruns demand. Negative sanctions instead of positive incentives should therefore prevail.

Thus the kind as well as the degree of control can be expected to vary across layers of the institutional hierarchy. Plainly, the kinds of productivity differ from level to level: Pages published means something different from pages typed. Not only the definition but also the extent of productivity should vary by career rank.

Positing a relationship between the kind and the amount of productivity mires us in a classical problem of social indicator research. Yet the claim that type of work affects amount of productivity is a modest one, if confined to the assumption that the range of permissible productivity is restricted at lower levels of the institutional hierarchy. By and large clericals are not rewarded for extraordinary performance extraneous to their job descriptions; but academic-researchers are expected, if not as a matter of routine then as a net result over a period of years, to perform exceptionally.

None of this contradicts everyday observation, but it does violate a key assumption of the human capital model. In the long run, artificial barriers to achievement, such as those represented by step changes between career paths, should fall before the momentum of education, experience, and so on. Our argument is that although the human capital model may apply to some career strata in the organization—in particular to the highest—it does not fit the lower strata, where variation in productivity is structurally constrained.

Our task is now to operationalize this hypothesis. The procedure is first to aggregate the six job categories into three career lines: academic-research, administrative-technical, and clerical. We then regress salary on the six predictors within each of the career lines. Although the replicative estimations are straightforward, they generate a mass of findings. It is therefore useful to systematize the alternative hypotheses in advance.

The first hypothesis (H_1) holds that career paths have no independent effect on either relative productivity or relative wages. The regression coefficients should be the same within each career path as those estimated from the baseline model minus job classification. The contributions of the human capital indicators and of the discrimination indicators should remain constant, indicating that career paths as such have nothing to do with differences in productivity and reward.

The second hypothesis (H_2) holds that career paths have an independent effect on relative productivity and on wages. Beta weights differ across career lines. In particular, the impact of the discrimination indicators is expected to be greater in the lower career strata, and the impact of the human capital indicators should be greater in the higher strata.

Table 2 gives the beta coefficients and the proportion of variation explained in salary separately for the academic-research, administrative-technical, and clerical strata. Table 3 presents the adjusted mean salary levels within each category of the predictors by career paths. For any one of the predictors the effects of the other predictors have been removed. Thus, the means are not the result of one-way analysis of variance. They are "net" means, with the remaining five predictors controlled.

The results suggest that the organizational hierarchy may have an impact on the range of productivity. A first, though not decisive, indicator of this constraint is that the coefficient of determination is quite high for the academic-research brand of Phalanstère (.88) but substantially lower for the subordinate strata (.51 and .64). By themselves, differences in the R-squareds do not undercut the universality of the human capital model.

Table 2. Results of Model (3)

Academic–Research $R^2 = .88$		Administrative–Technical $R^2 = .51$	
Predictor	Beta	Predictor	Beta
Seniority	.58	Seniority	.65
Prejob experience	.31	Education	.41
Education	.30	Sex	.27
Division	.06	Prejob experience	.16
Sex	.05	Race	.13
Race	.02	Division	.13
N = 102		N = 136	

Clerical $R^2 = .64$	
Predictor	Beta
Seniority	.65
Division	.21
Education	.18
Prejob experience	.18
Race	.07
Sex	.01
N = 84	

They reflect the narrower variance in the dependent variable, salary, within the administrative and clerical strata. It is the differential ordering of the predictors across career paths that damages H_1 and supports H_2.

Thus, for example, the human capital indicators are the only meaningful determinants of salary among academic-researchers. Significantly, it is only when we examine this group separately that the impress of pre-Phalanstère experience comes plainly into view. So far its role as a predictor of salary has been minor. Here, among the academic-researchers, it ranks second in importance. The preeminence of pre-Phalanstère experience indicates that the market in academic-research talent is far wider than that for administrators and clericals. At this level the personnel network is national, and experience outside Phalanstère counts; so senior researchers may be recruited directly to the top on the basis of reputations made beyond the walls of Phalanstère.

Seniority is paramount among the predictors of salary in the administrative and clerical ranks as well as among the academic researchers. It is the supreme variable of formal organizations. But once past this indicator, the determinants of salary differ by strata. Within the administrative-technical stratum, pre Phalanstère experience counts for less than it does at the academic-research level. The market in administrators, as in clericals, is comparatively localized. Sex assumes relatively great importance as a determinant of administrators' salary. As Table 3 shows, the differential favors males. The fact that sex is a more important predictor of salary among administrators than among researchers indicates the frailties of the human capital model where universalistic standards of evaluation are only partially adopted. Personnel in the administrative and technical ranks at Phalanstère implement rather than make the rules. The academic-researchers continue to make the key personnel decisions, and—at least vis-à-vis one another—they are kept minimally honest by the outside professional market.

Neither sex nor race matters much in the determination of clerical salaries. This is because most of the clericals are females, so that the indicator does not vary. And, as in the academic-research and administrative-technical strata, only a few of the clericals are members of minority groups, with the result that the direct effect of this attribute on salaries must also be small.

"Division" is the second most important determinant of clerical salaries. The prominence of this mundane indicator of institutional discrimination reflects the decentralization of operating units within Phalanstère and the consequently imperfect standardization of pay scales at the lower level of the organization.

In summary, it comes as no surprise that the absolute variation in salaries turns out to be greatest at the highest level of Phalanstère, that is, at the academic-research level. The human capital model—or its sociological counterpart, the functional theory of stratification—accounts easily for the range in rewards. It is more difficult to explain the reduced importance of the human capital indicators at the lower ranks of the organization. Productivity is exceedingly difficult to compare across job fam-

Table 3. Adjusted Mean Salary for Academic–Research, Administrative–Technical, and Clerical Personnel, by Six Predictors

	Academic–Research	Administrative–Technical	Clerical
Seniority			
1–3 years	$1,348	$ 797	$603
4–6 years	1,557	923	680
7–12 years	1,687	1,184	779
13–20 years	2,404	1,257	826
20+ years	2,823	1,460	–
Prejob experience			
18–22	$1,622	$1,031	$650
23–28	1,589	1,003	690
29–33	1,729	1,076	652
34–43	2,273	1,099	693
44–57	3,365	1,109	686
Education			
High school	–	$ 871	$705
B.A./B.S.	$1,471	1,089	678
M.A./M.S.	1,456	1,178	641
Ph.D.	1,936	–	–
Sex			
Male	$1,730	$1,214	$670
Female	1,639	1,010	673
Race			
White	$1,714	$1,048	$674
Minority	1,689	1,081	636
Division			
D_1	$1,740	$1,032	$674
D_2	1,614	1,059	718
D_3	1,687	1,047	666
D_4	1,717	1,011	721
D_5	–	1,116	639

ilies. At the subordinate levels of Phalanstère the extraneous factors of sex and bureaucratic division influence salaries more than they should by human capital standards. An inference compatible with the data is that this reflects a control structure with incentives and sanctions that differ by career levels. "Optimal" productivity may not be required below the academic-research stratum. It is therefore possible for factors such as sex and bureaucratic subdivision to have undue influence in the determination of salaries because salaries are not and need not be keyed to "inordinate" productivity. It would be irrational for many administrators and most clericals to overproduce.

Similarly, there are no obvious incentives for the true managers, the academic-researchers, to "overcorrect" for these discrepancies. Fairness is not necessarily related in axiomatic fashion to the net productivity of Phalanstère as a whole.

A few cautionary notes are in order. We have shown that sex bias in salaries exists at the middle stratum in Phalanstère but hardly, if at all, within the top and lower echelons. This indicates that institutional factors play a part in salary discrimination by sex. But it does not resolve the more complex issue of whether women are paid less than men at this level even though they produce equivalently or because they produce less. The data fit either interpretation, and it may be that they fit both interpretations. That is, some women at the middle level may lower their productivity as well as their aspirations, while others at the same level may perform superbly. The structural constraints we have measured are not a straitjacket on individual behavior. Once again it is important to remember that we have not measured productivity, the key behavioral variable.[5]

Men at the same administrative-technical level receive on the average higher salaries than women. It is not at all clear on theoretical grounds that they should produce more than females, unless they are viewed as breadwinners and the females primarily as noncareer, working wives. Furthermore, we do not know to what degree the "breadwinner-breadmaker" syndrome at Phalanstère is stereotype, shared norm, or fact. A true productivity measure would help determine the effect of these factors on salaries.

Thus although inferences based on organizational control fit the facts better than does the human capital model, we can argue only for its plausibility. The human capital model makes no distinction between sex bias as personal prejudice and sex bias as institutional discrimination. Theories of institutional sexism and racism depend on this distinction. But the data are not decisive on the issue. It is worth noting, however, that the evidence, although not absolutely convincing, favors institutional discrimination rather than personal prejudice as the operative negative factor affecting women at Phalanstère. In the first place, we have no attitudinal data on prejudice at Phalanstère. More important, all the evidence adduced thus far indicates that women are discriminated against as a group because of structural conditions, such as their lack of mobility. In brief, the exploitation of women at Phalanstère appears to be "inertial," a reflection of marketwide factors rather than the result of personal whim.

The virtue of organizational theory is to raise the possibility that women may be paid less than men because of relatively low productivity, which is structurally induced. Of course, the featherbedding or mild sabotage predicted by organizational theory should apply to men as well as women in blocked career paths. But if it is also true that women violate the human capital model by being less geographically mobile, then the combination of this constraint and truncated job lines would help account for the male-female pay differential as a function of unequal rather than equal productivity.

Common sense and methodological considerations also recommend caution in interpretation. It may be, as we have suggested, that the three tiers of Phalanstère represent qualitatively different career tracks. At the same time it is hard to disentangle this theoretical construct from the fact that the very size of the organization—the scarcity of openings toward the top—sets limits or opportunities both for mobility and for salary increases.

Also, in an important sense, our number of observations is not 322 but 1: the organization itself. We have just seen that subdividing the organization into three components reduces the number of cases for replicative analysis. Were we to proceed further, conducting the same analysis for each of the six job classifications, the number of cases would become perilously small in some of the categories for multivariate analysis. Because the range of the dependent variable is more constricted within some categories than others, estimates of the effects of the predictors on salary may be misleading. Reduction-in-variance methods cannot be applied uncritically without first considering the amount of variance that exists in the real-world dependent variable.

In summary, the most important implication of model (3) is that discrimination by sex and race is in part a structural problem and not merely a function of sex roles and racial stereotypes. The disadvantages of sex and race "per se" may aggravate the structural ceiling placed over subordinate career lines. At the same time it is important to recognize the possibly independent contribution of organizational control structures to sex and race differences in productivity and salaries. Males and whites in secondary career paths are also liable to be victimized by the differential reward structure.

Conclusions

Three models of institutional racism and sexism have been formulated and tested. All are variations on the human capital model. The first specifies salary as a purely linear additive function of productivity and discrimination measures. A non-negligible amount of sex bias was detected in the organization studied.

The second model tries to account for the failure of women who are discriminated against on the basis of sex to leave the organization in search of better conditions. The model specifies an interaction between sex and seniority. The results suggest that a trade-off occurs between the limited geographical mobility of females and the reduced productivity the organization expects of them.

The third model addresses the question of differential control of productivity across the three major career paths within the organization: the academic-research, the administrative-technical, and the clerical. The returns to productivity appear to be greater for those at the top of the hierarchy than for those in lower and truncated career paths.

What are the more general implications of these findings? First, it is instructive to read this study as an attempt to bridge he gaps between theory, models, and indicators. We have not een exclusively interested in the links between unmeasured ariables and empirical indicators. This version of the validity roblem is important, but it tends to gloss over the role of the- ry development and model specification. We have given prior- ty to these two tasks. The results are promising by accepted tandards of estimation. The R-squareds were quite large.

Second, we have found the logical properties of the hu- nan capital model useful in detecting institutional discrimina- ion. The problem of equal pay for equal work is viewed, under he terms of this model, as a problem of equal pay for equal roductivity. This alerts us to the fact that job classification nay be a poor indicator of actual productivity. People within he same job classes are not rewarded equally, even after dis- ounting the impact of education, seniority, and so on. It does ot follow, however, that women are discriminated against in alary terms despite productivity equal to that of males. This vould clearly violate human capital theory. It is also increasing- y difficult to get away with such overt discrimination, even if conspiracy of white males thought it were desirable.

It may be that women are paid less because they produce ess. The problem then is to determine why they fail to produce nore. Human capital theory provides no answers to this ques- ion, but it frames the question in the first place by pinpointing leviations from expected patterns.

Third, the human capital model is deduced from economic theory. Although it serves to systematize the issues, it is not capable of providing positive explanations for deviations from predicted outcomes. Strictly speaking, the organization of Phalanstère is residual noise. We turned to the insights of organ- izational theory (Westhues, 1976) after reaching the limits of the human capital model.

Organizational theory suggests that productivity differs not only in kind but also in quantity, vertically along hierar- chies. It suggests further that organizational efficiency is not the sum of productivity across individuals in the organization (Campbell, 1958). Productivity varies not only by level; the definition of productivity for the organization as a whole is also nebulous. It becomes confounded with the imperatives of control and survival.

Fourth, we have stressed that institutional discrimination is an interaction between gratuitous sex and race bias *and* organizational control structures. The fact that sex and race bias are gratuitous from the perspective of rational organizational theory as well as on the basis of the human capital model does not mean they are nonexistent within the organization. But such "pure" race and sex bias probably takes the form of personal prejudice; it is not institutional in any straightforward sense. Structurally induced race and sex discrimination is more subtle for being an integral part of the system of production.

This raises the question, finally, of whether it is easier or more difficult to remedy institutional than individual sexism and racism. It is impossible to answer a question of such generality with a universal rule. The central point is that affirmative action reforms will probably be relatively ineffective if divorced from organizational change incorporating occupational and career, as well as sex and race, factors.

Notes

1. For a critique of these models as applied to discrimination studies, see Van Alstyne, Withers, and Elliott (1977).

2. These results, including the proportion of variance explained, closely resemble those reported by Malkiel and Malkiel (1973).

3. It is not possible with MCA (as it is with multiple regression analysis) to include the additive effects of sex and seniority in the same model with their interaction effect. The fact that the difference in variance accounted for by the additive and combinatorial models is so small leads us to believe that *both* additive and interactive effects are present, even though their relative impact cannot be sorted out.

4. It should be emphasized that we cannot tell precisely why women with considerable seniority remain with the organization despite declining increments in salary relative to men. This is one point where a direct index of productivity would be extremely helpful, as well as some measurement of geographical mobility opportunities for females as opposed to males. Casual observation of careers at Phalanstère suggests that female mobility is in fact much lower than that for males, whatever the sex-related differences in productivity. Finally, the number of women with great seniority

at Phalanstère (for example, over fifteen years) is extremely small, with the result that the reliability of statistical tests in this range becomes precarious.

5. In the absence of further measures of organizational hierarchy, it is difficult to specify in detail the expected effects of "structural constraints" on productivity. But our major point can be stated simply without grievous distortion. It is that the opportunity to produce is limited at the lower rungs of the organization, that is, at the lower job classes; this limitation is clear relative to the theoretically unlimited nature of "creativity" at the academic-research level. In other words, we hypothesize that the possibility to produce increases exponentially instead of at a constant rate with upward changes in career lines. The argument is *not* simply that clericals cannot produce as much as academic-researchers (which is obvious enough) but rather that the productivity potential of job families varies disproportionately from one career line to the next.

7

Proportion of Black and White Army Officers in Command Positions

Peter G. Nordlie

The essential issue in considering approaches for reducing racism and sexism in organizations is how to change organizational practices that result in racial or sexual discrimination. Any successful effort to change such practices needs to begin with a demonstration that they exist and end with the documentation that they have been eliminated. This chapter will focus on the development and utilization of a management tool designed for a large-scale organization to diagnose the presence of institutional discrimination and to monitor the success with which such discrimination is being reduced within the organization.

This chapter is based on a study sponsored by the Army Research Institute (Nordlie and Thomas, 1975; Nordlie and Carroll, 1976). The objective of that study was to develop measures that could be used to examine changes in institutional

acial discrimination in the army. The purpose of developing
uch measures was to provide the basis for a management tool
hat could be routinely used to monitor the status of equal op-
•ortunity and treatment in the army.

One of the obstacles to developing such systems is that
acial issues have been so emotionally charged. Too often they
ave been perceived and defined in personal terms. Racial epi-
hets have been hurled; racism and bigotry have been charged;
nd attributions of racist motivation have been made. Minor-
ties have tended to see the white majority as being in total con-
rol of most organizations and fully aware of the policies and
practices the minorities perceive as discriminatory and racist.
Whites have tended to believe their organizatons function in the
way they claim they do—that good performance leads to advancement and proper rewards and that minorities are clamoring
for special privilege their performance may not merit. Managers
of organizations have found it difficult to chart a reasonable
course of action in such a charged atmosphere in which feelings
predominate and facts are obscured.

What is needed is a management approach that substitutes
facts for rhetoric and provides a way of determining the extent
equal opportunity is being successfully achieved as measured in
objective terms. This was the point of departure for the work
described here.

The study focused entirely on the phenomenon of *institutional* as opposed to *individual* discrimination. *Institutional discrimination* refers to the functioning of organizations and not
directly to individual attitudes or behavior. It occurs independent of the attitudes and motivation of individuals who may un-
knowingly perpetuate it. Institutional discrimination accounts
for the phenomenon wherein an organization continues to perpetuate discrimination even though its policies explicitly prohibit it and its leadership is sincerely committed to eliminating
it in all organizational practices. The most important characteristic of the concept of institutional racial discrimination is that
its presence is recognized by *effects* and not *intentions*. Based
on this key characteristic, institutional discrimination is formally defined as a difference in what happens to people in an organ-

ization that is associated with skin color, results from the normal functioning of the organization, and operates to the consistent disadvantage of persons of a particular skin color.

To examine institutional discrimination, then, one can look at what happens to people in a particular organization. In this specific case, what are all the actions taken or decisions made by the army that affect its individual members? These tend to be mainly personnel actions. Very generally, people are recruited, trained, promoted, assigned occupational specialities, assigned specific jobs, housed, provided services, administered military justice, reenlisted, discharged, and retired. These then are the areas to examine to see if there are consistent differences in what happens to people of different skin colors.

The study itself was able to utilize data on only one racial minority, blacks, because reliable data on other racial minorities were not available. The concept is usable, however, with respect to any defined group—including women—and can be used if such data are available.

It is important to note an important implication of the definition, namely that the measurement of institutional racial discrimination does not apply to any particular individual act; it applies only to the *direction* or *trend* of a *collection* of individual acts. One cannot tell, therefore, whether a particular individual's promotion or lack of it was or was not an institutionally discriminatory act; one can only tell whether in a given set of promotions there was or was not a measurable difference between promotions given to whites and blacks. Institutional racial discrimination, as defined here, can be measured only by examination of *populations* or *classes* of acts like promotions, dishonorable discharges, and assignments. This definition of institutional racial discrimination was used as the basis for specific quantitative measures. The objective was to create a practical tool that could be used to pinpoint specifically where differences in treatment existed and to reflect whether such differences declined, increased, or remained the same over time.

Typically, if one is interested in the subject of racial discrimination, one begins to compile statistics by race. For example, one might look at the racial composition of army officers in a given year. Suppose 4.2 percent of army officers were black. What does that say about discrimination? Such information is critically relevant to measuring discrimination, but by itself it does not provide any information about possible discrimination; it just indicates how many black officers there are relative to the total. By itself it does not indicate whether 4.2 percent black officers is evidence for the presence of a difference in treatment or the lack of it.

What is needed is a *standard* against which the actual percentage of black officers can be compared so one can say how much above or below the standard the actual percentage is. If the standard could be interpreted as being the number or percentage that would occur if there were no difference in treatment occurring on this dimension, then there would be a basis for saying by how much the actual number differs from the standard. In this study I proposed there is a meaningful basis for specifying such a standard; I call this standard the *expected number*.

The idea of expected number is borrowed from statistics. It is the result of applying the *null hypothesis* (the hypothesis that any difference one finds is attributable to chance variation alone) to any dimension of interest. Essentially, it is the number of blacks one would expect to be in a given category if skin color were a random variable with respect to being in that category. If the persons selected for a particular category were drawn randomly from an eligible population, the number of blacks selected would tend to be proportional to the number of blacks in the eligible population. That is what expected number means in this context; it has no meaning other than as a reference point from which to measure. Some confusion has existed on this point because of a tendency to regard the expected number as a goal. It might be accepted as a goal in a particular instance, but that is an entirely separate process and function from its usage as a reference point.

A hypothetical example may help develop this notion. Suppose interest focused on whether there is any difference in the selection of whites and blacks to attend senior services schools. If skin color were not related in any way to such selec-

tion, one would expect to find whites and blacks selected i
proportion to their total numbers in the eligible population
Thus if 4 percent of all eligible officers were black, one woul
expect about 4 percent of officers selected to be black. If ther
were two thousand officers selected and 4 percent of them wer
black, the expected number of black officers selected would be
determined by multiplying 4 percent times two thousand
which would yield an expected number of eighty. This expected
number is compared with the actual number to generate a par
ticular measure. The expected number will, of course, vary i
every particular instance, but it retains the same meaning. It i
the number that would result if color were not related to the
variable under consideration. The extent of the difference be
tween the actual number and the expected number is a measure
of difference in treatment associated with skin color.

In order to create a set of measures with the previously
described characteristics, I proposed the following formula
which can be applied to data on any dimension at any time.

$$\text{Difference Indicator} = \left[\frac{\text{Actual Number}}{\text{Expected Number}} \times 100 \right] -100$$

Where: Actual Number =   the number of blacks having the
                                  particular characteristics under con-
                                  sideration

      Expected Number =   expected percentage times the base
                                  population (total number of per-
                                  sons having the particular character-
                                  istics under consideration)

Dividing the actual number by the expected number creates
a ratio that expresses the extent to which the actual number is greater or less than the expected number. Multiplying by 100 converts the ratio to a more readily understood
percentage. Subtracting 100 from the product creates an indicator, which is zero when the actual and expected numbers
are the same. The meaning of such an indicator can thus be read
directly. If the indicator is zero or close to it, there is no evidence of difference in treatment on that dimension. If the indicator is over forty, the number of blacks found in a particular

ategory is 40 percent greater than would be expected if skin olor were not related to being in that category. If the indicator under forty, there are 40 percent fewer blacks in that category an would be expected if the null hypothesis were true. Notice at the general goal of equal opportunity programs is to drive l such indicators to zero. If all indicators were zero or close to (except for those dimensions over which the army has no con-ol), one would interpret that as evidence for the successful imination of that institutional racial discrimination measured y those indicators. If one examines the difference indicators or any particular dimension at different times, one can see im-ediately the extent to which the indicator is changing. This haracteristic permits ready diagnosis of those areas that are and re not changing in the desired direction.

In the original study, data were obtained on fifty-eight uch indexes. For some dimensions it was possible to obtain ata for as far back as 1962, but for others it was possible to go ack only to 1970. The data were obtained from the army's of-icer master tape record and enlisted master tape record. Al-hough the data are far too voluminous to present here in their ntirety, illustrative examples will be presented in the discussion f different uses of the system.

There are at least five major uses of such a management ool in an organizational change process. They are diagnosis and ssessment, hypothesis testing, policy development and clarifica-ion, education and training, and public relations. How the dif-erence indicator system has been used in the two primary uses, iagnosis and assessment and hypothesis testing, will be de-cribed briefly.

Diagnosis and Assessment

Diagnosis and assessment provided the study's original ationale. Army policy specifically stated that the identifica-ion and correction of existing equal opportunity discrepancies nd inequities is a matter of the highest priority (U.S. Army, 1973). It is this policy statement to which the difference indi-ator system is directly tied. The objective was to develop an

easily understood, quantitative system for measuring the natur
and extent of such inequities in the army and to use such a sys
tem for periodically monitoring change. Thus the system wa
envisioned as providing the army with a means for being ac
countable with respect to implementing the general policy.

Figure 1 illustrates the diagnosis and assessment applica
tion. As an example, difference indicators for separations of en
listed personnel from the army for the years 1970 through 197:
are plotted. Blacks are underrepresented among those separatin
from the army, which means blacks were less likely than white:
to leave the army during this time period. However, when th
type of discharge received by those who separated from the ar
my is examined, a consistent pattern emerges. Blacks are slightl
underrepresented among those receiving honorable discharges
Blacks are highly overrepresented among those receiving less thar
honorable discharges; and the more undesirable the discharge
the more likely that blacks receive it. In 1973, for example
blacks are overrepresented among those receiving dishonorabl
discharges by +158 percent, one of the highest indicators found
in the study.

It should be reemphasized that such indicators provide nc
information about *why* the difference exists; they only indicate
the magnitude of the difference associated with skin color. It is
a separate management task to determine in any given case wha
causes the difference.

Calculating difference indicators for successive points can
also show the extent to which the black-white difference on that
dimension is or is not decreasing to zero. Thus, not only can one
diagnose where potential areas of institutional discrimination
are occurring, one can also assess the degree of success being
achieved in reducing such discrimination.

Another example of the use of the indicators to examine
change over time is shown in Figure 2, which shows measures of
how randomly blacks are distributed across the enlisted and officer rank structures. This particular measure is derived from
individual difference indicators calculated for each grade and
rank separately. In order to create the single, summary measure
for each year plotted in Figure 2, it was necessary to adopt

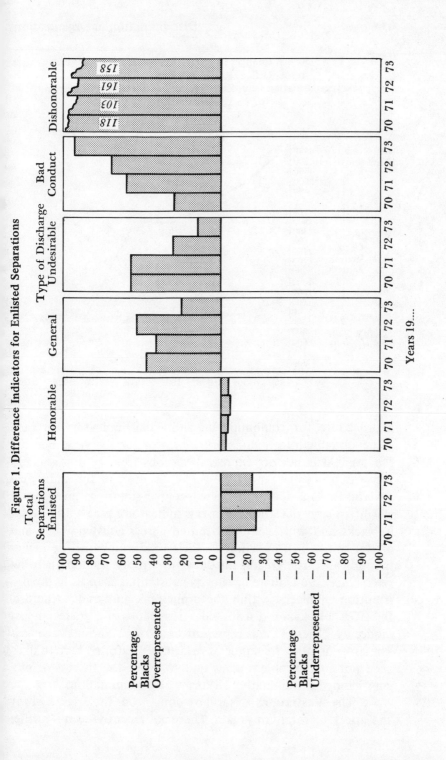

Figure 1. Difference Indicators for Enlisted Separations

Figure 2. Changes in Racial Representativeness
Across Officer Ranks and Enlisted Grades
(Average Deviation from Zero Squared of Difference Indicators
for Each Rank and Grade)

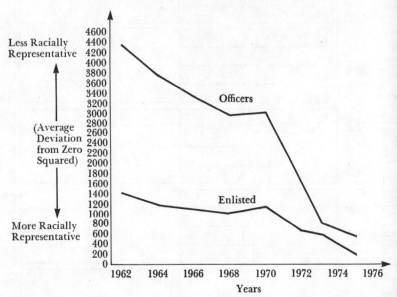

a procedure for combining the individual indicators for each grade or rank into a summary indicator for the year. Because the original indicators express deviations from zero, a straightforward procedure appeared to be to average the individual deviations. The deviations were squared simply to give greater weight to large deviations. For this indicator a zero would result if blacks and whites are distributed across enlisted grades and officer ranks in proportion to their total numbers. The higher the indicator, the greater the departure from a random distribution. Since 1962, there have been substantial changes in the distribution of blacks within the army rank and grade structure. By 1975, blacks are distributed across ranks and grades almost randomly. These curves represent large organizational changes. The army is using the kinds of measures illustrated here to diagnose potential problem areas and to assess the success of programs aimed at eliminating all forms of discrimination.

The illustrations so far have come from the original study and apply to total army data. There has recently been a further development of the system for application at lower levels of command. A handbook has been prepared with all the instructions necessary to collect the data, perform the required calculations, and graph the results for twenty-seven dimensions for army divisions, brigades, and battalions. The next illustrations are taken from the draft of that handbook.

Figure 3 shows the difference indicators for one quarter of the fiscal year for a hypothetical brigade (approximately twenty-five hundred persons). This is an example of a "time-slice" graph wherein all twenty-seven indicators for a particular time are compared. Another form of display of such indicators would be a graph that shows the difference indicators for all the subordinate units in a hypothetical division for a single dimension. This form of display facilitates the comparison of different units on the same dimension. A third type of visual display is a trend line that shows the difference indicator for a single dimension of a particular unit at different times and shows immediately how that indicator is changing. All these displays provide different ways of using the difference indicator system for diagnosis and assessment.

Hypothesis Testing

The second use of difference indicators is in testing hypotheses about what factors may have caused a particular black-white difference. This use will be illustrated by reference to some data on the difference in speed of promotion of white and black enlisted personnel. In this instance the format of the indicators is somewhat different because of the particular form in which the data were available, but the overall point would be the same if the data in this example were in the same format as in the previous examples.

When such a consistent and large black-white difference is observed, one is likely to be interested in whether the difference can be accounted for by variables other than race. One hypothesis this study examined was that level of education may be correlated with speed of promotion and white enlisted personnel may have consistently higher levels of education. If so, this factor may account for the black-white difference. This hypothesis

Figure 3. Illustrative Example of "Time-Slice" Graphic Display

Time Period: 1st Quarter FY '77-Oct., Nov., Dec. Unit: XXX Brigade

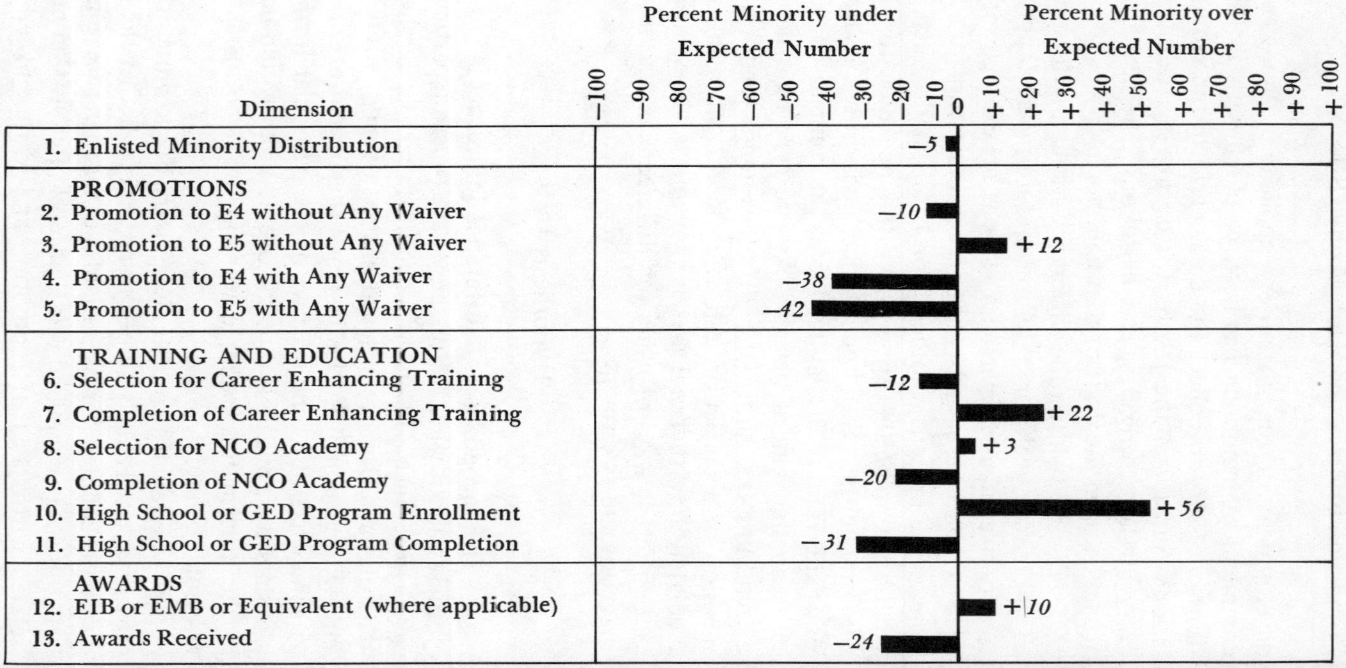

Percent Minority under Expected Number
Percent Minority over Expected Number
Dimension
−100 −90 −80 −70 −60 −50 −40 −30 −20 −10 0 +10 +20 +30 +40 +50 +60 +70 +80 +90 +100
1. Enlisted Minority Distribution
–5
PROMOTIONS
2. Promotion to E4 without Any Waiver
–10
3. Promotion to E5 without Any Waiver
+12
4. Promotion to E4 with Any Waiver
–38
5. Promotion to E5 with Any Waiver
–42
TRAINING AND EDUCATION
6. Selection for Career Enhancing Training
–12
7. Completion of Career Enhancing Training
+22
8. Selection for NCO Academy
+3
9. Completion of NCO Academy
–20
10. High School or GED Program Enrollment
+56
11. High School or GED Program Completion
–31
AWARDS
12. EIB or EMB or Equivalent (where applicable)
+10
13. Awards Received
–24

COMMAND ASSIGNMENT
14. Nonwhite Company Commanders — +8
15. Nonwhite 1st Sergeants — −7

NONJUDICIAL PUNISHMENT
16. Company Grade Article 15's — +56
17. Field Grade Article 15's — +44

UNPROGRAMMED DISCHARGES
18. Unprogrammed Separations — +33
19. Chapter 10 Separations — +23
20. Chapter 13 Separations — +5
21. Chapter 16 Separations — +4
22. Expeditious Discharge — +61
23. Courts-Martial — +219
24. Punitive Discharge — +58

REENLISTMENT
25. Bars to Reenlistment — +16
26. Career Reinlistments — +9
27. First-Term Reenlistments — +22

Figure 4. Months Above or Below Mean Months to Make Present Grade
by Race and AFQT Level—Enlisted Personnel (1975)

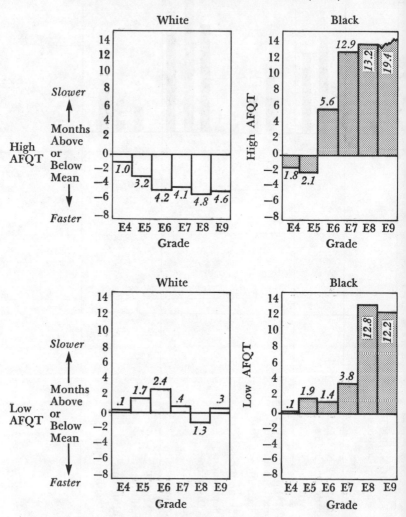

was tested by comparing the promotion times of blacks and
whites who had the same education level. It was found that education level did not account for the difference; whites were consistently promoted faster than blacks at every level of education.
The results of examining a second related hypothesis is given in

Figure 4, which relates Armed Forces Qualification Test (AFQT) score to speed of promotion. Figure 4 not only provides an example of hypothesis testing; it also illustrates the possibility of serendipitous findings. With a few minor exceptions whites are promoted faster than blacks at every grade for those with high AFQT scores and for those with low AFQT scores. The variable, AFQT score, does not therefore account for the black-white difference. But for whites, those with high AFQT scores are promoted faster than those with low AFQT scores, which is what one would expect. However, for blacks, those with low AFQT scores are promoted faster than those with high AFQT scores. The relationship is exactly the reverse for whites and blacks. Clearly, this is a phenomenon deserving further intensive study.

Other Uses of Difference Indicator Data

There certainly are additional uses for difference indicator data in an organizational change program, but I shall mention them only briefly here. One is in policy development and clarification. The army completely revised and reissued its affirmative actions plan on the basis of the results of the initial difference indicator study. Another use is as content for education and training programs on the subject of equal opportunity. Finally, it can be used in public relations activities to communicate the status of equal opportunity within an organization.

Conclusion

A practical system has been described for quantitatively measuring potential problems with respect to the status of equal opportunity within an organization. The indicator proposed is in the tradition of parity or equity indicators. It provides a manager with objective information on where in the organization and to what extent personnel decisions are resulting in outcomes associated with skin color. Used over time it can provide a manager with information about changes in the status of equal opportunity occurring within an organization.

Part Four

Studying Outside Influences on Organizational Staffing

~~~~~~~~~~~~~~~~~~~~~~~~~~~~~~~~~~~~

The next three chapters are not concerned with analyses conducted within a single organization. Rather, because they come more directly from a tradition of workforce analysis, they emphasize the occupational roles of people. However, these three chapters are included because they point toward an area that has to be systematically investigated with empirical data, namely, who from among a "relevant pool" in a particular occupation gets hired for positions within organizations? They are included not because they provide definitive answers but because they provide suggestive directions for further investigation of how people move into and out of organizational positions.

Benjamin Bowser suggests the existence of "vertical segregation," a concept that calls attention to the widespread existence of a new set of occupational roles for which blacks and other minorities are prepared and in a sense certified. Bowser contends these occupational roles have only nominal status and never command real power within an organization. Thus although jobs may exist at all hierarchical levels in the organiza-

172

tion, blacks are effectively segregated on a vertical dimension. To assess the extent of vertical segregation, Bowser suggests that occupational roles (and the positions into which persons are hired to perform those roles) must be measured for three factors: responsibility, authority and decision making, and degree of importance of the role for the organization. He also suggests an analysis of fixed ceilings for upward mobility within these vertically segregated occupational structures. Thus "tokenism" takes on a more precise meaning when empirical evidence resulting from these suggested analyses is considered.

Paula England and Steven McLaughlin designate sex segregation of jobs as the prime cause of overall inequality between average male and female earnings. Characteristic of the human capital approach, the authors' contention that sexism/racism is being practiced in the setting they researched is based on their inability to "explain away" differences in average income between men and women with the variables they used. However, they raise some interesting issues and suggest some novel approaches. Among these is the question of how it is that women end up in lower-paying or less-powerful jobs then men.

William Bridges provides a novel illustration of the use of log-linear contingency tables to analyze census and other types of social bookkeeping data. The task Bridges takes for himself is to reduce the vast array of models and techniques into a smaller or manageable analytical approach. Bridges concludes that although a researcher pays a high price for invoking this type of systematic analysis, there are substantial countervailing benefits. Among these is the fact that a large number of potentially explanatory variables can be simultaneously introduced into the analysis.

8

An Empirical Model for Measuring Racism in Large-Scale Organizations

Benjamin P. Bowser

Jim Crow practices in the South and racial covenants in the North were overt, obvious, and easily enforced. One did not have to go very far to find a convincing explanation of why blacks had poor housing, inadequate schools, high unemployment, and low incomes. As long as it was prescribed by law and manifest in the daily interaction between the races, racial discrimination, segregation, and prejudice would be sufficient reasons for blacks' collective and inferior place. When one is given a low ceiling for attainment in education and employment or is simply not allowed to attain higher-status participation in some aspects of American life, one has been victimized by a form of institutional racism best described as *horizontal segregation*. One is simply not allowed above a certain line.

As Myrdal (1944) predicted, formal racial discrimination was eventually outlawed—in 1954 and 1964. What is left is a complex and extensive range of informal and behavioral discriminations against blacks. Because discrimination was no longer reinforced by formal institutional sanctions, some believed that racial segregation might eventually become extinct in American life. This was both the promise and actuality of the New South. Closely related to the changes in American race practices during the 1960s was a period of relative economic growth; black gains were actually only fallout from this period (U.S. Department of Commerce, 1970, pp. 28–31). As the nation experienced an increase in prosperity, even the lot of those at the bottom improved. But in retrospect one can see these gains were made by some blacks while most experienced none and had heightened and unfulfilled expectations (see U.S. Riot Commission, 1968, pp. 230–280). The uprooting of segregationist political and public behavior was not accompanied by an equal uprooting of economic inequities.

Overt and formal discrimination were no longer practiced, so what could then account for the continued uneven progress in American life with regard to race—increasing ghettoization with higher mean incomes, desegregated schools but continued poor achievement, and voting rights but very little political influence? A host of victim-centered explanations have been offered, such as cultural deprivation, lack of delayed gratification, culture of poverty, and externalized locus of control (Leacock, 1971; Ryan, 1972). The notions of institutional and personal racism were the only explanations offered that suggested racial oppression had not ended with desegregation but had instead been only updated (Blauner, 1972, p. 41; Carmichael and Hamilton, 1967). It was an attempt to describe a new social order that no longer used overt, recognizable, and intentional racial discrimination but was just as effective in controlling the status and aspirations of blacks. When one considers that it required half a century for racial discrimination to become a compelling explanation for blacks' failures to achieve, it was remarkable that the idea of institutional racism was not subject to greater bitter disbelief than it was. Notions of institutional determinants of behavior not centered on specific individual's intentions have always had a rough time in American conventional beliefs, especially those regarding race and social class.

In the old order, blacks were simply not hired when whites were available. If they were already employed and new whites, such as immigrants, became available, blacks were displaced (Johnson, 1968, pp. 43–45; Wade, 1964, pp. 274–275). They were prohibited from equal employment with whites and could gain entry, temporarily, only as a reserve and "standby" labor pool. The new system, suggested by the idea of institutional racism, is only an update of changes that have taken place in the old one. Blacks now enter the labor force but on a restricted and selective basis—restricted in numbers and selective in roles. Now there are roles for blacks and other minorities on all levels of the occupational hierarchy. But they are parallel roles that most often give nominal status and appropriate incomes but no critical decision-making influence over the fate of the entire organization. One is a participant on all hierarchical levels but is still effectively segregated from the life of the organization. This new order is appropriately called *vertical segregation*.

If vertical segregation is a characteristic of institutional racism, can we illustrate its existence? Can we measure it? If it is a real trend, can it serve as a social indicator of institutional racism? Currently, there is no way to test directly for the existence of vertical segregation. A definitive examination would mean having to study the employment records of a sample of American companies, government agencies, and other organizations (Wallace, 1976). Our objective would be to see what is and what has been the racial distribution within each occupatinal grouping. Roles on each level (directors, management, staff supervisors, staff, labor) are subdivided according to their importance or lack of it in responsibility, authority, and decision making. This would tell us the difference between a vice-president for personnel and a vice-president for finance or between a supply room supervisor and a production shop supervisor. The latter in each example is more critical to the running of the company or organization. Though nominally on the same status level as their (most likely) minority counterparts, the finance and production roles are functionally more important and not as easily replaced as a personnel vice-president and supply room supervisor. In large-scale organizations there are also functional divisions, each having lines of upward mobility with different and unequal ceilings. Though the vice-presidents of personnel and of finance are nominally on the same level, it would be rare for the vice-president of personnel to become the company president.

If one cannot go into a particular set of companies because of limitations in staff, time, funds, and authorization, then one must rely on existing statistics of racial employment patterns. There are currently three major sources: U.S. Bureau of the Census reports of occupations and industries, U.S. Department of Labor surveys, and Equal Employment Opportunity (EEO) reports of minority and racial employment in American industries. But none of these three data sources "vertically" divides each occupational level into groupings of functional importance. Instead, each reports employment by functionally blind hierarchical groupings. For example:

White Collar	Blue Collar
(1) Officials and Managers	(6) Craftspersons
(2) Professionals	(7) Operatives
(3) Technical	(8) Laborers
(4) Sales	(9) Service
(5) Clerical and Office	

The two unequal vice-presidents would be summed as one figure under officials and managers (the first hierarchy); the two unequal supervisors would be summed as craftspersons (or in some cases as managers also). These statistics are excellent for studying the old order of horizontal segregation because they provide direct statistics on whether blacks and others are a decreasing or increasing part of any one occupational level. But they tell us nothing directly about vertical or interhierarchy segregation on each occupational level.

Institutional racism through vertical segregation has certain distinctive characteristics. First, all large-scale organizations can be illustrated as pyramids of occupational groupings of varied sizes. Figure 1 shows four hypothetical illustrations of possible biracial configurations within an organization.

Hypothetical models 2 and 3 (without upper-level "tokening") would be obvious illustrations of horizontal segregation; models 1 and 4 would be ideal illustrations of vertical segrega-

Figure 1. Four Models of Possible Biracial Configurations in an Organization

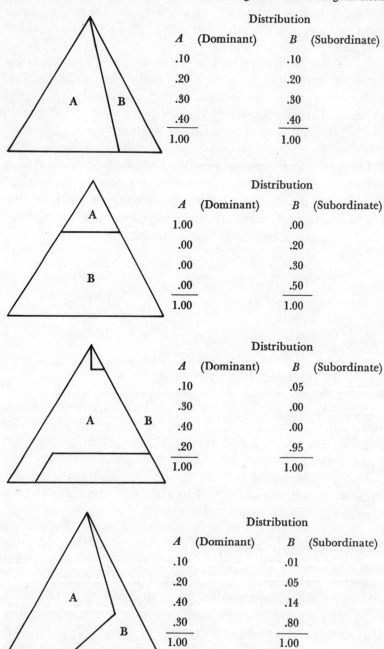

	Distribution		
A	(Dominant)	B	(Subordinate)
.10		.10	
.20		.20	
.30		.30	
.40		.40	
1.00		1.00	

	Distribution		
A	(Dominant)	B	(Subordinate)
1.00		.00	
.00		.20	
.00		.30	
.00		.50	
1.00		1.00	

	Distribution		
A	(Dominant)	B	(Subordinate)
.10		.05	
.30		.00	
.40		.00	
.20		.95	
1.00		1.00	

	Distribution		
A	(Dominant)	B	(Subordinate)
.10		.01	
.20		.05	
.40		.14	
.30		.80	
1.00		1.00	

tion. At this point a major problem becomes apparent. Because no existing data source can directly test the hypothetical models, we will have to enter a number of organizations and examine their employment records, as in the AT&T case, or we will have to find some other means of exploring the thesis. Given the diversity of types and kinds of organizations, we can assume most organizations would not voluntarily allow their records to be examined on such an issue. Thus it is more appropriate at this time (until we can get more comprehensive statistics from large organizations) to concentrate on identifying and characterizing organizations worth the time and effort to test these models. For now we must estimate to what extent vertical segregation may or may not exist from undifferentiated groupings.

Indicators

A social phenomenon that for a variety of reasons cannot be directly examined might be estimated by its related characteristics. There are many examples of this: Age and type of housing can indicate one's income; speech pattern and grammar can indicate the region one lives in and social class; or a combination of hair texture, body type, and skin color can be keys to one's physical racial inheritance. None of these related characteristics directly proves one is a particular income group, region and social class, or physical race. But the chances are that by identifying the differences in these related characteristics (indicators), one can correctly identify the other major characteristics. In a like fashion we will use several factors related to vertical segregation to estimate its presence or absence from a variety of organizations. There are several factors paralleling vertical segregation that may be used as possible social indicators.

1. Organizations that may be practicing vertical segregation, as in hypothetical models 1 and 4, have a disproportionately large number of blacks in semi- and unskilled blue-collar roles and a few blacks in white-collar positions other than sales and clerical.
2. Blacks in white-collar roles increase to a point and then remain a relatively small and stable proportion of each job cate-

gory. If many of the blacks in white-collar roles are tokens, then the number employed will remain stable and small.

3. Vertically segregated and token employment does not increase or decrease with the changes in overall employment. This is just the opposite of the historic pattern (Blauner, 1972, pp. 12–41).

The second factor can be monitored by observing changes in the occupational distribution of blacks in relation to the distribution of whites over more than one consecutive period. The following formula demonstrates this relation:

$$[(T2BOD_{1-9} - T1BOD_{1-9}) - T2WOD_{1-9} - T1WOD_{1-9})] + 100 = X \quad (1)$$

where

$T1, T1$ = Time 1, Time 2, first and second comparison
BOD_{1-9} = Black occupational distribution, [1] manager . . . [9] service
WOD_{1-9} = White occupational distribution, [1] manager . . . [9] service

The resulting value X is the percentage points (± 100), which increase or decrease with each occupational grouping of blacks in relation to the changes among whites. If vertical segregation is being practiced, there should be a slight relative increase of blacks in a hierarchical job category and stability despite further changes (increases or decreases) in white or black overall employment.

Formula 2 shows a way of measuring whether blacks are an increasing or decreasing proportion of the labor force between two periods. If the increase or decrease in the black proportion of the labor force is spread across each hierarchy according to the same rates from time 1 to time 2, then there has been no real change in black employment relative to white. The participation rate equals the percentage of total employment in each job category (note EEO reports). But more often participation rates do change; they are not apparent because they are masked by changes in the toal number of black and white employees. Formula 2 establishes whether the black participation for each hierarchy is affected by change in the black and white composition of the labor force.

$$\left(\frac{T2 \quad Bk.\ Pop.}{T2 \quad Tot.\ Pop.} \Bigg/ \frac{T1 \quad Bk.\ Pop.}{T1 \quad Tot.\ Pop.} \right) = Y \qquad (2)$$

$$\left(T2 \quad BPR_{1-9} - [Y\,(T1 \quad BPR_{1-9})] \right) + 100 = Z \qquad (3)$$

Tn: The same information gathered on n number of times (n = 1 or more)

Bk. Pop: Total black population in the organization

Tot. Pop: Total work force in the organization

BPR_{1-9} Black participation rate for each occupation hierarchy from official-managers down to service

Z: Percents on a baseline of 100.0 by which the actual rate of participation during time 2 exceeds or falls short of the rate of time 1 when one accounts for the changes in overall black employment

These formulas can be applied to U.S. Bureau of the Census, Department of Labor, EEO, or intraorganizational data. It is essential to have participation rates (percentage of black or white employment in each job category—official to service) and occupational distributions with total employment in a group as a base, thus indicating the percentage of persons employed in a particular job category.

What data should be presently used to examine these indicators? The EEO data are most appropriate; they are organized by participation rates and occupational distribution for selective major industries by nation, state, region, and Standard Metropolitan Statistical Area (SMSA). They are also time-seried and reported every three years rather than every ten. And fortunately, the data exist for the period when most organizations might have been "tokening" their white-collar hierarchies (job categories).

It is also important to use data from organizations (industries) whose racial employment practices are already known so that we have some way of ultimately judging the accuracy of these measures. Such a parallel series of studies was done by the Wharton School at the University of Pennsylvania during the late 1960s on the history and current position of blacks in selective U.S. industries. An overview of these reports suggests there are three kinds of industrial racial practices according to the type and age of a particular industry. The first consists of new "fast-growth" industries, in which most of the employees are highly trained and enter through professional education or high-skill craft unions (Northrop and others, 1971). This group is often called "post-industrial-era industries"; examples include aircraft manufacturing, aerospace, computers, synthetic products, insurance, and communications. The second type has a large blue-collar labor force and is more characteristic of most U.S. industries. Entry into this labor force is through craft and labor unions, while entry into management is through professional and college-level recruitment (Howard, 1970; Rowan, 1970). Examples of such industries are lumber, textiles, automobiles, chemical production, and farm machinery. The third group consists of older industries that have experienced technical obsolescence or deemphasis; examples include railroads, urban transportation, steel, and ship building. These have often been called "declining industries." Recruitment into the white-collar ranks in these industries is up through the blue-collar rank and file (Risher, 1970). What distinguishes the three industrial groupings are their age, the education of their work force, and the means of entry and elevation into white-collar management and technical roles. On one extreme the postindustrial industries recruit through universities; at the extreme other end the declining, labor-intensive industries recruit through their labor unions.

Given these variations in recruitment and advancement, each group of industries has its own dynamic for managing the entry of blacks and other minorities. Therefore two national industries in each of the three groups were selected from the EEO racial employment statistics, which were also studied by the Wharton School projects on racial policies of American industries.

Group I (postindustrial)	Group II (industrial)	Group III (declining industries)
Insurance	Textiles	Urban Transportation
Air Transportion	Lumber	Railroads

Table 1. Black Mean Participation Rates, 1966–1973

	1966	1969	1971	1973
Postindustrial				
Insurance	3.3	6.0	7.1	8.0
Air transportation	4.2	5.4	5.8	6.4
Industrial				
Textiles	7.9	12.0	14.6	16.9
Lumber	15.0	12.7	14.0	13.5
Declining industries				
Urban transportation	15.8	19.8	21.5	21.7
Railroads	7.9	7.5	7.5	7.2

As Table 1 demonstrates, the black mean participation rate, percentage of all employees who are black, increased from the postindustrial to dying industries; blacks are characteristically more highly concentrated in labor-intensive industries. From 1966 to 1973, the black participation rate in all but two industries (lumber and railroads) increased slightly.

At face value this reflects the increasing national diversity of black employment. But black participation rates are not separate from those of the white majority; if no regard is given to race, changes in one should be reflected by changes in the other. The black and white median occupational levels were computed; this is the category at which half of all blacks and then of all whites were above and below for each industry from 1966 through 1973.

As reported by the Wharton studies, from which Table 2 is constructed, changes in the median occupational levels for blacks and whites in urban transportation and railroads were one-to-one at all except one comparison. If one race increased or decreased its position, so did the other. In the industrials—textiles and lumber—the same pattern of change in the labor force occurred, but there were slightly more conflicts between the median occupational levels for each racial group. In the postindustrials—insurance and air transportion—there was very little coordination between changes in the two racial medians. Despite there being a good deal more individual and independent effort as a characteristic of jobs in this industrial group, the

Table 2. Median Occupational Level of Black and White Labor
by Industry, 1966–1973

Industry	1966		1969		1971		1973	
	B	W	B	W	B	W	B	W
Insurance	4.61	4.01	4.58	4.00	4.59	4.07	4.37	3.89
Air transportation	7.99	4.45	7.72	4.52	6.53	4.79	6.64	4.72
Textiles	6.84	6.37	6.62	6.32	6.63	6.31	6.58	6.25
Lumber	7.20	6.47	7.11	5.80	7.01	6.33	7.01	6.35
Urban transportation	6.62	6.15	6.43	6.06	6.54	6.19	6.48	6.07
Railroads	7.44	5.60	7.27	5.57	7.12	5.59	6.83	5.52

Note: Occupational levels were scored (1) managerial, official; (2) professional; (3) technical; (4) sales; (5) office, clerical; (6) craftspersons; (7) operatives; (8) laborers; (9) service.

black median should have experienced the same pattern of changes as the white. In comparison, as one goes from the declining to postindustrial, there is less coordination between changes in the status of the labor force by race. This might mean either of two things: More highly skilled industries continue to hire blacks into their labor force regardless of changes in their overall employment or many blacks are being hired into functionally different lines of employment on each level (vertical segregation). By observing median occupational distributions or participation rates, we cannot distinguish between these two alternatives.

One way we might establish the background of changes in the median occupational distribution is to take both the black and white medians and develop one statistic that reflects changes in both. Changes in the black occupational distribution would be related to changes in the white. This is the task of the first indicator. The values in Table 3 are residual percentages (on a 100.0 base) from the interaction between black and white occupational distributions. A score greater than 100.0 shows an increased rate of change for blacks over whites; a score less than 100.0 indicates that blacks are falling behind whites; and a 100.0 means stable movement with no relative change. (For copies of the complete tables by detailed occupational categories for each industry, contact the author.)

Table 3. Summation of Change Between Black and White
Occupation Sectors (Blue- and White-Collar)

Industry	Sector	1966–1969	1969–1971	1971–1973
Insurance	White	105.8	104.7	100.2
	Blue	104.3	104.4	100.4
Air transportation	White	109.1	104.0	103.0
	Blue	108.9	108.9	96.9
Lumber	White	86.8	109.8	100.8
	Blue	120.5	90.5	97.6
Textiles	White	98.8	99.0	97.6
	Blue	108.8	94.2	102.4
Urban transportation	White	108.4	93.4	104.4
	Blue	88.1	106.9	95.8
Railroads	White	103.9	102.2	100.9
	Blue	96.7	97.6	98.5

In all the white-collar industrial groupings there was a progressively slower elevation in the black occupational distribution relative to whites. But the blue-collar values show that black status within the labor rank and file continue to be unstable; only in the postindustrials was there a consistent pattern of decreases paralleling the white collar. These statistics illustrate that the recent prerecession blue-collar gains in black employment were only an expression of a larger white increase in the skilled to semiskilled sector. Apparently the market was right and the labor was needed. A small increase of blacks over whites in the white-collar sector (values over 100.0) accounts for an undetermined proportion of the overall increase in the black labor participation. The gains in the white-collar groups were larger than the losses in the blue-collar sector; but this does not point to improvement because there are relatively few persons in the white-collar sector. A notable trend is the lack of overall improvement but the stabilization of a low distribution of blacks in white-collar occupations—note the decreasing scores from 1966 to 1973. A small distribution is reflected in the short range of values greater than and less than 100.0 in Table 3.

What these figures also tell us is that in all but urban transportation the first two conditions for vertical segregation appear to exist; there is a relatively small distribution of blacks, tending neither to increase nor decrease in each white-collar occupational category. This point was explored further by analyzing participation rates to see if the last condition indicative of vertical segregation also exists; vertical segregation as token employment does not increase or decrease with the changes in overall employment. The second set of formulae was applied. The objective is to see if black white-collar participation rates (percentage of total employment in each job category that is black) increase or decrease. No change would mean that the additional blacks to enter each industry from 1966 to 1973 were spread across each occupational hierarchy in such a way that the early participation rates did not change. A value of 100.0 or more shows the extent to which more than the proportionate number of blacks entered that sector. A figure of exactly 100.0 indicates that blacks increased or decreased consonant with the change in total employment; a value less than 100.0 means the sector either did not absorb the increase in blacks employed (relative to the total) or lost blacks between time periods (see Table 4).

The white-collar sectors for the postindustrials (insurance and air transportation) added in 1969 slightly more than their proportions of the increased black participation rate by 1969. But by 1973, this rate of additions was exactly proportionate and decreasing. The blue-collar sector consistently did not add its proportion from one survey period to the next. The same pattern appears to be the case for the industrials (lumber and textiles) as well. Except for urban transportation there seems to be no difference between the behavior of each sector in each industry in which additional blacks entered the work force. In fact urban transportation serves as a test-worthy contrast. We know from the Wharton study on urban transportation that it was the only one of these industrial groups undergoing broadscale integration (Jeffress, 1970, p. 67). Its separation from the others is accurately reflected by the analysis.

None of the comparative statistics alone could definitely confirm the two major parallel characteristics of vertical segregation—a black increase and then stable occupational distribution plus no change in the overall rate of employment (participation rate). But a comparison of the three comparative periods

**Table 4. Change in Black Sector Participation Rates
Relative to Overall Change in Total Employment**

Industry	Sector	1966–1969	1969–1971	1971–1973
Insurance	White	102.4	100.2	102.0
	Blue	50.0	73.6	81.2
Air transportation	White	104.2	99.8	101.2
	Blue	91.1	98.2	88.8
Lumber	White	105.8	91.3	101.9
	Blue	132.2	72.2	99.2
Textiles	White	104.7	96.5	101.6
	Blue	91.7	97.8	95.8
Urban transportation	White	132.0	81.8	122.6
	Blue	83.1	98.5	93.8
Railroads	White	104.5	100.4	104.5
	Blue	104.5	93.7	96.0
Mean	White	108.9	94.9	105.6
	Blue	92.1	89.1	92.4

definitely suggests the first condition exists and partially suggests the second. Contrary to our expectations of vertical segregation, there is a slight increase in the white-collar work force. But it too is apparently decreasing; and if this trend has continued since 1973, then the third condition possibly now exists. If these indicators (X and Z) are accurate, possibly some form of vertical segregation is being increasingly practiced in industries that have varied characters and recruitment policies. Of course, this analysis is no proof of vertical segregation, but the results do match the findings of the Wharton studies of American industrial race policies. Where we differ is on the root process to which we ascribe these dynamics—discrimination (Wharton studies) versus institutional racism via vertical segregation.

What is interesting is how the EEO statistics at face value clearly show an improved situation in regard to horizontal segregation. But an examination of the patterns of change indicates the improvements are short lived and masked in unanalyzed interhierarchical movement and change. The more obvious of these maskings is how black blue-collar employment has increased, but relative to whites it has actually decreased and is less stable. The overall improvement is accounted for by the proportionately higher increase of black white-collar workers. But this increase has stabilized.

In sum, our sample of varied industrial groups is no longer practicing horizontal segregation; if this form of segregation is an operant definition of institutional racism, then they are not practicing it. What is needed are more precise statistics on the differential roles of minorities within each occupational category. We need not only their horizontal status from service to managers but also their vertical status across the organizations' functional divisions. Until such statistics are compiled, indirect and less conclusive social indicators will have to continue to be developed.

9

Sex Segregation of Jobs and Male-Female Income Differentials

Paula England
Steven D. McLaughlin

Words like "progress" come readily to the lips of commentators in discussions of the status of women. In a society that assigns job achievement such a central position in the value system it is not surprising that the increased proportion of women in the labor force is seen as evidence of progress toward equality for women. The 1970 census found 43 percent of U.S. women employed, whereas only 27 percent had been employed in 1940 (U.S. Bureau of the Census, 1973a). Indeed, the emerging pattern is for most women to be employed for many of their years, taking one or more breaks during their twenties and thirties for child rearing (Oppenheimer, 1970).

Note: This chapter is a collaborative synthesis of two papers prepared for the Research Symposium on Social Indicators of Institutional Racism/Sexism, Los Angeles, California, April 29–30, 1977. Authorship of this chapter is joint and equally shared. We would like to thank Toby Parcel and Charles Jaret for very helpful comments on earlier drafts.

Yet in the face of all this change two rather remarkable constants can be identified. The first is the extent to which occupations have remained sex typed. The magnitude of occupational segregation has remained virtually unchanged throughout recent history despite the dramatic increase in the number of employed women and in the female proportion of the labor force (Gross, 1968; Hooks, 1947; Oppenheimer, 1968, pp. 219–234). In fact, Oppenheimer (1970, 1973) has argued that increased female employment is due in large part to disproportionately increased demand for labor within those occupations already identified as "female." A second constant is the ratio of average male to female earnings. There has been no progress toward sex equality of earnings. In 1939, the median income of women who worked full-time year-round was 60.8 percent of the male median income for full-time year-round workers. By 1971, the median income of women had actually decreased slightly to 59.5 percent of the male median (U.S. President's Council of Economic Advisors, 1973).

Our contention is that these two constants are related in more than a coincidental fashion. The purpose of this chapter is to investigate how sex segregation of jobs is related to the gap between average male and female income. To say that low income for women results from segregation into predominantly female occupations can mean two distinct things. On the one hand it may mean that female occupations have low pay because they rank relatively low on those task attributes and training requirements associated with high income. On the other hand it may mean that predominantly female occupations provide less pay than is commensurate with their task characteristics and training requirements. This chapter shall show that both factors contribute to an explanation of the male-female income differential.

Sex Segregation of Jobs

Job here means a specific occupational title or task performed in a specific industry and in a specific establishment (for example, firm, public agency, or plant). Thus if one had a cross classification of occupations by industries by work places, each cell in the resulting matrix would be a job in the sense we use the term here. Examples of workers in the same job are typists in the same office, janitors employed by the same school, or textile operators in the same plant.

A cursory observation of the American labor force reveals that jobs as here defined are very often filled almost exclusively by either men or women. Although it is hard to find data simultaneously disaggregated by occupation, industry, and establishment, one can get an underestimated sense of the magnitude of job segregation by examining the distribution of men and women across census-detailed occupational categories.

Gross (1968) has shown, using the Index of Dissimilarity (Duncan and Duncan, 1955), that the extent of sex segregation across detailed occupational categories did not change substantially from 1900 to 1960 (Williams, 1976). In each decennial census year during this period approximately 70 percent of all males or females would have had to change detailed occupational categories in order for the proportion of women in each occupation to equal their proportion in the labor force. Blau (1975a) has shown that the magnitude of sex segregation continued at this level in 1970.

If we knew the number of men and women in each job, sex segregation would undoubtedly be revealed as more pervasive than is indicated by computing a segregation index across census occupational categories. Oppenheimer (1970) has shown for a few selected mixed-sex occupations that males and females are segregated into different industries within occupational categories. For example, male assemblers are concentrated in the automobile industry while female assemblers are concentrated in the textile or electronics industries. Blau (1975a) has shown that mixed-sex office occupations are often sex segregated by firm. For example, some firms may hire all women in the bookkeeping department while other firms in the same city hire exclusively males to do the same task. Thus although the data analyzed in this chapter pertain to occupations, the reader should bear in mind that the sex segregation of jobs is even more pervasive than that of occupations.

Within-Job Versus Between-Job Income Differences

What does the pervasiveness of the sex segregation of jobs reveal about the form taken by income differences between men and women? To answer this question, it is useful to divide the total sex differences in income into two parts: that resulting from men and women in the same job getting paid differently and that resulting from the distribution of men and women across jobs that differ in their average pay. We call the former differences within-job sex differences in earnings and the latter between-job or distributional differences.

This distinction between distributional and within-job sex differences is logically related to sex segregation: If the sex segregation of jobs were total (that is, no job had both men and women in it), then 100 percent of any observed sex difference in income would have to be distributional. There would be no within-job sex difference in earnings because no job would contain members of both sexes.

If all jobs were completely integrated (that is, contained numbers of men and women proportional to their numbers in the labor force), it would be impossible for any of the observed sex difference in income to be distributional or between jobs. Individuals' pay would surely differ according to which occupation they were in, but men and women would have identical distributions across high-paying and low-paying jobs. Thus although much of the total income variation among individuals would still be between jobs, 100 percent of any *sex* difference in earnings would have to result from men and women in the same job being paid different amounts. These within-job pay differences between men and women would be maximally visible to the workers involved.

Total sex integration of jobs allows the possibility of within-job income differences only, and total sex segregation of jobs allows the possibility of between-job differences in income only. The greater the magnitude of sex segregation of jobs, the higher the probability that most of the difference in income between men and women arises from differential distribution across jobs. Thus the pervasiveness of sex segregation can in itself be taken as indirect evidence that much of the sex differences in earnings is distributional.

Research Review

Much of the empirical evidence is consistent with the notion that a large part of the male-female income gap results from the concentration of women in lower-paying jobs rather than from men and women in the same job getting paid different amounts. When male and female earnings are compared within occupational categories, the income difference is much smaller than in the labor force at large (Cohen, 1971; Fuchs, 1971, 1974, pp. 23–26; Malkiel and Malkiel, 1973, pp. 693–705; Sanborn, 1964). Furthermore, men and women in the same occupation are often sex segregated by firm, with the firms hiring women for a given job paying a lower wage than the firms hiring men (Blau, 1975a; Buckley, 1971; McNulty, 1967). It is clear that the finer the job classification, the less the differential between men and women's incomes. At the same time, the finer the classification, the more segregation is revealed and thus the more income difference between the sexes is a consequence of between-job differences. As Fuchs (1971, p. 14) has pointed out, "Indeed I am convinced that if one pushes the occupational classification far enough one could 'explain' nearly all the differential. In doing so, however, one merely changes the form of the problem. We would then have to explain why occupational distributions differ so much."

Failure to grant equal pay for work in the same job is not a major cause of the sex differences in average earnings. For Fuchs this finding suggested that the relevant question becomes why it is that women end up in lower-paying jobs than men. Possible explanations include sex discrimination in hiring for well-paid positions or sex role socialization of women to consider themselves "secondary breadwinners" and thus not to seek highly paid jobs. Both explanations undoubtedly have some validity. However, the findings that most of the sex income gap is between jobs should shift our attention to a question Fuchs ignores as well as to the one he proposes. Rather than asking what causes women to be employed in lower-paying jobs than men, one can ask what it is that causes female jobs to pay less than male jobs.

Sociologists tend to view the income of a job as flowing from its functional task requirements, perhaps because of the dominance of the functional theory of stratification (Davis and Moore, 1945) as well as because of empirical evidence to support the contention. Unquestionably, these factors explain much of the variance in average earnings across jobs. However, it does not necessarily follow from this that the sex differences in average earnings flow from women being concentrated in jobs that are lower on the relevant income-producing attributes identified in theories of occupational income determination. Another possibility is that net of income-producing attributes of jobs, predominantly female jobs have lower earnings simply because women are employed in them. Stated another way, the income return experienced by the incumbents of occupations with a specific set of income-producing attributes may be lower for female-dominated jobs than for male-dominated jobs. An extreme example would be the fact that janitors receive higher pay than maids or charwomen despite virtual equivalence of the tasks performed by the males and females classified under these sex-segregated occupational titles. This form of sexism has gone virtually unrecognized.

An exception can be found in the work of Stevenson (1975). She divided occupational titles into major classifications according to the amount of formal education and specific vocational training required of the occupations's incumbents. She demonstrated that within each classification women tended to be segregated into a small number of occupations in which the wages were generally lower than the male occupations in the same classifications. Similarly, Treiman and Terrell (1975) utilized a regression analysis to demonstrate that occupations with a higher percentage of women have a lower wage rate for both male and female incumbents even when the average education of workers in the occupations was controlled. Because some measure of education has consistently been found to be one of the best predictors of earnings across individuals and occupations, these findings suggest it may be the presence of women in the occupation rather than the attributes of the occupations themselves that have led to their lower wages.

The approach taken in this chapter is to examine the effects of occupational income-producing attributes on the earnings of male and female incumbents in order to determine if the sex ratio of an occupation influences the average earnings of the occupation net of the functional characteristics of the occupational task. We build on the work of Stevenson (1975) and Treiman and Terrell (1975) by incorporating more complete measures of occupations' functional task requirements in our analysis.

Before proceeding with the analysis, let us review the line of reasoning upon which this research is built. We have pointed out that the extensive sex segregation of jobs is indicative of the fact that most of the differences in the average incomes of men and women come from the concentration of women in lower-paying jobs rather than from the failure to pay men and women in the same job at the same rate. We want to explore what it is about women's jobs that causes their relatively lower wages. On the one hand women may be concentrated in jobs with characteristics that generate income at a lower rate than the jobs in which males are concentrated. On the other hand employers may simply pay lower wages in jobs where women predominate, regardless of the nature of the task. The two possibilities are not mutually exclusive; if both contribute to the income differential, the task is to shed light on the relative importance of each factor in explaining the income differences between men and women.

Data and Measurement

The unit of analysis in this investigation is the occupation. We employed the *Dictionary of Occupational Titles* (DOT), published by the U.S. Bureau of Labor Statistics, as a source of information concerning the nature of the occupational task and the requirements made on the occupation's incumbents. The 1970 census was the source for the percentage male and median earnings of each occupation.

The basic coding scheme used to classify occupations in the DOT was based on the assumption that all jobs involve some relationship to people, to data, and to things. It was assumed that the nature of these relationships was continuous such that job functions proceeded from simple to complex with regard to each of the three dimensions. Taken as a set of indicators, these three variables represent a description of each job's content. (For a description of the history and rationale of the DOT job evaluation system see Fine and Heinz, 1958. See Appendixes A and B of Volume 1 of the DOT for a detailed description of all occupational characteristic indicators.)

In light of the roughness of the DOT measures, "data" was trichotomized to form an interval scale with the following levels: (1) the lowest level, in which there is no relationship to data at all or the worker needs only to compare readily observable characteristics; (2) the middle range of complexity, in which the worker performs such operations on data as computing, compiling, and analyzing; and (3) the highest level, in which data is coordinated for decision making or is integrated for the discovery of knowledge. Because it was not clear that the nine categories of complexity the DOT provided for the "people" and "things" dimensions were truly ordinal, both variables were dichotomized to form dummy variables to represent the presence or absence of an occupational relationship to people or things.

The third edition of the DOT presents measures of additional occupational characteristics. Among these additional data are worker aptitudes required for successful job performance, general and specific training required, and prevailing working conditions. General educational development (GED) was measured with a six-point scale reflecting the amount of formal and informal training necessary for average job performance. It was intended to tap the dimensions of education relevant to the development of reasoning ability, communications skills, and mathematics. The second training requirement, specific vocational preparation (SVP), was measured with a nine-point scale representing increasing amounts of time required to learn the techniques and skills of a specific occupation. It included vocatinal education, apprentice work, and on-the-job training.

For each occupation the requirement for the following aptitudes was recorded: intelligence, verbal skill, numerical skill, spatial comprehension ability, form perception, clerical perception, motor coordination, finger dexterity, manual skill, eye-hand-foot coordination, and color discrimination ability. Scores for each of these aptitudes were assigned to an occupation according to a five-point scale indicating increasingly higher requirments for that aptitude.

The DOT's measure of the job's working conditions included a five-point scale of physical strength, the presence or absence of a need to climb, stoop, talk, see, or handle objects. It also included indicators of the presence or absence of a requirement for the worker to experience extremes of hot and cold, loud noises, fumes, and of the job's requirement to work inside, outside, or both. All these variables except "talking" and physical strength were eliminated from the analysis because each of the eliminated variables was nearly constant rather than a variable across occupations. That is, each eliminated variable was almost uniformly present or absent from all the occupations included in this analysis. Physical strength was retained because it did vary, and "talking" was retained due to its correspondence with verbal skills requirement.

In addition to this extensive list of occupational characteristics it was necessary to obtain additional information regarding the average income and the percentage male of the occupation. Because the DOT contains no information regarding either income or the sex ratio of occupations, we utilized the 1970 published census data. In order to merge the two separate data sets it was necessary to match each 1970 census three-digit occupatinal code to a DOT occupational title. Although there was a close correspondence between the census classification at the professional level, the DOT was considerably more detailed than the census for managerial, sales, crafts, and operative occupations. This lack of correspondence required a careful reading of each DOT job description and a concurrent examination of the "Alphabetical Index of Occupations and Industries" (U.S. Bureau of the Census, 1970a) to determine the best possible match among several DOT titles for each census title. In a few cases the census title was too general to allow an accurate match (for example, "laborers not elsewhere classified"). In these cases we dropped the occupations from the analysis.

This matching procedure resulted in a data set containing the DOT occupational characteristic information along with the number of male and female incumbents in the experienced civilian labor force in 1970 and the median earnings of the men and women in the experienced civilian labor force who worked full-time for fifty to fifty-two weeks in 1969 for each of 378 detailed 1970 occupational titles. Although we use the terms "income" and "earnings" interchangeably throughout this chapter, all data analysis herein uses *earnings* of full-time year-round workers.

Creating Composite Indicators of the Occupational Characteristics

In order to examine the differential effects of the occupational characteristics on male and female earnings and to determine if percentage male has an independent effect on earnings, it is necessary to regress the occupational characteristics along with percentage male on median male and female earnings. Because a number of the occupational characteristics drawn from the DOT were from the same content domain (for example, the "talking requirement" and "verbal skill") and consequently were highly correlated, it was necessary to create composite indicators. Utilizing each DOT variable as an element in one regression equation would generate a problem of multicolinearity and thus produce unstable coefficients. This would result in misleading estimates of the relative contributions of the occupational characteristics to the explanation of median earnings. In response to this problem we created composite indicators of the nature of the occupational task with exploratory principal factor analysis utilizing an orthogonal, varimax rotation. All variables demonstrating a communality of less than .50 were dropped one at a time from the factor analysis. This procedure eliminated spatial comprehension ability, clerical skill, eye-hand-foot coordination, and color discrimination. The indicator of physical strength was not included in the factor analysis because it was regarded as a "nonskill" characteristic. Consequently, it was included as an occupational characteristic but regarded as a separate variable independent from the skill-related indicators included in the factor analysis. Table 1 presents the means, standard deviations, and zero-order correlation coefficients for all variables retained in the factor analysis. Table 2 displays the factor structure and communalities for the solution.

An inspection of the factor loadings reveals a remarkably "clean" solution in that each variable is clearly loaded on one factor and the set of variables loading heavily on each factor share a common substantive theme. Because the results of the factor analysis suggest a great deal of face validity, it is with some degree of confidence that we utilized the three resultant factors as indicators of the nature of the occupational task. Factor I is labeled "cognitive skill" because of the high loadings from data, the two measures of training required, and the aptitudes of intelligence, verbal skill, and numerical skill. Factor II is labeled "manipulative skill" because of the high loadings from form perception, motor coordination, finger dexterity, and manual skill. Factor III is identified as "social skill" due to its high loadings from the "people" and "talking" and a high negative loading from the variables assessing the job's relationship to things. Linear composite indicators of each of these factors were then created with factor score coefficients generated with a regression technique (Alwin, 1973, pp. 191–214; Harmon, 1967). These coefficients, when used in a standardized regression equation, form the best possible least squares estimation of the standardized factors. The computation of the factors results in the creation of three orthogonal (uncorrelated) dimensions of the occupation so that the problem of multicolinearity is minimized. As a product of this procedure the three factors have a mean of zero and a variance of one. In order to simplify the interpretation of later analyses, the fourth occupational characteristic (physical strength) was also standardized. These four variables complete the set of indicators of the nature of the occupational task.

Characteristics of Male and Female Occupations

Having assembled this set of indicators of the nature of the occupational task and the sex ratio for each occupational

Table 1. Correlations, Means, and Standard Deviations of the Selected Occupational Characteristics

	Data	People	Things	Talking	GED	SVP	Intelligence	Verbal Skill	Numerical Skill	Form Perception	Motor Coordination	Finger Dexterity	Manual Skill
Data	1.0												
People	.276	1.0											
Things	-.328	-.749	1.0										
Talking	.370	.686	-.633	1.0									
GED	.818	.292	-.357	.400	1.0								
SVP	.743	.125	-.083	.265	.816	1.0							
Intelligence	.728	.367	-.455	.437	.881	.710	1.0						
Verbal skill	.808	.415	-.513	.488	.875	.674	.921	1.0					
Numerical skill	.767	.223	-.326	.365	.855	.727	.875	.869	1.0				
Form perception	.395	-.150	.232	-.056	.469	.512	.432	.390	.507	1.0			
Motor coordination	.109	-.188	.329	-.227	.168	.250	.136	.092	.162	.636	1.0		
Finger dexterity	.271	-.070	.238	-.119	.351	.446	.296	.237	.355	.766	.860	1.0	
Manual skill	.102	-.197	.340	-.213	.176	.254	.100	.028	.177	.644	.684	.780	1.0
Mean	2.13	.386	.558	.466	3.81	5.63	3.44	3.29	2.88	2.83	2.77	2.67	2.78
Standard deviation	.85	.49	.50	.50	1.29	2.11	.987	1.10	1.18	.78	.63	.63	.63

Table 2. Varimax Rotated Factor Matrix
for Selected Occupational Characteristics

| | Factor I | Factor II | Factor III | |
	Cognitive Skill	Manipulative Skill	Social Skill	Communality
Data	.825	.095	.181	.722
GED	.918	.162	.202	.909
SVP	.795	.257	.016	.699
Intelligence	.870	.124	.305	.865
Verbal skill	.883	.061	.355	.910
Numerical skill	.892	.164	.157	.847
Form perception	.445	.698	-.168	.714
Motor coordination	.067	.849	-.140	.746
Finger dexterity	.223	.966	-.036	.984
Manual skill	.074	.791	-.172	.660
People	.131	-.075	.893	.821
Things	-.260	.286	-.786	.767
Talking	.319	-.158	.669	.574

title, we begin the analysis with an examination of the extent to which predominantly male and female occupations differ in the characteristics. Following this, we can proceed to an analysis of the extent to which these specific differences in occupational characteristics account for the lower income typical of the predominantly female occupations. Table 3 presents the mean values of the four occupational characteristics for each of three categories of occupational sex identification.

The sex identification of the occupations was determined by the ratio of male to female workers within each occupational title in 1970 (U.S. Bureau of the Census, 1973a). Unfortunately, no concensus exists regarding the operational rules for establishing "male" and "female" occupational categories. Following the work of Jusenius (1975), we labeled an occupation as typically male or female based on the proportion of the 1970 labor force that was female (38.1 percent). Any occupation in which women make up 48.1 percent of the workers (38.1 plus 10) or more was labeled a "female occupation." This group contained 82 occupations or 24 percent of the total set of occupations. All

Table 3. Mean Values of Occupational Task Characteristics
by Identification of the Occupation

| Occupational Characteristic | Female Percentage of Occupational Work Force | | |
	"Male" (Less Than 28.1%) (N = 247)	"Mixed" (28.1–48.0%) (N = 49)	"Female" (Over 48.0%) (N = 82)
Cognitive skill	.09	.37	−.50
Manipulative skill	.05	−.02	−.14
Social skill	−.26	.50	.47
Physical strength	.21	−.41	−.39

occupations in which female workers represented 28.1 percent (38.1 minus 10) or less of the occupations' incumbents were labeled "male occupations." This occupational category contained 247 (65 percent) of the occupations. The remaining 49 (11 percent) occupations in which women represented between 28.2 and 48.0 percent of the workers were labeled "mixed occupations."

In general these data suggest a set of nonlinear relationships between the sex ratio of an occupation and the demands of the occupational task. Occupations falling within the "mixed" category demonstrate the greatest demands for cognitive and social skill and require the least physical strength. Thus those occupations in which women have significant but minor representation (28–48 percent) tend to be the "thinking," nonmanual, and "social" occupations. As the occupation becomes female dominated (more than 48 percent female) or male dominated (less than 28 percent female), the mean cognitive skill requirement declines significantly. In terms of this dimension of the occupational task the mixed occupations require the most cognitive skill, followed by the male-dominated occupations, with the female-dominated jobs having the lowest requirement for this dimension.

There is little difference between the social skill requirements of the mixed and female-dominated jobs. Occupations in which women make up at least 28 percent of the incumbents tend to range high on the need for social skill. The male-dominated occupations, however, demonstrate a significantly lower demand for their skill.

The opposite relationship holds for the physical strength requirement of the job. Both mixed and female-dominated jobs require relatively little physical strength and the male-dominated jobs tend to demand more of this characteristic.

For the most part the findings regarding the social skill and physical strength dimensions correspond to the dominant stereotypes regarding men's and women's work. Women tend to work more with people in situations that require social skill, and males dominate the jobs demanding physical strength. The findings regarding manipulative skill, however, are not consistent with these stereotypes. There are no nontrivial differences in the amount of manipulative skill required in the male-, mixed-, or female-dominated jobs.

In general these data indicate that the relationship between occupations' sex ratios and all the dimensions of the occupational task are not systematic. All the relationships portrayed in Table 3 are largely nonlinear, and the pattern of nonlinearity depends on the particular dimension of the occupational task being measured. We shall see later that on the average (that is, when the nonlinearities in the relationship are "smoothed out") occupations with more males in them have somewhat higher demand for cognitive skill, less demand for social skill, and about the same demand for manipulative skill. The analysis now turns to an examination of the extent to which these occupational characteristics are related to income. Although there are differences in the nature of the task by the sex composition of the occupation, the extent to which these differences explain the between-job income differences remains an empirical question. Moreover, the impact of percentage male on income independent of the nature of the task is yet to be examined.

Occupational Characteristics and the Male-Female Income Differential

In this section we present the results of a regression analysis in order to provide some insight into the causes of the relatively low incomes characterizing predominantly female occupations. We juxtapose two possible explanations: Female occupations may pay less because the characteristics of the occupation-al tasks are such that they generate less income, or they may pay less than is commensurate with their task characteristics simply because they are female-dominated occupations. These two explanations are not mutually exclusive, but the objective of this analysis is to compare the explanatory power of each.

If the percentage of incumbents in an occupation who are male exerts a positive effect on the average income in the occu-pation, even when task characteristics of occupations are con-trolled, this is evidence that female occupations pay less than is commensurate with the task being performed in them. To see if this is the case, we regressed the average income in an occupa-tion on the four measures of the occupational task as well as the percentage male. In order to provide an indication of the effect of an occupation's sex composition on its income, it is necessary to use two separate regression equations. The first predicts aver-age female income in occupations from their functional charac-teristics and sex composition and the second equation predicts average male income in occupations from the same variables. If the two separate regression equations are not employed, mea-sures of the effect of sex composition on an occupation's earn-ings will be contaminated by the effects of within-occupation differences between men and women. Stated another way, by performing separate regression analyses on average male and fe-male income, we hold sex constant while viewing the effects of sex composition of occupations on the average income of either males or females in an occupation.

Thus using the three indicators of the nature of the occu-pational task derived from the factor analysis and the indicator of physical strength, we estimate coefficients for the following two regression equations:

(1) $MI = a_m + b_m CS_m + b_{2m} SS_m + b_{3m} MS_m + b_{4m} PS_m + b_{5m} PM + e_m$

(2) $FI = a_f + b_{1f} CS_f + b_{2f} SS_f + b_{3f} MS_f + b_{4f} PS + b_{5f} PM + e_f$

where: MI = median male income, FI = median female income, CS = cognitive skill factor, SS = social skill factor, MS = manipu-lative skill factor, PS = physical strength, PM = percent male.

The equations initially included all possible terms of interaction of the occupational task variables with percentage male. However, the addition of the interaction terms did not significantly improve the predictive power of the equations over and above the predictive power of the main effect. Consequently, they were omitted from the analysis.

We estimated the male equation by weighting each occupation by the number of males working in the job in 1969 and the female equation by weighting all occupations by the number of female incumbents. In the computations to estimate the coefficients for the male equation, an occupation counts as two cases if it has twice as many males in it as the average occupation does. Similarly, an occupation counts as three fourths of a case if it employs three fourths as many females in it as the average occupation. The justification for weighting in this aggregate analysis is that we want to prevent a few sparsely populated occupations characterized by unusual relationships between variables from dominating the results and leading to interpretations that do not typify the labor force as a whole. Of course, the weighting must be done for the relevant universe population (male in one case, female in the other). The same occupation will receive a different weight in the computation of the male equation than it does for the female equation. If this were not so, the two equations would be identical because the same occupational titles are the cases for both regression analyses. The results of these two regression equations are presented in Tables 4 and 5.

The positive coefficients associated with the percentage male in Tables 4 and 5 reveal that both males and females gain income as the proportion of males in an occupation increases. Both men and women get paid more in male-dominated occupations *controlling for the nature of the occupational task*. There are two possible interpretations of this link. The first is that the equations are misspecified such that there are occupational characteristics related to both percentage male and to income missing from the equations. If this is the case, percentage male may be acting as a surrogate of these other unmeasured occupational characteristics and consequently demonstrate a positive effect on the income of both males and females. Given the

Table 4. Regression of Male Median Income on the Occupational
Task Characteristics and Sex Composition

Means, Standard Deviations, and Zero-Order Correlations

	CS	MS	SS	PS	PM	MI
Cognitive skill (CS)	–					
Manipulative skill (MS)	-.01	–				
Social skill (SS)	.04	.05	–			
Physical strength (PS)	-.51	.14	-.43	–		
Percentage male (PM)	.07	.10	-.37	.37	–	
Male income (MI)	.65	.05	.30	-.50	.10	–
Mean	-.23	-.08	-.16	2.68	81.99	8,868.16
Standard deviation	.90	.93	.92	1.00	22.63	

Regression Results

	Standardized Regression Coefficients	Metric Regression Coefficients	Standard Error
CS	.51	1,994.7	166.7
MS	.05	175.9	132.7
SS	.28	1,044.8	153.8
PS	-.22	-768.1	172.0
PM	.248	37.9	6.1
Intercept		8,461.6	
R^2 = .56	F = 93.36		

Note: N = 378 occupations, each weighted by the ratio of the number of men in the occupation to the average number of men in the 378 occupations. The cases in the equations predicting male and female income are the same 378 occupations. Yet the means on the variables in Table 4 differ from those in Table 5 because of the weighting process. Each occupation in the male equation has been weighted by the number of men in it (divided by the average number of men in all occupations so that the average weight is 1 and N = 378). Analogously, for the female equations, each occupation is weighted by the number of women in it divided by the average number of women in all occupations. By this procedure, the means for the male and female equations differ as a direct function of the distribution of the sexes across occupations.

relatively high value of the coefficients of determination reported in Tables 4 and 5, it seems unlikely that most of the observed effect of percentage male on income is a spurious result of unmeasured occupational characteristics already in the equation.

Table 5. Regression of Female Median Income on the Occupational Task Characteristic and Sex Composition

Means, Standard Deviations, and Zero-Order Correlations

	CS	MS	SS	PS	PM	MI
Cognitive skill (CS)	—					
Manipulative skill (MS)	.04	—				
Social skill (SS)	.15	.08	—			
Physical strength (PS)	−.23	−.07	−.15	—		
Percentage male (PM)	.24	−.16	−.32	.33	—	
Female income (FI)	.75	.22	.01	−.13	.29	—
Mean	−.45	−.07	.51	1.97	29.71	4,776.23
Standard deviation	.69	.93	.86	.80	26.53	1,638.95

Regression Results

	Standardized Regression Coefficients	Metric Regression Coefficients	Standard Error
CS	.71	1,698.7	86.2
MS	.21	374.6	57.4
SS	−.07	−127.4	66.4
PS	−.01	−12.3	73.7
PM	.14	8.3	2.4
Intercept		5,406.7	
R^2 = .62	F = 119.74		

Note: N = 378 occupations, each weighted by the ratio of the number of women in the occupation to the average number of women in the 378 occupations.

The second and preferred interpretation is that the link between an occupation's sex composition and income is an aggregate form of discrimination. It is a form of discrimination that affects both men and women. Yet, because by definition women are more frequently in predominantly female jobs than males are, the overall effect of this aggregate discrimination is to lower women's wages relative to those of men's.

The between-occupational character of this discrimination makes it invisible. Sex differences in income within a job would be visible insofar as workers compare notes on their

wages, but between-job differences in pay are usually assumed
to be a result of attributes of the job. People do not perform
multiple regression analyses with their everyday observations, so
they cannot make the comparisons that reveal that the simple
presence of women in a job lowers wages. Thus it is sex segregation that makes invisible discrimination of this sort possible.

It is beyond the scope of this chapter to uncover the historical and social-psychological process through which job sex
labels have been translated into dollars. Employers may devalue
traditionally female work and feel it deserves a lower wage rate.
They may assume that women "need" money less because they
are "secondary breadwinners." These thoughts need not be conscious or explicit for wage decisions to be grounded in them.
Women may have internalized precisely the same ideas about
themselves that male employers have. Thus they may not bargain as hard for wages, individually or collectively. The fact that
this discrimination is largely between jobs discourges bargaining
because the relevant comparisons with higher male wages in
other occupations requiring similar skill are not obvious.

Establishing the positive net effect of percentage male
does not tell us whether this form of discrimination explains
more or less of the income difference between men and women
than the fact that the occupations in which women and men are
concentrated differ in their average level of income-producing
task characteristics. To make this assessment, we performed the
following manipulation with the regression results: For a given
predictor variable in the two equations we can ask what would
happen to one gender's income if the sexes exchanged means on
this variable but kept the same means on all other variables and
kept the same payoff rate to each occupational characteristic.
For example, we take the male mean on cognitive skill times the
slope for cognitive skill from the female equation and compare
this product with the female mean times the slope (or the rate
of return) from the female equation to determine what the effect would be on female incomes if they were to have the male
mean on cognitive skill but retain the female means on all other
variables. We can compare the effect of this on female income
with the dollar effect of a shift to the male mean on occupation-

Table 6. Effect on Male and Female Annual Dollar Earnings
of Substituting the Opposite Sex's Mean on Occupational Variables
into Own Sex's Equation

	Effect in Dollars on Male Earnings of Female Mean	Effect in Dollars on Female Earnings of Male Mean
Cognitive skill factor	−432.86	368.62
Social skill factor	703.13	85.73
Manipulative skill factor	1.93	−4.12
Physical strength	545.27	−8.76
Percent male	−1,982.23	435.03

al sex composition while holding constant the occupational task
characteristics of female occupations. In other words, we ask
the following two hypothetical questions: (1) How much would
female income be increased if women worked in occupations
having male mean occupational chacteristics? (2) How much
would female income be increased if women continued to work
in occupations with the same task characteristics but with the
sex ratio typical of the male worker? Table 6 shows the results
of such computations for all the variables.

The standardized regression coefficients in Tables 4 and 5
reveal that for both men and women the cognitive skill factor
explains more variance in income than does any other single occupational factor. We also note from comparing the female and
male means (see Tables 4 and 5) on this variable generated from
the weighting procedure that women are in occupations that on
the average require less cognitive skill than that required by the
occupations in which average males work. Table 6 shows that if
females raised the cognitive skill of their occupations to the
level of male jobs but did not change any other occupational
characteristic (including sex composition) and if they retained
the same payoff level for each increment of this occupational
characteristic (as measured by the unstandardized regression coefficient), women would gain $369 in median annual income. If
males lowered the mean cognitive skill of their occupations to
the level of the female mean but left all else about their occupation unchanged, they would lose $433 in annual median earnings.
The choice between these two dollar figures as the estimate of

the amount of the total income gap between men and women
explained by the difference in average cognitive skill required in
their occupations is arbitrary.

According to our composite indicator of social skill, females are concentrated in occupations with higher requirements
for this skill than are males. Does this help or hurt female incomes? The question is difficult to answer because the slopes
(unstandardized regression coefficients) indicating that payoff
to income from this factor are not only very different for males
and females, but they have different signs. For males, being in
an occupation with a high social skill requirement has a strong
positive effect on earnings; for females it has a weak negative
effect.

This suggests there may be two separate dimensions of
social skill that differ in their relationship to income and are
confounded by the indicator we have constructed. More specifically, there may be a dimension of social skill that involves the
supervision or management of people that is positively related
to income. Quite apart from this there may be a dimension of
less manipulative, more nurturant social skill that in the American occupational structure is less rewarded with income. Reviewing the construction of the indicator of social skills used here,
Table 3 shows the variable with the highest positive loadings on
this factor to be a measure of whether an occupation involves
dealings with people and whether it involves talking to people.
The variable with the highest negative loading on this social skill
factor is a measure of whether the occupation involves work
with things. Thus it is clear that our measure simply tells whether an occupation has a significant social dimension, not which
of the two social dimensions it involves or at what degree of
complexity along the two dimensions the occupation falls. In
the male equation a strong positive effect of the social indicator
on income indicates that men in supervisory or managerial positions receive higher incomes than men who primarily manipulate things in blue-collar production work. In the female equation the effect of the social factor on income indicates that jobs
involving people (including child care, waitressing, and reception work) pay slightly less on the average than clerical or production jobs, which involve little contact with people. These

people-oriented jobs are primarily nurturant rather than managerial. To be sure, more complex modes of nurturance, such as
teaching, nursing, or social work, pay better than such simple
service-oriented nurturant tasks as child care or waitressing; but
our measure does not register such differences in complexity.
The fact that the female mean on the social indicator is high,
then, means that women are more apt than men to be in jobs requiring some type of social relationship. Yet substituting one
sex's means into the other sex's equation, as we did for cognitive skill, does not make sense in light of the fact that the types
of social skill being measured in the male and female equations
are probably different dimensions. The fact that women tend
not to be in occupations requiring supervisory or managerial
kinds of social skill probably explains some of the sex income
gap, but we are unable to estimate how much with the data
available here. The development of separate measures of complexity for these two distinct dimensions of social skill would
help future researchers make such an estimation.

Turning to the composite manipulative skill factor, Tables
4 and 5 show very little difference between the male and female
mean. In addition, the effects of this skill factor on wages are
very small for women and not even statistically significant for
men. Thus it is clear that differences in the manipulative skill
requirements of male and female occupations do not explain
any nontrivial portion of the sex income gap.

In contrast to manipulative skill, male occupations have
a significantly higher mean requirement for physical strength
than female occupations. Contrary to popular opinion, this difference cannot explain any of the income difference between
men and women because requirement for physical strength does
not have a net positive effect on occupational earnings for either
males or females. Thus Table 6 shows that if the sexes exchange
means on their occupations' physical strength requirements, the
income gap between them would actually widen.

Let us return to a consideration of the net effect of occupations' sex composition on their earnings. We noted earlier
that the positive coefficients in both the male and female equations of percentage male indicates that occupations employing
a higher proportion of males pay higher wages to their male and

female employees than would be predicted on the basis of their requirements for cognitive, social, and manipulative skill and physical strength. Now we are able to use Table 6 to estimate how much this form of discrimination explains of the total income gap between the sexes in comparison to the amount explained by the different requirements of the occupations in which males and females are concentrated. Table 6 shows that if men and women exchanged means for occupational sex composition but kept their own means on all other occupational characteristics (and kept the slopes of their own equations), men would lose $1,982 in annual median earnings and women would gain $435. The choice between these numbers as estimates of the contribution of this form of sex discrimination to the total sex income gap is arbitrary.

However, even if we chose the more conservative estimate, $435, it is clear that this form of discrimination explains as much of the sex difference in income as the liberal estimate of the contribution to the income gap of the fact that women are in occupations with a lower mean requirement for cognitive skill. We determined previously that differences in the average requirements of manual and physical skills make no contribution to the income difference between men and women, so discrimination is obviously a larger factor than either of these. We cannot compare the contribution of this aggregate form of discrimination to the contribution of women's concentration in jobs low in managerial social skill because we do not have a measure of this skill variable.

It is clear that aggregate discrimination in the form of paying predominantly female occupations less than male-dominated occupations in which the nature of the task is the same is a large component of the between-occupation income gap. It may strike the reader that neither of the components we have isolated explains a sizable portion of the income gap: We have estimated the contributions of both aggregate discrimination and mean differences in cognitive skill requirements of male and female occupations at about $430 apiece. Together they explain less than $1,000 of a sex income gap that was about $4,000 in these 1969 data. The principal reason for this failure is probably the roughness of the occupational characteristic categories we have employed. This means that much of the sex income gap is within these occupational categories; however, as we argued previously, it is probably "between jobs," given the high degree of segregation by industry and firm within occupations. It remains the task of further investigations to determine how much of the between-job but within-occupation sex difference in income results from different job attributes (firms and industries) in which males are concentrated and how much of it results from discriminatory lower pay of the jobs in which females are concentrated. Based on this analysis, we would hypothesize that a substantial share of it is discriminatory low pay to the jobs in which females are concentrated.

10

Log-Linear Models of Sexism in Selected Industries

William P. Bridges

As studies of discrimination in modern society move beyond explanations based on individual properties, social scientists are pressed to specify where the exact locus of invidious treatment is. This is partly a problem in defining the level of society from which discrimination springs. In research on workplace discrimination, for example, numerous studies have shown important variation can be located at the national level (Fogarty, Rapoport, and Rapoport, 1971, pp. 47–159; Galenson, 1973), at the industrial level (Bibb, 1975; Bluestone, 1971; Oster, 1975), at the organizational level (Blau, 1975b; Lyle and Ross, 1973; Mennerick, 1975), and at the suborganization level (Bridges and Berk, 1977; Mennerick, 1975). These findings are perhaps best interpreted as an indication of the pervasiveness of inequality

Note: I wish to acknowledge the assistance of Baila Miller, Arnold Feldman, Richard Hay, and Houston Stokes. Any perversion of their contributions is the sole responsibility of the author.

rather than being seen as temporary anomolies that future re-search will clear up. Thus in a study of a large metropolitan labor market Baron and Hymer (1971, p. 97) summarize the character of racism in employment: "The racial divisions in the Chicago labor market are visible in many dimensions—by indus-try, by occupation, by geographic area, by firms, and by depart-ments within firms."

However, once a particular level of analysis is chosen, one still confronts the problem of determining which units discrimi-nate the most. A large manufacturing concern may have literally hundreds of departments scattered across a number of branches and divisions. Some may have admirable records and some may not.

To make matters worse, there are two kinds of discrimi-nation or, more precisely, discriminatory outcomes to which minority participants are subject. The first sort of discrimina-tion results in the minority's exclusion from or underrepresenta-tion in participation in the unit under consideration. To extend the earlier example, the shipping department of a firm may be entirely black and the accounting office may be entirely white. An equally important form of discrimination, however, results in the allocation of minorities to less-valued roles within these units even when they are allowed to participate. The kinds of processes operating in this fashion are as diverse as "tokenism," occupational stereotyping, or educational tracking. However, the results are similar in that minority participants are shifted into roles that carry less prestige, smaller paychecks, and other sorts of disadvantages. Thus if blacks were to be hired in both the shipping department and the accounting office, their chances of achieving supervisory status would probably be small.

This chapter describes the application of a set of tech-niques that allows the researcher to divide into two components the total amount of disadvantage minorities experience across units on a particular dimension. One component represents dif-ferences across units in representation per se and the second represents differences across units in the "success" rates of mi-norities within them. The latter component refers to the fact that blacks and other minorities might not be barred from achieving valued statuses (such as supervisor) in all units but only in some, causing variation across units in the distribution of roles within. In some settings the data may reveal wide disparities in how well different segments or units represent minorities, and in others the data may reveal that different segments or units also vary in how well minorities fare once they are allowed to participate at all. In addition the technique provides standardized, quantitative measures of how well or poorly individual units are doing in these two areas.

The specific methodology explored here is log-linear contingency table analysis as developed by Goodman (1970, 1971a, 1971b, 1972a, 1972b, 1973b). The major task is to reduce this vast array of models and techniques to a smaller, more manageable group that can be usefully applied to large data sets—that is contingency tables with hundreds or thousands of cells and individual cell frequencies up to ten thousand, or larger. A researcher pays high costs for invoking this systematic type of analysis in these situations; but there are countervailing benefits, namely, that effects normally appearing as findings of separate and discrete statistical analyses can, in a manner of speaking, be gathered under one "conceptual roof."

The restriction of using "available" data raises one substantial problem that can hardly be overlooked in discrimination research: Adequate data are rarely available to control for such important additional factors as the qualifications and expertise of the participants involved. Although there is no substitute for relevant data, I discuss a method that allows the researcher to test for the presence of mitigating circumstances. Essentially, this technique involves classifying units or organizational segments that are similarly situated with regard to the availability of suitable minority populations and examining the extent to which discrimination (of either type) happens more between or within these groups. For example, comparisons among departments of a firm in terms of the percentage of minority workers would be more telling if they were made within professional departments in branches in the urban Northeast, within unskilled departments in branches in the rural South, and so forth.

Data Analysis

Because the primary objective of this chapter is to illustrate a technique, I have chosen data more on formal grounds than on substantive ones. I examine two sets of contingency tables, one of which makes comparisons among organizations in their patterns of incorporating minority group members and the second of which makes comparisons between different industries. As noted, the method can be generalized to the situation where one is examining subunits within a specific organization.

The first table is a cross classification of full-time students in master's degree programs in graduate schools of social work by race by year in program by school (Council on Social Work Education, 1975, 1976). All students included were members of the cohort that began their second year of graduate studies in the fall of 1974. In analyzing these data, I presumed that being a second-year student was a more valued role than being a first-year student. Because the overwhelming number of these programs require two years, this assumption is justified by the fact that one who is in his or her second year is that much closer to obtaining a degree. Following the previously outlined protocol, I shall ask whether schools differ significantly in the proportion of minority students they enroll and whether they differ significantly in "promoting" students of different racial backgrounds. However, the word "promotion" cannot be used without qualification. As a cursory examination of the data makes clear, many social work schools have larger second- than first-year classes. In part this reflects the entrance of social work undergraduates directly into the second year of the program. Thus a change in the proportion of minorities between years within a cohort would reflect relative enrollment and completion rates of whites and minorities in joint programs as well as promotion rates in strictly graduate programs.

To put the issue somewhat differently, I am concerned with whether one needs to invoke the notion of school differences in promotion rates to understand the racial composition of graduate social work education in the United States. In addition, where I find significant school differences I shall make a preliminary attempt to identify what characteristics of the schools may be associated with them.

The second data set pertains to the pattern of participation of women in different occupational roles across industries in the U.S. labor force. The distribution of males and females across detailed occupation and industry categories was obtained from the 1970 Census of Population and Housing (U.S. Bureau of the Census, 1972a). The U.S. summary portion of this tape provides data broken down at the finest-grained level of census reporting, 441 occupations and 235 distinct industries.

Although there is a wide range of sources containing data on industrial characteristics, all data I used to group industries have been drawn from summaries of the 1967 economic census. In particular, *Enterprise Statistics, Volume 1, General Report on Industrial Organization* (U.S. Bureau of the Census, 1972b) was useful in providing readily comparable information on 144 different industries in the following major industry categories: mining, construction, manufacturing, wholesale trade, retail trade, and services. Each of the industries was initially classified according to the enterprise industrial classification, was then matched to standard industrial classification, and was ultimately translated to the industry categories used in the census of population and housing. Where population census categories were at a greater level of detail than the enterprise industrial categories, supplementary information was obtained from the relevant economic census volumes. Altogether the industries covered in this chapter employed about 40,475,250 workers or approximately 70 percent of the labor force in 1970 employed in the private, nonagriculture sector.

In analyzing this data set, I am particularly interested in how much different industries discriminate against women. This concern suggests that the occupation variable might be allowed to play the role played by the variable "year in school" in the first example. Because the occupational order contains an inherent hierarchical component, it is well suited for this task. To be an informative indicator, however, its complexity must be reduced. For analytical purposes it is useful to collapse the attribute into fewer than 441 categories. Although there are a number of possible categorization schemes (intervals on a prestige continuum, census-type groupings—professional, managerial, and so forth—average income groupings), I have intentionally chosen a different scheme. I classified the detailed census occupations according to the mean proportion of female each has across the entire labor force. There are several rationales for this procedure. First, there is a high level of congruence between an occupation having a large proportion of female incumbents and having a "female" stereotype attached to it, although the two should be kept analytically distinct. In short, these categories can be taken as a rough approximation of the sort of occupational roles women have traditionally "chosen." Second, these occupation groups differ systematically in terms of average reward and benefits (Bridges and Berk, 1977; Oppenheimer, 1970, pp. 99–101). Finally, the choice of grouping on the basis of the proportion of women employed in the occupation across all industries is useful in terms of the structure it imposes on the results of the contingency table analysis. That is, industry differences in the proportion of females employed will be "net effects" with the occupational composition of the industry "controlled." This is important because one would not expect to find as many women employed in an industry like coal mining, which has many miners, as in advertising, which has many secretaries. In addition, this classification method means that the "higher-order" effects will be tantamount to differences in the level of occupational segregation across industries. In other words, certain industries may be less likely to employ only women in jobs that tend to be women's jobs in most sectors of the economy.

If anything, this categorization scheme tends to be overcautious because it presumes that the industry's occupational distribution, in terms of male- or female-typed categories, is completely determined by exogeneous factors. Over the long

220   Discrimination in Organizations

run this assumption may not be completely adequate. Industries may, in fact, choose a job mix based on the sex compositions of the occupations in question. For the short-run analysis to be presented, I assume that industry differences in current levels of institutional discrimination can be indicated by differences in the proportion of women employed controlling for occupation (where occupations are classified into ten groups based on the percentage of female incumbents in the overall labor force).

Table 1 illustrates the organization of each of the sets as they enter the Goodman log-linear program. In each case the datum consists of a large contingency table; the first has 308 cells, the second, 576. The top half, which shows data on two of the seventy-seven schools of social work, shows that although each university has a similarly low proportion of minorities, the situation improves at one of them between the first and second year and worsens at the other. Subsequent analysis will determine whether schools in general reveal this sort of variation in class composition. Members of the following groups were classified as minorities: American Indian, Asian American, black, Chicano, Puerto Rican, and other U.S. The group labeled "white" was allowed to stand alone and foreign students were dropped from the analysis.

The bottom half of Table 1 illustrates the type of data used in the analysis of the sex composition of industries. The figures, which are actually input to the program, consist of the raw frequencies in the internal cells of the table. Eight of the total of 576 data entries are presented here. In this case the pattern is slightly different from the one above because the two industries differ markedly in the proportion of minority (women) members they have while the two social work schools had similar proportions of minorities. Moreover, there are even greater differences in the association of sex and sex type of job within the industries. Although men in both cases are largely restricted to male pursuits, 80 percent of the women employed in watch manufacturing hold jobs typically in the male domain, compared to 21 percent of women employed in liquor wholesaling. In sum, the data indicate that the level of sex segregation varies

Table 1. Illustrative Cross-Tabular Data

Race by Class Standing by School Graduate Schools of Social Work

| | SUNY Albany | | University of Kentucky | |
	First-Year Class[a]	Second-Year Class[b]	First-Year Class[a]	Second-Year Class[b]
Whites	80 (95%)	75 (94%)	45 (92%)	44 (95%)
Blacks and other	4 (5%)	5 (6%)	4 (8%)	2 (5%)
Total	84	80	49	46

Source: American Council on Social Work Education
[a] First-year class fall 1974
[b] Second-year class fall 1975

Sex By Job-Type by Industry

Industry

| | Liquor Wholesaling | | Watch Manufacturing | |
	Males	Females	Males	Females
"Male Jobs"	13,353 (96%)	536 (21%)	2,368 (96%)	2,469 (80%)
"Female Jobs"	594 (4%)	2,056 (79%)	100 (4%)	610 (20%)
Total	18,947	2,592	2,468	3,079

Note: Sizes given are estimate *sample* sizes. Population is five times larger.
Source: U.S. Bureau of the Census.

widely across these industries. The data analysis will examine
how typical these variations are.

The General Case

The log-linear models explain the pattern of cell frequencies that arises in a given observed contingency table. One need
not assume one of the variables is dependent because the model
is not explaining the distribution of a particular variable but the
distribution of cell frequencies across the different levels of all
variables. However, in some instances it is useful to constrain
the analysis by taking a particular variable as dependent, and
the system allows but does not require this presupposition.

In some ways the system can be thought of as a generali-
zation of the classical chi-square test of independence in an R x C
table. Both procedures share the logic of computing a set of
"expected frequencies" that are then compared to the observed
frequencies. The differences lie in the fact that the Goodman
sytem allows for types of effects other than those the standard
test of independence permits. It is therefore capable of being applied to tables of several dimensions rather than being restricted
to two-variable applications. A hint of the system's generality
is apparent even in a two-variable table. The Goodman technique posits the existence of four different types of effects:
total sample size, row marginal, column marginal, and interaction or association between the row and column marginal. The
usual chi-square test is really a test that the association effect is
zero. It can also be described as consisting of one model that
fits both the row and column marginal.

A second system characteristic is that it allows for the existence of interaction effects in tables with three or more dimensions. However, it posits the interaction effects as elements in
a hierarchical system, which means that if one is successful in finding an interaction effect in a three-variable table, one has necessarily assumed the presence of each of the two-variable associations as well. However, one need not presume that all the effects
present in a given model are of equal magnitude, and an important aspect of the Goodman system is the analysis of effect
parameters.

Effect parameters are structural coefficients that can be manipulated to reconstruct the cell entries in a contingency table. The effect parameters presented in this chapter are Goodman's lambdas. Essentially, they are transformations of cross-product ratios, generally their logs divided by a function of the table size (Bishop, Fienberg, and Holland, 1975, p. 18). The relationship to cross-product ratios is crucial because these ratios play a central role in other familiar measures of association, for example Yules Q (Bishop, Fienberg, and Holland, 1975, pp. 377–380). Thus although the Goodman system is hierarchical, the effect parameters allow some comparisons across system levels, and it is possible to observe weak interaction effects in conjunction with strong partial effects and vice versa.

Third, certain classes of system models are capable of being partitioned. There are several possible types of partitioning operations in the analysis of a given set of data. A very important type consists of breaking a general hypothesis into two subhypotheses, where one of the subhypotheses concerns the properties of a table of fewer dimensions than the table to which the general hypothesis applied. For example, the hypothesis that sex is independent of the joint distribution of industry and occupation, that is, the hypothesis that every industry-occupation combination will have the same proportion of males and females, can be partitioned into the hypothesis that industry and sex are independent in the two-way (zero order) table and the hypothesis that occupation and sex are independent of one another within the specific industries (Goodman, 1971a).

The presentation of hierarchical models is facilitated by using a notational shorthand that indicates which sets of marginal frequencies have been fitted to the data. The following models indicate the unit variable (school or industry) by the letter U, the minority variable (sex or race) by the letter M, and the positional variable (year in school or occupation) by the letter P. Thus the model that postulates the independence of sex and the joint occupation-by-industry distribution would be represented by (UP M). Figure 1 is a diagram of the key models to be analyzed.

Figure 1. Hierarchical Models

H_1 (UP)   (M)

|

↓   Between   Within

H_2 (UP)   (PM)   = (U_tP) (PM)   + $(U_tU_iP \ U_tMP)$

|

↓

H_3 (UP)   (PM)   (UM)

|

↓

H_4 (U_tU_iP) (U_tU_iM) (U_tPM)

Key

U $=$ unit variable

M $=$ minority variable

P $=$ position variable

Note: Variable U composed of two "subvariables," U_t or unit type and
      U_i or individual unit within type.

Initial concern is with only the models appearing in the
first three rows in the left-hand portion of the figure. The first
model can be regarded as a baseline model that postulates the
distribution of the minority variable is independent of the unit
and position variable. In the case of the social work data, were
this model to fit the observed frequencies, it would mean that
each class within each school would have the same proportion
of whites and nonwhites and no over- or underrepresentation
would be possible. The model in the second line allows for the
minority variable to be related to the positional variable; in the
example blacks might be systematically underrepresented in
second-year classes, but each school would have a similar distribution of minorities within class levels. That is, if 90 percent of
Chicago's first-year class were white and 95 percent of their
second-year class were, the same proportions would be observed
for UCLA, Smith, or any of the seventy-four other schools. This

model may be interpreted as either consistent or inconsistent with institutional discrimination; but the important finding would be that the discrimination, if it existed, was systemwide.

The third model is more complicated in that it allows for units to differ in terms of their "within-position" participation rates, for example, Columbia may have a lower proportion of minority group members at both class levels, but it does not permit differential success rates across schools. In other words, the association of race with class standing is required to be constant across all schools or units. Of course, this model itself may not fit, and there may be evidence of differential association between race and class standing by school.

Racism and Schools of Social Work

Table 2 presents the information required to evaluate these different hypotheses. The data shown in the third row indicate this model does in fact fit the data well. Thus the null hypothesis, which says there is no differential association of race with class standing across the different schools of social work, is acceptable. However, I have confirmed that there are large systematic differences in the racial composition of these graduate schools when class standing is controlled. Thus in line 5 of the table, where models 2 and 3 are compared, the partial association component has 1,503.0 likelihood ratio chi-square deviations associated with its seventy-six degrees of freedom, which is clearly statistically significant (Bishop, Fienberg, and Holland, 1975, pp. 126–127; Goodman, 1970, pp. 247–248). Line 4 presents a comparison that is useful for judging whether there is a "zero-order" relation between class standing and race. The data indicate there is. Finally, line 6 presents a sort of co-efficient of multiple-partial determination that tells how much of the association between race and school controlling for class standing is due to an effect that is constant across classes and how much is due to an interaction effect of race, school, and class standing—the differential success hypothesis that was just rejected (Goodman, 1971b, p. 55). Only 3 percent of the race and school association is due to three-factor interaction and is thus "trivial" substantively as well as statistically.

Table 2. Hierarchical Models of Race, Year in Program, and Social Work School Cohort Starting 1974

Model			$\chi^2 lr$	d.f.	P	Interpretation[a]
H_1	(UP)	(M)	1,561.14	153	.000	Total association of race with school and year in program
H_2	(UP)	(PM)	1,554.79	152	.000	Total association of race with school controlling year in program
H_3	(UP) (PM)	(UM)	51.79	76	>.5	Differential racial composition of first-year and second-year classes between schools
H_1-H_2	—		6.35	1		Zero-order association of class and race
H_2-H_3	—		1,503.0	76	.000	Partial association of school and race, controlling for year
$\dfrac{H_2-H_3}{H_2}$			.97			

[a] Interpretation given is that of the alternative rather than the null hypothesis.

**Table 3. Effect Parameters (Lambdas) from Saturated
Models for Race by School by Class Standing**

1	Grand mean	3.506	
2a	Race	.811 (54.3)[a]	
2b	Class standing	−.034 (−2.28)	
2c	School (range)	−1.25 (−5.26)	University of Nebraska
		1.306 (25.49)	Colombia University
3a	Race by class standing	−.026 (−1.725)	
3b[b]	Race by school (range)	−1.76 (−14.27)	Atlanta
		1.11 (4.31)	Yeshiva
3c	Class standing by school (range)	−.662 (−5.12)	Adelphi
		.359 (3.37)	Wisconsin/Milwaukee
4[c]	Race by class standing by school (range)	−.263 (−2.61)	Oklahoma
		.270 (2.08)	Adelphi

[a] Standardized values in parentheses.
[b] 45 of 77 significant, p <.05.
[c] 3 of 77 significant, p <.05.

Although the results just presented have given a flavor of the size of association between race, school, and class standing, they have provided few clues to the direction of the associations. For example, we may want to know whether the direction of the race and class standing association is such that minorities suffer differential attrition across all schools. Furthermore, we might ask which schools have high and low proportions of minorities. Here is where recourse to effect parameters is helpful.

Lines 1 and 2a through 2c of Table 3 are of little intrinsic interest in this context. However, line 3a contains a standardized value of −1.725, which, although not quite statistically significant at the .05 level, indicates an overall tendency for the second-year classes to have a higher proportion of whites than first-year classes. More important are the coefficients summarized in line 3b. These parameters are negative if a school has a disproportionate number of minorities (the three lowest belong to Atlanta, Howard, and UCLA) and positive if a school overrepresents whites (the three highest are Boston University, Catholic University, and Yeshiva University). Line 4 summarizes the coefficients corresponding to the three-factor interaction or hypothesis of differential success by race within school. As expected, few of these are significant; the negative value for Oklahoma says that the class composition of the 1974 cohort changed so that the position of nonwhites deteriorated between the first and second years. (It changed from 64 percent white to 85 percent white.) Things at Adelphi improved for minorities. It must be emphasized that these significant changes in class are exceptional; they do not add up to a significant pattern across all schools.

It can be argued that the pattern of results shown so far for U.S. schools of graduate social work do not convincingly document a pattern of institutional racism. After all, fewer minority group members are likely to apply to Catholic University than to UCLA. In addition, the qualifications of minority applicants to a school like Syracuse may be weaker relative to white applicants to Syracuse than is the case at the University of Hawaii. Ideally, it would be helpful to be able to take both of these refinements into consideration.

Although the data at hand contain nothing relevant to applicants' qualifications, we may be able to take into account factors likely to be related to the likelihood of minorities' applications. To test whether the factor of application rates was at all important, I assigned schools to different groups based on their geographic location. The location scheme involved cross classifying the percentage minority in the school's host state by the size of the standard metropolitan statistical area (SMSA) in which the school was located. Thus SMSAs were classified as over or under three hundred thousand and states were classified as having more or fewer than 10 percent minorities. This resulted in a group of forty-two schools in highly urbanized, high-percentage minority locales; a group of twenty-one highly urbanized, low-percentage minority locales; a group of eight less-urbanized, high-percentage minority locales; and a group of six less-urbanized, low-percentage minority locales.

Given the existence of these groups, table analysis can be carried out as follows. Rather than conceiving of the basic table as composed of one large table with dimensions 2 x 2 x 77,

I treated it as four tables with dimensions 2 x 2 x 42, 2 x 2 x 21, and so on. The Goodman system of hypothesis partitioning (Bishop, Fienberg, and Holland, 1975; Goodman, 1971a) informs us that the model in line 2 of Figure 1 can be partitioned into two component models, which are shown in the right-hand column. The component on the left refers to a collapsed table with smaller dimensions (in this case 2 x 2 x 4) in which school location group and class size are associated and in which race and class standing are associated but in which race is conditionally independent of school. This can be referred to as the "between-group" component of the association between school and race. If the hypothesis is true and our measurement of it adequate, then this component should be statistically significant. On the other side is a component that refers to the association of school and race within location groups. To the extent location is uniquely important this component should be small. The simplest way of estimating this component when groups are of unequal size, as they are here, is to estimate the first model of line 2 separately within each group and sum the result. This procedure is algebraically equivalent to estimating the model in the collapsed table and subtracting it from the value associated with first model on line 2.

Table 4 shows the chi-square values associated with each component. Both the between and within components are statistically significant at a low level of probability. Nevertheless, when the proper adjustment is carried out in column 4, only 8 percent of the total association of school and race is attributable to the school's location as measured here, which first confirms the idea that a school's location is related to its proportion of minority participants, a fact I would probably not wish to ascribe to institutional racism—at least on the part of the school. Second, there remains a large component that requires further investigation, perhaps best started by probing schools' actual application rates and their respective admission standards. Third, I have not been able to disprove the existence of institutional discrimination in participation rates, but I have severely restricted the idea of differential success of minority and ma-

Table 4. Partitions of Total Association of School and
Race Within and Between School Location Groups

Model	d.f.	$X^2 lr$	$\dfrac{X^2 t - X^2 w}{X^2 t}$	Interpretation
(UP) (PM)	152	1,554.79	100%	Total association of school with race
$(_iP)$ (U_tU_iM)	146	1,435.89		Association of school and race within school location groups
(U_tP) (U_tM)	6	118.90	7.6%	Association of school and race between location groups

jority participants once admitted. The partial effect parameter
was not statistically significant and there was no significant variation of this finding across schools.

Sexism and Industry

Table 5 is a counterpart to Table 2, providing similar assessment of the suitability of different hypotheses of the relation of sex, sex type of occupation, and industry. Apart from
the obvious difference in the order of magnitude of the chi-
square statistics, it is also possible to discern a different pattern
of results. In this case, the null hypothesis of equal sex - sex type
of occupation associations across industries can be rejected. In
other words, there is a differential tendency for women to hold
"women's jobs" and men to hold "men's jobs" across specific
industries. Not only is the chi-square value in line 3 significant,
but now 15 percent of the total association of sex with industry
is due to these differences in occupational sex typing.

Before turning to an examination of the effect parameters, one might question whether the significance of the model
in line 3 resulted from the accidental conjuncture of a few deviant industries with a particularly large sample size to produce
the impression of widespread differences when in fact they are
not present. One way of assuaging these doubts is to compare
this model's deviations with those from the similar model in
Table 2. To do this it is necessary to follow the procedure sug-

Table 5. Hierarchical Models of Sex, Occupation, and Industry, 1970 Census Data

	Model	$\chi^2 lr$	d.f.	Interpretation
H_1	UP M	3,845,934.6	287	Total association of sex with industry and occupation
H_2	UP PM	807,828.8	286	Total association of sex with industry controlling occupation
H_3	UP PM UM	154,562.1	143	Differential sex composition of occupation types across industries
$H_1 - H_2$		3,038,105.8	1	Zero-order association of sex and occupation type
$H_2 - H_3$		653,266.8	143	
$\dfrac{H_2 - H_3}{H_2}$		.85		

gested by Bishop, Fienberg, and Holland (1975, p. 330). The operation they recommend is to divide the Pearson chi-square statistic for comparable models by the total sample size to provide an index value for the relative size of the two values. Carrying out this procedure and multiplying each result by one thousand yields an index of 3.11 for model 3 of Table 2 (the social work analysis) and a value of 19 for model 3 of Table 5 (the industry analysis). In sum, as well as being statistically significant, the three-variable interaction is large compared to earlier effects.

Table 6 lists the effect parameters that correspond to the saturated model for the industry data. Starting at the two-variable level (lines 3a–3c), there are extremely large positive effects for the relationship between sex and occupation. This should not be particularly surprising because a large effect was built into the data by the method for classifying occupations. What is noteworthy is the uniform strength of the two-variable sex and industry relations. Both effects are partial with the occupational distribution of the industry controlled. Thus there is a strong indication that industries have a marked preference for workers of a particular sex even when the sexual stereotype of their occupational mix is considered. In line 4 the effect parameters corresponding to the significant three-variable interaction are summarized. The negative sign attached to the eating and drinking place industry signals this as an industry in which jobs are shared more equitably by the sexes than elsewhere. This is perhaps one case where within-industry patterns would be interesting to investigate. The cultural stereotype is that men tend to dominate most of the occupations in the more prestigious segments of the industry and women the least prestigious—a fact that may or may not be true empirically as the burger chains with their hordes of teenagers in unisex uniforms invade the field. Other industries with high negative coefficients are miscellaneous retailing and yarn, thread, and cloth manufacturing. More stereotyped are special trade construction, with its entrenched male unions, and other construction industries, motor vehicle retailing, and crude petroleum extraction.

Finally, to complement the partitioning of a conditional relationship shown in Table 4 for the social work data, these

Table 6. Effect Parameters (Lamdas) Set by
Occupation by Industry

1	Grand Mean	8.423	
2a	Sex	.219 (213.9)[a]	
2b	Occupation	.532 (520.1)	
2c	Industry (range)	-2.03 (-81.5)	Leather tanning
		3.01 (1432.0)	Eating and drinking places
3a	Sex by occupation	.789 (771.5)	
3b[b]	Sex by industry (range)	-.875 (-269.4)	Apparel manufacturing
		.735 (96.6)	Blast furnaces
3c	Occupation by industry		
	(range)	-.950 (-454.3)	Eating and drinking places
		.481 (114.)	Electrical machinery, NEC
4[c]	Sex by occupation by	-.251 (-119.5)	Eating and drinking places
	industry (range)	.618 (102.6)	Special trade contractors

Note: Standardized coefficients in parentheses.
[a] Standardized values in parentheses.
[b] 139 of 144 significant $p < .05$.
[c] 135 of 144 significant $p < .05$.

data can illustrate how one might partition a three-variable interaction or the occurrence of differential association across units.
Rather than use a variable like location to classify industries,
I have sorted them into two groups on the basis of their average
payroll. (The source of this information was the 1967 economic
census. See U.S. Bureau of the Census, 1972b.) The hypothesis
is that the lower the average payroll per worker in the industry,
the more likely it is to have high levels of occupational stereotyping. The rationale for this prediction is that low-wage industries are more exploitative and hence more likely to invoke labor
market segmentation as means of labor force control (Bluestone,
1971; Gordon, 1972).

The model to be tested in this case is diagramed in line
4 of Figure 1. Again I have subdivided the unit variable (in this
case, industry) into two variables—unit type U_t, having a high or
low average payroll, and the individual unit within type U_i.
There is no problem in treating this single dimension as two variables as long as one remembers that the individual unit variable
(U_i) is now vacuous and only refers to the arbitrary listing of an

industry within its payroll class. It will cause problems if one attempts to fit this variable without also fitting the unit type variable. Of course this analytical sleight of hand is only possible
when the groups of units are of equal size. Thus I convert
a table of dimension 2 x 2 x 144 into a table of dimension
2 x 2 x 72 x 2.

To test the hypothesis that groups of industries with similar average payroll levels have similar levels of occupational
segregation, I merely fit the model that allows for the relationship between unit type, position (occupation), and the minority
variable (sex) and that allows for all other effects included in
the model of line 3 in Figure 1. Although this is not a precise
partitioning of between and within components of differential
relationships, it does provide an estimate of the association between the group variable and the minority position relationship.
The results of this analysis are shown in Table 7. As expected,
the between component is quite large and average payroll, as
measured by a dichotomy, accounts for about 17 percent of the
differential relationship. However, when the effect parameter
that corresponds to this phenomenon is checked, we find the
value to be −97.12 (standardized lambda). The direction of this
effect means that a strong positive relationship between sex and
sex type of job is weaker under the positive condition of payroll,
which in this case was low-paying industries. In other words,
low-paying industries have a lower than average separation of
male and female workers. Thus although the payroll factor
makes a difference in the pattern of associations, its effect was
opposite in direction from that expected.

From the standpoint of a more general application of this
technique, what matters is not the specific result just obtained
but the fact that the groups tested might have been units in
some other entity that was grouped in some other fashion. For
example, this technique might have been applied to departments in a firm that had and had not been evaluated the previous
year for affirmative action compliance. Here the expectation
would be that units reviewed would show less association between minority and position than units not so reviewed. For
any set of groupings of individual units, whether of equal size
or not, the technique will allow one to test the notion that

Table 7. Partitions of Differential Association of Sex and Occupation
Within and Between Industry Payroll Groups

Model			χ^2 *lr*	*d.f.*
1. (U_tU_iP)	(MP)	(U_tU_iM)	154,562.1	143
2. (U_tU_iP)	(U_tMP)	(U_tU_iM)	127,683.7	142
3. $\dfrac{H_1 - H_2}{H_1}$			.17	

groups are internally homogeneous either with regard to the
level of absolute participation by minorities or the level of relative success or relative position.

Conclusion

In proposing any new application of an analytical technique, one has the obligation of assessing its strengths relative
to existing procedures. In the present case one would be most
likely to substitute the examination of standardized rates for
the examination of partial associations between unit and minority (as illustrated in the social work analysis) and of segregation coefficients for the examination of differential associations of minority and position across units. Each of these
measures, the rates or the segregation indexes, would then be
subjected to further analysis via regression analysis or some
other technique.

There are three main advantages of the techniques proposed here. First, they allow for an assessment of the importance of the two types of effects vis-à-vis one another. Thus
I can conclude that differential association was an important
occurrence in the distribution of women across industries and
occupations but was relatively trivial for the distribution of race
groups across schools of social work. Had I skipped this analytical procedure, I could easily have obtained measures of the disadvantage of minorities in moving to second-year status in social
work schools; but I would have had no way of assessing the
magnitude of the variance of this phenomenon across schools.

Second, the techniques are useful because they present
results that are part of an integrated system. One begins with
a total amount of association between a minority variable and

other related factors and successively whittles it down into meaningful components.

A third advantage of the system is its extreme sensitivity to higher-order interactions. Space limitation prevented the examination of a quantitative example, but a verbal exposition can illustrate the point as well. Suppose in the case of social work data that information was gathered in similar form on successive cohorts of students. I might wish to evaluate some additional hypotheses, namely: (1) Controlling for year in the program, schools differ from cohort to cohort in their inclusion of minorities. Thus I would be able to assess the notion of differential change across schools in minority opportunities for admission. (2) Schools differ across cohorts in their relative success rates for minorities. Given that the three-variable effect corresponding to this pattern was not present in the earlier data, it is unlikely that this complicated interaction would show up, but it is likely in other settings. Moreover, given the presence of any of these differences across individual schools, it is possible to examine how much particular groups of units are alike through the previously discussed partitioning technique.

On the minus side of the ledger regression analysis of standardized rates or segregation coefficients is more flexible when one has a true interval variable or a large number of independent variables. When there is a single qualitative attribute to examine, such as participation in an equal opportunity program, the partitioning type of analysis is at least as useful because it places the results in the context of a total amount of association. In sum, the log-linear technique is a heuristic screening device that identifies the level and locus of disproportions of minority participation. Its usefulness is most apparent when one is faced with a problem where interactions are likely. For example, is the relative rate of minorities' success deteriorating (or developing) across time, differentially across units, and where is there likely to be differential access to valued positions as well as differential access to participation per se?

Part Five

Investigating Representativeness of Women and Minorities by Organizational Level

〰〰〰〰〰〰〰〰〰〰〰

Representativeness within specific organizational sectors is the central theme of the three chapters in this part. The concern is whether a particular board of directors, committee, or organization is representative of either the constituencies it serves directly or of particular populations in society at large, whether or not they are directly served by the organization as customers, clients, patients, and so forth. These chapters provide excellent examples of existing technology for documentation of degree of representativeness. Upon that technology can later be built the study of mechanisms through which given types of population groups might obtain input into given types of organizations.

Anthony Hausner examines the racial and sexual composition of policy-making boards of health system agencies in order

237

to determine the degree to which they represent ethnic minorities and women. This type of analysis could be performed on all sorts of policy-making groups across any number of organizations, corporations, and institutions. Further, it could be done with respect to population groups other than women and minorities, for example, consumers or environmentalists. Especially in the case of national service organizations, it would seem vital that all interests obtain *representation* on policy- and decision-making boards; obtaining *representativeness* is an important first step toward the objective.

Jorge Schement examines the representativeness of Spanish-surname individuals within primary Spanish language radio (PSLR) stations in the southwestern United States. Asserting that PSLRs are a critical source of information for Spanish-speaking communities, Schement states that evidence of lack of *representativeness* in personnel increases the possibility of lack of *representation* of programming and broadcasting content of value to these communities.

David Nasatir and John Fernandez attempt to provide a working definition of "institutional racism/sexism" and a sensitive method for demonstrating its existence. They adapt the use of log-linear statistical models to their purpose and thus demonstrate the rich possibilities of this line of research. The particular example they use is that of ethnic composition of a graduate school. However, they assert that the technique can be used in any organizational situation where only a small proportion of the population is in a special organizational category; hence the technique is highly adaptable to studies of differential access to elite organizational positions.

11

Minorities and Women on Boards of Health Agencies

Anthony Hausner

The National Health Planning and Resources Development Act of 1974 (P.L. 93–641) is potentially a very significant health law. It attempts to build on the experiences of the Hill-Burton Program, the Comprehensive Health Planning Program, the Regional Medical Program, and the Experimental Health Services Delivery Systems Program. It seeks to combine their best features into one health planning and resources development effort. Administratively, the act specifies that Health Systems Agencies (HSAs) and State Health Planning and Development Agencies (SHPDAs) are to play a major role as planning, review, and approval bodies.

A major HSA responsibility is to develop health plans for their respective geographic areas. They also have the authority to approve the proposals for the use of almost all Public Health

Note: The data analyses were performed by the Orkand Corporation under Contract No. HRA–23–76–0210. Drs. Elliott Hurwitz and Sam Schildaus were key Orkand staff members of this contract. The author served as project officer for the government.

239

Service funds designated for local health services. Finally, they review and make recommendations to the SHPDA about proposals for new institutional health services and major capital expenditures, use of resources development funds, and the appropriateness of all existing health services. These decisions therefore control major portions of federal, state, and local expenditures for health services.

In the implementation of this legislation it is important that the needs of the disadvantaged, particularly minorities, be taken into account. The act specifically addresses this issue through one of its ten priorities concerning access to primary care services for medically underserved populations.

The goals of the Office of Health Resources Opportunity is to promote equal access to health careers and health services for the disadvantaged. Therefore this office and the Bureau of Health Planning and Resources Development (BHPRD), both of which are within the Health Resources Administration, recently undertook a project aimed at accomplishing several objectives related to the disadvantaged. One of the objectives of this project was to assess the representation of minorities, women, and other disadvantaged groups on the boards and staffs of the health planning agencies. A second objective was to develop a preliminary set of performance and impact criteria relative to the needs of the disadvantaged.

This chapter focuses on the representativeness of minority groups and women on governing boards and executive committees. Because the boards have the authority for all decisions the HSAs make, it seemed important to focus on the composition of the boards. Furthermore, the data on the boards were the first significant available data that indicate how well the HSAs are meeting their commitment to the disadvantaged.

Section 1512(b)(3)(c) of P.L. 93–641 specifies that consumer members of HSA governing boards and executive committees should constitute a majority, but not over 60 percent, and be "broadly representative of the social, economic, linguistic and racial populations [and] geographic areas of the health service area." Executive committees of less than twenty-five persons are formed when governing boards have more than thirty

Minorities and Women on Boards of Health Agencies 241

members. Executive committees can be delegated many of the board's responsibilities, so their composition may also be vital.

Section 1531 of the act specifies that a consumer is a person who is not a provider and has not recently been a provider, is not married to a provider, and has no fiduciary interest in a provider. A provider is a health practitioner, a representative of a health care institution, a health insurer, a health professional educator, or an allied health professional.

Relevant Terms

The purpose of this analysis is to determine whether Section 1512 (b) (3) (c) has been implemented. In order to do this, several concepts must be defined. For this analysis the following racial and ethnic groups were studied using the five mutually exclusive categories and definitions as endorsed by the Federal Interagency Committee on Education:

American Indian or Alaskan Native: A person having origins in any of the original peoples of North America (will be referred to as Native Americans).
Asian or Pacific Islander: A person having origins in any of the original peoples of the Far East, Southeast Asia, or the Pacific Islands. This area includes, for example, China, Japan, Korea, the Philippine Islands, and Samoa (will be referred to as Asian Americans).
Black/Negro: A person having origins in any of the black racial groups of Africa.
Caucasian/White: A person having origins in any of the original peoples of Europe, North Africa, the Middle East, or the Indian subcontinent.
Hispanic: A person of Mexican, Puerto Rican, Cuban, Central or South American, or other Spanish culture or origin, *regardless of race*.

The variables studied were sex and occupation. The Census Bureau's occupational codes plus the category of "not in the civilian labor force" were utilized in this analysis.

The concept of *representativeness* requires a comparison between the number of agency members who possess a given characteristic and the total number of agency members. The representativeness criterion in this case simply means having the same characteristic (for example, race). A black HSA board member is representative of the black community. The following formula defines the measure related to this concept.

$$\text{Representativeness}_A = \frac{\text{Number of HSA Members with Characteristics A}}{\text{Total Number of HSA Members}}$$

This measure varies from 0 to 100 percent. Representativeness is to be distinguished from *representation*, which incorporates issues such as the method of selection and the relationship between the board representative and constituents (for example, accountability). The full implications of representativeness can be seen in the concept of *parity*, which is the measure used to assess the term "broadly representative."

Parity is derived from Piatek (1971), who relates the level of agency representativeness to the characteristics of the local agency population. The following equation shows how the parity concept will be measured:

$$\text{Parity}_A = \frac{\text{Representativeness A}}{\dfrac{\text{No. of Individuals in HSA Population with Characteristic A}}{\text{Total Population of HSA}}}$$

This measure varies from 0 percent to infinity.

An example may clarify the concepts and measures of representativeness and parity. One HSA governing board may have five black members of a total of fifty board members; the level of black representativeness would be 10 percent. If the area population was 40 percent black, the parity measure would be forty divided by ten or 25 percent. If an HSA with the same population percentage of 40 percent black contains one black HSA member on the fifty-member board, the board representativeness would be fifty divided by one or 2 percent, and the parity measure would be forty divided by two or 5 percent of parity. This measure facilitates the interpretation of differences in HSA representativeness.

These comparisons will present baseline data at different levels of aggregation: by HSA, by U.S. Department of Health, Education and Welfare (DHEW) region, and nationally. Executive committees can be compared to the governing board and to the staff. Additionally, parity measures for racial/ethnic data can be compared between HSAs, between SHPDAs, between DHEW regions, and between individual HSA governing boards, their executive committees, and staffs.

Research Procedures

By July 15, 1976, 161 of the ultimate 202 HSAs had been conditionally designated by DHEW. On June 20, 1976, the director of BHPRD requested that the regional offices supply data by July 16 to the central office. The request was for the following information on the five racial-ethnic groups: sex, occupation, whether or not a member of the executive committee, consumer or provider member, and a number of related questions for each member of the HSA governing boards. The regional offices supplied almost all this information for 134 HSAs by August 1. Data on 29 of the conditionally designated HSAs were thus not included in this set, but data were included on 3 HSAs designated after July 15. Data were thus provided on 82 percent of the conditionally designated agencies and 67 percent of the ultimate number of agencies to be so designated. A reasonable proportion of agencies was reported for each region.

The forms sent to the regional offices contained the previously specified categories for all variables except occupation. For occupation the regional offices provided the specific occupation, profession, or title of the board member. The government contractor (Orkand Corportion) then classified the member's occupation using the Census Bureau's occupational codes.

Parity was analyzed using two procedures. The first procedure consisted of aggregating the total number of board members for all HSAs in the country. In the nationwide aggregate the percentage of the consumer members that belonged to racial and ethnic minorities was compared to the percentage of minorities among the national population.

$$\text{Parity}_{\substack{\text{Nationwide} \\ \text{Aggregate}}} = \frac{\dfrac{\text{National Total of HSA Consumer Members with Characteristic A}}{\text{National Total of HSA Consumer Members}}}{\text{Percentage of Individuals with Characteristic A in National Population}}$$

Only the parity of consumer representatives was analyzed because the act requires only that the composition of the consumer members to be broadly representative. Bureau of Census 1976 estimates of percentages of the different minority groups in the population, nationwide, were used for the nationwide aggregate analysis of parity.

The first step in the second procedure was to compare the percentage of minority consumer representatives for each HSA with the percentage of the minority within the population of each health service area. The only data on the minority composition of the population for each health service area were from the 1970 census. This procedure produced the percentage parity for each HSA.

$$\text{Parity}_{\text{HSA}} = \frac{\dfrac{\text{Number of Consumer HSA Members with Characteristic A}}{\text{Total Number of HSA Consumer Members}}}{\text{Percentage of Individuals with Characteristic A in Health Service Area Population}}$$

Two analyses were subsequently performed. First, the mean of the percentage parities of the HSAs was determined. In calculating the mean percentage representativeness and percentage parity, each HSA was given equal weight. Because the HSAs differ in size from each other, the mean percentage parity cannot be directly determined from the mean percentage representativeness. The second approach, using the percentage parities of the individual HSAs, was a frequency distribution analysis.

One underlying question of this research, which cannot be directly tested, is whether the various disadvantaged groups have become *politically enfranchised* (that is, have gained sufficient power to be able to exercise political leverage). If parity is achieved for a particular disadvantaged group, it would provide some indication that the group has become enfranchised.

As indicated previously, the purpose of this study is to determine if Section 1512 (b) (3) (c) has been implemented. The particular concern is with the usefulness of the concept of parity in addressing this issue and with a comparison of three different methods for analyzing the parity data.

Results

The average governing board contained 44 members, and the boards ranged in size from 15 to 161 members. For 66 of the 134 governing boards, executive committees were formed. The average size of these committees was twenty, with a range from seven to twenty-six. Consumers constituted on the average 52.8 percent of the governing boards and 53.1 percent of the executive committees, which is within the 50 to 60 percent range prescribed by the law. However, there were twelve HSAs that had less than 50 percent consumer members and two HSAs with greater than 60 percent consumer members on the governing boards. Finally, there were eight HSAs that had less than 50 percent consumer members on their executive committees and five HSAs had above 60 percent.

Minorities constitute about 19 percent of the consumer membership of governing boards nationwide. Blacks represent 78 percent of the minority members, with Hispanics the next highest at 16 percent. In terms of a nationwide parity analysis, minorities as a whole are slightly overrepresented. Blacks and Native Americans are the minority groups that account for this overrepresentation; Hispanics and Asian Americans are underrepresented. Women are also underrepresented. The same relationships hold for the executive committees. That is, the same groups are over- and underrepresented and by approximately the same amounts.

When each HSA is analyzed and means are calculated, the percentage representativeness figures are very similar to those determined from nationwide aggregations for each minority group and women for both governing boards and executive committees. (See Tables 1 and 2.) There are also several similarities between the individual HSA and nationwide aggregate analyses performed with the parity assessments. With only one exception the same groups are over- and underrepresented on the governing boards and executive committees.

For executive committees, minorities as a whole, Blacks, and Native Americans are overrepresented and Hispanics, Asian Americans, and women are underrepresented. For governing boards, minorities as a whole, Blacks, and Native Americans are overrepresented and women and Asian Americans are under-represented. This pattern replicates the results from the nation-wide analysis. The only exception is that on the average Hispanics were overrepresented from the HSA analysis but underrepresented in the nationwide aggregate analysis. (This is a mean and could be distorted by just one HSA having a very high figure. Furthermore, one HSA could have a very high figure because the population is a fraction of a percent.)

Tables 3 and 4 present frequency distributions of the percentage of parity for the HSAs. For this analysis a parity figure of less than 80 percent indicated underrepresentation and a parity figure of 120 percent or more overrepresentation.

Those HSAs with 0 percent parity but whose minority population was less than 5 percent of the area's population were excluded from the analyses. Zero percent representation is not significantly different from 5 percent, so it would not be appropriate to consider 0 percent representation as being underrepresented for those HSAs. Therefore HSAs with 0 percent parity and greater than 5 percent minority population (column 2 in Tables 3 and 4) were added to those HSAs between 1 and 80 percent parity in determining the total number of HSAs underrepresented.

For all minority groups there were twelve HSAs below 80 percent parity and seventy-nine HSAs above 120 percent parity. Thus far more HSAs were above than below parity (Table 3).

Table 1. Parity of Representativeness for Minorities and Women on HSA Governing Boards—HSA as Unit of Analysis

	Number of Board Members	Mean Percent Representativeness	Mean Percent in HSA Population[a]	Mean Parity Percent
Total minority	584	18.7	12.4	216.2
Native Americans	29	1.3	.4	168.5
Asian/Pacific Islanders	9	.4	.5	49.8
Blacks	455	13.6	9.8	239.2
Hispanics	91	3.5	7.4	107.6
Women	1,002	33.1	51.2	63.5

Note: Total number of boards = 134, total number of consumer board members = 3,111.
[a] Based on 1970 census.

Table 2. Parity of Representativeness for Minorities and Women on HSA Executive Committees—HSA as Unit of Analysis

	Number of Committee members	Mean Percent Representativeness	Mean Percent in HSA Population[a]	Mean Parity Percent
Total minority	140	20.4	13.8	215.0
Native Americans	12	1.9	.4	287.4
Asian/Pacific Islanders	1	.1	.5	16.6
Blacks	114	16.0	9.8	173.6
Hispanics	12	2.4	7.4	36.8
Women	202	28.7	51.2	56.1

Note: Total number of committees = 66, total number of consumer committee members = 684.
[a] Based on 1970 census.

Table 3. Frequency Distribution for Parity—HSA Governing Boards
(Number of Agencies)

	(1) 0[a] 0-5.0%	(2) 0[a] 5.0+	Percent of Parity (3) 1-80	(4) 81-120	(5) 121-200	(6) 200+	(7) NA
Total minority	19	7	5	21	28	51	3
Native Americans	110	0	1	1	2	16	4
Asian Americans	127	0	0	0	0	6	1
Blacks	27	8	4	26	23	41	5
Hispanics	98	1	3	0	0	21	2
Women	–	2	91	33	3	–	3

Total — 134 boards

[a] Zero percent parity has been divided into those for which the percentage of the population is less or greater than 5 percent for that particular minority group.

Table 4. Frequency Distribution for Parity—HSA Executive Committees

	(1) 0[a] 0–5.0	(2) 0[a] 5.0+	Percent of Parity (3) 1–80	(4) 81–120	(5) 121–200	(6) 200+	(7) NA
Total minority	8	5	5	9	16	23	—
Native Americans	56	0	0	1	0	9	—
Asian Americans	65	0	0	0	0	1	—
Blacks	16	4	4	8	14	20	—
Hispanics	57	0	1	1	0	6	—
Women	—	6	51	7	2	—	—

Total — 66 Committees

[a] Zero percent parity has been divided into those for which the percentage of the population is less or greater than 5 percent for that particular minority group.

For Native Americans there was one HSA below 80 percent and twenty-eight above 120 percent of parity; for blacks twelve were below and sixty-four were above; for Asian Americans none were below and six were above; for Hispanics four were below and twenty-one were above 120 percent of parity. Thus for each minority group there were also far more HSAs above than below parity.

In general there is more overrepresentation than underrepresentation for minority groups either individually or collectively, but these relations do not preclude the existence of twelve HSAs for which minorities were underrepresented. In contrast Table 4 indicates ninety-three HSAs in which women were underrepresented and only three in which they were overrepresented.

The interpretations made from the results of the frequency distributions were somewhat different from those of the nationwide aggregate analyses and the mean parity percentage figures. Both analyses indicated that Asian Americans were underrepresented. The nationwide analysis also indicated that Hispanics were underrepresented. Because the frequency distributions indicated overrepresentation for these groups, they provide the opposite interpretation. For the other minority groups and for minorities as a whole the results from the frequency distribution analysis are consistent with the other analyses—all indicate overrepresentation. The results are also consistent for women—all analyses indicate underrepresentation. Two factors account for the differences in some of the results between the various analyses. When the mean parity figures were calculated, the HSAs with minority population percentages near zero were included. These HSAs significantly reduced the mean parity figures and thus account for the differences in these figures compared to the previously reported frequency distribution results.

The inclusion of these HSAs in the nationwide aggregate analysis also accounts partially for the differences in the results of that analysis compared to the frequency distribution analysis. In addition the variation in the sizes of the governing boards and the populations in the health service areas are incorporated into the nationwide aggregate analysis and thus also are a factor in the differences between the results of that analysis and the frequency distribution analysis. Larger boards and larger populations contribute more to their respective parts of the equations than smaller boards and populations.

Thus it can be seen that limitations exist in the nationwide aggregate and mean parity analyses. For these reasons the results of the frequency distribution analyses are more appropriate summaries of representativeness and parity. Therefore the conclusion is that each of the minority groups was generally more overrepresented than underrepresented on the governing boards and that women were more underrepresented.

For all minority groups there were ten HSAs below 80 percent parity and thirty-nine HSAs above 120 percent parity. Thus, far more HSAs were above parity than below it (Table 5). The following relations existed for the different racial and ethnic minorities: Native Americans—no HSAs below 80 percent and nine above 120 percent; Asian Americans—no HSAs below 80 percent and one above 120 percent; blacks—eight below 80 percent and thirty-four above 120 percent; and Hispanics—one below 80 percent and six above 120 percent of parity. As with the governing boards, there is a greater degree of overrepresentation for each minority than there is underrepresentation.

Comparisons between the 134 governing boards and 66 executive committees revealed no significant differences in the percentages of HSAs above and below parity for the different minority groups. However, the percentage of HSAs for which parity for women was below 80 percent was greater for executive committees (86 percent) than for the entire governing boards (72 percent). This latter finding is consistent with the results from the nationwide aggregate and mean parity analyses.

The frequency distribution analyses also produced results similar to the mean parity and nationwide aggregate analyses for some of the minority groups. For minorities as a whole and for blacks and Native Americans all analyses indicated overrepresentation on executive committees. However, the nationwide aggregate and mean parity analyses indicated that Hispanics and Asian Americans were underrepresented while the frequency distribution indicated they were overrepresented.

Table 5. Representativeness of Minorities and Women Among Provider Members on HSA Governing Boards and Executive Committees

Unit	Number of Units	Total No. of Provider Members	Number and Percent Representativeness												
			Blacks		Asian Americans		Native Americans		Hispanics		Total Minority		Women	
			No.	%	No.	%	No.	%	No.	%	No.	%	No.	%
Governing board (HSA as unit of analysis)	134	2,820	138	3.9	6	.2	9	.4	33	1.6	186	6.2	533	18.4
(nationwide aggregate)				4.9		.2		.3		1.2		6.6		18.9
Executive committee (HSA as unit of analysis)	66	608	37	5.3	1	.1	1	.1	4	.5	43	6.1	108	18.0
(nationwide aggregate)				6.1		.2		.2		.7		7.1		17.8

Table 6. Representativeness of Minorities and Women for the Entire HSA Governing Boards and Executive Committees (Includes Consumers and Providers)

Unit	Number of Units	Total No. of Members	Blacks No.	Blacks %	Asian Americans No.	Asian Americans %	Native Americans No.	Native Americans %	Hispanics No.	Hispanics %	Total Minority No.	Total Minority %	Women No.	Women %
Governing boards	134	5,931	593	10.0	15	.3	38	.6	124	2.1	770	13.0	1,535	25.9
Executive committees	66	1,292	151	11.7	2	.2	13	1.0	16	1.2	183	14.2	310	24.0

The explanations provided for the governing board data as to the differences between these various analyses are also applicable to this executive committee data. Thus, as previously determined, the frequency distribution analyses are the most appropriate indicators of representativeness and parity. Therefore it can be concluded that each of the minority groups was generally overrepresented and that women were underrepresented on executive committees. Furthermore, women were even more underrepresented on the executive committees than on the boards.

Among provider members, minorities constitute on the average 6 percent of both HSA boards and executive committees. Women on the average constitute 18 percent for these two components (Table 6). The total percentage of minorities is about the same for the entire boards compared to executive committees. However, the percentage of blacks is greater for the executive committees than the boards; the reverse applies to the other minority groups. All these percentages for provider members are considerably lower than the percentages reported for consumer members. However, the law made no stipulation as far as representativeness of minorities and women for provider members, so there was less pressure on the HSAs to include these groups among providers.

There is also the factor of availability of minority providers. Consumers are selected from the general population, of which 18 percent are racial and ethnic minorities nationwide. Minorities are a much smaller percentage of the provider population. For instance, minorities contribute 9 percent of the nation's physicians. The fact that only 6 percent of the physicians on HSA boards are minorities is closer to the 9 percent minority physicians nationwide than the 18 percent minorities in the general population.

For the entire governing board, which includes both providers and consumers, minorities constitute 13 percent. Blacks represent the largest percentage at 10 percent, with Hispanics next at 2 percent. Women constitute 26 percent of the boards. For the entire executive committees, which include both providers and consumers, the percentage of minorities was 1 percent greater than for the entire board. Blacks constituted 12 percent, Hispanics 1 percent. The committees contained 24 percent women.

One caution must be exercised in comparing governing boards and executive committees. Comparisons were made between 134 boards and 66 committees. The committees are not a random sample. Exact comparisons, therefore, should be made between the 66 governing boards and their executive committees. However, time did not permit this analysis.

As pointed out earlier, data were collected on only 134 of the 202 HSAs. Even though a fairly representative number of HSAs was available from each region, there is at least one difference for those HSAs for which data were not available: They were designated later in the process. Whether this and any other differences will result in substantive effects on board representation is not known. Another limitation in the results is that it is not known whether the boards and executive committees had all their members at the time of data collection. Also noted previously, the small percentages in the population, particularly for Asian Americans, of the various minority groups has resulted in some distortions of the parity figures. However, none of these limitations should affect the validity of the results at this stage of the process.

Implications

The results of this study suggest that in recent years minority groups have become politically enfranchised so that generally they are more than adequately represented on the governing boards. These results are consistent with the composition of the Regional Medical Programs (RMPs), which had adequate minority representation on their Regional Advisory Groups (RAGs) in 1973.

In contrast, women and lower-status occupational groups appear not to be sufficiently enfranchised. However, the available data on women suggest that women have made gains between 1973 on the RAGs and 1976 for the HSAs.

Another theory to account for the differences in the results between minorities versus women and lower-status occupational groups is the "old boy network" theory, which proposes that professional men have a network of communication that excludes women. This network exists because of informal and formal social and professional organizations to which the men belong. According the the theory, women are not included because of their inexperience in team playing, lack of career orientations, and related factors (Henning and Jordan, 1976).

Parts of this theory would also be applicable to the lower-status occupational groups and/or low-income groups. These persons would also be excluded from the old boy network because of their lack of professional ties. The old boy network plays a major role in the acquisition of professional positions and the accrual of power in professional and political circles.

By percentage, minorities have been making greater gains into professional positions than whites. Minority males may thus be entering the old boy network, which in turn provides them connections with members of the boards and staffs of HSAs, which increases their opportunity to become board members. However, because women and lower-status occupational groups are not part of the network, they do not have the same opportunities to join the boards.

A third theory that may partially explain some of the results is the lack of sufficient financial incentives for low-income persons. The law specifies that board members be reimbursed for reasonable costs in attending board meetings. The department has not defined reasonable costs but has given transportation and child care as examples. Lower-status occupational groups and persons not in the civilian labor force include many low-income persons. For these persons the amount of reimbursement will only meet their financial outlay. Payment for their time as well as other costs may be an incentive that would help meet their needs and thus interest them in board participation.

The frequency distribution results indicated that the boards can be categorized into three types: overrepresented, underrepresented, or adequately represented as to minorities and women. Different degrees of representation on boards would also apply to lower-status occupational groups. There are a number of hypotheses that might account for the different degrees of representation. One is that boards that provide higher

levels of financial reimbursement will have greater representation of lower-status occupational groups than boards that provide lower levels of reimbursement. (Boards are authorized to
provide such reimbursement according to the legislation.)
A second hypothesis is that because public agencies are more
accountable to the public, they are more responsive to the different interest groups and thus will be more broadly representative than private, nonprofit agencies. A third hypothesis is that
if the public participates in the selection of board members at
open public meetings, the boards are more likely to be broadly
representative than if the public does not participate. The following variables should be considered in the selection of research
hypotheses: type of agency (private nonprofit or public, for
example); selection method; persons making the selection; financial reimbursements available to board members; whether board
members have served on other boards (indicates one method of
recruitment); recruitment methods; effects of the public on selection (for example, through public meetings); and relationships
and understandings between planning agencies and local governments, special interest groups, and so forth.

The factors that might account for the differences in
boards that are under- or adequately represented will be examined in a new study by the Department of Health, Education,
and Welfare. Several other analyses will be conducted in the department's continuing efforts to monitor the operations of the
health planning agencies. First, similar data will again be collected on the HSA boards, allowing for observations of changes
in board composition. Second, the department will be conducting several studies to address the issue of representation. Whom
do these consumers represent and what does this representation
entail? The previously mentioned study dealing with selection
methods and so on is one of these studies. Another study will
examine the issue of accountability. The third and most important area of investigation is to examine the actions or outputs of
these boards and their health planning agencies. One approach
is to examine the agencies' health system plans to see if they
adequately address the needs of minorities and other disadvantaged groups. Even more critical is the examination of the review

and approval decisions agencies make concerning new services, equipment, and such and applications for federal funds. The focal point of these decisions is in the area of certificate of need. It is of particular concern to know the location of each proposed project and the anticipated beneficiaries; for example, are projects located in areas where minorities and the poor reside? This area will be the focus of attention. There are a number of other research areas the department and/or other groups should address that are not currently planned for. One of these involves an examination of the effectiveness of different consumer board members, events occurring at the board meetings, and so on.

Conclusions

Consumers constitute, on the average, 53 percent of HSA governing boards and executive committees. This figure is within the prescribed 50 to 60 percent range. However, there were a few HSAs that were not within these limits. Based upon the frequency distribution analyses, the various minority groups were generally overrepresented on the boards and executive committees. There were, however, a few HSAs for which minorities were underrepresented. It should be noted that for many HSAs the minority populations were near zero. For these HSAs it was not appropriate to consider 0 percent representation as underrepresented and they were therefore not included in the analysis.

Women and lower-status occupational groups were generally underrepresented on the governing boards. There was an even greater tendency for these groups to be underrepresented on executive committees. It was also noted that there was significantly less minority and female representation among provider members as compared to consumer members.

All these comparisons could be made using the concepts of percentage representativeness and percentage of parity. Because there were many HSAs for which the minority populations were near zero, limitations existed in the results of analyses involving averaging. Thus frequency distribution analyses were considered the most appropriate summary of representativeness and parity.

12

Ownership and Employment Patterns in Spanish-Language Radio Stations

Jorge Reina Schement

For those Americans who speak Spanish as their first or only language, Spanish language radio is a critical source of information. In many communities throughout the southwestern United States Spanish language radio is the only source of information available to Spanish speakers. The absence of Spanish language newspapers, the relative absence of Spanish language television, and linguistic isolation from English language media place Spanish language radio in a role without precedent in any English language mass medium.

This chapter examines certain characteristics of Spanish language radio in an effort to determine possible patterns of institutional racism. Specifically, it focuses on personnel distribution by ethnicity as a contributing factor to institutional racism. It also examines wealth allocation resulting from differential personnel distribution in an effort to understand better

259

the social consequences resulting from these particular ownership and employment patterns.

This chapter is based on a survey of all forty-one primary
Spanish language radio (PSLR) stations identified as licensed in
Arizona, California, Colorado, New Mexico, and Texas. PSLR
refers to any radio station that broadcasts 50 percent or more
of its air time in Spanish.

Survey Data

Information on ethnic identity of station owner(s), percentage of station management with Spanish surnames, total station assests, ethnic identity of station chief engineer, percentage
of station employees with Spanish surnames, station owner's additional property holdings, name and rank of the market in
which the station is located, the station's advertising rate, and
percentage of local station time broadcast in Spanish was collected from station files of the Federal Communications Commission (FCC) in Washington, D.C.

The locations by state of the forty-one PSLR stations in
the Southwest are shown in Table 1. The concentration of stations roughly parallels the population densities of the various
states. PSLR stations are most likely to be found in markets
with high concentrations of Spanish-speaking people; Los
Angeles, San Antonio, and San Francisco have the three highest
concentrations of stations in the Southwest. Twelve of the forty-
one PSLR stations in our sample (29 percent) were located in
the ten largest markets. Markets ranked eleventh through twen-
tieth in size contained eleven PSLR stations (27 percent). Markets small enough to be ranked twenty-first through seventy-fifth
in size contained nine PSLR stations (22 percent). Neverthless,
an additional nine stations are located in markets too small to
be ranked, indicating the continued service of Spanish language
radio to rural areas.

Most of these stations broadcast all or nearly all their
time in Spanish. The type of license allocated by the FCC and
the personal preference of the owners greatly affect absolute
broadcast times, so the range of hours per station devoted to

Table 1. PSLR Stations by State

State	Number	Percent of Total No. of PSLRs in Southwest	Chicano Population of State[a]	Percent of Total Chicano Population in Southwest
Arizona	4	9.8	333,349	5
California	16	39.0	3,101,589	50
Colorado	2	4.8	286,467	5
New Mexico	4	9.8	407,286	7
Texas	15	36.6	2,059,671	33
Total	41	100.0	6,188,362	100

[a] Population figures taken from Current Population Reports, "Persons of Spanish Origin in the United States," Series P-20, No. 283, U.S. Bureau of the Census, March 1975.

Spanish language programming varies from 44 to 168 hours per week. Nevertheless, PSLR is composed mainly of stations that broadcast in English only incidently.

Two variables, advertising rate and total assests, are key indicators of a station's importance in the marketplace. Advertising rate, the cost of buying one minute of broadcast time on a station, represents the actual market power of the station because it is the only measure of what price the station's time brings on the open market. Furthermore, advertising rate is an important indicator of power vis-à-vis other stations because in one combined measure it represents audience size and characteristics and implies the relative influence of the station's messages. Seventy-nine percent (thirty-two of the forty-one PSLR stations in our sample) have an advertising rate of fifteen dollars or less per minute. Only 9 percent (four stations) of the PSLRs have an advertising rate of more than twenty-five dollars per minute.

Most PSLR stations (85 percent) have total assets less than or equal to $500,000. The bulk of PSLR stations contain very modest total assets and advertising rates, although a few appear to have much greater total assets and command very high advertising rates. These few stations form a nucleus of power that dominates Spanish language radio.

I chose ownership as a variable for investigation because of conditions unique to broadcast management. First, most stations have small staffs. Both PSLR and English language radio (ELR) average between fifteen and twenty-five employees, so owners are potentially more visible and influential. Second, in such small operations management decisions are more likely to be personal and involve the owners; in nearly all the stations suveyed the owner(s) listed themselves as personally involved in day-to-day station operations. Third, the structure of FCC regulations places all responsibility for failure to meet regulations or to carry out the station's responsibilities on the owner; in instances of failure to comply with regulations, it is the owner who is fined or loses the license. Thus ownership is a key variable toward understanding power and influence within the station.

Ownership is also important in understanding the role of racism in PSLR. Though ethnic identity of the owner is not necessarily an indicator that the quality of broadcasting will be better or worse or that there are racist employment practices within the station, it is an indicator of the Chicano community's penetration into a very important media position in a medium with extraordinary influence. The Chicano community, like other minority communities, has generally not exercised control over the institutions that operate in its midst. The measure of PSLR owner ethnic identity is a measure of the community's ability to control a key institution within it. When this latter point is considered in light of the active management role most station owners take, it offers a gross indication of likely community isolation or involvement in station operations.

Ten owners (24 percent) with Spanish surnames and thirty-one owners (76 percent) with Anglo surnames were identified. Eight Anglo-owned stations represent 55 percent of all PSLR total assets. Among stations with less than $100,000 total assets, there is a rough parity between assets held by the Spanish surname and the Anglo owners. Beyond $500,000 in total assets there are no Spanish surname–owned stations. Two Anglo-owned stations have total assets over $1 million, one with assets over $1.6 million. In terms of assets, Anglo-owned stations accrue much more wealth (84 percent of all total assets) than do their Spanish surname counterparts; a small core of Anglo-owned stations has achieved a dominant position within the PSLR system.

Moreover, 64 percent ($6,419, 016) of the total assets of all Anglo-owned stations are controlled by eight of these stations.

There is a similar differential distribution of advertising rates by ownership. The six highest advertising rates for Spanish surname–owned stations fall between $7 and $15 per minute; the six highest advertising rates for Anglo-owned stations fall between $21 and $50 per minute—the three highest being $42, $45, and $50. The income differences these various advertising rates indicate are quite large; a small difference in rates creates a large difference in potential income. As with assets, a few stations, all owned by Anglos, exert disproportionately higher market powers and market domination.

This Anglo economic domination is not limited to PSLR. Out of eighty-one additional broadcast properties held by all owners, Anglo owners hold seventy-six (94 percent). There are twelve Anglo station owners with a greater number of broadcast properties than any Spanish surname owner. There is only one case of a Spanish surname owner with three additional broadcast properties, but there are four cases of Anglo station owners with ten or more additional broadcast properties. In this instance the disparity in ownership patterns is distinct. A clear concentration of ownership exists in the hands of a few persons (men), all of whom are Anglos. It appears that Anglo station owners, especially a few large and powerful station owners, own more stations, control more assets, command higher advertising rates, and have more additional property holdings than anyone else.

Particularly significant is that this wealth is generated from the Spanish-speaking community only. Their listenership is measured and converted into advertising rates. Without a measurable Spanish-speaking audience, no radio station could attract advertisers and thus make a profit. Furthermore, it is the continued evidence of successful advertising campaigns on PSLR that ensures these stations' continued profits. Though it is not clear that there is an actual transfer of wealth from the Spanish-speaking community to the Anglo community through the vehicle of owners' ethnic identities, it is clear that wealth from the Spanish-speaking community is supporting the entire commerical Spanish language radio structure. Therefore even though it would be difficult to pinpoint the flow of PSLR-generated wealth in or out of the Chicano community, it is clear that a few Anglo owners are in a position to accrue the great majority of PSLR-generated wealth, as implied by the distribution of assests and advertising rates.

In discussing wealth and personnel, the study focused on differential distribution by ethnicity within occupational categories. Consequently, three categories of employment were examined: managers, engineers, and general employees.

Fully one-third of all PSLR stations have no Spanish surname managers. Only five stations (13 percent) have management teams where Spanish surname managers are in the majority. Of those five stations four have Spanish surname owners; only one Anglo-owned station has a primarily Spanish surname management team. But even stations with Spanish surname owners do not have strong Spanish surname representations; five of the nine stations with Spanish surname owners have Spanish surname managers in the minority, although all Spanish surname-owned stations have at least one Spanish surname manager (see Table 2).

Of all forty stations reporting, only one (also Spanish surname–owned) had a Spanish surname chief engineer. All engineers require FCC certification, though the chief engineer is responsible for the technical operation of the station. Of particular interest here is the very low penetration by Spanish surname personnel. It is probable that the need for certification has had an influence on the low representation by persons of Spanish surname; however, it is not clear how important this reason is because all announcers also require certification and there is an abundance of Spanish surname announcers. Certainly the necessity of speaking Spanish ensures a quantity of Spanish surname announcers. In addition the engineering exams are technical, making them potentially more difficult for someone who has been in a discriminatory educational system. Even so, the presence of only one identified Spanish surname chief engineer appears unusually low.

In contrast to the number of Spanish surname managers, the number of Spanish surname personnel reported by PSLR

Table 2. PSLR Station Managers with Spanish Surnames

Percent of Mgmt. with Spanish Surnames	Number of PSLR Stations	Percent of Total PSLR Stations	Anglo-Owned/Span. Sur.-Owned (A/Ss)
0	13	34	13/0 (A/Ss)
1–25	3	8	3/0
26–50	17	45	12/5
51–75	2	5	1/1
76–100	3	8	0/3
Total	38	100	29/9

(3 stations not reporting)

stations is large. Of the 417 PSLR employees reported, 268 (64 percent) had Spanish surnames. It appears that news persons, announcers, and receptionists speaking fluent Spanish make up a large portion of these employees (see Table 3).

An interesting sidelight to these findings is the case of the one station in the survey for which there are detailed data on part-time employment. This station reports twenty-four nonmanagerial or engineering employees—ten full time and fourteen part time. The station also reports sixteen Spanish surname employees in this group of twenty-four. Of the sixteen Spanish surname employees, thirteen are part time. Of the eight Anglo employees, only one is part time. Thus an apparent Spanish surname majority is questionable when closely examined. In this case it seems that Spanish surname employees hold the least secure and possibly least lucrative positions. Therefore it seems employee data must be very cautiously accepted as a direct indication of greater participation by Spanish surname employees.

Conclusion

The aspects of racism examined in this chapter illustrate the multifaceted nature of the problem and militate against a simple conclusion. Moreover, PSLR is a complex subsystem within the larger system of American broadcasting. Three inferences reflect this complexity.

Table 3. PSLR Employees with Spanish Surnames

Percent of Employees with Spanish Surnames	Number of PSLR Stations	Percent of Total Stations Reporting	Anglo-Owned/Span. Sur.-Owned (A/Ss)
0–25	0	0	0/0 (A/Ss)
26–50	6	21	5/1
51–75	8	29	8/0
76–100	14	50	10/4
Total	28	100	23/5

(13 stations not reporting)

First, differential distribution by ethnicity exists at numerous ownership and employment levels in PSLR. Unequal representation was found among owners, managers, and engineers. In the lowest employment category, that of general employee, there was a substantial representation of Spanish surname individuals. However, the findings in this last category may be misleading, as the case of one station indicated.

It is possible to infer from these findings that ethnic representation in PSLR is actually quite high because it is greater than the representation of Spanish surname individuals in the society at large. However, such an inference ignores the unique role of Spanish language radio within the Spanish-speaking community. PSLR's primary cause for existence is the Spanish-speaking listener; moreover, it draws the content for its broadcasts from that very same Spanish-speaking community. Thus the low representation of Spanish surname individuals within the organizational structure of PSLR is noteworthy, especially when one considers the even greater lack of representation at the higher decision-making levels.

Second, differential distribution of influence was inferred from evidence of differential access to the more powerful positions within PSLR. A few Anglo owners occupy the strongest market positions by owning the biggest stations and by holding more additional properties than anyone else. This places them in a position to exercise more power in the marketplace than those owners with smaller stations and fewer additional properties.

Similarly, fewer Spanish surname individuals have access to management and engineering positions. Moreover, Spanish surname managers are almost totally excluded from the larger, more powerful stations. Only in the lowest employee category are Spanish surname personnel abundantly represented; however, this is the employment level with the least influence in decision making.

I am not implying that Anglo owners and managers are incapable of making quality broadcasting decisions or of understanding the needs of the Spanish-speaking community or that it is categorically better (or somehow morally right) to replace Anglo personnel with Spanish surname personnel. A greater representation of personnel from the Spanish-speaking community would, however, probably exert a beneficial effect on the quality of broadcast decisions, especially in those cases where there are no Spanish surname personnel in decision-making capacities. Although in individual cases a Spanish surname person might be less sensitive than any Anglo, I assume that most Spanish surname personnel will bring with them certain sensitivities and understandings of community problems that will benefit station operations in the "public interest." Thus the differential distribution observed at the upper levels of broadcast management seem significant, and Spanish language broadcasting would probably benefit from an increase in the number of Spanish surname personnel at decision-making levels.

The ownership structure is not at issue here; rather it is the potential for operating in the public interest that differential distribution of owners by ethnic identity implies. Effective representation of Spanish surname persons in management positions is assumed to have a positive effect on operations and thus enhance the owner's ability to operate in the public interest.

Third, personal wealth derived from participation in PSLR was found to be distributed by ethnicity. Anglo ownership of the wealthiest and most powerful stations indicates that profits from those stations accrue to Anglo owners. Moreover, Anglo owners also hold far more numerous additional properties than their Spanish surname counterparts, thus enhancing Anglo wealth and influence within the Spanish language radio industry.

By contrast, Spanish surname owners have the smallest and poorest stations and draw only a small portion of the total prof-its generated by the Spanish language radio industry.

Because PSLR derives its sole rationale for existence from the participation of the Spanish-speaking audience and because all advertising revenues are the result of Spanish-speaking listenership, wealth derived from PSLR represents a form of community capital transfer. Though I am not implying that all income derived from PSLR activities is deposited in the Anglo community, the majority of all PSLR income is in fact derived from the Spanish-speaking community, so there exists the potential for a capital transfer from one community to the other. Even accepting the possibility that some or much of PSLR profits are reinvested in the Chicano community, the high differential distribution in ownership probably represents some capital loss to the Spanish-speaking community.

The significance of the findings regarding wealth and ownership is that they provide a gross view of the social consequences of PSLR-generated wealth in contributing to the problems of relative poverty in the Spanish-speaking community. I do not address the issue of whether a large number of Spanish surname owners would contribute to Chicano community wealth or assume that all Anglo owners are in the business of bleeding the Chicano community. This chapter indicates the possibility of the existence of capital transfers, through broadcasting, out of the Chicano community. In so doing, the information from the survey on which it is based contributes to an initial understanding of the possible economic impact of primary Spanish language radio.

This same economic impact is present within PSLR in the form of possible institutionally discriminatory outcomes. The patterns of differential personnel and wealth distribution are indicators that Spanish surname owners, managers, and employees are at a distinct disadvantage vis-à-vis their Anglo counterparts. Ironically, this disadvantage exists in an institution totally devoted to and sustained by the Spanish-speaking community.

I make the following recommendations for future research in PSLR. There is a need for more information on the issue of PSLR community responsibility. Future studies should focus on program content of PSLR as a measure of whether station programming is meeting community needs. Additionally, there is a need to focus on the relationship between Anglo and Chicano personnel in meeting community needs; the question of the value of substituting Latino broadcasters for Anglo broadcasters, only partially addressed in this chapter, needs careful examination.

Data gathered on owners' other properties raise the issue of PSLR's links to other institutions. Analysis of PSLR as a subsystem within the Chicano community or as a subsystem within American broadcasting should contribute to our knowledge of information flow, capital transfers, and development within the Chicano community.

This chapter did not touch the problem of comparisons between English and Spanish language radio. There is a need to examine the regulations of PSLR vis-à-vis ELR. Because of the special circumstances of potential cultural isolation between ownership and audience in PSLR, comparative regulation practices should be examined to evaluate whether the audience community's needs are being served. There is a further need for such comparisons in order to gain a better perspective on the operational practices of each medium.

Finally, there is a great need for case studies of PSLR stations. There is a need to apply a holistic approach in examining PSLR operations. By gathering micro views of stations as organizational entities, it is possible to observe the dynamics that can later be addressed at the systemic level. In addition, case studies can shed light on the large and small station, each of which has its own problems.

PSLR contains both a promise and a peril. It holds a promise of becoming an effective tool for community self-development and of contributing to the equalization of relationships between Anglos and Chicanos. But it also holds a peril by maintaining information and wealth control in the hands of the Anglo community. The future of successful relationships between the two communities depends in part on greater Chicano community access to the media that broadcast to it and on greater Anglo community recognition of the special needs of the Spanish-speaking community.

13

Use of Log-Linear and Hierarchical Models to Study Ethnic Composition in a University

David Nasatir
John P. Fernandez

Few would deny that institutional racism/sexism is an evil. Yet there is disagreement about the precise meaning of the phrase, and efforts to prove its existence often result in complicated court cases. This chapter attempts to provide a working definition for the term and a sensitive method for demonstrating its existence. The general approach employs a statistical model developed by Leo S. Goodman in a series of papers (1970, 1972a, 1972b, 1973a, 1973b, 1973c) and elaborated on by James Davis (1974), Otis Dudley Duncan (1975), and others.

270

We selected Goodman's system because it is particularly useful in the study of situations where crucial factors, such as gender or minority status, are considered dichotomous attributes. It is also a great utility in the study of situations where only a small fraction of the total population is in a special category. Thus it may be employed in the study of differential access to elite positions (such as graduate school, high-level managerial positions, or government appointments), differential allocation of scarce resources (such as scholarships, services of specialists, or specialized equipment), and differential sanctions (such as rapid promotions, special bonuses, or harsh sentences). The utility of the approach is not limited to these circumstances. It is readily applicable to situations where the category of interest is occupied by a large part of the total population but members of specified minorities are not represented in proportion to their expected numbers (first-time enrollments of Chicanos in community colleges in the Los Angeles area, for example, or special admission scholarships for females).

Goodman's techniques of log-linear analysis and hierarchical modeling also provide a method for choosing among alternative theories to explain the existence, persistence, or change in incidents of racism/sexism in organizational contexts. Thus the techniques may be useful in efforts to assess the relative importance of specific elements in a complex web of factors that ultimately result in an incident of racism/sexism.

A Working Definition of Racism/Sexism

We define *racism* as a cultural ideology that espouses the view that one race of people is inherently superior to another race of people. In the United States the white population has developed and nurtured a cultural ideology that minorities, especially blacks, are inherently inferior. Whites have sufficient power and control of societal institutions to support this ideology even to the point where it is accepted by many members of the minority population.

In the past, racism and sexism were overt and nonsophisticated. For example, if corporations hired or promoted women at all, they did so only into lower-level management positions that constituted female ghettos. This was done with the sanction of the larger society. When corporations excluded blacks or other minority groups, they also did so with societal approval.

Since the civil rights movement, the Civil Rights Act of 1964, and subsequent executive orders, racial and sexual discrimination are no longer legal. If exclusion of minorities and women is acceptable to society, then it is acceptable in neo-racist/neosexist actions and occurs in the context of institutional actions that are racist and sexist in their consequences. Racism/ sexism has become much more refined than in the past. It is more covert and sophisticated, with many subtle and complex attitudinal and institutional components, and might be better described as *neoracism* and *neosexism*.

Corporations no longer refuse to hire or promote women into various managerial levels because of their sex; now their excuse is that the women are not qualified or are not the most qualified applicants. Organizations do not claim that minorities, especially black, are not advancing as rapidly as possible because of their race but rather because they are "culturally deprived." The argument that the subcultures of minority groups limit their members' potential for full participation in the larger society is a crucial element of neoracism/neosexism.

Neoracism/neosexism involves attitudes particularly characteristic of white males. *Institutional racism/sexism* is a process of exclusionary procedures, rules, and regulations. Although institutional racism/sexism can be an instrument for neoracism/ neosexism by the individual interpretation of rules and regulations, most often such rules were formulated without the specific intention of exluding minorities and women. However, in our white-male-oriented society, most institutionalized procedures and rules have been made with white males in mind. Thus conformity to the operating norms of institutions has resulted in the almost total barring of minorities and women from equal and full participation in the society in which they are nominally full citizens.

Institutional racism/sexism is evident in the "old boy network" through which many positions are filled and which tends to institutionalize the selection mostly of white males for high-status positions. Testing and assessment procedures that do not take into account the cultural biases of the test and assessment criteria, that is, procedures that have been tested and validated only by white males, are crucial elements of institutional racism/sexism.

Blauner (1972, p. 9) cogently analyzed the insidiousness of such a racist structure by describing its effects on well-meaning individuals as they inadvertently perpetuate the unjust system: "The *people* of goodwill and tolerance who identify racism with prejudice can therefore exempt themselves from responsibility and involvement in our system of racial injustice and inequality by taking comfort in their own 'favorable' attitudes toward minority groups. . . . The error in this point of view is revealed by the fact that such *individuals* of goodwill and tolerance help maintain the racism of American society and in some cases even profit from it."

Racism/sexism manifests itself in many ways. However, this chapter is restricted to consideration of those circumstances where the distribution of statuses, rewards, punishments, opportunities, or resources is not independent of the race, ethnicity, or gender of the recipients. We are interested in differences resulting from all those processes by which greater burdens are placed on one population than another. The differences are reflected in a small return per unit of a group's own psychic, social, political, and economic investments.

The indicators used to detect racism/sexism may include such diverse attributes as occupational titles, admission status, pay rates, jail sentences, or scholarships as well as the conventional indicators of race, sex, and ethnicity. The measurement problems associated with these indicators are well known: How descriptive is a job title, for example, or what criteria will be used to classify a subject as a Chicano?

Errors in classification of individuals, even though they may be unintended, can produce profound shifts in the apparent distribution of minority group members within organizational categories, particularly when the numbers employed for comparisons are small. When there are only five full professors in a department, for example, inaccurate classification of only one will change the reported distribution of minority employees by 20 percent. These are difficult problems and they may have a profound effect on any effort to establish the existence of racism or sexism. A full development of these topics, however, must be left for another time.

Racism/sexism as used here includes no requirement of intent to discriminate, no postulate of prejudicial attitudes, hostile stereotypes, or even consciousness of different characteristics of individual recipients. It is not an individual act but a state or condition resulting from an act or acts. When such states are brief and transitory, they are of less interest than when they demonstrate permanence by stability, growth, or slow decay. The transitory condition will be referred to as *artifactual racism/sexism* because it is most often produced as an artifact of definitional, measurement, or computational procedures. Persistent or slowly changing situations will be considered essential to the definition of institutionalized racism/sexism. The institutionalized phenomenon may occur in any kind of setting, including (but not limited to) such formal organizations as government, industry, education, or the military. Institutionalized racism/sexism is characterized by the routine and ordinary quality of the activities that produce disparities in the distribution of the indicator attributes. The problem of distinguishing institutionalized from artifactual racism/sexism is treated later in this chapter.

Demonstrating the Existence of Racism/Sexism

Most efforts to demonstrate the existence of racism/sexism focus upon comparing the observed value of a statistic, such as a proportion, with the total range of values that could occur for that statistic with a sample of that size. Conclusions are then drawn based on the likelihood of encountering the distribution of values obtained for the sample if the only source of variations to be considered in examining the observed distribution is that derived from chance factors in the sampling process and it is assumed that these factors had been operating in a completely random fashion (Wolf and Reidel, 1973). These are rather strong assumptions, but the difficulties that arise if they are not made account for their widespread adoption. Thus it is usually presumed (often without good cause) that the value obtained for the observed statistic was not influenced in any way by measurement problems or data-processing and computation errors.

Recent advances in the effort to demonstrate the existence of racism/sexism have been made, primarily by success in the efforts to clarify conceptually the relevance of the universe from which the observed data are presumed to have been drawn. Thus the proportion of graduate students from ethnic minorities is compared with the proportion of college graduates from that group rather than the total proportion of the world's population from that group. More and more emphasis is being placed on the "relevance" of the comparison population (Baldus and Cole, 1977).

The usual method of demonstrating racism/sexism, then, is to establish that the distribution of an attribute in the organizational context is unlike its distribution in the relevant pool. Because it may not be possible for the sample statistic to match the population figure exactly, for simple algebraic reasons, some difference from zero is usually acceptable when comparing sample and population characteristics. Just how much of a difference, of course, is a matter for debate. When sample sizes are very large, very small deviations may be unlikely to have occurred due simply to factors operating randomly in sample selection. However, statistically significant differences may be so small that they are of no substantive interest whatsoever unless they are viewed as evidence of the existence of a causal pattern —an important point to which we shall return. In contrast, very large differences due to random sampling frequently occur between sample and population when sample sizes are small. The simple presence or absence of a difference must therefore be compared to some referent before a statement can be made about the presence or absence of racism/sexism. The magnitude as well as the likelihood of an observed difference must be considered.

The usual referent is an estimate of the standard deviation of the sampling distribution without much consideration for the meaning of the size of such a unit in the specific case under study. An observed difference, even a large one unlikely to have occurred due to random factors in the sampling process, may not be sufficient to declare the existence of institutionalized racism/sexism, however, because the circumstances might simply be a transient anomaly or, more likely, an artifact of measurement or computation. Evidence is also required to show the phenomenon persists over time. It is for this reason that the use of regularly gathered, methodologically standardized, and routinely published data is so important for the identification of institutionalized racism/sexism. Data of this kind, often known as "social indicators," provide the basis for comparisons over time; and it is precisely this aspect of social indicators that is so vital to the demonstration of instutionalized racism/sexism.

Using social indicators to demonstrate the evidence of institutionalized racism/sexism, then, we should be able to demonstrate the significant departure of an observed statistic from some ideal benchmark and show that this departure is stable or changing slowly over time. When this is done, we can attempt to isolate the specific policies, arrangements, practices, and actions within an organizational context that might be manipulated to reduce or eliminate undesired discrepancies from the ideal. Thus we could see, for example, if a change in admission policy actually resulted in a relative increase in minority student enrollment independent of fluctuations in total enrollment or in the distribution of enrollment among departments or schools.

Static and Dynamic Demonstrations of Institutionalized Racism/Sexism

If a *pattern* of circumstances can be identified that would, if continued, lead to the development or support of racism/sexism, a great step will be made toward demonstrating the institutionalization of the phenomenon. The more complex the pattern, that is, the more elements it contains, the more convincing the demonstration. Demonstrations of this kind are usually static in their use of data from a single moment. They approximate a dynamic model of the racism/sexism process by projecting from a *process* model of the context under study. This is usually accomplished by showing that disparities observed at one level are currently paralleled by similar disparities at lower or prior levels within the organizational context or process. This suggests that even though selection factors may operate in a fashion uninfluenced by attributes such as race or gender at one level of organizational functioning, the resulting distribution at that level would, over time, reflect the operation of such factors at some lower or prior level. The earlier activity results in distortion of the relevant pool so that the final decision, although unbiased, still produces a racist or sexist outcome.

Although the attribution of a dynamic, or process, analysis to data obtained at a single point is a common practice, its dangers are well known and quickly singled out by those attempting to deny the existence of institutional racism/sexism in a given case. Efforts to show an increase in the proportion of women and minorities who will be occupying high-status positions by demonstrating an increase in their numbers in low-status positions ignores the possibility of differential rates of promotion. It is therefore important to distinguish between the analysis of data from different stages in a process gathered at the same time and data on the results of that process gathered at different times in order to develop an appropriate explanation for an observed instance of racism/sexism. Even when this has been done, however, it is still necessary to choose among competing explanations.

How should the problem of establishing the existence of institutionalized racism/sexism be addressed in a context where alternative explanations are put forth to account for associations in the joint distribution of those attributes selected for analysis and the race, ethnicity, or gender of the population under study? The *existence* of the association may be acknowledged, but the causes of the observed association may be debatable. Is it the result of differential recruitment, for example, or of differential selection? How can the degree of change over time be assessed when examining the contribution of selected factors to the production of the observed indicators whether we have data from a single moment or from several points in time? Statistical techniques commonly employed for this purpose require assumptions about the nature of the attributes and their distribution that may not be easily met or in some cases may produce results difficult to interpret in a practical context. Many conventional techniques, such as comparing differences in means, require data that may be properly characterized by interval or ratio scales of measurement. The meaning of a regression coefficient or beta weight in a path analysis is not immediately obvious when a crucial variable such as ethnicity may have only the characteristics of a nominal scale. Use of Goodman's techniques provides an easily interpretable aid in developing answers to the question of causality without the need for such assumptions.

Consider the following example. According to the fall ethnic survey data routinely gathered by the office of the vice-president for planning, 91,449 students enrolled in the University of California system in the fall quarter of 1971 responded to an ethnicity survey. Most of them (68,252) were undergraduates and relatively few (16,347) were minority students. Had "the situation" changed by 1974? If so, how important were changes in undergraduate enrollments (prior in the process) and how important were other causes associated with the changing times? Examining the data for 1971, we see that the odds are about 1 in 4.5 that an undergraduate in the system was a "minority" student and about 1 in 4.6 that a graduate student was. If the undergraduate pool in the UC system represents the relevant pool for comparison (a debatable point, but a typical assumption in using available data), we might expect the graduate figure to look more like the undergraduate figure a few years later. Data are presented in Table 1 showing the actual distribution encountered for the fall of each year from 1971 to 1974. Is there any evidence of institutionalized racism/sexism? Is there any reason to believe the phenomenon is abating? How do you tell?

Table 1. University of California Enrollments,
Fall Quarters, 1971-1974

		Minority	Nonminority	Total
1971	Undergraduates	12,232	56,020	68,252
	Graduates	4,115	19,082	23,197
	Total	16,347	75,102	91,449
1972	Undergraduates	14,658	62,885	77,543
	Graduates	5,309	22,142	27,451
	Total	19,877	85,027	104,994
1973	Undergraduates	17,265	66,662	83,927
	Graduates	6,497	23,437	29,934
	Total	23,762	90,099	113,861
1974	Undergraduates	18,271	67,290	85,561
	Graduates	6,956	23,115	30,071
	Total	25,227	90,405	115,632

Source: University of California, Office of the Vice-President for Planning.

Examination of Table 1 reveals several points worthy of comment. While the total enrollment of the university increased from 1971 to 1974, so did the odds that a student would be from a minority group; minority enrollments increased proportionately more than nonminority enrollments. The rate of growth was not constant, however, and an attempt to project future developments using a linear model would be risky. However, the relative importance of changes in the undergraduate pool as a contributor to changes in the proportion of minority graduates, as compared to changes in total enrollment over time, is not clear. How well could the observed distribution of students be estimated, for example, if we ignored the effects of changing enrollments or the effects of changing proportions of minorities or the interactions between these factors? Use of Goodman's system provides an answer. The answer in this case is that without considering both factors and their interaction it would be difficult to estimate the number of minority graduate students in 1974 with a degree of accuracy akin to what might be obtained had only random factors been operating in a sampling process. Had estimates been made knowing only the change in total enrollment, only the change in the proportion of graduates, or only the change in the proportion of minorities, the results would have been substantially in error.

This example illustrates two difficulties associated with the effort to use social indicator data in the study of institutional racism/sexism. First, had a dynamic projection been made based only on observation of the distribution of cases at two stages in the organizational process under study, the results would have been in error. Obviously, many factors operate in this case to produce minority enrollments in graduate school. Without considering the variety of causes for the end state, it is dangerous to consider those factors for which data are readily available because they are routinely produced for administrative purposes. Social indicators, although they may be available, may be misleading when used for making predictions by extrapolation. More sophisticated causal models are required for this purpose.

The second point the example illustrates is the difficulty of using a conventional statistical model to assess systematically the role played by several factors associated with changes in minority graduate enrollment. What difference does it make, if we are trying to predict the number of minority graduate students in a given year, if we only consider the overall distribution of minority students, only the distribution of graduates, and only the total number of students year by year? By how much, precisely, can an estimate be improved by considering combinations of these factors? Which combinations make the most difference? How much difference does each combination make? Answers to questions of this type provide the basis for studying the causal web of factors that produce racism/sexism. With knowledge of the structure of the causal web in a specific case, we can address the location of discrimination in the organizational process and develop rational strategies for change.

Hierarchical Models in the Study of
Institutional Racism/Sexism

One difficulty in translating the figures in a cross tabulation into words is the tendency (when there are three or more

variables) for the relationship between two of them to be different with different categories or combinations of categories of
the other variables. The ability to demonstrate that the relationship between minority status and graduate status does not
depend upon the year, for example, would make the translating
task much easier. If we have data that are a sample of the entire
population, as we do in the example, it is very likely that some
of the variation in the relationship between minority status and
graduate status might be due to the sampling process itself. This
is true, of course, even though no sampling process was intended.
Thus even though the population consists of all students enrolled
in the nine campuses of the University of California system, the
sample consists of those responding to the university's ethnicity
survey. Let us assume that the pattern of nonresponse would
permit us to treat the obtained data as if it were a random
sample.

Although it is common practice to assume a random pattern of nonresponse to surveys of this type in order to obtain
a standard of comparison for assessing the relative magnitude
of shifts in the enrollment process, there is no evidence to support such an assumption and many reasons to believe it may be
untenable. There are manifestly different participation rates in
other aspects of university life, so it seems reasonable to assume
there might also be systematic differences in responses to the
survey associated with gender and minority group status. The
assumption of random nonresponse is invoked here only to
demonstrate a common technique utilizing the data at hand.
The question, then, is whether the interactions observed are so
small that it is fairly likely they could have occurred by chance
factors in sampling. Or do the differences really reflect systematic relationships between variables in the larger population?

To decide this question, we employ Goodman's technique to reproduce all the relations among the variables except
for specific interaction effects that we wish to test for their statistical significance, that is, the size of those effects compared
to the size that might be expected by fluctuations due to random factors in the sampling process. Once this is done we may
compare the distribution of cases actually observed with the dis-

tribution generated by ignoring selected interactions. We may use the resulting differences to calculate a chi-square statistic that in turn permits an estimate of how often a discrepancy of the size encountered might be found if the rules used in the attempt to reproduce the relations were actually true but fluctuations due to random factors were operating.

If the discrepancy is large (would only occur by chance, at the most, five times in a hundred, for example), then the rules used in the attempt to reproduce the observed data would be presumed inadequate. If the overall discrepancy is so small that differences of the size obtained could be expected to occur at least fifty times out of a hundred, just by random fluctuations in the sampling process, then the rules (or model) used to reproduce the data actually observed could be considered adequate. Leaving out selected interactions in the model and still being able to reproduce the observations suggests that the interactions are not really present in the population. The fluctuations observed are apparently due to other factors operating in a random fashion.

This idea can be extended to provide a basis for choosing among competing models for explaining observed distributions. The degree to which the different models are capable of reproducing the observed data can be tested by the chi-square technique and any difference found attributed to the differences in the components of the models. Systematic application of this procedure permits assessment of the relative importance of specific factors in creating the most suitable model.

Goodman (1972b, pp. 1080–1083) and Davis (1974) outline the steps for creating models for contingency tables where the cell frequencies produced are maximum likelihood estimates of what the actual frequencies would be if the model were a true reflection of reality and there were no sampling error or random fluctuation involved. In this approach no lower-order relationship is excluded if a higher-order one that contains it is included in the model. This procedure involves successive approximations where cell frequencies are created by considering, one by one and in combination, the overall or marginal distributions of all the factors in the model. The process can be very tedious and is best accomplished by a computer. A program for this purpose (ECTA) is readily available. The analyst must suggest the models to be tested, that is, which factors and combinations should be included and which ones excluded. Alternative models thus created are then compared for adequacy.

Concerned analysts occasionally may have a strong feeling for the general relevance of various factors in the production of racism/sexism, but the exact details of how these factors might interact may not be well worked out. ECTA can be employed to analyze the adequacy of all the models possible with the variables under consideration, although there may be quite a few. Examination of the chi-square statistic produced for each model provides an excellent guide for selection among alternatives. Precise methods for choosing among alternatives are presented by Goodman (1970) along with strategies for generating models. The model with the fewest elements and greatest accuracy in reproducing the observed data is usually the prime candidate for selection.

One way to approach this problem is by careful consideration of the model itself. ECTA can quickly and cheaply produce the "fully saturated" model for any set of variables to be analyzed. This is the model that employs every variable and combination of variables. The general form of the model is:

> Frequency of
> cases in a   = Constant X Grand Effect Parameter
> specific cell

where the constant is a kind of average cell frequency, and the grand effect parameter is the product of components representing each level of each factor or combination of factors. Analysis of the components of the grand effect parameter can quickly suggest the relative contribution of each factor and combination of factors. Elimination of those components that contribute very little to the model can be systematically undertaken by an assessment of the model's relative loss of accuracy compared to the simplicity gained by including fewer components.

The "effect parameters" Goodman's iterative process produces, referred to earlier, can be produced for any model and

Table 2. Parameters for Fully Saturated Model
of University of California Enrollment Data

Variables	Components of Grand Effect Parameter
Constant = 18574.401	
Year	
1971	0.820
1972	0.975
1973	1.102
1974	1.135
Enrollment status	1.677
Minority status	0.500
Enrollment status × year	
1971	1.025
1972	0.996
1973	0.988
1974	0.991
Minority status × year	
1971	0.931
1972	0.971
1973	1.035
1974	1.069
Enrollment status × minority status	0.988
Enrollment status × minority status × year	
1971	1.015
1972	1.003
1973	0.995
1974	0.986

are shown in Table 2 for the model with all components present
(the saturated model) using the enrollment data from Table 1.
The parameters calculated by employing the ECTA program reflect the ratio of frequencies in selected sets of cells within Table 1. Thus in Table 2 the value of 0.500 shown as the minority
status component of the grand effect parameter is derived from
the ratio of minority to nonminority students. The figure of
0.988 shown for the enrollment status × minority status component is derived from the ratio of the odds for being a minority student among undergraduates as compared to the odds for
being a minority student among graduates.

The grand mean effect, noted before, is the geometric mean or "average" cell size in the model. The effect parameters tell by how much a specific cell will deviate from this mean due to the effect of a given variable.

The sum of the products of the effect parameters and the grand mean effect will provide the frequency for a specific cell (if the reciprocal of the value given is substituted for the parameter itself when the "second" level of a dichotomous variable is being considered). Thus examination of the effect parameters for the fully saturated model can suggest the relative importance of each variable in the total web of interrelationships. On this basis it is possible to eliminate one variable at a time, or specific interactions among variables, and then, using a chi-square test, assess how well the resulting model generates the appropriate cell frequencies.

Examination of the parameters in the bottom section of Table 2 suggests that the relation between minority status and enrollment status shifted direction over the four-year period under study so that the odds of a student being a graduate has declined more for minority than for nonminority students—the ratio of these ratios was greater in 1971 than in 1974. The major part of this change took place between 1971 and 1972 with large changes in total enrollment, but the trend continued when the rate of change in overall enrollment slowed down.

University recruitment of minority graduate students as part of the minority student body apparently had not kept pace with these efforts among nonminority students even though the absolute number of minority graduate students had continued to grow. Yet the relationship appears "small." Would it be plausible, then, to ignore the shift in the relationship between graduate status and minority membership over the years as suggested by the comparatively small size for these effect parameters? Could one conclude that no changes had taken place in university actions but that the minor fluctuations observed were due to chance alone?

If it is assumed that there is no need to take the changing relationship between graduate and minority status into account, it is still possible to estimate the enrollment distribution over the years. The results produced by this model (shown in Table 3) differ from the observed values by an amount considerably greater than what might have been expected had only chance factors been in operation.

This suggests the model that ignores the relationship between graduate and minority status is inappropriate. By trying every possible alternative, it is possible to show that there is no adequate model (using only race, status, and year) to predict enrollment distributions simpler than the fully saturated model. In that model each component of the grand effect parameter reflects the relative importance of the factors (and their combinations) to the overall model for predicting the distribution of minority students among graduates and undergraduates for each year considered. The greater the difference between the effect parameter and the value 1.000, the greater is its contribution to production of the final result. Thus the importance of enrollment status was greater in 1971 than in 1972 and greater in 1974 than in 1973, although the *direction* of the contribution had changed between 1972 and 1973. Examination of the components of the grand effect parameter also shows that when creating a model to re-create the distribution of enrollments, the relative contribution of the minority status component in 1971 was greater than that of enrollment status at that time. Contributions of both factors changed over the years: Indeed, the direction of their contributions reversed in four years, although the relative contribution of minority status was still greater.

Use of Goodman's technique, then, has helped in assessing the relative contribution of overall growth, minority growth, and changes in the proportion of graduates enrolled in producing an increase in minority graduate enrollment in the University of California system. Despite the increased enrollment of minority undergraduates as part of the general increase in enrollments in the UC system in the four years under study, this growth was less than might have been expected and the growth of minority graduate students was not what might have been expected considering the general expansion of the institution and the increase of minority members at the "earlier" or undergraduate level in the process.

Table 3. University of California Enrollments, Fall Quarters, 1971–1974 and Enrollments Predicted Using the Model Requiring Marginal Distributions for Enrollment Status and Year to Fit the Original Data and for Minority Status and Enrollment Status to Fit the Original Data

		Minority		Nonminority		Total
		Actual	Predicted	Actual	Predicted	Actual
1971	Undergraduates	12,232	11,958.35	56,020	55,749.34	68,252
	Graduates	4,115	4,388.65	19,082	19,352.66	23,197
	Total	16,347	16,347	75,102	75,102	91,449
1972	Undergraduates	14,658	15,540.65	62,885	63,116.82	77,543
	Graduates	5,309	5,336.35	22,142	21,910.18	27,451
	Total	19,967	19,877	85,027	85,027	104,994
1973	Undergraduates	17,265	17,382.65	66,662	66,881.84	83,927
	Graduates	6,497	6,379.35	23,437	23,217.16	29,934
	Total	23,762	23,762	90,099	90,099	113,861
1974	Undergraduates	18,271	18,454.35	67,290	67,108.99	85,561
	Graduates	6,956	6,772.65	23,115	23,296.01	30,071
	Total	25,227	25,227	90,405	90,405	115,632

Note: Likelihood ratio chi-square = 46.65 for 6 degrees of freedom.
Source: University of California, Office of the Vice-President for Planning.

A plausible alternative causal model was generated by eliminating a specific relationship shown empirically to be of relatively little importance. Yet a test of this model revealed that the cost of simplifying the original conceptual scheme was an unacceptably high level of error in predicting specific kinds of enrollment. Thus we may conclude that the interactions among the three variables—enrollment status, minority status, and year—are of sufficient size that to ignore small lower-order relations (such as graduate and minority status) is misleading. To model the enrollment distribution with any degree of precision, we must consider all the variables simultaneously. Policy designed to improve minority status must do so too.

We have, then, an example of how the Goodman system may be used both to clarify the structure and to test theories of causation in the study of institutionalized sexism and racism.

Part Six

Analyzing Institutions of Social Control

≋≋≋≋≋≋≋≋≋≋≋≋≋≋≋≋≋≋≋

The four chapters in this part are each concerned with a particular aspect of the criminal justice system: They each deal with institutions of social control in our society and are presented in the order in which a person would be processed through the criminal justice system.

The chapter by Daniel Mendoza de Arce and Omar L. Peraza presents an overview of the criminal justice process and examines ways institutional discrimination can come into play in this process. Their purpose is to develop a general scheme that can be used to discern all the inputs into the decision-making process and thus identify the points at which to look for discrimination or to intervene to counteract it. They emphasize the problem of developing "independent" social indicators of racism or sexism. Of particular interest is their assertion that although some court decisions are not in themselves discriminatory, they do serve to perpetuate the patterns of disadvantage incorporated into the process at earlier stages.

James O'Reilly presents an inexpensive method of measuring the racial, ethnic, class, and sexual composition of jury systems. His method does not provide information on *representation* of particular interest; it demonstrates the degree to which the jury is *representative* of various populations. O'Reilly notes that although the available pool of potential jurors might be

289

representative of the community, this does not mean that the jury itself will be. Numerous contingencies prevent relatively powerless populations from serving on juries.

Ilene Bernstein, John Cardascia, and Catherine Ross go far beyond merely asserting sex status of defendants as an important variable in processing criminal defendants; they seek to determine how and through what mechanisms sex status affects formal outcomes in the criminal justice system. One of the strengths of their chapter is its examination of the process through which the outcome decisions passed in order to determine if there were any differences by sex. This should serve as the focus of much future study, identifying as it does the critical systemic points at which inputs relevant to institutional discrimination might be made. It remains to be seen whether differential treatment of male and female criminal defendants is justified in light of their differential capacity for rehabilitation, if it is found that they are indeed differentially rehabilitatable.

Shirley Brown presents the results of her research into whether the criminal justice system works to the disadvantage of black persons seeking to be paroled. Among the questions Brown raises is whether the type of facility (custodial or treatment) in which the person has been incarcerated makes a difference on the decision to parole. She considers whether public opinion toward custodial and treatment facilities influences the degree to which the potential parolee is viewed as a threat.

14

Institutional Discrimination in Criminal Justice Processes

Daniel Mendoza de Arce
Omar L. Peraza

When researchers study how and on what basis defendants are sentenced, they commonly "control" for the offense by holding it constant. In doing so, however, they presume that the definition of the crime found on the books is an objective, "factual" account. We propose this is a grievous error, for the presumed identity of the crime lies only in the account of some overt behaviors that have reached the judge—often without the guarantee of the operation of the adversary system. As Quinney (1974, pp. 41–42) suggests, the constructs of the specific offense as well as of the alleged criminal—created and adhered to by court officers—play an important part in subsequent decisions (sentencing, for instance). Therefore the process or the dynamic by which these definitional constructs, which lend meaning to the offense, are developed should be subjected to careful study.

We view this chapter as a pioneering effort that we hope will lead to new discoveries in the field rather than a verification study. Our interest is in the potential effect of racial/ethnic discrimination—intended or unintended—in terms of the input into the decision-making processes in the courts at various formal stages in the processing of the alleged criminal. How, for example, might such intervening variables as the psychological (predispositional) or situational factors serve to inhibit or release discriminatory behavior on the part of social control agents involved in the process? Clearly, then, we believe that although judges may be consistent in the sentencing of cases of "approximately equal gravity" (Green, 1961, p. 99), there is still a strong possibility that serious discriminatory effects are in some sense embedded in the criminal process.

The objectives of this research are (1) to get a general overview of the criminal process in terms of possible discriminatory practices, (2) to learn about the ways cases may get loaded with relatively covert discriminatory practices when they reach decision at each of the formal stages of the criminal process, (3) to investigate the interplay of the psychological to the institutional variables, and (4) to coordinate for these purposes research techniques that have not yet been used together in the literature on the subject.

We then propose a method to analyze the forces that contribute to the shaping of all inputs that affect the final decision-making process in the courts. In this way we can establish the extent to which opposing tendencies, such as those leading to discrimination and those counteracting it, conflict and determine which have the higher probability of dominating. This method should take into account the peculiar social environments of each of these inputs. The next step would be to analyze the weight of each factor in the final sentence decision. No matter how similar or dissimilar the outcomes may be in terms of length of punishment administered, the discriminatory nature of the act could thus be established. Mechanisms are then to be identified to study the processes whereby prejudice—considered as a trait, perhaps normal, embedded in the individual's personality or better as a set of potential definitions of the situation—gets awakened and grows in certain specific networks of social relationships to manifest discrimination.

This conceptualization poses important methodological problems regarding possible sources of discontinuity between the psychological, the social-psychological, and the sociological approaches. When strictly positivistic views are abandoned regarding the first two approaches, qualitative research becomes paramount for the task of tracing the logical-meaningful links between phenomena that will eventually lead to the comprehension of the linkages between statistically found antecedents and their consequences, thereby ruling out many sources of spuriousness and improving our predictive capacity (Mendoza de Arce, 1975, pp. 143–144). Modern sociological research cannot dispense with such theoretical breakthroughs as the phenomenological, the ethnomethodological, and the "hard" symbolic interactionistic, which emphasize respectively the cultural/social construction of reality and meaning and the relative freedom of the subject with regard to his or her own psychological background and the social situations or settings (Mendoza de Arce, 1975, p. 138). An adequate science of the social world must take all this into account. However, scientists in these fields should look for tools in that frontier research carried out by "traditional" social scientists who have used all the safeguards of the positivistic method of validation but who have also shown a sensitivity for the phenomenological world that surrounds the "hard facts" or realities of the scientific world vision.

Besides any measure of *institutional racism* (those processes by which greater burdens are placed on one ethnic population than another such that one population receives far less return per unit of its own psychic, social, political, and economic investments) that U.S. courts may have, they are influenced by environmental sources of discriminatory behavior. There are differential rates of contact with the law enforcement and legal agencies according to ethnic membership; these are a consequence of both push and pull factors.

We conceptualize those factors in two general categories, using the concept of *colony* as defined by Chambliss and Seidman (1971): first, definitions of what is considered proper or

improper behavior held by the police and other officers, which
are in conflict with the culture of the colonized group, especially in the definition of what a "reasonable man" is and what his
behavior would be in any particular situation and, second, lack
of access to resources for those colonial enclaves where the
"middle-class" value system has already, in greater or lesser degree, made its way. These factors introduce discrimination in
the core of the law and in the very heart of the definition of the
particular offense, no matter how faithfully objective and factual the information provided by the agencies about the offense
may be.

The definition of the law as being sometimes discriminatory in both its formulation and its application would entail
a thorough analysis of acculturation and cultural contacts between ethnic communities. Such an analysis would constitute
a precondition for the adequate assessment of the degree of discrimination involved in the application of the law to people in
different cultural contexts. This would require, however, a sys-
tematization of a large body of essentially incomplete and culturally bound data regarding acculturation of ethnic minorities
in the United States. A task of such magnitude does not seem
feasible at this point.

The controversy between the principles of *equity* and
equality helps shed light on the difficult dimension of unintended discrimination. Although subjective intent may not be
present, there is objective intent to discriminate whenever equality is imposed without regard to the particular cultural characteristics created by both history and the operation of the colonial law. Objective intent to discriminate also operates when
equality is imposed together with a rationale that emphasizes
making up for previous disadvantages, that is, *equity*, based on
factors that the metropolis holds as beyond its responsibility.

Decisions in the criminal justice process may be described
according to a basic general schema that includes a measurable
outcome, a person who produces it (group decisions constitute
a negligible part of the penal process), a more or less detailed
written statement that points to the provision of grounds for
the decision, and different formal as well as informal sources of

input. These inputs include written as well as oral accounts by other officers about the defendant and the offense and interventions by "interested persons," the community, and the press (Chambliss and Seidman, 1971, p. 447). The law in the case of the judges and prosecutors, and the scientific and practical knowledge in the case of the probation officers and psychiatrists, provide the general coordinates within which the decision makers exercise discretion. Interpretation of those norms, as well as the discretional activity, are nonetheless regulated by social norms that condition the relationship between all previously mentioned factors as well as their weight in determining the outcome. Institutionalized practices in social interaction engaged in by the different persons involved in the criminal justice process regulate the possible ways the variables related to personality (characterological and personality traits) as well as other psychological factors (value and attitudinal data) will shift from mere potentiality to actuality and the ways and limits of their manifestation in terms of overt discriminatory practice and, at the level of the decisions, differential treatment. The outcome or decision at any stage of the criminal justice process, even in cases where it contains objectively measurable and comparable differential treatment, may be due to different factors.

In the last instance all court decisions are mediated by the personalities of the court officers, including their legal normative orientation, their value orientation (which finds an outlet in the wide discretion they are allowed regarding both the sentence and the reason invoked), the information about the offense and the offender, and the outside pressures (Chambliss and Seidman, 1971, p. 452). Our model emphasizes the prior action of personality factors, considered as a frame of reference to locate the offender and the offense within a set of preexisting actual or potential categories. It also emphasizes the influence of those factors in recorded accounts which are amenable to content analysis with the aid of semantic techniques and which may be considered, to some extent, projective or expressive data and thus amenable to Rokeach's content analysis of values (Rokeach, 1974). These documents, especially important in the case of presentence and other reports by caseworkers for certain fel-

onies, should in turn be reinterpreted according to the normative and value categories of those who write them as well as
those to whom the recommendations are made and should
therefore be also content analyzed according to them. These
factors, together with what may remain of the factual information about both the offense and the offender, the pressure of
outside "interested persons," and public opinion, contribute to
the creation of semantic definitions about both the criminal and
the offense, which contain in various degrees factual elements,
value orientations, and normative orientations. The "discrimination load" may then increase or decrease as a result of the operation of all these forces, always within the limits set up by the
framework of institutional racism.

The relationships between the three categories of factors
involved—namely, the personality traits of the officer, the recorded statement issued, and the decision—may be considered
simultaneous indicators of discrimination, which could result in
a three-value variable on an ordinal scale or in more refined
mathematical expressions. Thus we argue for the testing of the
relationship between the criteria the court officers use to make
their decisions and differential treatment of racial/ethnic minority group defendant cases at the following stages of the penal
process: prosecution (including charges, reductions, and entry
plea), recommendation of probation officer, and sentencing (including granting and length of probation, jail and prison sentences, parole, and revocation of probation and parole).

The Model

From the very first moment the suspect or offender comes
in contact with the law enforcement and criminal justice system,
factual elements about the offense and the criminal (already
containing a certain measure of discrimination) are interpreted
according to the officers' world vision. This encompasses a value
orientation (that may include important prejudicial elements)
and a normative orientation regarding both legal and social
norms, which may also be discriminatory, even in its purely legal
component. This is true because the law itself as a category, its

interpretation and application to the particular case and the latitudes of discretion involved in many bureaucratic decisions, may harbor discriminatory potential. Conformity or deviance from social norms affects the definition of the situation mainly according to the social setting in which the act or decision is performed (Liska, 1974, pp. 261–272). Thus the element of role performance must also be added to the personality and social factors that condition control reactions by agencies.

Thus we contend that future research on racial/ethnic discrimination in the courts should address itself to the analysis of the "factors of criminal prosecution" through both attitude and value tests. Value orientation as part of the court officers' personalities should be measured through multiple-item indicators. We recommend Rokeach's rank-ordering value test (Rokeach, 1974, p. 27) in the cases of judges and prosecutors and content analysis of their written statements. These data should be complemented by semantic differential tests. This will allow us to study not only the psychological conditioning of the courts' decision makers but also their processes of attributing meaning to written statements coming from other sources (that is, presentence reports). Moreover, it should yield a measure of intent to discriminate, if it exists, and should help clarify the mechanisms by which this translates into overt behavior. Unstructured interviews may prove particularly useful in the cases of caseworkers (probation and parole officers) and psychiatrists as an additional tool that may reduce problems arising from the phenomenon of role selection and the intrusion of awareness factors linked to the familiarity of the subject with tests.

We assume that intent to discriminate cannot be measured without taking into account the psychological and connotative meaning of prejudiced attitudes in the subject. This is another way to say that the weight of other attitudes that make up the subject's response capacity must also be measured and correlated to the indicators of prejudice.

The construction of the previously mentioned questionnaire and structured interviews should then be supplemented by instruments scaled according to Osgood's semantic differential techniques (Rokeach, 1974, pp. 49–51) to measure difference in connotative meaning and to provide attitudinal profiles for each work semantically analyzed. Due attention should be paid to concept hierarchies and the thinking process of mediational clustering, that is, what Rokeach (1974, p. 50) has termed "psychological significance" of words understood as a wider type of connotation that refers to other words, attitudes, and values to which the measured word may be related. It seems that in order to uncover the meanings in human discourse the researcher must pay attention to the context of the word. As Rokeach (1974, p. 1339) points out, these questionnaires should be projective tests that illuminate the internal complexity of the subject's mind, not just reactive responses to the external stimulus of the words, and yet have a definite outcome that can be compared.

Self-reports of delinquency organized following the guidelines of Hardt and Bodine (1965) and Clark and Tifft (1966) will be developed to be administered when feasible for the purpose of delineating the factual element of the offense. We assume that its measurement requires the development of highly reliable instruments inasmuch as there are obvious reasons why the "factual element of the offense" will never be completely ascertained. However, a careful analysis of the offender's personality may, to a certain extent, contribute to validate the affirmations contained in the self-report.

The Allport-Vernon-Linzey test (Allport and others, 1960) provides elements that should be used to measure attitude toward the law—which may or may not be based in its underlying values of security and equality—no matter how they may affect the person's other interests and values, such as equity (normative orientation) and its subordination to other value considerations (value orientation). The degree to which equity enters into the decision maker's value system, as well as its forms or meanings, is an important indicator of unintended discriminatory potential. Another important indicator in this context is the subject's knowledge about the history and culture of the ethnic/racial minorities and capacity to understand their psychology. A test can easily be devised to measure this dimension.

The law is just one among the various "surface structures" or norms that give order to social situations and is therefore a part of subjacent latent structures of much wider scope. The world of practices, formal as well as informal, that structures everyday relations in the courts deserves study. The analysis of these practices and the assessment of their importance for a theory of institutional racism may be done with the help of such concepts as "situational patterning" (Kohn and Williams, 1956, pp. 164–174). Situational patterning may affect the expression of prejudice from the very moment the putative offender comes in contact with the law enforcement and court officers, thereby influencing the depiction of the offense as well as the offender. Although, as Green (1961) has observed, many possible verbal and nonverbal expressions of prejudice that are not likely to get expressed in the decisions may take place in face-to-face interaction in court settings, it is important to observe the conditions under which they may actually make their way into the more structured situations surrounding the decisions.

Conclusion

This chapter delineates the contours of an empirical model to measure the nature, scope, and forms of racism within the criminal justice system. It is general and needs elaboration in each of its parts. We hope it will help in assessing the impact of the now voluminous research in the effects of discrimination. Our approach is useful for showing the limitations of the all too familiar procedure some sociologists engage in, namely, computing the amount of variance explained by race/ethnicity without forcing its way into the lower orders in the regression equation, thereby treating race as if it were not related to the other independent variables, or merely computing degrees of disparity in sentencing for specific crimes. Both techniques are misleading inasmuch as they fail to account for the role of discrimination in defining the nature of the offense and the intimate relationships between ethnicity and the other inputs that enter the decision processes. We are interested in equal dispensation of justice and believe that research like that outlined here would result in intervention programs that would reduce variations in treatment and increase the operating efficiency of the courts.

15

Jury Representation by Neighborhood

James M. O'Reilly

A relatively simple and inexpensive method of measuring the racial, ethnic, sex, and class composition of jury systems is needed because (1) the representativeness of juries is of fundamental constitutional and practical importance to the fairness and legitimacy of American justice; (2) the actual degree of representation of major social and demographic groups has only infrequently been measured, even though the available evidence indicates serious underrepresentation of socially disadvantaged groups; and (3) the cost and complexity of the measurement method most often used, the survey, is an important reason so few empirical studies have been done. An inexpensive alternative method of measuring jury representation based on the analysis of representation by residential area, rather than by the individual-level characteristics, is presented. This method is illustrated using data on six North Carolina counties.

Note: The research reported here was supported in part by the Program in Demography and Ecology, Duke University, operating under grant 5T01GM01291 from the NIGMS of the National Institutes of Health and by a grant from the NAACP Legal Defense and Educational Fund, Inc. The author gratefully acknowledges the assistance and advice of Richard T. Campbell, Charles Hirschman, Lawrence Landerman, and Joel Smith.

The Problem

The principle that juries should reflect the social and demographic makeup of their communities is a cornerstone of the American justice system. Representative juries fulfill two key functions in the administration of justice that together serve to legitimate the legal process for both society at large and the defendant. First, by reflecting a broad range of beliefs and opinions spanning the variety of elements that make up the community, the jury is supposed to embody the conscience of the community. Second, by including members with many different backgrounds and points of view, the jury is thought to understand better the context and circumstances of the specific case.

Just what constitutes a representative jury has changed and evolved over the years. The contemporary legal view according to Van Dyke (1977, pp. 12–13) is, "A jury that includes a representative cross-section fulfills the needs of impartiality, reliability, and legitimacy essential to the jury system. Such a system provides a modern definition of 'peer' and 'community' by recognizing that no one should be excluded from jury service on the basis of poverty, race, sex, age, nationality, or religion, and by insisting that all persons be equally represented on jury panels to ensure their impartiality and independence. The Supreme Court first recognized the importance of such a jury in 1940, and it reaffirmed its position 1975 when it declared that 'selection of a petit jury from a representative cross-section of the community is an essential component of the Sixth Amendment right to a jury trial.' "

The practical importance of representative juries to trial outcomes has been demonstrated in a variety of ways. Many experimental studies have found a relationship between the social and psychological characteristic of jurors and their decisions in simulated court cases (Erlanger, 1970, pp. 352–353; Stephan, 1975). More direct evidence of the impact of jury composition is offered by experiences in the city of Baltimore and a large judicial district in Los Angeles. In both cities major changes in the methods of selecting jurors in the early 1970s produced juries that included sharply higher proportions of the poor and minorities. And in both cities conviction rates then dropped substantially (Van Dyke, 1977, pp. 33–34, 375–382). Finally, the importance of jury composition is affirmed regularly in courtrooms as opposing lawyers attempt in *voir dire* to seat on juries people whose personal and demographic characteristics seem most favorable to their side and in the recent increase of systematic jury selection efforts using social science techniques (Berk, Hennessy, and Swan, 1977).

Despite the constitutional and practical importance of representative jury systems, relatively little research has been done to measure the degree of cross-sectional representation of important social and demographic groups. This is especially true of the state court systems, where the bulk of the criminal and civil trials take place. Van Dyke attempted to compile the results of all available state court studies for the period since 1970 from published court reports, case records, and legal and social science journals. His research managed to find only sixty studies involving fifty counties in twenty-five states. These studies in general show sharp underrepresentation of minorities, women, blue-collar workers, the less educated, and persons with low incomes. A similar lack of information existed for the federal court system until Van Dyke obtained the representational figures available from court questionnaires for about two-thirds of the nation's U.S. district courts. The results in the federal courts, whose jury selection methods are often held up as a model, were essentially the same as that of the state courts (Van Dyke, 1977, pp. 293–371). Thus the available evidence indicates to Van Dyke (1977, p. 23) that "most courts in the United States still have a long way to go before truly representative juries are the rule."

Many of the jury studies that have been done grew out of highly publicized "political" cases, such as those of Angela Davis, Joan Little, the Attica Prison inmates, and anti-Vietnam War activists. The principal method for measuring jury representation in such cases, and in most of the lesser-known ones Van Dyke cites, is the sample survey. A random sample of the jury population is drawn and the social and demographic characteristics of each person are determined through a telephone or in-person survey. The proportions of minority, female, young, and lower-class jurors are then compared with the jurisdiction's adult population in those groups shown in the census. Although this method is simple in concept, actually executing a survey of suffi-cient size and quality to be persuasive in court can be quite ex-pensive and demanding. The difficulties in implementing a survey probably explain why they are so rare. However, a relatively sim-ple and inexpensive type of survey of jury representation is pos-sible in some states. Many states, particularly those in the South covered by the Voting Rights Act, keep records of the race, sex, and, at times, ethnicity of all registered voters. Therefore if the voter rolls are the major source for a master jury list, the indivi-dual-level jury representation can be measured by looking up those characteristics on the voter records for a sample of jurors. This method has been used recently for a number of counties in North Carolina and elsewhere. A computer program that takes the census population data and jury counts by race and generates and documents all the needed representation statistics is available from the author.

An examination of the institutional process of jury selec-tion is necessary both to understand why the jury system so of-ten fails to meet its constitutional obligations and to explore how to correct its problems. Three phases of the system are important: the choice of the source lists of names from which to make up the jury pool, the process of excusing and eliminat-ing persons drawn from the jury pool to arrive at the group of persons who show up in court for selection as jurors in specific cases, and the process in court of selecting from among this group the jurors to hear specific cases—the *voir dire* proce-dure. Each element independently and cumulatively affects jury composition.

I shall examine in some detail how the workings of the first two phases may affect the jury participation of the poor, blacks, and other minorities. The kinds of changes in the insti-tutional mechanisms that might improve representation at the source and excusal stages are addressed later. Because the mea-surement method proposed here is less relevant to the *voir dire*

phase, I shall not deal with it other than to point out that
a number of studies have found the pattern of challenges often
also diminishes the representation of the same less-favored
groups (Van Dyke, 1977, pp. 152–160).

Sources

The initial step in jury selection is the creation of a jury
pool or master list of persons eligible for selection as jurors. This
typically involves simply taking one or more broad-based source
list, such as the local voter registration rolls or tax lists, and
deleting those legally ineligible to be jurors: nonresidents, convicted felons, mental incompetents, and so forth. If impartially
administered, this culling procedure usually affects only a relatively small number of people and is not likely to be a major
source of bias in the resulting jury pool.

The representativeness of the sources selected is the
key to the quality of representation in the jury pool (Kairys,
Kadane, and Lehoczky, 1977). Voter lists are the main source
of jurors' names in most states. They are conveniently accessible,
often in computer form, and avoid the bias resulting from such
discretionary methods as the "key-man" system, in which local
leaders propose jurors based on personal acquaintance or subjective judgment (Van Dyke, 1977, pp. 85–88).

The problem is that the poor and minorities are usually
substantially underrepresented on voter lists. The November
1974 Current Population Survey of the Bureau of the Census
found, for example, that nationally underregistration was related, often quite strongly, to being black, of Spanish origin,
under thirty, not being a high school graduate, being unem-
ployed, from a blue-collar occupation, having a low income, and
not being married. The rate of registration for men and women
was essentially the same (U.S. Bureau of the Census, 1976a).

For decades political scientists and sociologists have studied why socially and economically disadvantaged groups register
to vote at lower rates than more favored groups. The explanations offered are quite diverse. They include the economic: Registration and voting impose costs in terms of acquiring information on how elections affect one's interest, and the relative costs

are greater for the less advantaged (Downs, 1957); the psychological: Political interest is a personal characteristic reflecting the salience of politics to one's personality (Campbell, 1966); the sociocultural: Voting activity is a function of the absorption of prevailing civic norms and results from contact with the integrative forces of society (Smith, Turk, and Myers, 1962); the demographic: The poor and minorities change residences more often and have a younger population; and the political: The political system differentially serves the interests of the majority and middle class (Alford and Friedland, 1975).

More representative sources than the voter lists are not easily found, however. Such seemingly broad-based lists as tax rolls, city directories, driver registration lists, and telephone directories also typically contain a built-in bias favoring higher-status groups.

From a constitutional point of view, though, the particular reason a list is unrepresentative is not important. Juries, and therefore their sources, are required to reflect the major segments of the community—whether or not certain groups are easily accessible to the court's administrative apparatus.

Excuses and Attrition

Once the jury pool or master jury list is prepared and a group of persons is selected to serve as jurors for a term, those persons must be induced to serve. This involves first locating and notifying them and then granting or refusing requests to be excused. Each element can alter the makeup of the resulting group of jurors who serve. Very often a substantial part of those called do not end up serving. In the six North Carolina counties studied, 47 to 58 percent of those called did not serve.

Problems of notifying those called depend to a large extent on the currency of addresses on the jury pool source list and on the diligence of court officials in attempting to locate those jurors not found at the address on the source. Voter lists especially may contain names of many persons who have moved since registering to vote without changing their address or re-registering. Attempts to summon those persons will then be problematic. This may differentially dilute the representation of blacks and other minorities particularly. Blacks are less likely to register in the first place, so they are less likely to reregister; yet blacks are more likely to need to reregister because they have higher rates of intracounty migration than whites (Simmons, 1968). Out-of-date sources also will contain the names of many deceased and not contain those persons who recently moved into the community or new adults.

Thus the seeming level of representation on a jury list based on out-of-date sources may be higher than the level of the group in the pool actually available for service. In the six North Carolina counties many of the persons picked from the jury pool could not be located. This pattern was especially strong in counties that relied most heavily on the voter list, which is updated only every four years. Counties using the personal property tax list, which is updated yearly, showed a lower proportion of jurors called who were not found.

Excuses also produce sizable attrition. In principle the courts permit a person to be excused from jury duty because of ill health or severe personal or economic inconvenience. In practice many courts grant almost any request, often reasoning that anyone who does not want to be a juror would be a poor juror if forced to serve. This, of course, denies the principle that jury service is a universal obligation of citizenship.

Two reasons probably account for most efforts to be excused: the costs in money and in time. Most states pay jurors less than $15 a day, an hourly rate less than the minimum wage. For an employed person the cost of a typical jury term of a few weeks can thus be substantial. It is not uncommon for some employers to make up all or part of the difference between jury pay and normal wages, but studies show that such policies are most likely to apply to higher-level employees and to workers in unionized industries (Van Dyke, 1977, pp. 112–118). Not only are blue-collar and service workers less likely to have their lost pay made up, but for those in nonunion and small firms absence from work for jury duty may mean losing one's job.

The time required for jury duty affects the total economic cost for the employed as well as the amount of personal inconvenience for the rest. Jury terms vary widely from state to state, ranging from one to two days in Texas to three months or more in a number of states. The typical term is between two weeks and a month (Van Dyke, 1977, pp. 116–118). A study for the National Institute of Law Enforcement and Criminal Justice (1974, pp. 6–7) concluded that lengthy jury terms were a major cause of evading and being excused from jury service, thus restricting the representativeness of juries and often producing a pattern of "professional jurors."

Overall, then, it seems that at both these institutional phases of the jury selection system substantial underrepresentation of the less-advantaged tends to be built into the process. The poor and minorities are underrepresented in the sources, and then they are forced to bear a heavier relative, if not absolute, cost in order to serve.

Measuring Jury Composition by Residential Area

The following is an alternative to the survey method for measuring the jury representation of four frequently underrepresented groups—blacks, lower socioeconomic groups, persons of Spanish origin, and women. Except in its application to women, this method is based on an elementary pattern of American society, namely, the residential segregation of the races, classes, and ethnic groups. The strength and persistence of residential segregation means that knowing where a person lives also describes with reasonable accuracy that person's race, class, and ethnic background. Therefore a systematic examination of the distribution of jurors by neighborhood can reveal the makeup of the jury system for those characteristics that differentiate neighborhoods.

The logic of this approach is as follows: (1) A jury system made up of a cross section of the community is one in which every eligible person has an equal chance of being selected. (2) Because residence bears no relationship to eligibility, jurors should be distributed in proportion to an area's population of eligible persons. (3) The difference between an area's actual number of jurors and the number it should have based on its proportion of eligible persons measures the degree to which the jury system fails to resemble the community cross section. (4) The extent of concentration of specific social and demographic groups in over- or underrepresented areas indicates the degree of proportional representation of those groups in the jury system.

Put less formally, this method begins by locating the census tracts in which a random sample of jurors live. The number of jurors in each tract is then compared with the number each tract would be expected to have based on its proportion of the total area's adult population eligible for jury service. A rate of representation for each tract is then computed by subtracting the expected from the observed number of jurors and then dividing by the expected to get the percentage of over- and under-representation weighted for the tract's population size. For example, a tract containing 10 percent of the jurisdiction's eligible population would be expected to have one hundred jurors in a jury sample of one thousand. If only fifty jurors in the sample were found to live in that tract, its rate of representation would be –50 percent (50 minus 100) divided by 100 equals –50 percent). Finally, the rates of representation of all tracts are examined for their relationship to other tract characteristics, such as degree of black, Spanish-heritage, or low-income concentration. This permits an interpretation of the "ecological" or aggregate representation of the poor or minorities on juries.

Census tracts are subareas of Standard Metropolitan Statistical Areas (SMSA) with an average population of about four thousand. They were created to provide comparable statistics for small, neighborhood-sized units of metropolitan areas. Census tracts are an appropriate unit for this type of investigation because in urban areas particularly they delineate the prevailing pattern of residential segregation of the races, ethnic groups, and economic classes with substantial accuracy. That in fact is the major criterion for their definition. According to the U.S. Bureau of the Census (1970b, p. 86), "tracts are originally designed to be relatively homogeneous with respect to population characteristics, economic status and living conditions."

Because this method allows all the data to be collected from the jury records without contacting and interviewing individual jurors, measuring jury composition is substantially faster and cheaper than surveys. The only information to be collected are jury lists from official court files and tract characteristics from published census reports. The plotting of juror addresses by census tract can be done using maps, directories, or geographic computer files available from the Census Bureau or in public libraries.

A second advantage is that jury lists usually include information on the persons summoned for jury services (jurors called) and whether those persons actually showed up at the courthouse for jury service (jurors served). The representation of jurors called will describe closely the sources used in making up the jury pool; the representation of jurors served measures the output end of the process, the legally and practically more important group of persons available to be seated on individual juries. Differences between the representation of jurors called and jurors served will indicate, at least roughly, how the intermediate administrative procedures dealing with excuses and failure to find persons drawn from the pool affect jury composition. The study of this intermediate process often can be further refined because the court records frequently contain information on why jurors failed to serve: whether they were excused, for what reason, or if they were not found. Thus the impact of the granting of excuses and the quality of the source list addresses on representation can be examined.

Tract measurement, however, also imposes some limitations that surveys do not. Most important is that only characteristics varying appreciably from tract to tract can be used to explain underrepresentation of tracts. For example, because the age structure does not usually differ much between tracts, there is no way to detect underrepresentation of young people or of the elderly even though most survey investigations have found substantial underrepresentation of both (Van Dyke, 1977, pp. 35–39). Sex, although similarly invariant between tracts, is not a problem because the sex of individual jurors can be determined from the first name or honorific on the jury lists. Because the honorific is not always available, a test was run on the accuracy of predicting sex from only the first name using a sample of 298 Durham, North Carolina, registered voters; 286 (96 percent) were correctly predicted.

The tract method also raises questions about the quality of the census data—whether they are accurate initially and whether population shifts since 1970 render them seriously inaccurate years later. These questions were examined in detail. The overall conclusion is that neither the undercount of certain groups nor the passage of time in most cases invalidates tract findings of jury underrepresentation among the disadvantaged.

Another limitation is that the method can only be applied to the 237 SMSAs tracted for the 1970 census. However, for most potential applications this is not a major problem because 70 percent of the U.S. population in 1970 and even higher proportions of the black and Spanish-heritage populations lived in SMSAs.

The method as applied to measuring the representation of blacks, the poor, and women in North Carolina would be equally useful for the study of representation of Mexican Americans, Cuban Americans, and Puerto Ricans in metropolitan areas where they constitute a substantial part of the population. There is good reason to do so because in general persons of Spanish origin are even less likely than blacks to be included on the primary source of jury pools, the voter registration rolls. The 1974 Current Populations Survey found that nationally only 35 percent of adults of Spanish origin were registered to vote, compared to 62 percent of all adults and 55 percent of blacks (U.S. Bureau of the Census, 1976a).

The same census tract data used for the North Carolina investigation are available for persons of Spanish heritage in either printed volumes or on the computer summary tapes. One important additional factor should be taken into account, however. Many persons of Spanish origin are not citizens and therefore not eligible to vote or to serve on juries. In 1974 only about 1 percent of the black and non-Spanish white adults said they were not citizens, but 26 percent of the Spanish-origin adults said they were not citizens (U.S. Bureau of the Census, 1976a). Therefore the best estimate of the population actually qualified for jury service would be the group of adult citizens not living in institutional quarters. Fortunately, the adult citizen population is tabulated by tract on the computer summary tapes, and that group could be multiplied by the proportion of the tract's population not living in institutions to get the qualified population. Finally, interpreting individual-level relationships from aggregate data presents special problems.

Analyzing Tract Data

Tract measurement creates difficulties in analyzing area representational patterns so that the actual participation of major groups of the community are clearly described. There are two important issues there. First, what kinds of statistical conclusions can one make about, say, the jury representation of blacks or the poor from the relationship of representation rates and the social and demographic makeup of the tracts? Second, how can the statistical findings be presented with sufficient clarity so that lay persons can comprehend the nature and magnitude of the measured pattern?

Statistical Conclusions

The question of the kind of inferences that are justified about groups and individuals from aggregate, area data arises because the measurement level does not directly correspond to the substantive level of concern. As Robinson (1950) demonstrated, the correlation of a relationship measured at the aggregate level is often much greater than the corresponding one between individuals who make up the aggregate. This is because aggregate or ecological correlations depend on the marginal frequencies of the within-area correlations but the individual correlations depend on the internal frequencies of the within-area correlations. Grouping by area therefore often masks the within-group variation and may spuriously raise the measured relationship. According to Hannan (1971, p. 5), Robinson's conclusion that ecological correlations cannot be substituted for unavailable individual-level measures "has become firmly entrenched in the methodological canon."

However, subsequent methodological investigation has demonstrated some procedures and conditions under which aggregate data can be used confidently to address relationships at the individual level. Duncan and Davis (1953) showed that a systematic examination of the marginals of aggregate cross classification can produce absolute upper and lower bounds on the individual-level correlations. These upper and lower limits become increasingly narrow as the area units used become smaller. Goodman (1953, 1959) expanded the methods of obtaining bounds and demonstrated that under certain conditions linear regression techniques at the aggregate level can provide unbiased estimates of the individual-level relationships. According to Hannan (1971, p. 67), Goodman's procedure "may not be overly problematic if we can assure ourselves that only independent variables were manipulated in the grouping process." Blalock (1964) also showed that a key consideration in using linear regression is how the grouping procedure affects the variation in the dependent variable.

Hannan presents the most recent and comprehensive investigation of the problems of aggregation bias and cross-level inference, drawing on the work of sociologists and economists. Hannan's conclusion relevant to the method of tract-level analysis of jury representation are that regression estimates are likely to be unbiased by the use of aggregate data if (1) the grouping procedure does not systematically manipulate the variation in the dependent variable, (2) the grouping procedure does not systematically confound the variation in two or more conceptually distinct independent variables, and (3) the relations involved are linear both at the individual and aggregate levels.

How well does the tract-level measurement technique satisfy the conditions demanded for use of linear regression with aggregate data? Concerning the effect of tract measurement on the dependent variable, the misrepresentation rates, there seems to be no reason the area unit should affect the rates of representation. The rates are based on the areas' proportion of the eligible population, which is a standard used by the Supreme Court (Van Dyke, 1977, p. 60). The issue of confounding conceptually distinct independent variables is not a problem because it is primarily simple bivariate relationships one is interested in—namely, are blacks, the poor, or persons of Spanish heritage substantially underrepresented? However, confounding can become troublesome when one tries to answer more subtle questions, such as the magnitude of the independent effect of an explanatory variable net of the effect of other variables. Very often with aggregate data there is a high degree of intercorrelation among social and demographic characteristics that makes it difficult to disentangle the independent impact of specific variables.

The question of linearity can be answered only by examining a specific empirical situation. For the six North Carolina counties already analyzed, the relationships of percentage black and percentage of families with incomes below the poverty line were generally linear with respect to representation rates. Of twenty-eight separate bivariate regressions five showed nonlinearity significant at the .05 level when the independent variable was squared and added to the equation. Fortunately, simpler statistical measures often can be used to supplement the regression results if nonlinearity seems to be a potential problem. These procedures will be covered in the next section.

In general, then, the tract method of jury analysis seems to meet the major conditions required for using linear regression to infer the individual representation. But one other feature of aggregate analysis needs to be mentioned. Hannan (1971) points out that the variance of the aggregate regression coefficients will be greater than that of the corresponding individual-level estimates in proportion to the ratio of the within-group variation relative to the between-group variation of the independent variable. Thus the greater the within-tract homogeneity of an explanatory variable, such as the proportion black or poor, the greater the confidence one can have in the estimated magnitude of the relationship with the dependent variable. Therefore the regression measures of the misrepresentation of blacks should be more precise than for socioeconomic groups. A number of studies have confirmed that blacks in urban areas are segregated to a very high degree (Taeuber and Taeuber, 1965; Van Valey, Roof, and Wilcox, 1977). Residential segregation by education, occupation, or income, although not as intense as that by race, is still sizable and consistent among at least the larger cities (Farley, 1977).

Clarifying the Findings

Although regression coefficients provide valid measures of jury representation, their lack of intuitive meaning to persons not versed in statistics creates a problem when the purpose of the investigation is to persuade judges, court officials, or other policymakers that there may be serious faults in the jury system. A regression analysis of the relationship between the percentage of blacks in the tracts and jury representation will state that as a tract's percentage black increases by X percent, representation decreases by Y percent, with a given margin of error. But such precise statistical statements are often mistakenly viewed, even by the U.S. Supreme Court, as of little relevance to the substantive issue of the degree to which faults in a jury system threaten a defendant's chances for a fair trial and due process (Finklestein, 1966).

The challenge then is to present the findings in simple and nontechnical terms. The principal approach I used in the analysis of six North Carolina counties begins with simple tables of misrepresentation rates by categories of the explanatory variables, such as percentage black or poor, in order to show the pattern of the relationship found in the regression analysis. The misrepresentation rate gives the relative probability of being included in a jury population for residents of different areas. Thus if the misrepresentation rate for tracts that are more than 40 percent black is –33 percent, those resident are one-third less likely to be jurors than the average person in the jurisdiction. Van Dyke (1977) and Kairys, Kadane, and Lehoczky (1977) agree that this rate is the proper legal and mathematical measure of jury representation.

The second step attempts to show the substantive impact of the misrepresentation rates on juries and the groups in question. Although this cannot be shown with a single number with tract data, an accurate sense of the situation can be gained, particularly for highly segregated groups such as blacks and probably the Spanish population, by some simple statistics. Within categories of the explanatory variable the proportion of the total group in the jurisdiction is computed along with the proportion of persons in the category who are members of the group. For example, a table showing that the area's tracts that are more than 40 percent black are underrepresented in the jury pool by –33 percent indicates that a serious problem may exist in the cross-sectional representation of the jury system, but it does not tell the practical magnitude of the problem for blacks. However, if it is also pointed out that those tracts as a group are 80 percent black and they contain three-quarters of the county's total adult black population eligible for jury service, then a much stronger case is made that black underrepresentation materially affects jury makeup. A number of variations on this approach to illustrating the findings are possible, depending on the nature of the issue at hand.

Jury Representation in Six North Carolina Counties

I applied the previously described method to six large urban counties in North Carolina to examine the jury composition for the 1974–1975 judicial biennium. The counties and their principal cities are Cumberland (Fayetteville), Durham (Durham), Forsyth (Winston-Salem), Guilford (Greensboro), Mecklenburg (Charlotte), and Wake (Raleigh). They contain 28 percent of the state's population and 30 percent of the black population. Random samples of from five hundred to nine hundred names from jury records were obtained from the courts. The addresses were located by tract for more than 95 percent of the samples in the six counties.

An important feature of these data is that the sources used to make up the two-year jury pools covered by the samples varied from county to county. North Carolina law requires that both the voter list and the county personal property tax list be used, at least minimally, as sources. The proportions of each used and the decision to draw on other sources, however, are left to the local officials. In each county for the period covered by these data only the two legally required sources were used. The proportion of voter and tax names used varied widely. For the five counties where it was possible from official records to determine the proportions used, the ratio of voter to tax names was Durham, nine voter to ninety-one tax; Forsyth, eighty-nine to eleven; Guilford, forty-eight to fifty-two; Mecklenburg, ninety-four to six; and Wake, ninety-nine to one.

As noted earlier, sex is the only juror characteristic that could be determined at the individual level from the jury list. Across the six counties no systematic pattern of representation by sex was found either among the jurors called or among those who actually served. In four counties (Forsyth, Guilford, Mecklenburg, and Wake) the differences between the percentage female of the total adult population in the 1970 census and the percentage female in the jury samples ranged from +2 percent to –4 percent for jurors called and from +2 to –6 percent in jurors served. The other two counties did have substantial deviations from the countywide female proportions. Durham had a lower proportion of women than expected in both the jury pool and the group of jurors served, by –13 and –19 percent, respectively; for Cumberland the corresponding figures were +10 percent in jurors called and +17 percent in jurors served, even when the Fort Bragg military area was excluded.

No simple explanation is apparent for the Durham and Cumberland findings. The substantial underrepresentaion of women in Durham is most likely linked to the heavy use of the tax list as a source because in many husband-wife households taxable property is listed under the husband's name only. The lack of a parallel pattern in Guilford, where half the names came from the tax list, suggests that this explanation alone is not sufficient. Interpreting the overrepresentation of women for Cumberland is even more difficult because we do not know the source proportions and because of the strong likelihood of local anomalies due to the dominating presence of the Fort Bragg military installation.

The findings on the degree of area or tract representation for jurors called and jurors served for the six counties individually and for the six as a group are given in Table 1. The chi-square statistic measures the likelihood of the observed pattern

Table 1. Chi-Square Values for Jury Representation by Tracts in Six North Carolina Counties, 1974–1975

	Cumberland	Durham	Forsyth	Guilford	Mecklenburg	Wake	Total
Jurors called	202	121	105	151	177	154	910
Jurors served	121	92	80[a]	96[b]	105[a]	76[a]	569
Tracts	37	34	59	78	75	55	338

Note: A significant chi-square value means the pool of jurors (called or served) is not representative of all tracts (neighborhoods) in the country.

[a] Statistically significant at .05 level.

[b] Not significant at the .05 level. All other values significant at the .01 level.

of jurors occurring if the jury system reasonably reflected the geographic distribution of the population. The statistic is computed by squaring the difference of the observed minus the expected, then dividing the expected and summing over all tracts.

The expected number of jurors for each tract was computed by taking the tract's proportion of the county's total noninstitutional population eighteen years and older and multiplying by the number of persons in the sample. The noninstitutional population was used rather than the full adult population because it drops from consideration persons living in prisons, college dormitories, military quarters, and other institutions. Such persons are likely to be either not permanent residents of the county or not qualified for jury duty for other reasons. Failure to drop the institutional populations can inflate measures of misrepresentation in areas containing colleges with sizable dormitory populations or military bases (Taeuber and Taeuber, 1965, p. 229).

As indicated in Table 1, the chances are less than one in a hundred that the jury pools in these six counties are geographically representative. Adequate representation of jurors served for five of the six counties and overall is also quite unlikely, with two counties showing probabilities of less than .01 and for three more between .01 and the customary level of statistical significance of .05. Only with the jurors served group in Guilford is the probability greater than .05 that the geographical pattern is representative.

The fact of geographic misrepresentation is significant because, as mentioned earlier, a community's major social and demographic groups generally live in different areas. Therefore unequal area representation suggests that important segments of the community are not equally included in the jury populations.

The relationship of race and poverty to jury misrepresentation was measured by the regression of tracts' rates of representation of the percentage black of the track adult noninstitutional population and on the percentage families in the tract with incomes below the poverty line. As is evident from Table 2, race and poverty are negatively related to the level of representation in every county for both jurors called and jurors served.

Table 2. Regression Results of the Effects of Tract Percent Black (Black) and Percent of Families with Incomes Below the Poverty Line (Poverty) on Rates of Jury Representation in Census Tracts for Six North Carolina Counties, 1974–1975

	Cumberland	Durham	Forsyth	Guilford	Mecklenburg	Wake	Total
			Jurors Called				
Black							
b	-.39	-.69	-.39	-.47	-.64	-.46	-.51
	(.36)	(.19)	(.18)	(.22)	(.14)	(.24)	(.08)
Beta	-.18	-.53	-.29	-.24	-.48	-.26	-.32
R^2	.03	.28	.08	.06	.23	.07	.11
Poverty							
b	-1.4	-2.3	-1.0	-2.6	-1.8	-1.5	-1.6
	(.77)	(.46)	(.58)	(.80)	(.36)	(.59)	(.23)
Beta	-.30	-.66	-.22	-.35	-.50	-.34	-.35
R^2	.09	.43	.05	.12	.25	.12	.12
			Jurors Served				
Black							
b	-.68	-.55	-.36	-.36	-.46	-.59	-.46
	(.48)	(.23)	(.20)	(.23)	(.16)	(.27)	(.09)
Beta	-.23	-.40	-.23	-.18	-.32	-.28	-.26
R^2	.05	.16	.05	.03	.10	.08	.07
Poverty							
b	-2.1	-1.9	-1.5	-2.2	-1.8	-1.6	-1.7
	(1.0)	(.57)	(.63)	(.84)	(.40)	(.70)	(.26)
Beta	-.33	-.51	-.31	-.29	-.46	-.30	-.33
R^2	.11	.26	.09	.08	.21	.09	.11

Notes: Standard errors of the coefficients are in parentheses; b represents unstandardized regression coefficients; Beta represents standardized regression coefficients.

The unstandardized regression coefficients, the b's, indicate the percentage point change in the representation rate associated with a 1 percent change in the percentage black or percentage in poverty. Thus in the first column of row 1 the regression coefficient of percentage black in Cumberland means that as percentage black increases by 1 percent the rate of representation of tract residents in the jury pool drops by nearly .4 percent. Viewed in a slightly different way, this coefficient means that an all-black tract in Cumberland is likely to have a rate of representation among jurors called that is 39 percent lower than an all-white tract. It is clear then that black underrepresentation in both the jury pool and among jurors who served is sizable and fairly consistent from county to county. As shown by the total column for the six counties taken together, all-black tracts in North Carolina's major urban counties are likely to have a 51 percent lower rate of representation in the jury pool and a 46 percent lower rate among the jurors served compared with all-white tracts. Five of the twenty-eight linear regressions reported in Table 2 showed significant nonlinearity when the independent variables were squared and added to the equation: jurors called on poverty for Mecklenburg, Wake, and total and on percentage black for Mecklenburg, and jurors served on poverty for total. In each case the nonlinear pattern consisted of sharply falling representation rates until the tracts' percentage of families living in poverty or percentage black reached about 20 percent and a flat or mildly negative relationship thereafter. To simplify the presentation of the North Carolina examples, subsequent analyses of these nonlinearities using alternative functional forms are omitted. The linear coefficients, although less precise in these three instances, still reasonably summarize the overall relationship.

The regression coefficients of poverty indicate that in the six counties together high-poverty tracts (those with more than 25 percent of the families with incomes below the poverty line) are underrepresented by −27 percent in both jurors called and jurors served compared with nonpoverty tracts. The smallest level of underrepresentation of high-poverty tracts is −25 percent in jurors called in Forsyth and the largest is −65 percent in jurors called in Guilford. It is interesting to note that although the chi-square test of geographical representation of jurors served in Guilford is not significant, the negative relationships of race and poverty for jurors served in Guilford are both substantial. All-black tracts are underrepresented by –36 percent compared to all-white tracts, and high-poverty tracts by –55 percent compared to nonpoverty tracks. Aggregate data such as those used here complicate the problem of statistical inference. Significance levels as reported directly in Table 1, and by way of the standard errors of the regression coefficients in Table 2, are based on assumptions of simple random sampling. Yet the estimates of representation in both tables are based on far more information than the simple number of tracts in a county. For example, in Guilford the chi-square measure of geographic representation of jurors called and jurors served all just barely fail to attain conventional significance levels based on seventy-seven degrees of freedom, the number of tracts minus one. However, the distribution of jurors is based on 685 observations for the called and 285 for the served, and the information on percentage black is from the census of the whole population, not a sample. Thus these departures from the normal assumptions mean that the reliability of the estimates are far greater than the ordinary significance tests indicate. This is supported for Guilford by Table 3. The thirteen nearly all-black tracts, which contain 74 percent of the county's adult blacks, are underrepresented by –31 percent in jurors called and –30 percent in jurors served. This indicates a far different pattern of black jury representation from one suggested by a rigid interpretation of the regression standard errors, which would say that one cannot reject the hypothesis that there is no relationship between jury representation and the tract's proportion black. For these reasons the interpretations of the regression coefficients are based on the far more reasonable assumption that all the statistical estimates are reliable both in terms of the direction and the magnitude of the substantive relations.

At this point the major pattern of representation of blacks and the poor in both the jury pools and jurors served is clear. Underrepresentation of both groups is substantial for each

Table 3. Rates of Jury Representation for Six North Carolina Counties, 1974–1975, by Category of Tract Percent Black, in Percentages

Percent Black	Cumberland	Durham	Forsyth	Guilford	Mecklenburg	Wake	Total
0–1	(4)	(2)	(23)	(24)	(31)	(13)	(97)
Called	49	20	17	7	20	31	19
Served	68	4	24	18	17	28	23
1–5	(5)	(7)	(10)	(14)	(6)	(11)	(53)
Called	60	13	–6	15	17	22	16
Served	61	19	–14	11	–5	24	13
5–15	(5)	(6)	(11)	(19)	(7)	(12)	(60)
Called	–24	28	–4	5	10	–5	2
Served	–45	29	–9	–3	–6	–8	–5
15–40	(16)	(8)	(2)	(8)	(11)	(10)	(55)
Called	–13	7	–38	4	–31	–34	–17
Served	–13	–3	–52	3	–26	–28	–17
40–100	(7)	(11)	(13)	(13)	(20)	(9)	(73)
Called	–6	–37	–18	–31	–35	–16	–27
Served	–10	–32	–20	–30	–20	–17	–23
Percent black in 40–100% black tracts	77	80	90	80	84	83	83
Percent of country's eligible blacks in 40–100% black tracts	45	75	87	74	77	53	70

Note: Number of tracts in each category in parentheses.

of these large urban counties. Now we turn to the related but secondary issues of the relative effects of race and poverty and the possible impact of differences between counties in their choice of jury pool sources.

Examining Table 2 again for jurors called, it seems evident from the standardized regression coefficients (Beta) that the absolute level of black underrepresentation was not especially influenced by the source used. Durham and Mecklenburg show an equally strong negative effect of percentage black, and Mecklenburg used predominantly the voter list as a source while Durham relied equally heavily on the tax list. The three other counties for which we have information on the source mix also had similar weaker direct effects for race; and two, Forsyth and Wake, used mostly voter names while Guilford took equally from the two sources.

The absolute level of jury pool underrepresentation of the poor, however, is appreciably greater in the two counties using names primarily from the tax lists compared to the three counties relying mainly on the voter list. This is not surprising even though every adult in the state is required to register for the personal property tax each year. The poor who do not own real estate or a car generally owe little or nothing in taxes; therefore there is no practical reason for them to register and no incentive for tax officials to seek out the unregistered. For those who own homes or vehicles, however, accurate records are kept to ensure they register and pay taxes.

Looking at changes in representation between the called and served stages for each county in Table 2, one finds that for blacks underrepresentation declined modestly at the served level in three counties, increased in two, and was unchanged in the other. For poverty tracts, underrepresentation declined in two, increased in two, and was unchanged in two. Although no clear pattern related to the source mix is evident, these changes support the case for examining both the called and served groups. It is reasonable to expect that the intermediate institutional phase might be particularly important where the jury pool is fairly representative because then there would be more of the disadvantaged facing the economic burdens of service. Furthermore, the fact that the two phases—the picking of sources and excuses and failing to find jurors called—are related and to some degree may interact does not mean that improvements in one phase without changes in the other will be futile. These data suggest that a major part of any representation gain in the jury pools would probably be transmitted through to better representation of jurors served.

Overall these regression results indicate that of the two legally required sources in North Carolina, the voter list is the better one, but only in a highly qualified sense. The voter list's principal virtue is that it seems to underrepresent the poor somewhat less than the tax list while being no worse than the tax list in excluding blacks. Both do an equally dismal job representing blacks.

Although questions on the relative effect of poverty and race and the way the effects seemed to have been created are important, they should not be allowed to obscure the central fact revealed by Table 2: Juries in North Carolina's most populous counties do not faintly resemble the community cross sections required by the Supreme Court for the elementary constitutional right to a fair trial by a jury of one's peers. Tables 3 and 4 provide a better sense of just how substantial the impact is of this pattern on jury representation.

Table 3 gives the percentage over- and underrepresentation in the six counties and overall for five levels of percentage black in the tracts. The pattern closely parallels that found in the regression analysis. All-white and predominantly white tracts are sizably overrepresented and predominantly black tracts are heavily underrepresented. Of most significance, however, are the last two lines, which show that, with the exception of Cumberland and Wake, more than three quarters of the total eligible black population in the counties lives in the heavily underrepresented tracts that are more than 40 percent black; and these tracts are almost completely made up of blacks. Thus in Durham 75 percent of the county's eligible blacks live in eleven tracts whose population is 80 percent black, and those tracts are underrepresented by –37 percent in jurors called and by –32 percent in jurors served.

Table 4. Rates of Jury Representation for Six North Carolina Counties, 1974-1975, by Category of Tract Percent of Families with Incomes Below the Poverty Level, Percentages

Percent Poverty	Cumberland	Durham	Forsyth	Guilford	Mecklenburg	Wake	Total
0–5	(0)	(6)	(13)	(23)	(31)	(16)	(89)
Called	—	15	25	24	27	39	27
Served	—	11	25	26	22	37	25
5–10	(7)	(10)	(25)	(28)	(16)	(15)	(101)
Called	13	24	5	10	-4	4	8
Served	17	29	12	8	-10	1	9
10–15	(9)	(7)	(5)	(16)	(9)	(7)	(53)
Called	12	2	-26	-31	-51	-19	-20
Served	6	-9	-46	-26	-37	-16	-20
15–25	(11)	(4)	(7)	(6)	(5)	(8)	(41)
Called	5	-17	-26	-20	-29	-40	-19
Served	12	-15	-23	-34	-0	-36	-14
25+	(10)	(7)	(9)	(5)	(14)	(9)	(54)
Called	-15	-56	-27	-46	-42	-23	-33
Served	-27	-52	-43	-39	-40	-18	-36
Percent poverty in 25+ poverty tracts	37	34	39	33	37	33	35
Percent of total county poverty families in 25+ tracts	34	39	37	20	41	38	35

Note: Number of tracts in each category in parentheses.

In the six counties as a group more than two thirds of the eligible blacks live in the seventy-three tracts with virtually all-black populations (83 percent black), and these neighborhoods are underrepresented in jurors called by -27 percent and in jurors served by -23 percent.

The parallel relationship of poverty and representation is given in Table 4. Low-poverty tracts are consistently and heavily overrepresented and high-poverty ones are heavily underrepresented. For the six counties as a group, high-poverty areas, that is, those with more than 25 percent of the families in poverty, are underrepresented by -33 percent in jurors called and -36 percent in jurors served.

In summary, the following conclusions are justified concerning jury representation in the six counties for the 1974–1975 judicial biennium: (1) Blacks and the poor are consistently and substantially underrepresented in both the jury pools and jury boxes in every county. (2) The primary reason for this underrepresentation is the sources used to make up the jury pool, the voter registration and personal property tax lists. (3) Neither list, by itself or combined, reasonably reflects the community cross section.

Conclusion

In this chapter I sought to demonstrate a relatively convenient and simple method for measuring jury representation. The need for such a method and for investigations of jury makeup in the multitude of U.S. court systems is obvious, given the evidence of widespread and serious underrepresentation of socially disadvantaged groups. It is members of just those groups, of course, who most frequently find their futures in the hands of the disproportionately white, middle-class, and middle-aged juries. The previously mentioned experiences in Baltimore and Los Angeles in which substantially improved jury representation produced dramatic declines in conviction rates demonstrates that jury representation is not an idle or abstract issue.

Clearly, the most effective way to change this situation is not to rely on the scrupulousness and vigor of judges and court administrators in living up to their responsibilities. Rather, the resources and tools to challenge the current system must be placed in the hands of those being injured. That is the purpose of the method presented here.

Challenging the judicial system to recognize the failure of its jury selection process is fundamental. But at the same time this raises the question of just how to change the sources and administrative arrangements. A detailed examination of these issues is included in Van Dyke (1977). A few points can be briefly made here drawing on Van Dyke (1977), Kairys, Kadane, and Lehoczky (1977), and my own experience in the area.

First, better sources than the voter and tax lists must be developed. Although such alternatives to the voter lists as city directories, telephone directories, or lists of licensed drivers all are likely to contain major errors in coverage that create bias against the disadvantaged, their biases most likely do not all cut along the same lines. Thus the combining of a number of broad-based lists would likely result, after duplicates are eliminated, in the representation of greater proportions of the disadvantaged than any list would by itself. Such a method was used in Denver County, Colorado, in 1974. The total voter, drivers license, and city directory lists were combined and duplicate names eliminated by computer. The result was a master list twice the size of the voter list and substantially larger than either of the other two lists (Van Dyke, 1977, pp. 102–103). Although no study was apparently done to determine if the resulting master list significantly improved representation, it seems quite reasonable to assume it did because the final list much more closely approached the total number of eligible adults in the population. Such a procedure seems quite promising, especially in medium and larger cities where such lists are likely to be computerized.

Second, efforts must be made to reduce the impact of excuses and the failure to locate persons selected from the jury pool. The sacrifice jurors must make to serve, both in money and time, must be reduced. Not only should juror pay be raised to more realistic levels, but legal and other measures are needed to guarantee that jury service does not cost an individual his or her job and to encourage or require employers to make up the

Discrimination in Organizations

difference between jury pay and normal wages. Briefer jury terms will reduce both the economic and noneconomic burdens of jury service. The National Institute of Law Enforcement and Criminal Justice (1974) recommends a number of methods for selecting and summoning jurors that make terms of one week or less administratively feasible. Shorter terms, according to the institute, "make it possible for more people to participate as jurors and to serve with less personal disruption. They are also less likely to become 'professional jurors'" (pp. 6-7). The institute's manual on jury administrative procedures also describes a number of specific ways to reduce the confusion, waiting, and herding of jurors that make service personally distasteful for many. Not only must the individual burdens be ameliorated, but judges and other court officials who dispense the excuses must become aware of the impact of the casual granting of excuses from service. Jury duty, as the name suggests, is not a voluntary service but an obligation of citizenship that courts need to ensure is borne equally and equitably by all.

Finally, court systems routinely need to collect and make public data on the makeup of juries on all relevant social and demographic dimensions so that less direct measurement methods are not needed.

16

Defendant's Sex and Criminal Court Decisions

~~~~~~~~~~~~~~~~~~~~~~~~~~

Ilene Nagel Bernstein
John Cardascia
Catherine E. Ross

Since the onset of the women's liberation movement, social science has witnessed the proliferation of empirical research focusing on sex differences in the variety of phenomena being investigated (Hochschild, 1973; Rosenberg and Bergstrom, 1975). The rationale for this new focus is that most prior research is limited to male samples (Holmes and Jorgensen, 1971). Thus the possibility of discovering differences in patterns of results by sex is often precluded (Hochschild, 1973). Furthermore, it is assumed that in many areas of social life sex differences

Note: Partial support for this research was provided by a Daniel and Florence Guggenheim Research Fellowship to Ilene Nagel Bernstein during her residence at Yale Law School. We would like to thank the Vera Institute of Justice for making these data available and Richard Berk, Sheldon Stryker, and Austin Turk for comments on earlier drafts.

manifest themselves in discriminatory practices, which are presumed to result in women being treated disadvantageously solely because of their sex. The question is not just whether differential treatment exists but also the degree to which it results in outcomes disadvantageous to women.

In criminology, Ward, Jackson, and Ward (1969), Babcock (1973), Brodsky (1975), Simon (1975b), and Harris (1977) argue that the inattention to sex as a relevant variable has serious negative consequences. First, a variety of theories of crime causation have been developed with little or no attention to the single variable that "appears to explain more variance in crime across cultures than any other variable" (Harris, 1977, p. 4). The result is, "general theories of criminal deviance are now no more than special theories of male deviance" (Harris, 1977, p. 3). Second, the theoretical perspective that focuses on formal societal responses to criminal deviants similarly ignores the relationship between sex status and the response of deviance-controlling agents. With a few exceptions (see for example, Bernstein and others, 1977b; Green, 1961; Martin, 1934; Nagel, 1969; Nagel and Weitzman, 1971; and Swigert and Farrell, 1977) this is true as well for the empirical research that bears on this interactionist perspective (Rubington and Weinberg, 1973). The result is that little is known about the determinative role of sex in societal responses. Because characteristics of the individual deviant are thought to be salient in the labeling process (Becker, 1963; Schur, 1971), the failure to consider sex as a defendant attribute poses a serious theoretical limitation. Third, to the extent that sex status mediates the relationship between other sociological variables (for example social class, race, and prior deviance experiences) and both crime causation and formal societal responses, the extant theory and research needs to be reexamined.

The research reported herein directly attends to three questions. First, are societal responses to male and female criminal deviants isomorphic or does the inclusion of females alter the pattern of relationships heretofore noted in prior research? Second, in comparing the response to females to the response to males, is one sex group more or less likely to be the recipient of a favored response? Third, does sex status interact with other independent variables in such a way as to mediate, that is, change the relationship ordinarily found between these other variables and societal responses?

Sex Status and Deviance Processing

In a general sense the justification for assuming that sex status will affect deviance processing outcomes is based on its logical relevance to the conflict and interactionist perspective. Specifically, sex status can be thought of as relevant to social power, to stereotypic expectations and responses to alleged deviants, and to a deviant's ability to negotiate the imposition of deviance labels. For example, in terms of power, Turk (1969), Quinney (1970), and Chambliss and Seidman (1971) argue that the relative autonomous power of an individual will affect deviance processing outcomes, with the less powerful societal members being the more likely recipients of the least favorable outcomes. If one makes the simplistic assumption that females are generally less powerful, one might expect female deviants to fare less well in deviance processing outcomes. However, to the extent that one concedes that power is partly situational and that general powerlessness can be advantageous in some settings, it becomes unclear whether we should expect that being female is advantageous or disadvantageous when one is being responded to as an alleged criminal. To elaborate, if being less powerful in society helps to generate a more sympathetic (and thus less harsh) societal response, then the lack of general power can be said to provide a measure of relative power in some specific settings. If, however, one assumes that general power is always transsituational, then one would assume that relative powerlessness will always be disadvantageous.

Becker (1963), Kitsuse and Cicourel (1963), Erikson (1964), Schur (1971), Rubington and Weinberg (1973), and Swigert and Farrell (1977) argue that the outcomes of deviance processing are partly a function of the values, tolerances, and expectations that processing agents hold for certain types of deviance and deviants. And these values, tolerances, and expectations are likely to be affected by an individual's ascribed and achieved statuses. Because sex is a major ascribed status (Angrist, 1969), typifications based on stereotypic assumptions about sex roles may be likely to affect deviance processing decisions.

Newman (1966), Blumberg (1967), Schur (1971), and Bernstein and others (1977) argue that a deviant's "negotiator" abilities often affect deviance processing outcomes. The thesis is that certain individuals, by virtue of their statuses and/or experience, are better able to negotiate so as to avoid the imposition of a negative deviance label. Warner, Wellman, and Weitzman (1971) suggest that females may be better negotiators because they use their "feminine" characteristics to manipulate actors to respond favorably to them.

Although sex status can logically be fit into the interactionist and conflict perspectives, with the exception of Turk's (1969) notion of derivative power, none of the works ordinarily construed as representative of these perspectives directly addresses sex status as a relevant variable. Moreover, the general lack of specificity of the propositions in these perspectives, as pointed out in Gibbs (1966, 1972), Gove (1975), Tittle (1975), Bernstein, Kelly, and Doyle (1977), and Bernstein and others (1977), makes it unclear whether ultimately the appropriate hypothesis to deduce is that females are preferentially treated or that they are the subjects of discrimination.

Two theses have been articulated, both of which focus exclusively on the relationship between sex status and processing outcomes vis-à-vis criminal deviants. Of interest is that although the two perspectives make differential attributions of *intent* to processing agents (punitive versus protective), the predicted *outcomes* are not clearly dissimilar. Simon (1975b, p. 446) summarizes the two hypotheses: The first is the "paternalistic" or "chivalry" thesis; the second is the "evil woman" thesis. The paternalistic thesis posits that women are preferentially treated in the criminal justice system because deviance processing agents (for example, judges and prosecutors) find it difficult to be punitive toward women when they liken them to other women they know because a less severe response is chivalrous and/or because severe sanctioning of women is impractical given their housewife-mother roles in society. The empirical evi-

dence to support the paternalistic position is scant. Reckless and
Ray (1967) report its occurrence, but their conclusion is not
based on multivariate analyses of criminal justice decisions in
which important variables (for example, release status pending
case disposition) other than sex have been controlled. Nagel
(1969) and Nagel and Weitzman (1971) report findings of preferential treatment for women, but again both studies fail to
control simultaneously for other important variables (such as
prior criminal record). Moreover, the sample in Nagel and Weitzman (1971) is comprised of litigants in personal injury and divorce cases rather than alleged criminal deviants. Thus even if
the findings of a paternalistic response holds in a replicated
multivariate analysis, it may be an occurrence specific to civil
(rather than criminal) proceedings. The litigant in a divorce case
is quite different from the alleged deviant in a criminal case.
(Simon 1975b) examines the zero-order relationship between
sex status and conviction rates and tentatively rejects the preferential thesis. However, the fact that her presentation includes
no control for the variety of variables known to be correlated
with conviction (for example, prior criminal record, seriousness
of prosecution charge, and release status pending case disposition) limits acceptance of her conclusion, too. Swigert and
Farrell (1977), in a study of homicide, report that women are
less likely to be convicted of more serious charges; and they
speculate that this preferential treatment is a "social pedestal"
effect. Although they do use multivariate techniques, the fact
that they combine acquittals and dismissals with conviction
charge severity into one rank-order dependent variable leads us
to question the validity of their findings. Bernstein and others
(1977) find that factors affecting adjudication decisions (dismissals) differ from those affecting sanctioning decisions (sentence severity). Thus to combine these outcomes into one rank-
ordered scale seems questionable. Until we know whether sex
status is related to adjudication, sentence severity, or both, we
cannot conclude that paternalistic responses to women are the
predominant response mode.

There is also an important negative consequence of a paternalistic response. Singer (1973) and Temin (1973) argue that
paternalistic responses have given rise to differential treatment

both in legal statutes and criminal justice practices that clearly discriminate *against* females. As examples they cite the practice of institutionalizing girls for offenses less serious than those for which boys are institutionalized and imposing longer sentences on females than males convicted of the same offense. Although these occurrences purportedly arose from the belief that females were better candidates for rehabilitation, the result of this practice may be that females are the recipients of the harsher outcomes (Wheeler and Hughes, 1968; Tittle, 1974).

In sum, the paternalistic pattern generally predicts preferential treatment, but Nagel and Weitzman (1971), Singer (1973), Temin (1973), and Simon (1975b) are all careful to note the potential of paternalistic intent resulting in disadvantaged outcomes for women.

The second thesis, the "evil woman" thesis, posits that women are responded to more negatively because their criminal deviance violates stereotypic sex role expectations. For example, females are not expected to engage in dangerous criminal activities such as armed robbery. Moreover, they may be presumed to be basically "less evil" than males and thus less criminogenic. Thus when a female is prosecuted for a "nonfemale" crime (that is, not prostitution), she may be presumed to be *really evil*. In reviewing the history of traditional responses to criminal deviants, Rasche (1975, p. 15) notes, "very few women were labeled 'evil,' but when such labeling occurred, it was with a vengeance." Lombroso (1893) noted that women rarely fell into his "born criminal" category; but when they did, the assumption was that they were even more evil than the equivalent male.

Somewhat consistent with this evil woman thesis is Bernstein and others' (1977) finding that women are convicted of more serious offenses than their male counterparts, controlling for the seriousness of the offense for which they were prosecuted. Similarly, several studies on sentencing (for example, Foley and Rasche, 1976) report harsher sentences for women. However, with the exception of Bernstein and others (1977), as before, these studies are limited by their failure to control for the variety of other variables that might alternatively explain the relationship between sex and severe societal response outcomes. Clearly, the effect of sex remains very much undefined.

In accordance with our review of the sparse and limited theoretical and research literature, we define our research as exploratory. Yet our exploration is guided by the preferential versus discrimination hypothesis. Under that rubric we address two questions. First, are women the more likely recipients of more or less severe criminal outcomes, based solely on their sex? Second, can inferences about paternalism or the evil woman thesis be drawn by examining the bases upon which the different outcome decisions are made?

Dependent Variables

Because the processing of criminal deviants occurs in a series of stages (Blumberg, 1967; Rosett and Cressey, 1976; Schur, 1971), it is more appropriate to examine sequential decisions than to examine one decision at one isolated stage. Furthermore, decisions at prior deviance processing stages affect subsequent decisions. Thus a processual model of analysis that examines sequential decisions, where the sample for whom the decision is relevant changes with each decision, is recommended (see Bernstein, Kelly, and Doyle, 1977; Swigert and Farrell, 1977). Ideally, processual analyses start at the point of entry into the processing system. In the case of criminal defendants one might argue this is the arrest. Unfortunately, however, our data begin at the point of entry into the court, which implies we cannot attend to sex differences that may have resulted in differential arrest patterns or to their consequences as the defendants pass through the various stages associated with court processing outcomes.

We examine three dependent variables. First, the *adjudication decision* (Y_1) focuses on whether the defendant's case is fully prosecuted and results in a conviction *or* the case ends in a dismissal. Although acquittals would have been relevant here, too, defendants whose cases were acquitted were excluded because there were too few cases. Of seven thousand defendants arraigned in the four-month period of observation, twenty-two were acquitted. Because 10 to 50 percent of defendants prosecuted are ultimately dismissed (see Bernstein, Kelly, and Doyle, 1977; Hagan, 1975; Zeisel, de Grazia, and Freidman, 1975), and dismissed defendants are not subjects for sentencing decisions, it is critical to examine this deviance processing outcome alone.

Second, for defendants whose cases are not terminated by a dismissal we examine the *severity of the sentence* (Y_2). Sentence severity is analyzed as a dummy dichotomous dependent variable. Probation and incarceration are categorized as "harsh" sentences, and fines or suspended sentences (for example, conditional and unconditional discharges) are categorized as "less harsh." The determination of harsh versus less harsh is in accordance with the order specified in interviews with judges, defense attorneys, prosecutors, and auxiliary criminal justice personnel.

Although we preferred to examine differences in defendants sentenced to imprisonment versus those sentenced to nonimprisonment, the fact that so few women were sentenced to prison makes this kind of analysis inappropriate. Moreover, our interviewees repeatedly stressed that probation is often as serious a sanction as prison, although we interviewed no defendants to corroborate this *consistently* reported assertion.

Y_1 and Y_2 are useful for examining sequential processual points through the criminal justice process, but a strong argument can be made for constructing an outcome measure heretofore not used in criminal justice processing research, that is, time imprisoned *either* before adjudication (in detention) or after adjudication (in prison). The rationale is that the *process of the administration of justice often serves as the sanction* (Feeley, 1977). To illustrate, Bernstein, Kelly, and Doyle (1977) found that defendants who had spent a considerable amount of time in jail (detention) while awaiting the final disposition of their cases were often likely to have their case terminate by dismissal. They explain this seemingly strange relationship by noting that judges may subtract the time the defendant has spent in detention from the additional time the defendant would receive were he or she sentenced. Further, the judge subtracts an equivalent to what the defendant would get off for "good behavior." Once those subtractions have been summed, it may be more cost effective to dismiss the defendant than to expend further time and money in continuing to process the defendant. Importantly, the process is equated with a sanction. To the extent that males and females differ in their pretrial release experience (see Table 2, X_6), measuring time imprisoned the way we specify here allows us to examine what might otherwise be an obscured artifact of court processes. Moreover, it also allows us to examine an informal sanction apart from the more traditional concentration on formal societal response outcomes, that is, the sentence.

Sample

The sample consists of all male (N=2,627) and female (N=338) persons arraigned in state criminal or supreme court in a major American city in New York State between December 1974 and March 1975. Defendants whose cases were not completed during the data-collection period were excluded because we needed data on adjudication and sentencing. Defendants whose cases were finally disposed of at their first court presentation were excluded. In an analysis of males arrested for felonies, Bernstein, Kelly, and Doyle (1977) found defendants finally disposed of at their first court presentation are responded to in different ways than those processed in the more traditional way. Thus it made little sense to merge these groups here. Future analyses of sex differences will analyze these defendants' experiences.

Furthermore, our interest in sex differences caused us to exclude defendants prosecuted for sex-linked crimes, such as prostitution, abortion, or rape. The total sample (N=2,965) includes defendants prosecuted for assault, homicide, burglary, arson, larceny, robbery, theft, forgery, mischief, obstruction of justice, narcotics, and possession of a dangerous weapon.

Data

For each of the 2,965 defendants court record data were recorded daily for the judicial disposition of every court appearance (for example, bail status and charge reductions). Data on the defendant's criminal history (prior arrests and prior convictions, for instance) were recorded from state criminal records, and data on demographic characteristics of the defendant (race, age, education, and so forth) were obtained from personal interviews conducted with the defendant by a pretrial services agency officer during the six- to twenty-four hour period immediately following arrest and before the defendant's first court appearance. Data on the characteristics of the charged criminal offense (such as type of offense and number of charges) were recorded from court records. In addition to the quantitative data, supplementary and complementary qualitative data were collected during on-site observations of court proceedings and through interviews with judges, prosecutors, defense attorneys, and auxiliary court personnel.

Analysis

The data are analyzed using dummy variable regression procedures. Johnston, Savity, and Wolfgang (1972) make the case for regression using dummy dichotomous dependent variables. Because we define our work as exploratory, nominal independent variables are effect coded in accordance with Kerlinger and Pedhazur's (1973) argument that comparison made between any one category and the mean of the other categories is more appropriate in exploratory research than comparisons between one category and some arbitrarily selected left-out category.

We followed two procedures for analyzing each of the three dependent variables. First, to examine the effect of sex on the favorability of the processing outcomes, we regress each dependent variable on the independent variables, including a dummy variable for sex. Second, to determine whether dependent variables other than sex differentially affect the favorability of the outcomes, we separate males and regress each dependent variable on the independent variables, once for females and once for males. To determine whether these sex differentials are significant, we use a test of significance for interaction terms in the analysis of covariance framework. In order to test for significant interactions we recode all independent variables back into traditional dummy variable terms (that is, change them from effect coding of $-1/1$ to $0/1$). We then proceed within the usual ANCOVA framework in testing the difference between coefficients for males and females.

The decision as to which independent variables to include is largely based on prior research (Berk and Rossi, 1977; Bernstein, Kelly, and Doyle, 1977; Bernstein and others, 1977; Burke and Turk, 1975; Hagan, 1975; Swigert and Farrell, 1977) and our court observations.

The analyses include (1) variables related to the defendant's social attributes, for example, marital status, family composition (children and adults), age, race, and employment status; (2) variables that might affect reactor's expectations for and perceptions of certain deviants, such as the type of alleged offense, the defendant's prior criminal record, whether the defendant was charged with possession of a dangerous weapon, and whether the alleged offense is for a person or property crime; (3) variables related to the organizational imperatives of the deviance processing agency, for example, whether the defendant has other cases pending in another court action and whether the defendant is processed in supreme court or in criminal court; and (4) variables summarizing the results of prior deviance processing decisions, such as the defendant's release status prior to the final disposition of the case. Variables related to the alleged offense, such as the seriousness of the charge for which the defendant was prosecuted, as well (Bernstein, Kelly, and Doyle, 1977).

Results

Looking at the simple bivariate cross tabulation of final case disposition by defendant's sex, Table 1 shows that females are more likely than males (66.3 percent to 57.2 percent) to have their cases dismissed. Moreover, among convicted defendants females are more likely to receive the least harsh (suspended) sentence (16.9 percent to 9.1 percent) and less likely to receive the harshest (prison) sentence (4.7 percent to 14.7 percent). One might argue that this female advantage is a function of women being prosecuted for less serious crimes. However, the cross tabulation of the severity of the arrest charge by sex (see X_1 in Table 2) indicates that our sample of males

Table 1. Final Disposition of Defendant's Criminal Case by Sex

Disposition	Males	Females
Case dismissed	57.2% (1,502)	66.3% (224)
Suspended sentence	9.1 (239)	16.9 (57)
Time served	1.4 (38)	0.9 (3)
Fine with no prison default	.8 (22)	1.2 (4)
Fine under $50 with prison default	2.9 (75)	1.5 (5)
Fine over $50 with prison default	7.5 (198)	3.3 (11)
Probation	6.4 (167)	5.3 (18)
Prison	14.7 (386)	4.7 (16)
Total	2,627	338

Note: $\chi^2 = 37.41; p < .001$.

and females is equally distributed along the severity of charge dimension. Furthermore, males and females arrested are equally likely to be charged with possession of a dangerous weapon (see X_2, Table 2) and equally likely to be charged with committing a personal (violent) crime (see X_5, Table 2). Second, to examine whether being female increases the likelihood that a defendant will fare better on the three outcome variables, controlling simultaneously for all independent variables earlier delimited, we turn to the multivariate analyses presented in Table 3.

Table 3 presents the standardized and unstandardized regression coefficients for the three dependent variables. Standardized (betas) and unstandardized regression coefficients (b's) are presented for all regression equations. The standardized coefficients provide a means to order the saliency of the effects of the independent variables (that is, the larger the beta, the more salient the effect). The unstandardized coefficients (because we are using dummy dependent variables) provide estimates of the conditional probability of the independent variable on the dependent variable. To elaborate, if the b for sex on the dependent variable Y_3 (spending any time imprisoned) is .16, the probability of spending any time imprisoned is 16 percent greater for males than it is for females, controlling for the other variables in the equation.

Because the dependent variables are dichotomized, the unstandardized regression coefficient may be interpreted as the increment in the marginal probability of an outcome, controlling for other independent variables. The nominal independent variables are effect coded, so the *difference in the probability of a particular outcome is twice the unstandardized regression coefficient*.

Because our research is defined as exploratory, we use the more liberal significance level of .10 to indicate a relationship worthy of attention. Moreover, in the case of dichotomous dependent variables, standard errors of regression coefficients may be inflated (Goldberger, 1964), so the more liberal .10 significance cutoff reduces the likelihood of ignoring an important finding.

According to Table 3, sex has a significant positive relationship to both sentence severity (Y_2) and whether a defendant spends any time imprisoned (Y_3). That is, males are predicted to be more likely (12 percent) to receive a harsh sentence (Y_2) and even are more likely (32 percent) to spend any time imprisoned (Y_3). Sex is not found to have any significant relationship to the probability of having one's case dismissed (Y_1). The entire set of independent variables explains very little variation in the probability of case dismissal. Bernstein, Kelly, and Doyle (1977) find the decision to dismiss a case (versus full prosecution) is based on factors substantially different from those affecting formal sanctioning decisions applied to convicted defendents. They contend the dismissal decision is largely a function of evidence and the value of the case to the court. Unfortunately, the indirect indicators of evidentiary concerns and case value used by Bernstein, Kelly, and Doyle (1977) are not available for this research. Future research aimed at exploring sex differences in dismissal decisions should probe this question further.

Because sex does have an additive effect on Y_2 and Y_3 and the amount of explained variance is nontrivial, we turn next to the question of sex differences in the process leading to these outcomes. Table 4 presents the zero-order relationships and the standardized and unstandardized regression coefficients for males and females. To examine sex differences in the process

Table 2. Frequency Distributions for Exogenous and Endogenous Variables for Males and Females

Notation	Variable	Scale	Percent Frequency Males	Percent Frequency Females	χ^2 for Male/Female Differences
Y_1	Adjudication	Dismissed (0)	35.5	36.0	$p > .50$
		Fully prosecuted (1)	64.5	64.0	
Y_2	Sentence severity	Less severe (0) (suspended sentence, fine)	77.0	90.0	$p < .001$
		More severe (1) (probation, prison)	23.0	10.0	
Y_3	Pre- or postadjudication imprisonment time	No imprisonment time (0)	44.0	72.0	$p < .001$
		Imprisonment time (1)	56.0	28.0	
X_1	Severity of arrest charge as defined in penal case	Violation (1)	.1	0.0	$p > .50$
		Unclassified misdemeanor (2)	0.0	0.0	
		B misdemeanor (3)	2.0	2.0	
		A misdemeanor (4)	19.0	20.0	
		E felony (5)	12.0	13.0	
		D felony (6)	35.0	40.0	
		C felony (7)	15.0	12.0	
		B felony (8)	12.0	10.0	
		A felony (9)	4.0	3.0	
X_2	Arrest charge includes possession of weapon charge	No (−1)	97.0	98.0	$p > .25$
		Yes (1)	3.0	2.0	

X_3	Prior arrest record but no prior convictions	No prior arrests (−1)	26.0	50.0	$p < .001$
		Prior arrests and convictions (0)	29.0	10.0	
		Prior arrests but no prior convictions (1)	46.0	40.0	
X_4	Prior arrests and prior convictions	No prior arrests (−1)	26.0	50.0	$p < .001$
		Prior arrests but no prior convictions (0)	46.0	40.0	
		Prior arrests and prior convictions (1)	29.0	10.0	
X_5	Type of most serious charge	Property (−1)	61.0	61.5	$p > .50$
		Personal (1)	39.0	38.5	
X_6	Release status pending final case disposition	Detention ≥ 30 days (1)	16.0	8.0	$p < .001$
		Detention < 30 days (2)	29.0	14.0	
		Bail made (3)	3.0	1.0	
		Released on own recognizance (4)	52.0	77.0	
X_7	Defendant has other open cases	No (−1)			$p > .05$
		Yes (1)	87.0		
X_8	Court in which case was processed	Criminal court (−1)	92.59	94.0	$p > .25$
		Supreme court (1)	7.5	6.0	
X_9	Defendant's race	Nonwhite (−1)	88.0	90.0	$p > .30$
		White (1)	12.0	10.0	
X_{10}	Defendant's age	Interval	Mean 26.4	28.2	$p < .001$
			s.d. 9.13	8.70	
X_{11}	Defendant's employment status	Unemployed (−1)	59.0	77.0	$p < .001$
		Employed (1)	41.0	23.0	

Table 2. Continued

Notation	Variable	Scale	Percent Frequency Males	Females	χ^2 for Male/Female Differences
X_{12}	Defendant's marital status	Single, widowed, divorced (–1)	63.0	73.0	p < .01
		Common law, married (1)	37.0	27.0	
X_{13}	Family composition	No children (–1)	87.0	62.0	p < .001
		Children with defendant and another adult (0)	12.0	12.0	
		Children, defendant, and no other adult (1)	1.0	26.0	
X_{14}	Family composition	No children (–1)	87.0	62.0	p < .001
		Children, defendant, and no other adult (0)	1.0	26.0	
		Children with defendant and another adult (1)	12.0	12.0	
X_{15}	Defendant's sex	Female (–1)		11.0	
		Male (1)	89.0		

Table 3. Unstandardized (b) and Standardized (β) Regression
Coefficients of Exogenous Variables on
Y_1, Y_2, and Y_3 for Total Sample

Variable		Dismissal (Y_1)		Sentence Severity (Y_2)		Any Time Imprisoned (Y_3)	
		b	β	b	β	b	β
X_1	Severity of arrest charge	-.02	-.06[a]	.04	.13[b]	.05	.14[b]
X_2	Weapon	.03	.02	-.05	-.04[c]	.07	.05[a]
X_3	Prior arrests, no convictions	-.04	-.06[a]	-.01	-.02	.01	.01
X_4	Prior convictions	.02	.03	.09	.14[b]	.14	.20[b]
X_5	Personal	-.04	-.09[b]	-.03	-.06[a]	.01	.01
X_6	Release status	.01	.02	-.13	-.32[b]	—	—
X_7	Number of open cases	.01	.02	.01	.02	.04	.10[b]
X_8	Supreme court	.21	.23[b]	.27	.36[b]	.16	.16[b]
X_9	Race	-.04	-.05[a]	-.03	-.04[c]	-.04	-.05[b]
X_{10}	Age	-.00	-.01	-.00	-.07[b]	-.00	-.02
X_{11}	Employment status	-.03	-.05[a]	-.01	-.02	-.01	-.01
X_{12}	Marital status	.00	.01	-.01	-.02	-.01	-.03
X_{13}	Children, no other adult	.07	.07	.02	.02	-.12	-.11[b]
X_{14}	Children, and other adult	-.05	-.06	-.02	-.02	.07	.10[a]
X_{15}	Sex	.04	.03	.06	.04[c]	.16	.10[b]
R^2		.068		.410		.186	
N		2972		1993		2972	
Intercept		.088		.637		.232	

[a] $p < .05$.
[b] $p < .01$.
[c] $p < .10$.

resulting in severe sentences (Y_2) and the probability of spending any time imprisoned (Y_3), we compare the unstandardized regression coefficients for males to those for females for each of the two dependent variables.

Table 4. Zero-Order Correlations and Unstandardized and Standardized Regression Coefficients for Exogenous Variables on Y_2 and Y_3 for Males and Females

| | | Sentence Severity (Y_2) | | | | | | Any Time Imprisoned (Y_3) | | | | | |
| | | Male | | | Female | | | Male | | | Female | | |
	Variable	r	b	β	r	b	β	r	b	β	r	b	β
X_1	Severity of arrest charge	.339	.048	.144	.234	.006	.020	.227	.055	.157[a]	.129	-.001	-.002
X_2	Weapon	.076	-.055	-.044[b]	.089	-.060	-.044	.107	.071	.049[b]	.064	.083	.049
X_3	Prior arrests, no convictions	.105	-.006	-.011	.041	-.010	-.024	.121	.009	.016	.128	.037	.078
X_4	Prior convictions	.254	.086	.135[a]	.185	.046	.085	.271	.142	.211[a]	.194	.051	.076
X_5	Personal	.162	-.036	-.00	.164	.013	.033	.130	-.001	-.002	.162	.078	.167[c]
X_6	Release status	-.473	-.127	-.317[a]	-.480	-.096	-.252[a]						
X_7	Number of open cases	.139	.003	.009	.233	.050	.132	.184	.041	.091[a]	.207	.075	.149[c]
X_8	Supreme court	.470	.269	.354[a]	.559	.303	.459[a]	.234	.148	.158[a]	.274	.253	.259[a]
X_9	Race	-.064	-.031	-.040[c]	.039	-.019	-.030	-.070	-.041	-.053[b]	-.014	-.043	-.058
X_{10}	Age	-.094	-.004	-.083[a]	-.095	-.001	-.014	-.005	-.001	-.015	-.117	-.004	-.078
X_{11}	Employment status	-.074	-.006	-.013	-.172	-.044	-.010	-.043	-.012	-.023	-.079	.004	.007

X_{12} Marital status	-.027	-.004	-.008	-.122	-.049	-.117	.020	-.007	-.013	-.152	-.091	-.178[a]
X_{13} Children, no other adult	-.024	.011	.008	-.137	-.002	-.005	-.018	-.214	-.162[a]	-.152	-.067	-.129
X_{14} Children, and other adult	-.018	-.015	-.012	-.102	-.015	-.028	.009	.118	.158[a]	-.097	-.047	-.072
R^2	.397			.478				.162			.206	
N	1768			220				2627			338	
Intercept	.698			.543				.292			.652	

[a] p < .01.
[b] p < .05.
[c] p < .10.

First, with respect to sentence severity (Y_2), more variance can be explained for females than for males. That this is probably the result of the relatively few number of females is suggested by the fact that for females only two of the fourteen independent variables have effects significant at .10 (eight are significant for males). There appear to be very few differences between males and females. There are three statistically significant interaction effects: sex and prior convictions, sex and prior arrests but no convictions, and sex and open cases pending in another court. According to Table 4, the adverse effect of prior convictions on sentence severity (where prior convictions increase the probability of a more severe sentence) is stronger for males than for females. The beneficial effect of having no prior convictions (thereby reducing the probability of a severe sentence) is stronger for females than for males. And the adverse effect of having other pending cases (where pending cases increase the probability of a severe sentence) is stronger for females than for males. The two factors that have the strongest effects on the sentence severity decision (the defendant's release status pending final disposition and whether the case was prosecuted in supreme court) are equally relevant for males and females. Finally, the direction of findings is consistent with prior research using male samples on the determinants of sentence severity. That is, the harsher sentence is likelier for defendants (1) charged with more serious crimes, (2) who have prior convictions, (3) who have been detained for longer periods of time prior to case disposition, (4) who have other pending cases, (5) who are processed in supreme court (the only court empowered to sentence offenders to prison terms of more than one year), (6) who are nonwhite, and (7) who are older. Additionally, similar to other recent multivariate analyses of sentencing (Bernstein, Kelly, and Doyle, 1977; Burke and Turk, 1975; Hagan, 1975), the effects of race, age, employment status, and the like are small in comparison to the effects of the alleged offense, the defendant's criminal record, and organizational variables relevant to court processing.

Second, with respect to spending any time imprisoned (Y_3), there are more significant differences between males and females than in Y_2, and the differences seem greater. The five significant interaction effects are sex and marital status, sex and severity of arrest charge, sex and prior convictions, sex and personal crimes, and sex and pending cases in another court. The beneficial effect that accrues to married defendants is stronger for females than for males. The adverse effect of prior convictions is stronger for males than for females. And the adverse effect of open cases is stronger for females than for males. Although these interactions are significant because of the differences in the strength of the relationships, two interaction effects are relevant to effects different in strength *and* direction. First, the severity of the offense, a variable that has a strong effect for males (that is, those charged with more severe offenses are likelier to spend some time imprisoned), has no significant effect for females; and the sign is opposite. If this finding is robust, it means that females charged with felonies are neither more nor less likely to be imprisoned than those charged with misdemeanors or violations. This is a striking departure from prior research. Moreover, looking at the effect of the type of crime (personal versus property), we find a strong adverse effect for females charged with personal crimes but no significant effect for males similarly charged. What is striking here is that females are found to be more harshly treated for personal offenses. Again, this is a departure from prior research (Bensing and Schroeder, 1962; Bernstein, Kelly, and Doyle, 1977; Garfinkel, 1949), that reports that personal crimes among the socially disadvantaged, which is characteristic of the population of defendants here, ordinarily evokes a less rather than more harsh societal response than crimes against property.

Discussion

The first question addressed was whether the determinants of societal responses to criminal deviants, as examined here for three criminal justice outcomes, are isomorphic for males and females. More specifically, does the inclusion of females in the sample of defendants examined alter the pattern of relationships noted in prior research? Because sex had no significant ef-

fect on the first outcome, that is, whether a case is fully prosecuted (Y_1), and moreover the entire set of independent variables
explained little of the variance in this outcome, we refrain from
commenting on whether the outcome for males is differentially
determined from the outcome for females. Future research will
have to probe this question more deeply.

Examination of the second outcome (sentence severity for
convicted defendants, Y_2) revealed some differences between
males and females, but those differences were minor and few.
They were differences largely in the magnitude of the effects of
the independent variables rather than differences in direction.
Moreover, the general pattern of relationships between the independent variables and this dependent variable was remarkably
similar for males and females.

Of interest is that on the third dependent variable, the
likelihood that a defendant will spend any time imprisoned
(Y_3), there were considerable differences between males and
females. Thus for this particular outcome the response to females is not isomorphic with the response to males. Before interpreting these differences, we need to elaborate on how they
are manifested.

First (see Table 4) for males, the pattern of relationships
between the independent variables and this dependent variable
is very similar to what one would expect given the findings reported in prior comparable studies. That is, the harsh outcome
(spending time imprisoned) is more likely to be experienced by
male defendants (1) charged with more serious offenses, (2)
charged with possession of a dangerous weapon, (3) with prior
convictions, (4) who have open cases pending in another court,
(5) who are processed in supreme court, and (6) who are nonwhite. To this list we add the finding that for males having children at home with no other adult present *reduces* the likelihood
of spending any time imprisoned. For females, however, the
pattern of relationships between these same variables and the
likelihood of experiencing this harsh outcome is quite different.
Three differences are striking. First, the severity of the offense,
a variable almost always found to have a very strong determinative effect, has no significant effect. Second, prior convictions,

also a variable ordinarily found to have a strong determinative effect, is trivial in size and nonsignificant. Third, the defendant's marital status, a variable *not* ordinarily found to be strong or significant, is both strong and significant. Finally, although the finding is not as striking, the adverse effect of prior convictions is weaker for females than for males.

The fact that prior convictions is so much stronger for males than for females (for males the *b* is .14 compared to the *b* of .05 for females) may be a function of males having prior convictions for *more offenses* and for *more serious offenses*. By coding the variable as we do here, the variation in the number of prior convictions and the severity of the offense for which the defendant was convicted (felony versus misdemeanor) is obscured. Unfortunately, problems of multicolinearity precluded coding the data into separate categories of prior felony convictions, prior misdemeanor convictions, and the like. We know that males have more prior convictions and more convictions for felonies, so it may be that the effect is stronger because the record is more severe. However, the alternative hypothesis, that for males accumulating disadvantageous statuses increases the severity of outcomes whereas for females there is no such accumulation, cannot yet be rejected. To the extent that females are increasingly convicted and convicted of more severe offenses, data collected several years from now may be able to resolve this question.

The fact that the severity of the offense has a strong effect for males and no effect for females, whereas the type of offense (person versus property) has a strong effect for females and no effect for males, is curious, especially the adverse effect of being charged with a personal crime for female defendants. One interpretation is that to the extent interpersonal violence is presumed to be "unladylike," females so charged may be subjected to this harsher outcome for their inappropriate sex role behavior. In Turk's terms, they may have lost whatever power they derived from being a woman by acting in a manner atypical of and unbecoming to women. If this speculative hypothesis is accurate, it may suggest that a kind of sex discrimination exists *among* the population of women defendants, where those engaging in inappropriate sex role behavior are the recipients of more harsh outcomes. Such an explanation would be consistent with the evil woman thesis earlier delimited.

The finding that marital status has no significant effect for males and a strong and significant effect for females, where married females are considerably less likely than their unmarried female counterparts to spend any time imprisoned, is also suggestive of a kind of sex discrimination among the population of female defendants. Two speculative interpretations come to mind. First, married females may derive a certain advantage by being able to present themselves as occupants of traditional roles; their unmarried counterparts, however, are neither occupants of this traditional role status nor able to point to a stable dyadic relationship to which they would return were they not imprisoned. Second, the court agents (judges, prosecutors) may not wish to break up a marital dyad where such a breakup would leave the man without a woman. Of interest is that the same marital state does not affect the outcome for males. If it is the concern for the "lone man" that is responsible for this effect, we are left to ponder what that says about the lack of concern for the "lone woman." Future research should probe this question further.

Conclusion

To summarize, we are unable to comment on whether the dismissal decision is differentially determined by sex because the independent variables are poor predictors of whether a case is fully prosecuted. On sentence severity, the decision to sentence a defendant more or less harshly is determined similarly for males and females by consideration of the same factors. Thus for this particular outcome we have little reason to conclude, as did Harris (1977), that theories based on male experiences are rendered inappropriate by the inclusion of females. However, on the more innovative societal responses outcome measure, the likelihood of spending any time imprisoned, the females experience differs substantially from that of males. The major theoretical implication is that societal response theory needs to expand its thesis to include sex stereotypic assumptions as a potential determinant of societal responses, at least in the case of female deviants. Moreover, the concept of power needs to be refined so as to elaborate on the variety of types of power that accrue to individuals as a result of status characteristics and the conditions under which these varied power dimensions are operable assets.

The second question addressed was whether sex status affects societal response outcomes, more specifically, whether one or the other sex statuses increases the net probability of a defendant's receiving a favorable outcome. Sex has no independent effect on the question of full prosecution versus dismissal (Table 3). Females are neither more nor less likely than males to be dismissed. On sentence severity (Table 3) sex has a significant effect, where females are more likely than males to be less severely sentenced. This is consistent with the paternalistic thesis, which argues that women are the recipients of preferential outcomes solely on the basis of sex status consideration. Finally, on the likelihood of spending any time imprisoned, there is evidence of the same preferential pattern for women; and it is even stronger.

The fact that female defendants receive preferential outcomes when compared to comparable male defendants is, as stated, consistent with the paternalistic thesis earlier described. However, at this juncture we do not know why this occurs. The fact that female defendants whose offense/offender pattern deviates from sex stereotypic assumptions are less favorably responded to than their *female* counterparts whose offense/offender pattern is more traditional suggests that the benefits accruing to a female defendant by virtue of her sex may be decreased or lost if her deviant behavior contradicts other sex stereotypic expectations. That is, a paternalistic response, because it is itself based on sex stereotypic ideas, may be cancelled out by behavior perceived to be in violation of other sex stereotypic assumptions.

To conclude, we raise the following questions. To the extent that sex stereotypic assumptions are held, what is the nature of these assumptions, and how and where do they fit into the interactionist thesis about the societal response to criminal defendants? Moreover, what is the relationship between sex stereotypic assumptions and power, and does this relationship manifest itself in ways suggestive of institutional sexism? Finally, to the extent that institutional sexism is evident in the criminal courts, what policy reforms are suggested?

This research was a preliminary effort to examine some pressing questions. We hope this exploratory effort will give some direction to the study of the questions outlined above.

17

Race and Parole Hearing Outcomes

Shirley Vining Brown

Recent interest in the criminal justice system has raised questions about whether the police, judicial, and correctional agencies in fact operate under a system of equal justice with respect to all offenders. There is evidence that minority group offenders experience differential treatment in their contacts with the police and the courts and in the rate at which they are sentenced to prison (Beach, 1932; Bullock, 1969; Wolfgang and Cohen, 1970). Female and juvenile offenders from minority groups have experienced disparate treatment as well (Axelrad, 1952; Burkhart, 1973; Goldman, 1963).

One of an offender's most important experiences during incarceration is the decision made at the first parole hearing. However, correctional experts and lay investigators tacitly agree that the parole administration process is an arbitrary system that permits wide discretion in parole decisions. One questions why and how this can happen when there are available scientific measures devised by actuarial sociologists to aid decision makers in the parole selection process. In reference to this very issue,

Note: The data are part of a larger study supported by Graduate Research Fellowship grant 72 NI 99 1060 from the Law Enforcement Assistance Administration, U.S. Department of Justice.

Johnston, Savitz, and Wolfgang (1962) note that although these
predictive instruments exist to offer more accuracy in predicting
parole success, parole officials rarely use such techniques to
determine an inmate's readiness for parole. Instead many boards
continue to arrive at parole decisions in an assemblylike fashion,
rendering judgments that are capricious and often unfair (Mitford, 1971). Thus although some believe that parole discretion
is due to the negative reaction of parole officials to the use of
parole prediction devices (Hayner, 1958), others take the position that parole discretion is due to the parole board's lack of
accountability to other agencies (President's Commission on
Law Enforcement and the Administration of Justice, 1967).
Whatever the precise dynamics are that produce parole disparities, it is clear that some groups are more disadvantaged than
others by the present system of administering paroles.

Wolfgang's (1964) analysis of racial bias in the national
parole statistics for 1964 revealed that approximately 10 to 14
percent more whites than blacks were annually granted some
form of conditional release from prison in the United States.
Data from the California Department of Corrections reveal that
among prisoners released for the first time in 1967 and 1968
the median length of time served was five months longer for
blacks than for whites in seven offense categories. During the
same time period the median length of time served by Chicano
inmates was six months longer than white inmates in four offense categories (Wright, 1973). The same pattern is seen in data
for female offenders confined in the California system. Holt
(1971) found that black female offenders served a median length
of time averaging five months longer than white female offenders in twelve offense categories. Explicitly or implicitly, these
studies support the belief of some (Wright, 1973) that institutional racism is a pervasive fact of prison life. However, they tell
us nothing more about the parole disadvantage of minority
group offenders than the color of their skin. There is reason to
believe that more can be determined about parole disparities if
we examine closely such variables as the type of institution in
which the inmate is confined.

In this chapter, *institutional racism* refers to the conceptualization given the term by Jones (1972, p. 131), that is, insti-

tutional racism exists when "racist consequences accrue to institutional laws, customs, or practices . . . whether or not the individuals maintaining the system have racist intentions."

Using the *first parole hearing outcome* as an indicator of institutional racism, the study reported in this chapter addresses two central questions: First, does race make a difference in the parole hearing outcomes of black and white first offenders? Second, does the institution of confinement affect the nature and degree of extant racial disparities in parole hearing outcomes?

Theoretical Considerations and Research Findings

Contemporary theories of organizational behavior have moved away from a classic Weberian conceptualization of organizations to theories that recognize differences in organizational goals, technology, and structure (Perrow, 1970). Perrow's conceptual framework specifically focuses on technology as a major independent variable that influences the choice of goals and structures of "people-changing" organizations—those that "work not only with or through people but also on them" (Street, Vintner, and Perrow, 1966). Based on Perrow's thesis, organizations in the very same line of business (for example, correctional institutions) can differ radically in their operations and in their method of handling people. This is due to differences in their perception of the "raw material" (inmates) worked on, the technology used to transform this raw material, and whether the task is well understood or not well understood, as well as whether the task is uniform and stable or nonuniform and unstable (Perrow, 1970). Basically, Perrow contends that organizations strive to increase the compatibility between their technology, goals, and structures and other characteristics of their organization's character. In effect, then, variations in organizational outputs (treatment outcomes, recidivism rates, and so forth) are the product of compatible organizational factors that differ between generically similar organizations, such as prisons.

For example, when correctional institutions are differentiated according to custody (classified along a custodial-treatment continuum), there are important differences in their operations and their handling of inmates (Perrow, 1970). Custodial

institutions show less tolerance and less particularism toward
inmates, and treatment institutions reflect more of these characteristics. This is because institutions with rehabilitative goals
tend to perceive inmates as unique individuals and respond accordingly. Protection of the community and containment are
comparatively less important, so more effort is put on resocial-
izing inmates by means of complex, esoteric techniques so they
can successfully return to the community. To realize this goal,
the professional staff has more influence on correctional decisions (decentralized structure), inmates are allowed greater flex-
ibility to develop internal controls, and the openness of the
institution results in a more congenial relation between inmates
and staff. The net effect for all inmates is a higher self-esteem
and a greater chance of being rehabilitated. Thus irrespective of
an inmate's race, one would expect inmates to be treated more
individually and consequently one would expect fewer differences by race in correctional outcomes.

Custody-oriented institutions (mixed-goal and custodial)
are primarily concerned with the tasks of security and inmate
control. Because orders come directly from the top at these
institutions, their structures are more centralized. External
security is visible when one observes the physical environment
and the larger custodial staff used at these institutions. Inmates
are perceived as needing discipline, conformity, and hard work.
In the jargon of inmates, prison officials try to "keep the joint
quiet." The end result is little or no emphasis on inmate rehabilitation. Moreover, inmates of different races may be seen
as similar at these institutions, but only to their respective racial
groups (Wright, 1973). I have reported elsewhere (Brown, 1975)
that urban inmates (a euphemism for minority inmates) are perceived as being more difficult to understand than other inmates
in custodial institutions. If they are also treated differently, this
would explain the larger outcome differences between racial
groups in custodial institutions.

Empirical evidence to support this conceptualization of
correctional organizations comes primarily from comparative
studies of juvenile institutions. Two studies (Sarri, 1962; Street,
Vintner, and Perrow, 1966) report that juvenile inmates in

treatment institutions more often express positive attitudes about their institution and staff than juvenile inmates in custodial institutions. Moreover, these studies found that rehabilitative efforts were more successful with juveniles confined in treatment institutions. In institutions where there is a bifurcation of treatment and custodial goals, it has been noted that outcomes generally depend on which goal is predominant (Sarri, 1962).

Weeks' (1958) study of juvenile treatment outcomes is of special interest because it shows that the relation between race and correctional outcomes varies by type of institution. His data revealed that when the treatment outcomes of black and white juveniles were compared, (1) there were clear differences between the races within both the treatment and custodial institutions; (2) there were also within-race differences between the two institutions; and (3) the degree of difference between the races varied according to the institution of confinement (differences in treatment outcomes were clearly larger between the races at the custodial institution). Thus this study lends more support to the assumption that racial disparities in parole hearing outcomes vary by custody level. It also provides further evidence to support Perrow's comparative perspective on organizational analysis.

Adult correctional research has also revealed differences by custody level. Glaser's (1964) study of recidivism in the federal prison system consistently found that parolees from minimum-security prisons had the highest success rates and differences between medium- and maximum-security prisoners were less substantial (a finding similar to the small differences in outcomes observed by Sarri, 1962, in mixed-goal and custodial juvenile institutions).

Ohlin's (1956) analysis of solidarity opposition among inmates also reflects differences by custody level; inmate solidarity was found to be greatest in maximum-security institutions.

These studies indicate two things. First, correctional institutions are not a discrete type of organization but, like other organizations, manifest differences that make them more or less bureaucratic in structure. Second, they suggest that more can be determined about the relation between race and correctional outcomes by examining how the type of institution impacts on this relation. Based on these theoretical and empirical considerations and the need to understand more about the nature of institutional racism in parole board practices, the comparative approach provides a useful framework for speculating about the influence of organizational factors on differential parole hearing outcomes.

It is conceivable that there are two ways the institutional variable could influence a parole board's actions. The first explanation assumes that corrections is an interdependent system where the outputs of one part of the system determine the inputs of other parts. This open–systems perspective assumes that racism is transmitted from the institutions to the parole board by means of institutional assessments that are recorded by prison personnel and become part of the inmate's permanent file. Most correctional departments require prison counselors to prepare a written report that summarizes and evaluates the inmate's adjustment and overall progress at the institution. Some correctional departments also require counselor recommendations for parole in the reports submitted to the board. If these reports and recommendations contain racially biased information and if the board is greatly influenced in its actions by these reports, it would be perpetuating the perversity of these assessments, which could have racial implications.

The second explanation has to do with the board itself. Hayner (1958) states that parole boards are sensitive to public opinion against paroling high-risk inmates (serious offenders) and therefore tend to act more cautiously on such cases. Although research has shown that property offenders are more likely to violate parole than serious offenders (Beattie, 1953; Ohlin, 1951), from the standpoint of the parole board the questions raised when high-risk inmates are considered for release are more serious. Therefore, independent of the information received from the institutions, parole release rates should reflect the custody level of the institution of confinement because high-risk inmates are generally confined in maximum-security institutions in a differentiated system of corrections. In any case one would expect that racial disparities in parole hearing outcomes will reflect the influence of the institution of confinement if Perrow's thesis on particularism versus universalism holds true for rehabilitative and custodial institutions. In other words, institutional racism is built into the parole administration process by the very fact that the discretionary process could lead to racial bias due to unscientific selection procedures and the lack of accountability and where custody level influences the selection process, there is a considerable reduction in the minority inmate's chances for parole because racial minorities are disproportionally confined in most correction institutions (U.S. Congress, House, Subcommittee #3, 1972). Therefore the implication for racial bias in the parole selection process is straightforward: If there is differential treatment of inmates by custody level and by race, it follows that racial differences in parole hearing outcomes will increase as custody level increases.

Although this research explores only black-white parole hearing outcomes, the comparative approach is equally useful for examining the parole disadvantage of other racial minorities (Chicanos, Puerto Ricans, and Native Americans) in correctional systems where they are confined in appreciable numbers.

This research is based on a sample of 547 black and white male first offenders randomly selected from the total population of all male first offenders who were twenty-three years of age and under and who had been paroled or discharged for the first time from one midwestern state prison system between 1969 and 1972. Other races were less than 1 percent of the population and were too small for comparison. Female offenders are also omitted because all females are housed in one facility in the state.

To ensure variation in organizational characteristics, three institutions in this state were selected nonrandomly for comparative purposes: a minimum-, a medium-, and a maximum-custody institution. Space limitations preclude a full description here, although details of the department and the institutions are reported elsewhere (Brown, 1975).

The minimum-custody institution was a small facility (two hundred capacity) situated on a beautiful lake site. There were no visible signs of security anywhere on the grounds of this institution. Inmates sent here are primarily trustworthy youthful first offenders, although an occasional older inmate considered trustworthy may be assigned here for a short time prior to parole. Inmates enjoyed freedom of movement and participated in self-government. The rehabilitative ideology of the counseling staff was accepted by both the custody staff and the administrators, which was reflected in certain policies at the institution. It is noteworthy that correctional officers are integrated into the treatment program and are addressed as "Mr." rather than by the militaristic terminology (corporal or sergeant) used at the other institutions.

The medium- and maximum-custody institutions were much larger facilities (750 to 1,300 capacity, respectively). Although both were highly concerned with security, the latter by far had the most controlled and contained environment. Inmates sent to the medium-custody institution are generally property offenders (petty larceny, breaking and entering, and so forth) whom officials perceive to be in need of security, discipline, and education. However, the official concern over security and discipline attenuates educational efforts at the institution because prison instructors are an integral part of the control system.

Inmates convicted of serious crimes (murder, rape, or armed robbery) as well as property offenders are sent to the maximum-security prison if a need for close security has been determined on the basis of their juvenile history of escapes. Thus at both institutions inmates are continually monitored by human (custodial staff) and nonhuman (electronic devices) means. Professional counselors at these institutions have little or no influence on correctional policies and appear to be there just to legitimize the use of public funds allocated for treatment programs. At both institutions disturbances that occurred in the late 1960s have been the motivating force behind the increased salience of custodial goals. This is most apparent in the pressure brought to bear on the administration to hire more correctional officers by the unionized custodial staff. The threat of strikes has influenced the goals toward more custody and less treatment, as reflected in the addition of 34 new custodial positions (increasing the force to 118 officers) at the medium-security institution and 17 new positions (increasing the force to 211 officers) at the maximum-security institution. In contrast, the counseling staff numbers eight and twelve (medium- and maximum-security prison, respectively) when up to full strength.

The inmate populations of all the institutions ranged from 50 to 75 percent black, but racial minorities made up only 10 percent of the staff at two of the three institutions and 20 percent at the medium-custody institution. Compared to other state systems this department of corrections is reputed to be penologically progressive and concerned with racial equity. However, interviews with staff and inmate (black and white) revealed potentially serious racial problems at all institutions. I used the *first parole hearing outcome* to determine if these problems could be picked up in parole board decisions.

Under state law each inmate in this state must be considered for parole after serving a minimum term, less allowances for good time. Minimum sentences are set by the court at the time of sentencing and are outside the control of the parole board.

There were four possible outcomes from the parole process: The inmate could receive a special parole because of unusual or meritorious circumstances, a regular parole, a deferred parole (usually for two to six weeks while obtaining information), or parole could be denied. Because the special and deferred categories had too few cases and the outcome was generally affirmative, a simple collapsing of these categories produced the dichotomous measure of parole outcome used in this analysis: Inmates were either *denied* (continued in custody) or *not denied* (given a regular, special, or deferred parole).

The choice of institutional variables was straightforward. Both the inmate's institutional adjustment rating and the counselor's parole recommendation were said to be crucial for the parole hearing and were included in all parole eligibility reports.

Counselor recommendations were of three types: The inmate was recommended for parole, was not recommended, or the counselor abstained and gave no recommendation. Because there were too few cases among inmates who were given no recommendation for parole, this category was collapsed with inmates who were recommended in the analysis. The effect of collapsing these categories was to reduce the likelihood of differences in the paroles between those *recommended* and those *not recommended* for parole.

Counselors rated inmates' adjustment according to their overall assessment of their behavior as excellent, good, fair, or poor. The same collapsing procedure used to create the recommendation variable was used to create the institutional adjustment variable: Inmates were considered *well adjusted* (rated excellent or good in adjustment by counselors) or *less well adjusted* (inmates rated fair or poor in adjustment by counselors).

Because inmates from the minimum-custody institution were oversampled and because the races might be disproportionately represented in the aggregate (institutional samples), proportional representation of the average population size and racial composition of each institution had to be ensured. To get a true estimate of the parole outcomes of the races at each institution, I applied a set of weights reflecting the racial composition of the three institutions to the conditional probability of being *denied* or *not denied* parole from prison. I used chi-square and multiple-classification analysis (Andrews and others, 1973) to examine the effect of the institutional type on the relations between race and parole outcomes.

During interviews with system officials I was informed that most institutions in the state were overcrowded between 1969 and 1972, the period for which the data were collected. As a way of relieving this situation the majority of all inmates eligible for parole were said to be released on their regular goodtime date (and a few were released earlier under arrangements with the courts). This information was confirmed by the findings (see Table 1) that most inmates were released at the first parole hearing. However, even though nearly all inmates were released during this period, the relations between type of institution and parole outcome is monotonic, that is, the percentage denied parole increases as the custody level of the institutions increase.

This finding lends support to the assumption that custody level has some effect on the parole board's decisions. However, at this point there is no way of knowing whether the institu-

Table 1. Parole Recommendation by Race and Institution,
in Percentages

Institution	Race	No Parole	No Recommendation	Parole	N^a
Minimum	Black	14.4	3.1	82.5	97
	White	11.8	2.6	85.5	76
			$\chi^2 = .29$, p = .86		
Medium	Black	17.8	11.0	71.2	73
	White	19.1	4.5	76.4	89
			$\chi^2 = 2.4$, p = .29		
Maximum	Black	27.2	12.0	60.9	92
	White	12.8	6.4	80.8	78
			$\chi^2 = 8.0$, p = .02		

[a] Excludes twelve minimum-security cases, sixteen medium-security cases, and fourteen cases from maximum security with missing data on parole recommendation.

tional effect on paroles is the result of information contained in parole reports or the board's sensitivity to public opinion. It is clear, however, that even when the parole chances of all inmates are higher than normal, there is more caution about releasing inmates from custodial institutions.

Because most inmates had a high probability of parole during this period, those denied parole were of even more interest. In particular I speculated about whether the effect of having a greater chance for parole was to make less likely any difference in the parole outcomes of blacks and whites at the two custodial institutions. The data revealed this was not the case.

Although there was almost no difference in the paroles of blacks and whites at the minimum-custody institution, 12 and 15 percent more blacks than whites were denied at the medium- and maximum-custody institutions, respectively. Moreover, the magnitude of the percentages denied in the aggregate at these institutions is primarily due to the larger percentage of black inmates denied by the parole board.

Apart from these general findings, an examination of the effect of institutional assessments on this relation may give more insight into the observed results.

The parole board's action could reflect the influence of institutional assessments, particularly the counselor's recommendations for parole. White inmates were recommended for

Table 2. Parole Hearing Outcome by Counselors' Recommendations
Race, and Institution

Institution/Race/ Recommendation	Parole Hearing Outcome				
	Denied	Not Denied	N^a	χ^2	p
Minimum					
Black					
Recommended	2.4%	97.6%	83	.9	<.30
Not recommended	7.1	92.9	14		
Total	3.1	96.9	97		
White					
Recommended	1.5	98.5	65	.1	=.70
Not recommended	–	100.0	9		
Total	1.4	98.6	74		
Medium					
Black					
Recommended	15.0	85.0	60	.0	=.95
Not recommended	15.4	84.6	13		
Total	15.1	84.9	73		
White					
Recommended	4.2	95.8	71	.6	<.30
Not recommended	–	100.0	17		
Total	3.4	96.6	88		
Maximum					
Black					
Recommended	10.6	89.4	66	30.8	<.00
Not recommended	68.0	32.0	25		
Total	26.4	73.6	91		
White					
Recommended	10.4	89.6	67	1.1	=.30
Not recommended	22.2	77.8	9		
Total	11.8	88.2	76		

[a] Excludes forty-eight cases with missing data on parole outcome/recommendations.

parole by counselors slightly more often than black inmates; although I was unable to account for this difference as definitely due to race. Thus if the board responded to recommendations without regard to color, it would still be perpetuating their adverse effect on parole of black inmates.

Although the relation between parole recommendations and the parole board's action was straightforward in the aggregate, things were much more complex for the experiences of the races within institutions (see Table 2). At the minimum- and medium-custody institutions nearly everyone was recommended for parole and the recommendation does not appear to make much difference for either race. Although nearly everyone is recommended at the maximum-security prison, blacks who are not recommended are about five times more likely to have parole denied than blacks for whom parole is recommended.

With the exception of maximum-custody inmates, particularly black inmates, the findings only weakly support the assumption that inputs (recommendations) originating from the institutions have a decisive effect on parole hearing outcomes. This may be unusual, but the pressures created by overcrowding apparently operated to the advantage of most inmates during this period.

If one reconstructed the data in Table 2, one would find no real differences between blacks and whites at the minimum-custody institution in either recommended category. However, blacks at the medium-custody institution are more often denied parole than whites, even though the difference is only significant (p = .03) for those recommended for parole.

The pattern differs for maximum-custody inmates. Race has no effect on the paroles of recommended inmates (p = .59) at this institution: About the same percentage from both races were denied by the board. But for those not recommended, over 45 percent more blacks were denied at the first parole board hearing (p = .02). Table 1 reveals that 14.4 percent more blacks than whites are not recommended at the maximum-custody institution, so the parole board's action has increased the disadvantage for black inmates by 32 percent (45.8 minus 14.4 percent) in this sample. A similar trend is picked up when the effect of institutional adjustment is considered.

The number of misconduct reports an inmate accrues during incarceration has often been cited as an important contributing factor in parole decisions. Counselors at the institutions here considered incorporated misconduct behavior in the adjustment ratings reported in the parole eligibility reports. The institutions differed in what they considered an act of misconduct, which rendered this variable an inaccurate predictor of parole.

Table 3. Parole Hearing Outcome by Adjustment,
Race, and Institution

Institution/Race/ Adjustment	Parole Hearing Outcome				
	Denied	Not Denied	N^a	χ^2	p
Minimum					
Black					
Well-adjusted	4.8%	95.2%	42	.0	=1.0
Less well adj.	4.8	95.2	21		
Total	4.8	95.2	63		
White					
Well-adjusted	3.6	96.4	28	.09	>.70
Less well adj.	—	100.0	22		
Total	2.0	98.0	50		
Medium					
Black					
Well-adjusted	8.2	91.8	49	8.9	<.01
Less well adj.	40.0	60.0	15		
Total	15.6	84.4	64		
White					
Well-adjusted	1.7	98.3	60	.3	>.50
Less well adj.	—	100.0	16		
Total	1.3	98.7	76		
Maximum					
Black					
Well-adjusted	14.8	85.1	54	9.8	<.01
Less well adj.	45.4	54.4	33		
Total	26.4	73.6	87		
White					
Well-adjusted	5.0	95.0	40	3.1	>.05
Less well adj.	18.5	81.5	27		
Total	10.4	89.6	67		

[a] Excludes thirty-seven cases (medium), twenty-nine (maximum), and seventy-four (minimum) with missing data on parole outcome/adjustment.

For example, inmates at the minimum-custody institution were written up for "wasting food" and "in shower too early," trivial offenses not reported at the other institutions. Consequently, minimum-custody inmates had a higher rate of misconduct in their files than inmates at the other institutions. At the same time, minimum-custody inmates were more often released on parole. No significant differences by race were found in the number of misconduct reports issued at the institutions.

An examination of adjustment ratings shows that an inmate's institutional adjustment has no real effect on the paroles of either race at the minimum-custody institution (see Table 3).

However, adjustment has a different effect on paroles at other institutions. Maladjusted black inmates at the medium-security institution are about five times more likely than well-adjusted black inmates to be denied parole. In contrast, there is only a slight difference in the proportions denied among well-adjusted and poorly adjusted white inmates at this institution. Adjustment has an effect in the expected direction on paroles for both races at the maximum-security institution, although the effect is much stronger for blacks than for whites.

When adjustment is held constant (Table 3), there are no large differences by race in either adjustment group under minimum custody or for well-adjusted inmates at the other two institutions.

However, at the more custodial institutions it is clear that among intractable (less well adjusted) inmates black inmates are more disadvantaged by the parole board's action, as shown by the significantly higher proportions denied parole at both institutions. Compared to the large differences (40 percent) between the races at the medium-custody institution, the smaller difference (27 percent) at the maximum-custody institution appears to be influenced by an interaction between intractable behavior and being a high-risk inmate (maximum security). This is not surprising. These parole hearings were held during a period (beginning in 1968) when the national atmosphere strongly supported the "law and order" theme. If the parole board believes prison conduct is predictive of the inmate's outside conduct and if Hayner (1958) is correct about the board's sensitivity to public opinion, this finding suggests that public opinion against paroling intractable inmates may be operative here. Thus in addition to racial bias, which also reflects the "law and order" sentiment (Wilson, 1973, p. 149), the parole board's concern over the conduct of high-risk inmates appears to have reduced the relative advantage of whites over blacks at the maximum-custody institution.

These results suggest that although institutional assessments have a differential effect on the paroles of black and white

Table 4. Percent Paroled by Race by Selected Independent Variables, Using Multiple-Classification Analysis, in Percentages

Independent Variables	Black Mean	Black Adjusted Mean	Black N	White Mean	White Adjusted Mean	White N
Institution:						
Minimum	96.3	91.5	81	98.4	97.7	62
Medium	80.3	76.6	61	96.2	97.0	78
Maximum	68.3	75.8	82	86.8	88.8	68
Juvenile history						
N.A.	a	a	3	a	a	3
None	85.0	84.7	153	92.3	91.3	130
Some	75.0	75.2	68	96.0	97.9	75
Type of offense:						
Least serious	a	a	5	a	a	6
Moderate	81.6	81.4	152	93.6	94.6	140
Most serious	80.6	81.8	67	93.5	91.6	62
Time served:						
1–18 months	78.1	80.3	146	92.8	93.8	139
19–36 months	88.5	84.3	78	95.7	93.8	69
Institutional adjustment:						
N.A.	89.6	83.9	48	92.9	90.8	51
Well-adjusted	87.8	85.0	115	96.3	95.5	108
Poorly adjusted	73.9	83.7	61	89.8	93.2	49
Parole recommendation:						
No recom.	85.2	75.7	27	93.9	95.2	33
Recommended	83.3	84.1	162	92.5	92.7	147
Not recom.	71.4	75.4	35	100.0	98.1	28
Total	81.7	81.7	224	93.8	93.8	208

Note: This table is based on the 432 cases having data on parole outcome and total time in prison, but excluding 10 cases who served more than thirty-six months in prison.
[a] Too few cases.

inmates, the differences are not substantial enough to cause the parole disparities between the races. The adversity found for black inmates appears to result from the parole board's actions. To charge that this adversity was caused by racial bias may be a specious argument. Perhaps the parole board's actions were influenced by factors not yet accounted for. Therefore I looked at other factors (type of offense, juvenile history, and time served in prison) that are commonly assumed to have an influence on paroles (Hayner, 1958).

Using multiple-classification analysis (MCA), I accounted for all variables considered important for parole (see Table 4). Contrary to what is commonly assumed, type of offense, juvenile history, and the amount of time served in prison had no effect on parole. The data show that parole is primarily a function of the institution of confinement and race.

Clearly, the net effect of being black decreases an inmate's chances for parole because 12 percent more whites than blacks in this sample were paroled from prison (93.8 and 81.7 percent, respectively). One could argue that black inmates are more serious offenders than white inmates because a higher percentage of blacks in the sample were in this offense category (32 percent versus 15 percent). If this is true, the 8 percent (91.4 minus 83.3) difference is an overestimate of racism. However, Table 4 also shows that type of offense has no real effect on paroles. Furthermore, except for custody level (institution), blacks and whites who are paroled are quite similar on all characteristics.

The net effect of being confined in different institutions explains from 9 to 12 percent (94.5 minus 85.1, 94.5 minus 82.6) of the difference in the paroles of all inmates reviewed by the board. The same analysis by race revealed that the adversity of being confined in custodial institutions was greater for blacks than for whites. For example, 16 to 28 percent (96.3 minus 80.3, 96.3 minus 68.3) more black inmates from the minimum-custody institutions were paroled than black inmates from the medium- and maximum-custody institutions, respectively. The corresponding percentage difference between white inmates were 2.2 and 11.6 percent (98.4 minus 96.2, 98.4 minus 86.8). Because institutional assessments have only a minor impact on

Table 5. Expected Versus Actual Proportions
Paroled by Race, Standardized for Selected
Characteristics, in Percentages

Race and Expected Versus Actual Parole Probability	Proportions Paroled
Black	
Expected	89.2
Actual	81.7
White	
Expected	93.8
Actual	93.8

Note: This table is based on 432 cases having data on parole outcome and total time in prison, excluding 10 cases serving thirty-six months in prison. Proportions are the result of applying to black inmates the same MCA equations as applied to white inmates.

paroles, this latter finding is revealing. Again, this points to the argument raised earlier that racism may coincide with the parole board's sensitivity to public opinion; that is, given that parole officials are sensitive to the public's concern about paroling high-risk inmates and this sensitivity is accompanied by racist attitudes about paroling minority group inmates, racial differences will widen as custody level increases.

To explore the difference further, I asked one final question: What proportion of black inmates could be expected to be paroled if parole decisions for blacks were made exactly the same as they were made for whites? Given the characteristics of black and white inmates, I would expect 4.6 percent (93.8 minus 89.2) more whites than blacks to be paroled (see Table 5). However, 12.1 percent (93.8 minus 81.7) more whites were paroled, indicating that more than 7.0 percent of the difference is the net effect of race (12.1 minus 4.6). This finding further supports the assertion that the discretionary power parole boards exercise results in capricious and unfair parole decisions.

Conclusion

The focus of the forgoing analysis was on the institutionalized inequities experienced by minority group inmates in the course of being processed for parole. By using a comparative framework I showed that the extent of parole disadvantage for a black inmate in this state depended partially on the particular institution where the inmate "did time." It is important to keep in mind that the adverse effects described for blacks in this chapter are modest at best. However, to find any racial differences at all during a highly favorable period for parole and in a progressive state is significant in itself.

The consistency of the findings points to a systematic bias against paroling black inmates from higher custody institutions. It is not known if whites' greater parole advantage is due only to the parole board's racial bias or to additional factors not accounted for by these data. The difference may be due to the sentencing judge's failure to sanction the paroles of blacks or to blacks having fewer employment opportunities (two factors upon which paroles are often contingent). Inmates in need of employment before release and inmates needing the sanction of the sentencing judge are given deferred paroles in this state. The reader may recall that the deferred parole category was included in the category of all inmates paroled from prison.

Because predictor variables are viewed as determinants rather than controls, these findings have important implications for correctional research. They imply a need to study the normal, routine functioning of correctional agencies rather than the interpersonal aspects of race relations within correctional environments. They indicate a need to investigate how institutional racism is distributed in a correctional system rather than assuming it is concentrated in one area or is pervasive throughout the system. From the standpoint of organizational theory, the findings also imply a need for more investigations to determine more about how parole boards use institutional assessments. The findings were mixed and inconclusive in this effort. However, where parole officials tend to follow counselor recommendations, how they act on these recommendations clearly indicates their actions increase the adverse effect on minority group inmates' parole chances.

There are many implications for correctional policy, but only one is offered here. Whether or not the disparities observed in this study were the result of discretion and racial bias, there is a need to monitor the activities of all parole boards to ensure the integrity of this process. A periodic audit focusing on the equity of processing practices should be undertaken by audit units external to the system. These auditors might be responsible to the governor of the state or to an agency designated to oversee this process.

Finally, these audits should provide more data on the causes of the parole disadvantage experienced by minority group inmates. Parole discrimination generates large costs (social and monetary) to inmates, to the community, and to state and federal governments. In the interest of reducing these costs it is imperative that state and federal agencies assume more responsibility for eliminating noncorrectional effects on parole decisions.

Part Seven

Conclusion

~~~~~~~~~~~~~~~~~~~~~~~~~~~~~~~~~~~~~~~

In this book's final chapter, Rodolfo Alvarez explores a variety of potential future directions for research in the continuing quest to develop more effective social indicators for measuring and monitoring the multiple dimensions of institutional discrimination. Chapter Eighteen is organized around the five major distributive justice issues—participation, financial rewards, organizational power, opportunity, and psychic involvments—which were analyzed in the first chapter and addressed by the empirical research presented in the other chapters in this book. Assuming the excellence of these chapters, Alvarez critiques the authors' work to identify issues that need further empirical research and conceptual sharpening so that this volume sets the stage for new applications of social indicators to the question of distributive justice within organizations.

18

Future Directions
in the Study
of Institutional
Discrimination

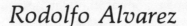

Rodolfo Alvarez

The study of institutional discrimination (its conceptualization, empirical investigation, and theoretical explication) is at the leading edge of contemporary social science. If studying institutional discrimination clarifies the processes by which given populations are excluded from participating in organizations and, if partially included, the ways reward distribution to various participant populations is affected by specifiable conditions, significant gains in the study of how general social systems actually operate will have been made. As the authors in this book amply demonstrate, we have come far in this effort to expand our knowledge, but we have yet a long road to travel. No one chapter has tackled the whole job; but each has empirically addressed one or another of the issues raised by the conceptual overview in Chapter One. Nevertheless, the social indicators employed to measure organizational elements, the statistical techniques used to analyze the data, and the theoretical perspectives used to explicate the issues in question together represent the leading edge of the state of the art in the study of institutional discrimination.

This chapter critically reviews the studies presented in this volume in order to prepare for the next round of empirical studies. I identify some aspects of the work presented that need further scholarly attention. Out of this critical review may come some directions for future research.

This chapter is organized around the five major distributive issues raised throughout this book; these are the distribution of participation, financial rewards, organizational power, opportunity, and psychic involvements. Each of the chapters has addressed two or more of these distributive issues; each issue has been addressed centrally in at least one chapter and tangentially in at least one of the other chapters. The objective in this final critical summary is to raise the kinds of questions that will stimulate these and other researchers to do further work in the construction of appropriate social indicators, data-analysis techniques, and theoretical explanations of the phenomenon addressed here as institutional discrimination. A side effect of this critical summary might be to give the practicing manager a stronger resolve to resist the temptation to abdicate responsibility to the so-called "experts" and their statistical tools. Much remains to be discovered in the attempt to understand how institutional discrimination works and how it affects the rest of the social system within which it is found. Perhaps the strongest and wisest admonition that can be given to the practicing manager is to move forward toward implementation of egalitarian inclusiveness based on justifiable principles, to move cautiously in a spirit of discovery with the constant assistance of the researcher's findings, but above all to move forward. The result of such efforts may well be the discovery of more efficient and effective ways of accomplishing organizational objectives never before thought even remotely related to institutional discrimination.

Participation

Populations' participation in organizations can be approached through analysis of their physical distribution according to four different aspects of organizational structure: vertical, horizontal, sectorial, and locational. Unless members of specified populations in question are at least minimally distributed in each of these four dimensions of organizational structure, it is highly unlikely that members of the populations in question will believe their own particular self-interests are receiving adequate representation (advocacy) in the formation and implementation of organizational policies. Thus we need better social indicators of both *representativeness* (physical distribution of populations) and *representation* (social distribution of advocacy for special perspectives). The lay wisdom among human rights and civil rights activists is that unless a particular population has representativeness as a participant within all internal dimensions of organizational structure, it is highly likely to be discriminated against in the making and carrying out of organizational policy. Even organizations whose central mission is the protection of the civil liberties and civil rights of women or minorities are suspect unless members of the population being served are participating in the organization presumably safeguarding their interests. Thus physical distribution is critical.

How is the adequacy of physical distribution to be measured? Two chapters in this volume, one by Nasatir and Fernandez, the other by Nordlie, consider measurement of physical distribution of populations. Nordlie invokes a baseline standard as his point of reference; Nasatir and Fernandez choose a comparative standard. The point of reference chosen from which to measure physical distribution as the measure of participation in the organization will affect, at least in part, the degree to which the organization appears to practice institutional discrimination. For example, if the proportion of blacks in the general population of the United States is chosen as the point of reference, then the proportion of army generals is likely to be lower to a statistically significant extent, leading to the conclusion that institutional discrimination is widespread in the army. But if the proportion of black army colonels is taken as the point of reference, then the proportion of black generals might not be viewed as evidence for institutional discrimination. Nasatir and Fernandez deal with the concept of a comparative standard by calling for a specification of the "relevant availability pools" from which candidates for particular types of organizational positions are drawn. Nordlie refers to these pools as the "eligible population." The log-linear and hierarchical models Nasatir and Fernandez use seem to handle the issue much better from the point of view of powerful statistical analyses than the simpler proportional comparisons Nordlie uses. Further, efforts to adapt these powerful statistical models for use within formal complex organizations seem to be highly indicated.

Neither the Nasatir nor the Nordlie chapters centrally addresses a question of critical relevance to the study of institutional discrimination: How do minorities and women get into the "relevant availability pools" in the first place? If there are institutional barriers to their entry into the long chain of organizational events that ultimately leads to becoming a colonel (or assistant professor in the case of universities), those facts can be obscured by focusing on the lack of statistical disparity between the proportion of black colonels who get promoted to general versus the proportion of whites promoted to that rank (or whites who achieve tenure status, and so forth). Both the chapters by Nordlie and by Nasatir and Fernandez clearly demonstrate the most basic and comprehensive approach that must be taken to provide systematic research evidence on the kinds and degrees of physical distribution of minorities and women within organizations. It well may be that responsible public policymakers will simply have to take such basic descriptions of physical distribution as *prima facie* evidence of the presence or absence of institutional discrimination and place the burden of proof to the contrary on the organization in question.

Precisely because physical distribution of specified populations is the most tangible evidence of the degree of participation by those populations in the making and implementing of organizational policies, it becomes critical to obtain sophisticated measures and descriptions of physical distribution within all dimensions of organizational structure. Four dimensions of organizational structure are listed in Chapter One: vertical, horizontal, sectorial, and locational. Social indicators for two types of measurement tasks are needed; the idea of a "comparative standard" may turn out to be essential. First, there is a need to measure physical distribution from the point of reference of comparison to a known relevant availability pool of candidates for positions *within* any one of the four dimensions of organizational structure. A variety of points of reference can be chosen from which to evaluate physical distribution within each dimension of organizational structure. A different pool will surely have to be selected to evaluate vertical distribution up the hierarchical ranks of an organization as compared to that chosen to evaluate horizontal distribution within the same rank. Different points of reference are needed to evaluate equality of distribution within the marketing department (sector) versus within the research or engineering sector; similarly, a corporation's manufacturing plant in Los Angeles will require a different point of reference than that used for the plant that manufactures the same product in Bangor, Maine. The point is that much more research is needed to arrive at some standard set of generally acceptable reference points from which to measure physical distribution of specified populations *within* each of the four major aspects of organizational structure. A second and perhaps more important measurement task presupposes solution of the first one. That is, once a solution is found to the problems of measuring equality of distribution *within* each of the four dimensions of organizational structure, there is still the problem of comparative measures of equality of distribution *between* the four dimensions of structure. Again perhaps log-linear statistical models will be useful tools. The problem is raised here in order to call attention to a major direction for the next round of research projects. Clearly, an organization may achieve an acceptable level of equity in the physical distribution of women or minorities along any one or combination of two or more dimensions of organizational structure without necessarily achieving it along all four dimensions.

Participation of specified populations (women or minorities) through their physical distribution along various dimensions of organizational structure makes it possible to raise a second major aspect of the study of inequality. *Social* distribution within organizational structure is far more complex and difficult to measure than physical distribution. The two distributional concepts are independent; even if acceptable levels of physical distribution were achieved along all four dimensions of organizational structure, it would still be possible to find evidence of institutional discrimination in the participation of women or minorities in terms of their social distribution within the organization and of the distribution of "social goods" to them by the organization. The distribution of social goods (finances, power, opportunity, and psychic rewards and punishments) will be discussed subsequently in some detail. Here the focus is on the social distribution of specified populations within organizations in the sense of the degree to which the interests of a given population receive "representation" or advocacy within the organization.

Bowser, for example, raises a new area for research by introducing the concept of "vertical segregation." He suggests the existence of a "new order" within organizations such that although blacks and other minorities are allowed into all levels of the organizational hierarchy, they are disproportionately placed in nominal roles that entail no real power in the system. It is unclear whether Bowser is referring to the classical distinction between "staff" and "line" positions or whether he refers to placement of minorities into "parallel" segregated positions without real power but that are nevertheless apparently equal to positions with real power into which whites are disproportionately placed. Bowser points out that roles must be subdivided according to three factors: responsibility, authority and decision making, and the importance (or lack of it) of the role in these domains. He also points out that each various functional division within an organization has its own lines of upward mobility. Each line has a fixed ceiling for minorities. Future research into these suggestive areas may produce new insights.

Bowser, for example, asserts that vertical segregation must be measured indirectly. That may be a critical observation calling for the development of special kinds of social indicators. Presumably, current statistics do not yield the data needed to evaluate degree of vertical segregation and discrimination. Dubeck makes a somewhat similar point in her chapter. A good deal of creative insight is needed to develop social indicators of vertical institutional discrimination, perhaps by dividing each occupational grouping into levels of functional importance. Another approach to following up on Bowser's observations is to classify organizations into various kinds of industries for comparative research on degree of discrimination in fast-growth, postindustrial industries (aerospace); the classical industrial-era industries (textiles); and declining industries (railroads).

Bowser's chapter also raises another important aspect of social distribution: the need for social indicators of the degree to which black employment in white-collar roles is "token." Tokenism can refer to either physical or social distribution. Token employment of minorities can refer to the fact that they are extremely underrepresented in a statistical sense by comparison to some relevant pool of available potential employees. But tokenism can also refer to the fact that socioeconomic-political interests of a given population receive more apparent than real treatment by the organization. The chapters by Hausner and by Schement partially address this issue in their concern with the composition of boards of directors. Beyond the physical presence of minorities or women on boards of directors, there is the question of representation. Because such boards constitute the quintessential policy-making structures of organizations, we need empirical social indicators by which to measure the degree to which policies substantively address the needs of minorities and women or provide only a superficial, token treatment. As discussed in the first chapter, a board may have minority or women members but not provide any representation of these groups' interests. The reverse is also possible: A board without any minority or women members may in fact provide very strong representation of their interests. Hausner's observations are critically important for future research on the development of social indicators of social distribution aspects of participation. For example, we need to develop ways of measuring accountability of the organization to its various constituencies: managers, workers, customers, clients, suppliers, neighbors, minorities, women, and so forth. It may not be feasible or even desirable to have *representativeness* from each constituency on the board of directors, but it may be feasible to have some measure of how each of their various interests is advocated or *represented* in policymaking and implementing. Hausner provides some important directions for future research by noting the need to examine the actions and outputs of boards and of planning agencies generally. This issue is critically raised in Schement's chapter. He asserts that primary Spanish language radio (PSLR) stations are a major source of critical information for Spanish-speaking communities and that institutionalized discrimination is likely to occur in broadcasting and programming activities unless this minority is physically represented among owners and members of boards of directors. Schement makes a number of excellent suggestions for the development of social indicators of institutional discrimination in social participation of this minority in this type of organization. For example, he suggests content analysis of PSLR news programs. The point is well taken although the case study approach he proposes is not likely to reveal the desired information. To get reliable evidence on discrimination against the interests of Spanish-speaking communities, it might be necessary to do a comparative study of programming and commercials of Anglo-owned and -managed PSLRs *versus* Anglo-owned and Spanish-surname-managed *versus* Spanish-surname-owned and Anglo-managed *versus* Spanish-surname-owned and -managed. In short, although his suggestions do not fully address the issue, Schement's suggestions point the way toward ultimately confronting directly the questions of how to create social indicators of social *representation* as well as of physical *representativeness*. Merely because a PSLR is not owned or managed by Spanish-surname persons does not necessarily mean its programming and commercials go counter to the interests of the Spanish-speaking community. Schement points out the need to develop independent social indicators of that community's needs so as to determine comparatively the empirical relationship between representativeness and representation.

Financial Distribution

Research on financial distribution within the study of institutional discrimination has been traditionally guided by some version of the "equal pay for equal work" hypothesis. When it is found that the evidence does not support the hypothesis, the usual recourse is to search for other variables from within the "human capital model" to explain or account for the differences in financial distribution to the populations in question. The human capital model refers to the differential distribution of rewards to people according to their accumulation of such human capital variables as education or job experience and other special characteristics acquired by individuals that presumably enhance their capacity to deliver a higher quantity and/or quality of performance than workers characterized by lesser amounts of human capital. A problem that arises from research done with the human capital orientation is that it appears the more technically proficient the anlaysis, the more likely the results are to demonstrate statistically significant disparity in the financial distribution between the comparison populations. Whether this is due to the lack of precise instruments (social indicators) for measurement of variables suggested by the human capital approach or because what is needed is the introduction of variables outside the human capital approach is not yet clear. The fact remains that so far most studies that take into account comparable levels of education, job experience, and job seniority for the comparison populations show the minority or female population to receive fewer financial rewards than the majority male population. The suggestions made in the first chapter is that the achievement variables the human capital approach suggest are insufficient for explanatory purposes. Perhaps sponsorship and ascribed characteristics directly relevant to the task being performed by individuals need to be introduced into the analysis simultaneously with the achieved characteristics suggested by the human capital model. This approach has the advantage of leaving open the possibility of discovering explanatory variables outside those traditionally used in the human capital approach and consistently found not to account fully for variation in the distribution of material rewards.

Moreover, such human capital indicators as job seniority are usually introduced into the analysis of wage distribution without taking into account the organizational context within which they occur. For example, some organizations deliberately maintain a very high rate of mobility from one position to another while other organizations experience very little mobility. A general measure of seniority such as that used by McDonough, Snider, and Kaufman, which does not take the organizational context into account, might be less adequate than one that does. Another social indicator McDonough, Snider, and Kaufman use is prejob experience, constructed by subtracting year of birth from year hired. Prejob experience by itself, as a characteristic of individuals rather than of the organizational structure in question, tells us very little if we are not aware (and we usually are not because hardly any data on the following questions are gathered) of qualifications such as what experience at what level of performance in what prior sequence of positions is required for promotion into the position for which wages are being compared. Much further research creativity is required to develop more refined social indicators that take into account where prejob experience was obtained and how relevant it is to the job for which hired. A great deal more effort is required on the part of researchers using the human capital model to refine their measurement instruments and their use. Not only may the crudeness of the social indicators used account for some of the lack of explanatory value, but also accounting for lack of progress is the general reluctance to move beyond traditional human capital variables related to personal achievement, on to other categories of variables such as ascribed task-relevant attributes as well as task-relevant characteristics of sponsorship. Such variables are more important in some organizational contexts than in others. Ethnicity and good relations with a community constituency may be more important to the role of police officer on the beat than to some other kinds of jobs. Such ascribed and sponsorship variables can have task relevance even in the performance of more professional roles, such as that of professor of history or of bank president. The development of social indicators for these types of variables may permit significant advances in the analysis of how financial rewards are distributed within organizations.

Power Distribution

Power is sometimes exercised in organizations without regard to the hierarchical level or the formal specifications of the position a person occupies in the organization. It is not unusual to find that one or two vice-presidents in an organization are far more powerful than others. That acquisition of power is sometimes formally awarded to a position, but in other cases the greater power of particular position incumbents is not formally assigned to their positions. To what extent women and minority persons get a proportionate share of power, a variable independent of the status of the positions of which they are incumbents, is an important element in the study of institutional discrimination.

Degree of access to organizational power by specified populations within an organization is a theme raised in Kanter's chapter. Kanter's insightful analyses of power and of the excess of it are intertwined with the more general concepts of opportunity, which will be discussed later in this chapter. Here only the issue of how power is distributed within organizations is treated. This is an extremely difficult research area because it presumes that power is a known and quantifiable variable. The very fact that Kanter is reduced to defining power as "clout" to get things done demonstrates the need for operational measures of power in the study of organizations. The first chapter of this volume presents a definition of power that may lend itself to the construction of social indicators that will permit empirical measurement of this crucial phenomenon in organizational analysis.

Among the questions researchers are asking is whether power is differentially distributed to populations within organizations on the basis of race or sex. It is frequently said that the affirmative action movement has been instrumental in creating new, perhaps redundant, roles within organizations so it is now pertinent to ask whether a position is functionally "token" or "decisional." That is, in order to achieve some degree of compliance with federal regulations for affirmative action in hiring practices, it is said that women and members of racial minorities are hired for positions at all levels of an organization but that such positions are essentially redundant inasmuch as incumbents of these positions have no power to get things done. The older lay term for this is "window dressing"; the newer is "tokenism." There is a considerable need for empirical social indicators of the kind and degree of power available to incumbents of particular types of organizational positions.

How much available power an incumbent actually uses is still another issue. To the extent that these can be converted into measurable phenomena, it will then be possible to ascertain whether women and minorities are in fact assigned disproportionately to relatively powerless positions. But such claims and counterclaims will remain a useless exercise until we have the appropriate measurement tools (social indicators) by which to determine the type and amount of power available to specific position incumbents and the degree to which they exercise it. Tools for measuring the three classical Weberian dimensions of power (coercive, utilitarian, and normative) are all but nonexistent in the organizations literature. These conceptual dimensions are invoked in theoretical analyses (Etzioni, 1961), but it is difficult to find extensive use of any measurement tools for empirically based analyses. Tools for this purpose would advance organizational analysis considerably independent of their utility for the study of institutional discrimination.

Opportunity Distribution

The study of status attainment processes within organizations can usefully be divided into two principle areas of investigation: the distribution of *actual* opportunity and the distribution of the *perception* of opportunity. These two types of distribution might very well be found to vary independently of each other; specified populations might be found to have more actual opportunity than they perceive themselves to have while others might perceive themselves to have more than is actually the case. The chapters by Kanter and by Rosenbaum advocate a conceptual approach that promises to bring the study of access to opportunity structures by women and minorities into the mainstream of organization research. One such issue is the effect of an organization's structure on behavior and attitudes toward achievement by individuals depending upon their own representativeness within the organization. Dubeck discusses this issue with perhaps greater depth than either Kanter or Rosenbaum.

Dubeck introduces the concept of "opportunity status" of women in organizations; although this concept needs considerable refinement if it is to be effectively used for research purposes, it may offer a way to start understanding the ways distribution of minorities and women in organizations impacts upon other elements of organizational structure and function. She measures and compares the proportion of women in white-collar clerical positions and the proportion in nonclerical white-collar positions. Although it is essential to do so, she does not at this initial stage differentiate between lower, middle, and upper levels of management in computing proportions. Nevertheless, the organization can thus be characterized as having a high or low opportunity status for women or minorities. That conception of the organization may itself have a reflexive impact upon other aspects of organizational functioning as much for those populations as for white males, but perhaps most importantly for the broad variety of publics with which the organization must interact in its environment: customers, suppliers, government, competitors, and the general population of organizational citizens within the business community wherein the organization must create goodwill in order to operate successfully with dignity.

Recruitment Practices

Paula Dubeck has stressed the importance for the organization of sex stereotyping in managerial recruitment. She notes
that although there is a high correlation between images of *male*
and of *manager*, there is no such relationship between images of
female and *manager*. A great deal of further research is necessary
to identify more clearly the characteristics of a good manager
and the cultural stereotypes traditionally used in managerial
recruitment. It may be that organizations have had a built-in factor causing managerial inefficiency due to cultural stereotypes
that emphasize some dominant male attributes that may in fact
"mask" the characteristics that actually make for good management.

Status Attainment Processes

Dubeck, like Kanter, points out the need for further research on both formal and informal social networks through
which people are attracted to entry positions in organizations
and through which they gain access to promotion and organizational resources. She discusses the ramifications of not belong-
ing to networks and the goods and advantages that accrue to
those who become part of the network. Network analysis should
become a major avenue of research contributing to an understanding of mobility *within* and *between* organizations.

Dubeck also calls attention to the need for research on
the relationship between criteria employed to recruit candidates
for organizational positions and the subsequent impact those
same criteria have on long-term promotion and mobility within
the organization.

The chapter by Reskin and Hargens is a model of the
kind of research that must be done to understand differences in
social mobility experiences between men and women (minority
versus white, and so forth) within particular organizations.
Rather than looking simply at the *outcome* (number of male
versus female "successful" scientists), they investigate the processes through which each of the groups achieves success. Some

of the findings this research generates indicate there are differences between the processes of accumulation of advantages by men and by women. An example is the now standard observation that the eminence of the sponsor directly affects the career of the former student; Reskin and Hargens discover that it affects women more than men. Future research should explore and specify the mechanisms by which this disparity comes about.

The chapter by Reskin and Hargens unveils two of the most perplexing difficulties currently confronting researchers on institutional discrimination: the difficulty of operationalizing what is meant by the existence of sexism/racism. First there is the conceptual problem of when the phenomenon exists. For example, simply because a women gets a tenured position at a moderately prestigious university in no way demonstrates that she was not denied a similar or even better position (or perhaps not even considered) because of her sex at any number of other more prestigious institutions. A second problem needing much further work is that of how to develop "independent" social indicators of racism/sexism. Reskin and Hargens are forced to use social indicators of discrimination, of organizational position, and of professional performance in the organizational position, which in themselves are "contaminated" or biased because they incorporate past sexist or racist practices. Using professional citations to rate the worth of a woman's scientific productivity, for example, already incorporates prior sexist practices against citation of work by women scientists. A bias against allocation of predoctoral and postdoctoral fellowships to women makes the use of such an indicator questionable in establishing the standing of women scientists by such social indicators. The point is that much research needs to be done to develop independent social indicators or at least to state explicitly that indicators used are heavily biased and may result in an exaggeration of subsequent findings.

Rosabeth Kanter and James Rosenbaum advocate a conceptual approach that promises to bring access to opportunity structures by sexual and racial populations into the mainstream of research on organizations. Kanter urges consideration of more than the simple questions of equal pay for equal work or of the equity of recruitment practices. She suggests that advancement prospects and degree of access to organizational power by particular groups of individuals within organizations be examined. She then attempts to identify the major problems and subtleties of measuring opportunity and power distributions. Her major objective is to direct sociologists to fertile areas for future research. One such issue is the effect of an organization's opportunity structure on individuals' attitudes and behavior. Kanter also addresses the idea of job ladders within organizations, contending that the amount of advancement reflected in each step within the organization can vary greatly. Thus opportunity is not simply a matter of counting the number of upward steps possible from a particular starting position; it is important to measure the "value" that step represents in terms of the organizational resources available to an incumbent of the position. Her chapter also points to the very considerable need for further research on the development and consequences of networks within organizations. Networks are critical in the study of institutional discrimination because their explication may clarify the pathways to career development and the ways some get access to power and others do not.

James Rosenbaum provides more specific, more technical research suggestions for the study of opportunity structures within organizations. He points out that most current research looks at discrimination in terms of wages and appointment to organizational levels through what has come to be called the human capital approach; this emphasizes the supply side of labor markets. Rosenbaum suggests combining this approach with one that studies the demand side of labor markets as well. Education as a personal attribute of the candidate for a position may be more important for some positions than for others; thus it becomes an essential factor or social indicator for one type of occupation but not for the analysis of another. Rosenbaum also points out that we need more research on the phenomenon of "historical carry-over effects"; that is, some women and minorities are promoted "too fast" or through inappropriate "steps," which subsequently may preclude their access to higher positions because they lack the proper organizational experience. Analysis of these contingencies is important as much for the development of organizational theory and clarity of research results as for effective long-term cultivation of managerial talent in general and for minorities and women in particular.

A point neither Kanter nor Rosenbaum raises that is related indirectly to the topics they discuss is the question of how tokenism affects not just the token individual's future in terms of potential for upward mobility or access to power and other organizational resources but also in terms of how tokenism affects the organization itself. Does tokenism really give the organization a good "public face"? Does having minorities and women in visible but noncentral or nonimportant areas of the organization negatively affect such essential organizational dimensions as the general morale of the rest of the organization and of the tokens themselves? How does it affect organizational effectiveness in society or the efficient use of resources within the organization itself? If women and minorities are brought into ever higher levels of management, will the image of what constitutes a good manager to be transformed to include cultural traits not previously considered desirable in managers? What will be the long-term consequences of such transformation of the cultural meaning of management and managers?

Psychic Reward and Punishment Distribution

The contraposition between physical representativeness and social representation discussed previously also has important implications for the distribution of psychic rewards and punishments within organizations. O'Reilly's chapter has as its principal objective the inexpensive measurement of representativeness on juries. However, implicit in O'Reilly's discussion is the idea that the degree of physical representativeness of minorities or women on a jury may very well have an impact on the jury's decisions; thus development of social indicators to measure representation may very well open up an entire new area of research. Among questions that need exploration are the psychological impact of jury composition upon various types of participants in the system: adversary parties, judge, jury, and so forth. Research on questions of this kind will surely be called for as technical measurement problems progress beyond the mere assessment of representativeness.

The chapter by Bernstein, Cardascia, and Ross does not take representativeness of the jury into account in analyzing differential sentencing for men and women. They invoke a direction of analysis that may point the way toward exploring ways culture impacts on the distribution of rewards and punishments. When the offense for which a woman is convicted is nontraditionally associated with women, the sentence is much harsher than when it is one with which women are traditionally associated. Bernstein, Cardascia, and Ross leave unattended the question of whether the differential sentencing of women and men is discriminatory on legitimate or illegitimate bases. Perhaps rather than being sexist these differentials in sentencing accurately reflect the greater likelihood of rehabilitation on the part of women; we have no evidence either way.

Judges and processing agents have a number of opinions concerning what types of individuals are "hardened" versus "nonhardened" criminals. They have to have a normative frame in order to make the decision they are called upon to make. What we investigators must do is determine if these normatively shaped opinions are credible and should be used as the basis for decisions concerning case dismissal, sentencing, parole, and even initial apprehension. Another example is the "Judge Armstrong" theory, which asserts that in crime the male is usually the dominant individual and tends to "lead" the woman into the crime. The question is whether this could in fact usually be true. The same point holds for other reasons officials give for the preferential treatment of women, such as "the family gets broken up if the mother is jailed" or "they are better subjects for probation." These points may very well be true and they might consequently be legitimate discriminatory criteria. The value of such studies as Bernstein, Cardascia, and Ross's is that in attempting to document the existence of differential treatment, they bring sociologists to these sorts of questions. Thus though the first step might be an admittedly rough one, it is truly an important one, leading to increasing conceptual sophistication in this area.

       Shirley Brown's chapter proceeds along lines parallel to that of Bernstein, Cardascia, and Ross except that she compares parole decisions for black and white offenders. Brown examines the ways secondary discrimination is exemplified in decisions that perpetuate traditional ways of treating blacks in the allocative process versus parole decisions that create new patterns of disadvantage for them. Brown also holds constant the type of offense to compare parole outcomes. In common with the chapter by Mendoza de Arce and Peraza, Brown's chapter attempts to bring into the analysis of differential outcomes both elements of culture (that is, public opinion) and organizational characteristics. Like all the chapters in Part Five, the chapters by Brown and Mendoza and Peraza reflect the need to develop social indicators of the psychic rewards and punishments experienced by some populations within organizations. Although the stimulation for the development of these indicators might be to further the study of institutional discrimination, in the long run the entire field of research on organizations is likely to benefit from this work. The study of morale and its impact upon productivity, for example, is a research area likely to be advanced by the development of social indicators for systematic research on the distribution of psychic rewards and punishments within organizations.

References

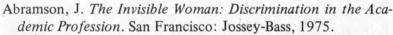

Abramson, J. *The Invisible Woman: Discrimination in the Academic Profession.* San Francisco: Jossey-Bass, 1975.

Alford, R. R., and Friedland, R. "Political Participation and Public Policy." In A. Inkeles, J. Coleman, and N. Smelser (Eds.), *Annual Review of Sociology.* Vol. 1. Palo Alto, Calif.: Annual Reviews, 1975.

Allison, P. D., and Stewart, J. A. "Productivity Differences Among Scientists: Evidence for Accumulative Advantage." *American Sociological Review,* 1974, *39,* 596–606.

Allport, G., and others. *Study of Values.* Boston: Houghton Mifflin, 1960.

Althauser, R. P., and Wigler, M. "Standardization and Component Analysis." *Sociological Methods and Research,* 1972, *1,* 97–135.

Alvarez, R. "Informal Reactions to Deviance in Simulated Work Organizations: A Laboratory Experiment." *American Sociological Review,* 1968, *33,* 895–912.

Alwin, D. F. "The Use of Factor Analysis in the Construction of Linear Composites in Social Research." *Sociological Methods and Research,* 1973, *2,* 194–214.

American Chemical Society. *Directory of Graduate Research.* Washington, D.C.: American Chemical Society, 1957.

American Chemical Society. *Directory of Graduate Research.* Washington, D.C.: American Chemical Society, 1959.

American Chemical Society. *Directory of Graduate Research.* Washington, D.C.: American Chemical Society, 1961.

395

Andrews, F. M., and others. *Multiple Classification Analysis.* Ann Arbor: Institute for Social Research, University of Michigan Press, 1973.

Angrist, S. "The Study of Sex Roles." *Journal of Social Issues,* 1969, *25,* 215–232.

Antonovsky, A. "The Social Meaning of Discrimination." *Phylon,* 1960, *21,* 81–95.

Astin, H. S. *The Woman Doctorate in America: Origins, Career, and Family.* New York: Russell Sage Foundation, 1969.

Astin, H. S., and Bayer, A. E. "Sex Discrimination in Academe." *Educational Record,* 1972, *53,* 101–118.

Axelrad, S. "Negro and White Male Institutionalized Delinquents." *American Journal of Sociology,* 1952, *47.*

Babcock, B. "Introduction: Women and the Criminal Law." *The American Criminal Law Review,* 1973, *11,* 291–308.

Bachman, J. G., Smith, C. G., and Slesinger, J. A. "Control, Performance, and Satisfaction: An Analysis of Structural and Individual Effects." *Journal of Personality and Social Psychology,* 1966, *4,* 127–136.

Baldus, D. C., and Cole, J. W. "Quantitative Proof of Intentional Discrimination." *Evaluation Quarterly,* 1977, *1,* 53–85.

Baron, H., and Hymer, B. "The Dynamics of the Dual Labor Market." In D. Gordon (Ed.), *Problems in Political Economy.* Lexington, Mass.: Heath, 1971.

Bauer, R. A. (Ed.). *Social Indicators.* Cambridge, Mass: M.I.T. Press, 1966.

Bayer, A. C., and Astin, H. S. "Sex Differentials in the Academic Reward System." *Science,* 1975, *188,* 796–802.

Bayer, A. E., and Dutton, J. E. "Career Age and Research-Professional Activities of Academic Scientists." *Journal of Higher Education,* 1977, *48,* 259–282.

Beach, W. G. *Oriental Crime in California.* Palo Alto, Calif.: Stanford University Press, 1932.

Beattie, R. H. *California Male Prisoners Released on Parole, 1946–49: A Study of the Parole Experience of this Group as of January 1, 1953.* Sacramento, Calif.: Department of Correction and Adult Authority, 1953.

Becker, G. *Human Capital.* New York: Columbia University Press, 1964.

Becker, H. S. *Outsiders*. New York: Free Press, 1963.

Bensing, R. S., and Schroeder, O., Jr. *Homicide in an Urban Community*. Springfield, Ill.: Thomas, 1962.

Bergmann, B., and King, J. "Diagnosing Discrimination." In P. A. Wallace (Ed.), *Equal Employment Opportunity and the AT&T Case*. Cambridge, Mass.: M.I.T. Press, 1976.

Berk, R., and Rossi, P. "Reforms in the Treatment of Convicted Offenders." In R. Berk and P. Rossi (Eds.), *Prison Reform and State Elites*. Cambridge, Mass.: Ballinger, 1977.

Berk, R. A., Hennessy, M., and Swan, J. "The Vagaries and Vulgarities of 'Scientific' Jury Selection." *Evaluation Quarterly*, 1977, *1*, 143–158.

Bernstein, I., Kelly, W., and Doyle, P. "Societal Reaction to Deviants: The Case of Criminal Defendants." *American Sociological Review*, 1977, *47*, 743–755.

Bernstein, I., and others. "Charge Reduction: An Intermediary Stage in the Process of Labeling Criminal Defendants." *Social Forces*, 1977, *56*, 62–84.

Bibb, R. "Blue Collar Women in Low Wage Industries: A Dual Labor Market Approach." Paper presented at 70th annual meeting of the American Sociological Association, San Francisco, 1975.

Bishop, Y. M. M., Fienberg, S., and Holland, P. *Discrete Multivariate Analysis: Theory and Practice*. Cambridge, Mass.: M.I.T. Press, 1975.

Blalock, H. M. *Causal Inferences in Nonexperimental Research*. Chapel Hill: University of North Carolina Press, 1964.

Blau, F. "Pay Differentials and Difference in the Distribution of Employment of Male and Female Office Workers." Unpublished doctoral dissertation, Harvard University, 1975a.

Blau, F. "Sex Segregation of Workers by Enterprise in Clerical Occupations." In R. Edwards and others (Eds.), *Labor Market Segmentation*. Lexington, Mass.: Heath, 1975b.

Blau, P. M., and Duncan, O. D. *The American Occupational Structure*. New York: Wiley, 1967.

Blau, P. M., and Schoenherr, R. A. *The Structure of Organizations*. New York: Basic Books, 1971.

Blauner, R. *Racial Oppression in America*. New York: Harper & Row, 1972.

Bluestone, B. "The Characteristics of Marginal Industries." In M. D. Gordon (Ed.), *Problems in Political Economy*. Lexington, Mass.: Heath, 1971.

Blumberg, A. S. *Criminal Justice*. Chicago: Quadrangle Books, 1967.

Boudon, R. "Educational Growth and Economic Equality." *Quality and Quantity*, 1974, *8*, 1–10.

Boudon, R. "Comment on Hauser's Review." *American Journal of Sociology*, 1976, *81*, 1175–1187.

Boulding, K. E. "Toward a Theory of Discrimination." In P. A. Wallace (Ed.), *Equal Employment Opportunity and the AT&T Case*. Cambridge, Mass.: M.I.T. Press, 1976.

Breiger, R., Boorman, S., and Arabic, P. "An Algorithm for Clustering Relational Data with Applications to Social Network Analysis and Comparison with Multi-Dimensional Scaling." *Journal of Mathematical Psychology*, 1975, *12*, 328–383.

Bridges, W., and Berk, R. A. "Sex, Earnings, and the Nature of Work." Unpublished paper, Department of Sociology, University of Illinois, Chicago, 1977.

Brodsky, A. (Ed.). *The Female Offender*. Beverly Hills, Calif.: Sage, 1975.

Broverman, I. K., and others. "Sex Role Stereotypes: A Current Appraisal." *Journal of Social Issues*, 1972, *28*, 59–78.

Brown, S. A. "Race as a Factor in the Intraprison Outcomes of Youthful First Offenders." Unpublished doctoral dissertation, University of Michigan, 1975.

Buckley, J. "Pay Differences Between Men and Women in the Same Job." *Monthly Labor Review*, November 1971.

Bullock, H. A. "Significance of the Racial Factor in the Length of Prison Sentences." In R. Quinney (Ed.), *Crime and Justice in Society*. Boston: Little, Brown, 1969.

Burke, P., and Turk, A. "Factors Affecting Post-Arrest Dispositions: A Model for Analysis." *Social Problems*, 1975, *22*, 313–332.

Burkhart, K. W. *Women in Prison*. New York: Doubleday, 1973.

Caballero, C. M., Giles, P., and Shaver, P. "Sex Role Traditionalism and Fear of Success." *Sex Roles*, 1975, *1*, 319–327.

Campbell, A. "Surge and Decline: A Study of Electoral Change." In A. Campbell and others (Eds.), *Elections and Political Change*. New York: Wiley, 1966.

Campbell, D. T. "Common Fate, Similarity, and Other Indices of Entities." *Behavioral Science*, 1958, *3*, 14–25.

Cassell, F. H., and others. "Discrimination Within Internal Labor Markets." *Industrial Relations*, 1975, *14*, 337–344.

Chambliss, W., and Seidman, R. *Law, Order, and Power*. Reading, Mass.: Addison-Wesley, 1971.

Carmichael, S., and Hamilton, C. *Black Power*. New York: Random House, 1967.

Clark, J., and Tifft, L. "Polygraph and Interview Validation of Self-Reported Deviant Behavior." *American Sociological Review*, 1966, *31*, 516–523.

Cohen, M. "Sex Differences in Compensation." *Journal of Human Resources*, 1971, *6*.

Cole, J. R., and Cole, S. *Social Stratification in Science*. Chicago: University of Chicago Press, 1973.

Coleman, J. C. "The Mathematical Study of Change." In H. M. Blalock and A. B. Blalock (Eds.), *Methodology in Social Research*. New York: McGraw-Hill, 1968.

Collins, R. *Conflict Sociology*. New York: Academic Press, 1975.

Council on Social Work Education. *Statistics on Social Work Education in the United States: 1975*. New York: Council on Social Work Education, 1975.

Council on Social Work Education. *Statistics on Social Work Education in the United States: 1976*. New York: Council on Social Work Education, 1976.

Davis, J. A. "Hierarchical Models for Significance Tests in Multivariate Contingency Tables: An Exegesis of Goodman's Recent Papers." In H. L. Costner (Ed.), *Sociological Methodology: 1973–1974*. San Francisco: Jossey-Bass, 1974.

Davis, K., and Moore, W. "Some Principles of Stratification." *American Sociological Review*, 1945, *10*, 242–249.

Department of Commerce. *Social Indicators*. Washington, D.C.: U.S. Government Printing Office, 1973.

Doeringer, P., and Piore, M. *Internal Labor Markets and Man-*

power Analysis. Lexington, Mass.: Heath, 1971.

Downs, A. *An Economic Theory of Democracy.* New York: Harper & Row, 1957.

Duncan, O. D. "Partitioning Polytomous Variables in Multiway Contingency Analysis." *Social Science Research*, 1975, *4*, 167–182.

Duncan, O. D. and Davis B. "An Alternative to Ecological Correlation." *American Sociological Review*, 1953, *18*, 665.

Duncan, O. D., and Duncan, B. "Residential Distribution and Occupational Stratification." *American Journal of Sociology*, 1955, *60*, 493–503.

Edwards, A. L. *Techniques of Attitude Scale Construction.* New York: Appleton-Century-Crofts, 1957.

Erikson, K. "Notes on the Sociology of Deviance." In H. Becker (Ed.), *The Other Side: Perspectives on Deviance.* New York: Free Press, 1964.

Erlanger, H. S. "Jury Research in American." *Law and Society Review*, 1970, *4*, 345–370.

Esther, S. E. "Women as Leaders in Public Education." *Signs*, 1975, *1*, 363–386.

Etzioni, A. *A Comparative Analysis of Complex Organizations.* New York: Free Press, 1961.

Farley, R. "The Residential Segregation of Social Classes, United States Urban Areas: 1970." Paper presented at annual meeting of the Population Association of America, Montreal, 1977.

Feeley, M. "Sentencing in the Lower Courts of Connecticut." Unpublished paper, 1977.

Fielder, F. E. "Style or Circumstance: The Leadership Enigma." *Psychology Today*, 1969, *2*, 38–46.

Fine, S., and Heinz, C. A. "The Functioning Occupational Classification Structure." *Personnel and Guidance Journal*, 1958, *37*, 180–192.

Finkelstein, M. O. "The Application of Statistical Decision Theory to the Jury Discrimination Cases." *Harvard Law Review*, 1966, *80*, 338–376.

Fogarty, M. P., Rapoport, R., and Rapoport, R. *Sex, Career, and Family.* London: Allen & Unwin, 1971.

Foley, L., and Rasche, C. "A Longitudinal Study of Sentencing Patterns for Female Offenders." Paper presented at the American Society of Criminology Meeting, Tuscon, Ariz., 1976.

Freedman, M. *The Process of Work Establishment*. New York: Columbia University Press, 1969.

Fuchs, V. "Differences in Hourly Earnings Between Men and Women." *Monthly Labor Review*, 1971, *94*, 9–15.

Fuchs, V. "Women's Earnings: Recent Trends and Long-Run Prospects." *Monthly Labor Review*, 1974, *97*, 23–36.

Galenson, M. *Women and Work: An International Comparison*. Ithaca: New York State School of Industrial Labor Relations, Cornell University, 1973.

Garfinkel, H. "Research Note on Inter- and Intra-Racial Homicides." *Social Forces*, 1949, *27*, 369.

Gibbs, J. "Conceptions of Deviant Behavior: The Old and the New." *Pacific Sociological Review*, 1966, *9*, 9–14.

Gibbs, J. "Issues in Defining Deviant Behavior." In R. A. Scott and J. Douglas (Eds.), *Theoretical Perspectives on Deviance*. New York: Basic Books, 1972.

Glaser, B. G. *Organizational Careers: A Sourcebook for Theory*. Chicago: Aldine, 1968.

Glaser, D. *The Effectiveness of a Prison and Parole System*. Indianapolis, Ind.: Bobbs-Merrill, 1964.

Goldberger, A. *Econometric Theory*. New York: Wiley, 1964.

Goldfarb, R. S., and Hosek, J. "Explaining Male-Female Wage Differentials for the 'Same Job.'" *Journal of Human Resources*, 1976, *9*, 98–107.

Goldman, N. *The Differential Selection of Juvenile Offenders for Court Appearance*. Washington, D.C.: National Council on Crime and Delinquency, 1963.

Goodman, L. "Ecological Regressions and Behavior of Individuals." *American Sociological Review*, 1953, *18*, 663–664.

Goodman, L. "Some Alternatives to Ecological Correlation." *American Journal of Sociology*, 1959, *64*, 610–625.

Goodman, L. "The Multivariate Analysis of Qualitative Data: Interactions Among Multiple Classifications." *Journal of the American Statistical Association*, 1970, *65*, 226–256.

Goodman, L. "Partitioning of Chi-Square, Analysis of Marginal

402   References

Contingency Tables, and Estimation of Expected Frequencies in Multidimensional Contingency Tables." *Journal of the American Statistical Association*, 1971a, *66*, 339–344.

Goodman, L. "The Analysis of Multidimensional Contingency Tables: Stepwise Procedures and Direct Estimation Methods for Building Models for Multiple Classification." *Technometrics*, 1971b, *13*, 33–61.

Goodman, L. "A Modified Multiple Regression Approach to the Analysis of Dichotomous Variables." *American Sociological Review*, 1972a, *37*, 28–46.

Goodman, L. "A General Model for the Analysis of Surveys." *American Journal of Sociology*, 1972b, *77*, 1035–1086.

Goodman, L. "The Analysis of Multidimensional Contingency Tables When Some Variables are Posterior to Others: A Modified Path Analysis Approach." *Biometrika*, 1973a, *60*, 179–192.

Goodman, L. "Causal Analysis of Data from Panel Studies and Other Kinds of Surveys." *American Journal of Sociology*, 1973b, *78*, 1135–1191.

Goodman, L. "Guided and Unguided Methods for the Selection of Models for a Set of T Multidimensional Contingency Tables." *Journal of the American Statistical Association*, 1973c, *68*, 165–175.

Gordon, N. M., Morton, T. E., and Braden, I. C. "Faculty Salaries: Is There Discrimination by Sex, Race and Discipline?" *American Economic Review*, 1974, *64*, 419–427.

Gove, W. *The Labeling of Deviance: Evaluating a Perspective*. New York: Wiley, 1975.

Granovetter, M. *Getting a Job*. Cambridge, Mass.: Harvard University Press, 1974.

Gray, A. *The Socialist Tradition from Moses to Lenin*. New York: Harper & Row, 1968.

Green, E. *Judicial Attitudes in Sentencing*. London: Macmillan, 1961.

Grinker, W. J., Cooke, D. D., and Kirsch, A. W. *Climbing the Job Ladder: A Study of Employee Advancement in Eleven Industries*. New York: E. F. Shelley, 1970.

Gross, E. "Plus Ça Change. . . ? The Sexual Structure of Occupations Over Time." *Social Problems*, 1968, *16*, 198–208.

Hagstrom, W. O., and Hargens, L. L. "Mobility Theory in the Sociology of Science." Paper presented at Cornell Conference on Human Mobility, Ithaca, N.Y., October 31, 1968.

Hannan, M. T. *Aggregation and Disaggregation in Sociology.* Lexington, Mass.: Heath, 1971.

Hanushek, E., and Jackson, J. *Statistical Methods for Social Scientists.* New York: Academic Press, 1977.

Hardt, R., and Bodine, G. *Development of Self-Report Instruments in Delinquency Research.* Syracuse, N.Y.: Syracuse University Press, 1965.

Harmon, H. H. *Modern Factor Analysis.* Chicago: University of Chicago Press, 1967.

Harris, A. "Sex and Theories of Deviance: Toward a Functional Theory of Deviant Type-Scripts." *American Sociological Review*, 1977, *42*, 3–16.

Hauser, R. M. "Review Essay: On Boudon's Model of Social Mobility." *American Journal of Sociology*, 1976, *81*, 911–928.

Hauser, R. M., and others. "Structural Change in Occupational Mobility Among Men in the United States." *American Sociological Review*, 1975, *40*, 585–598.

Hayner, N. S. "Why Do Parole Boards Lag in the Use of Predicting Scores?" *Pacific Sociological Review*, Fall 1958.

Henning, M., and Jordan, A. *The Managerial Woman.* New York: Doubleday, 1976.

Hochschild, A. "A Review of Sex Role Research." *American Journal of Sociology*, 1973, *78*, 1011–1129.

Holmes, D., and Jorgensen, B. "Do Personality and Social Psychologists Study Men More than Women?" Government Reports Announcement No. 25. Washington, D.C.: U.S. Government Printing Office, 1971.

Holt, N. Unpublished study in E. O. Wright (Ed.), *The Politics of Punishment.* New York: Harper & Row, 1971.

Hooks, J. M. "Women's Bureau Bulletin No. 218." Washington, D.C.: U.S. Government Printing Office, 1947.

Howard, J. *The Negro in the Lumber Industry.* Philadelphia: University of Pennsylvania Press, 1970.

Hughes, E. C. "Dilemmas and Contradictions of Status." *American Journal of Sociology*, 1945, *50*, 353–359.

Hughes, E. C. *The Sociological Eye*. Chicago: Aldine, 1963.

Jeffress, P. *The Negro in the Urban Transit Industry*. Philadelphia: University of Pennsylvania Press, 1970.

Johnson, J. *Black Manhattan*. New York: Atheneum, 1968.

Johnston, N., Savitz, L., and Wolfgang, M. *The Sociology of Punishment and Correction*. New York: Wiley, 1972.

Jones, J. M. *Prejudice and Racism*. Reading, Mass.: Addison-Wesley, 1972.

Jusenius, C. L. "Occupational Change, 1967–1971." In U.S. Department of Labor, *Dual Careers*. Washington, D.C.: U.S. Government Printing Office, 1975.

Kairys, D., Kadane, J. B., and Lehoczky, J. P. "Jury Representativeness: A Mandate for Multiple Source Lists." *California Law Review*, 1977, *65*, 776–827.

Kanter, R. M. "The Impact of Hierarchical Structures on the Work Behavior of Women and Men." *Social Problems*, 1976, *23*, 415–430.

Kanter, R. M. *Men and Women of the Corporation*. New York: Basic Books, 1977a.

Kanter, R. M. "Some Effects of Proportions on Group Life: Skewed Sex Ratios and Responses to Token Women." *American Journal of Sociology*, 1977b, *82*, 965–990.

Kashket, E. R., and others. "Status of Women Microbiologists." *Science*, 1974, *83*, 488–494.

Kerlinger, F., and Pedhazur, E. *Multiple Regression in Behavioral Research*. New York: Holt, Rinehart and Winston, 1973.

Kitsuse, J., and Cicourel, A. "A Note on the Uses of Official Statistics." *Social Problems*, 1963, *11*, 131–139.

Klaw, S. *The New Brahmins*. New York: Morrow, 1968.

Kohn, M. L., and Williams, R. M. "Situational Patterning in Inter-Group Relations." *American Sociological Review,* 1956, *21*, 64–74.

Kornhauser, W. *Scientists in Industry*. Berkeley: University of California Press, 1962.

Kundsin, R. B. (Ed.). *Women and Success*. New York: Morrow, 1974.

Land, K. C., and Spilerman, S. (Eds.). *Social Indicator Models*. New York: Russell Sage Foundation, 1975.

Leacock, E. (Ed.). *The Culture of Poverty*. New York: Simon & Schuster, 1971.

Leavitt, H. J. "Some Effects of Certain Communication Patterns on Group Performance." *Journal of Abnormal and Social Psychology*, 1951, *46*, 38–50.

Liska, A. E. "Emergent Issues in the Attitude-Behavior Consistency Controversies." *American Sociological Review*, 1974, *39*, 261–272.

Lockheed, M. "Female Motive to Avoid Success: A Psychological Barrier or a Response to Deviancy?" *Sex Roles*, 1975, *1*, 41–50.

Lombroso, C. *The Female Offender*. New York: Philosophical Library, 1893.

Long, J. E. "Employment Discrimination in the Federal Sector." *Journal of Human Resources*, 1976, *11*, 86–97.

Long, J. S. "Productivity and Academic Position in the Scientific Career." *American Sociological Review*, 1978, *43*, 889–908.

Lyle, J. R., and Ross, J. L. *Women in Industry: Employment Patterns of Women in Corporate America*. Lexington, Mass.: Lexington Books, 1973.

McFarland, D. "Putting Goal-Oriented Actors into Harrison White's Vacancy Chains." Paper presented at the 71st annual meeting of the American Sociological Association, 1976.

McNulty, D. "Differences in Pay Between Men and Women Workers." *Monthly Labor Review*, 1967, *90*.

Malkiel, B. G., and Malkiel, J. A. "Male-Female Pay Differentials in Professional Employment." *American Economic Review*, 1973, *63*, 693–705.

Martin, R. *The Defendant and Criminal Justice*. University of Texas Bulletin No. 3437. Austin: Bureau of Research in the Social Sciences, University of Texas, 1934.

Mendoza de Arce, D. "Positive Science, Analytical Reason, and the Human World." *Sociological Analysis and Theory*, 1975, *5*.

Mennerick, L. "Organizational Structure of Sex Roles in a Non-Stereotyped Industry." *Administrative Science Quarterly*, 1975, *20*, 570–586.

Merton, R. "Priorities in Scientific Discovery." *American Sociological Review*, 1957a, *22*, 639–659.

Merton, R. "Science and Democratic Social Structure." In R. Merton, *Social Theory and Social Structure*. New York: Free Press, 1957b.

Merton, R. "Insiders and Outsiders." *American Journal of Sociology*, 1972, *78*, 9–47.

Miller, S. M., and Rissman, F. "The Working Class Subculture: A New View." *Social Problems*, 1961, *9*, 86–97.

Mitchell, T., and others. "The Contingency Model: Criticism and Suggestions." *Academy of Management Journal*, September 1970.

Mitford, J. "Kind and Usual Punishment in California." *The Atlantic Monthly*, 1971, *227*, 45–52.

Moses, J., and Boehm, V. "Relationship of Assessment Center Performance to Management Progress of Women." *Journal of Applied Psychology*, 1975, *60*, 527–529.

Myrdal, G. *An American Dilemma*. New York: Harper & Row, 1944.

Nagel, S. *The Legal Process from a Behavioral Perspective*. Homewood, Ill.: Dorsey Press, 1969.

Nagel, S., and Weitzman, L. "Women as Litigants." *Hastings Law Journal*, 1971, *23*, 171–198.

Nagel, S., and Weitzman, L. "Double Standard of American Justice." *Society*, 1972, *9*, 18–25.

National Institute of Law Enforcement and Criminal Justice. *A Guide to Juror Usage*. Washington, D.C.: U.S. Government Printing Office, 1974.

Newman, D. J. *Conviction: The Determination of Guilt or Innocence Without Trial*. Boston: Little, Brown, 1966.

Nordlie, P. G., and Carroll, R. M. "Differences in Speed of Promotion of Blacks and Whites with Education and AFQT Score as Control Variables." *Research Problem Review* (Army Research Institute), December 1976, pp. 76–114.

Nordlie, P. G., and Thomas, J. A. *Measuring Changes in Institutional Racial Discrimination in the Army*. Technical Paper No. 270. Arlington, Va.: Army Research Institute for the Behavioral and Social Sciences, 1975.

Northrup, H. and others. *The Negro in the Air Transport Industry*. Philadelphia: University of Pennsylvania Press, 1971.

Oaxaca, R. "Male-Female Wage Differentials in the Telephone
Industry." In P. A. Wallace (Ed.), *Equal Employment Opportunity and the A.T.&.T. Case*. Cambridge, Mass.: M.I.T. Press,
1976.

Ohlin, L. E. *Selection for Parole*. New York: Russell Sage Foundation, 1951.

Ohlin, L. E. *Sociology and the Field of Corrections*. New York:
Russell Sage Foundation, 1956.

Oppenheimer, V. K. "The Sex-Labeling of Jobs." *Industrial Relations*, 1968, *7*, 219–234.

Oppenheimer, V. K. *The Female Labor Force in the United
States: Population Monograph Series, No. 5*. Berkeley: University of California Press, 1970.

Oppenheimer, V. K. "Demographic Influence on Female Employment and the Status of Women." *American Journal of
Sociology*, 1973, *78*, 946–961.

Oster, S. "Industry Differences in Discrimination Against Wom-
en." *Quarterly Review of Economics*, 1975, *89*, 215–229.

Patterson, M. "Some Limitations of Traditional Research on the
Benefits of Higher Education: The Case of Women." In L.
Solomon and P. Taubman (Eds.), *Does College Matter?* New
York: Academic Press, 1973.

Perrow, C. *Organizational Analysis*. Monterey, Calif: Brooks/
Cole, 1970.

Piatek, E. S. "Program Analysis Memorandum, No. 28," Nov.
24, 1971. RMP Service, Department of Health, Education,
and Welfare, 1971.

President's Commission on Law Enforcement and the Administration of Justice. *The Challenge of Crime in a Free Society*.
Washington, D.C.: U.S. Government Printing Office, 1967.

Quinney, R. *The Social Reality of Crime*. Boston: Little, Brown,
1970.

Quinney, R. "The Social Reality of Crime." In A. S. Blumberg
(Ed.), *Current Perspectives of Criminal Behavior*. New York:
Knopf, 1974.

Rasche, C. "The Female Offender as an Object of Criminal Research." In A. Brodsky (Ed.), *The Female Offender*. Beverly Hills, Calif.: Sage, 1975.

Reckless, W. C., and Ray, B. A. *The Female Offender*. Consultants' report presented to the President's Commission on Law Enforcement and Administration of Justice, 1967.

Reskin, B. F. "Sex Differences in the Professional Life Chances of Chemists." Unpublished doctoral dissertation, University of Washington, 1973.

Reskin, B. F. "Sex Differences in Status Attainment in Science: The Case of The Post Doctoral Fellowship." *American Sociological Review*, 1976, *41*, 597–612.

Reskin, B. F. "Scientific Productivity and the Reward Structure of Science." *American Sociological Review*, 1977, *42*, 491–504.

Risher, H. *The Negro in the Railroad Industry*. Philadelphia: University of Pennsylvania Press, 1970.

Robinson, W. S. "Ecological Correlations and the Behavior of Individuals." *American Sociological Review*, 1950, *5*, 351–357.

Roe, A. "Women in Science." *Personnel and Guidance Journal*, 1966, *44*, 784–787.

Rokeach, M. *The Nature of Human Values*. New York: Free Press, 1974.

Rosen, B., and Jerdee, T. H. "Influence of Sex Role Stereotypes on Personnel Decisions." *Journal of Applied Psychology*, 1974, *59*, 9–14.

Rosenbaum, J. E. *Making Inequality*. New York: Wiley, 1976a.

Rosenbaum, J. E. "Organizational Selection and Employee Careers." Proposal to Manpower Administration, Department of Labor, 1976b.

Rosenbaum, J. E. "Employees' Adaptations to Opportunity." Mimeograph, Department of Sociology, Yale University, 1977.

Rosenbaum, J. E. "Tournament Mobility: Career Patterns in a Corporation." Paper presented at the 73rd annual meeting of the American Sociology Association, San Francisco, August 1978a.

Rosenbaum, J. E. "Organizational Career Mobility: Promotion

Chances in a Corporation During Periods of Growth and Contraction." Unpublished paper, 1978b.

Rosenberg, M., and Bergstrom, L. *Women and Society*. Beverly Hills, Calif.: Sage, 1975.

Rosett, A., and Crassey, D. *Justice by Consent*. Philadelphia: Lippincott, 1976.

Rowan, R. *The Negro in the Textile Industry*. Philadelphia: University of Pennsylvania Press, 1970.

Rubington, E., and Weinberg, M. *Deviance: The Interactionist Perspective*. New York: Macmillan, 1973.

Ryan, W. *Blaming the Victim*. New York: Vintage Books, 1972.

Sanborn, H. "Pay Differences Between Women and Men." *Industrial and Labor Relations Review*, 1964, *17*, 534–550.

Sarri, R. C."Organizational Patterns and Client Perspectives in Juvenile Correctional Institutions." Unpublished doctoral dissertation, University of Michigan, 1962.

Schein, V. E. "The Relationship Between Sex Role Stereotypes and Requisite Management Characteristics." *Journal of Applied Psychology*, 1973, *57*, 95–100.

Schein, V. E. "Relationships Between Sex Role Stereotypes and Requisite Management Characteristics Among Female Managers." *Journal of Applied Psychology*, 1975, *60*, 340–344.

Schinnar, A. P., and Stewman, S. "A Non-Stationary Opportunity Model for Organizational Careers." Paper presented at the 71st annual meeting of the American Sociological Association, New York, 1976.

Schur, E. *Labeling Deviant Behavior*. New York: Harper & Row, 1971.

Schwartz, E. *The Sex Barrier in Business*. Atlanta: Georgia State University, Publishing Services Division, 1971.

Simmons, J. W. "Changing Residence in the City." *Geographical Review*, 1968, *58*, 623–652.

Simon, R. J. *The Contemporary Woman and Crime*. Rockville, Md.: National Institute of Mental Health, 1975a.

Simon, R. *Women and Crime*. Lexington, Mass.: Lexington Books, 1975b.

Singer, L. R. "Women and the Correctional Process." *American Criminal Law Review*, 1973, *11*, 295–308.

Smith, J., Turk, H., and Myers, H. P. "Understanding Local Political Behavior: The Role of the Older Citizen." *Law and Contemporary Problems*, 1962, *27*, 280–298.

Sørensen, A. B. "The Structure of Intragenerational Mobility." *American Sociological Review*, 1975, *40*, 456–471.

Specht, D. A., and Warren, R. D. "Comparing Causal Models." In D. R. Heise (Ed.), *Sociological Methodology 1975*. San Francisco: Jossey-Bass, 1974.

Spilerman, S. *Careers, Labor Market Structure, and Socioeconomic Achievement*. Madison, Wisc.: Institute for Research on Poverty, 1977.

Stephan, C. "Selective Characteristics of Jurors and Litigants: Their Influences on Juries." In R. J. Simon (Ed.), *The Jury System in America: A Critical Overview*. Beverly Hills, Calif.: Sage, 1975.

Stevenson, M. "Relative Wages and Sex Segregation by Occupation." In C. Lloyd (Ed.), *Sex Discrimination and the Division of Labor*. New York: Columbia University Press, 1975.

Stevenson, M. "Internal Labor Markets and the Employment of Women in Complex Organizations." Unpublished paper, Center for Research on Women, Wellesley College, 1977.

Stewman, S. "Two Markov Models of Open System Occupational Mobility: Underlying Conceptualizations and Empirical Tests." *American Sociological Review*, 1975, *40*, 298–321.

Strauss, A. *Mirrors and Masks*. New York: Free Press, 1959.

Street, D., Vintner, R., and Perrow, C. *Organizations for Treatment*. New York: Free Press, 1966.

Swigert, V., and Farrell, R. "Normal Homicides and the Law." *American Sociological Review*, 1977, *42*, 16–32.

Taeuber, K., and Taeuber, A. *Negroes in Cities: Residential Segregation and Neighborhood Change*. Chicago: Aldine, 1965.

Tannenbaum, A. S., and others. *Hierarchy in Organizations: An International Comparison*. San Francisco: Jossey-Bass, 1974.

Temin, C. "Discriminatory Sentencing of Women Offenders: The Argument for ERA in a Nutshell." *The American Criminal Law Review*, 1973, *11*, 355–372.

Thompson, J. D., and McEwen, W. J. "Organizational Goals and Environment: Goal Setting as an Interaction Process." *American Sociological Review*, 1958, *23*, 23–31.

Thurow, L. C. "Education and Economic Equality." *Public Interest*, 1972, *28*, 66–81.

Thurow, L. C. *Generating Inequality: Mechanisms of Distribution in the U.S. Economy*. New York: Basic Books, 1975.

Tittle, C. "Prisons and Rehabilitation: The Inevitability of Disfavor." *Social Problems*, 1974, *21*, 385–395.

Tittle, C. "Labeling and Crime: An Empirical Evaluation." In W. R. Gove (Ed.), *The Labeling of Deviance*. New York: Halsted Press, 1975.

Treiman, D. J., and Terrell, K. "Women, Work, and Wages—Trends in the Female Occupational Structure Since 1940." In K. Land and S. Spilerman (Eds.), *Social Indicator Models*. New York: Russell Sage Foundation, 1975.

Turk, A. *Criminality and the Legal Order*. Chicago: Rand McNally, 1969.

Turner, R. "Sponsored and Contest Mobility and the School System." *American Sociological Review*, 1960, *25*, 855–867.

U.S. Army. Army Regulations No. 600–21, "Race Relations and Equal Opportunity." September 1, 1973.

U.S. Army. Army Affirmative Actions Plan. Washington, D.C.: Office of the Secretary, June 24, 1975.

U.S. Bureau of the Census. *Alphabetical Index of Occupations and Industries*. Washington, D.C.: U.S. Government Printing Office, 1970a.

U.S. Bureau of the Census. *1970 Census User's Guide*. Washington, D.C.: U.S. Government Printing Office, 1970b.

U.S. Bureau of the Census. *Census of Population: 1970 Occupation by Industry*. Final Report PC (2)–7c. Washington, D.C.: U.S. Government Printing Office, 1972a.

U.S. Bureau of the Census. *Enterprise Statistics, 1967. Vol. 1: General Report on Industrial Organization*. Washington, D.C.: U.S. Government Printing Office, 1972b.

U.S. Bureau of the Census. *Census of the Population: 1970, Subject Reports*. Final Report, Occupational Characteristics. Washington, D.C.: U.S. Government Printing Office, 1973a.

U.S. Bureau of the Census. *Current Population Reports*. P–20, No. 293. "Voting and Registration in the Election of November 1974." Washington, D.C.: U.S. Government Printing Office, 1976a.

U.S. Bureau of the Census. *Data User News*. Vol. 11. Washington, D.C.: U.S. Government Printing Office, 1976b.

U.S. Congress, House. Subcommittee Report No. 3. of the 1972 Committee on the Judiciary Prisons, Prison Reform, and Prisoners' Rights. Michigan 92nd Congress, 2nd Session, 1972.

U.S. Department of Commerce, Census Bureau. *Census of Population: General Social and Economic Characteristics for Texas*. PC (1)–C45. Washington, D.C.: U.S. Government Printing Office, 1970.

U.S. President's Council of Economic Advisors. *Economic Report of the President*. Washington, D.C.: U.S. Government Printing Office, 1973.

U.S. Riot Commission. *Report of the National Advisory Commission on Civil Disorders*. New York: Bantam Books, 1968.

Van Alstyne, C., Withers, J., and Elliott, S. "Affirmative Inaction: The Bottom Line Tells the Tale." *Challenge*, 1977, *9*, 39–41, 60.

Van Dyke, J. M. *Jury Selection Procedures*. Cambridge, Mass.: Ballinger, 1977.

Van Valey, T. L., Roof, W. C., and Wilcox, J. E. "Trends in Residential Segregation: 1960–1970." *American Journal of Sociology*, 1977, *82*, 826–844.

Vanneman, R. "The Occupational Composition of American Classes." *American Journal of Sociology*, 1977, *82*, 783–807.

Vetter, B. M. "Women in the Natural Sciences." *Signs*, 1976, *1*, 713–720.

Wade, R. *Slavery in the Cities*. New York: Oxford University Press, 1964.

Wallace, P. A. (Ed.). *Equal Employment Opportunity and the AT&T Case*. Cambridge, Mass.: M.I.T. Press, 1976.

Ward, D., Jackson, M., and Ward, E. "Crimes of Violence by Women." In D. J. Muhuilhill (Ed.), *Crimes of Violence*. Washington, D.C.: National Commission on the Causes and Prevention of Violence, 1969.

Warner, S., Wellman, D., and Weitzman, L. "The Hero, the Sambo, and the Operator: Reflections on Characterizations of the Oppressed." Paper presented at the 66th annual meeting of the American Sociological Association, 1971.

Weeks, A. *Youthful Offenders at Highfields*. Ann Arbor: University of Michigan Press, 1958.

Weisbrod, B., and Karpoff, P. "Monetary Returns to College Education, Student Ability, and College Quality." *Review of Economics and Statistics*, 1968, *5*, 491–497.

Weisstein, N. "Adventures of a Woman in Science." *Federation Proceedings*, 1976, *35*, 2226–2231.

Westhues, R. "Class and Organization as Paradigms in Social Science." *American Sociologist*, 1976, *11*, 38–49.

Wheeler, S., and Hughes, H. "Agents of Delinquency Control: A Comparative Analysis." In S. Wheeler (Ed.), *Controlling Delinquents*. New York: Wiley, 1968.

White, H. C. *Chains of Opportunity: System Models of Mobility in Organization*. Cambridge, Mass.: Harvard University Press, 1970.

White, H., and Boorman, S. "Social Structure from Multiple Network I." *American Journal of Sociology*, 1976, *81*, 730–780.

Wilensky, H. L. *The Welfare State and Equality*. Berkeley: University of California Press, 1975.

Williams, G. "Trends in Occupational Differentiation by Sex." *Sociology of Work and Occupations*, 1976, *3*.

Willie, C. "Perspectives on Black Education and the Education of Blacks." In L. Solomon and P. Taubman (Eds.), *Does College Matter?* New York: Academic Press, 1973.

Wilson, W. J. *Power, Racism, and Privilege*. New York: Free Press, 1973.

Wise, D. "Academic Achievement and Job Performance." *American Economic Review*, 1975, *65*, 350–366.

Wolf, M., and Reidel, M. "Rape, Judicial Discretion and the Death Penalty." *Annals of the American Academy of Political and Social Science*, 1973, *407*, 119–133.

Wolfgang, M. *Crime and Race*. New York: Institute of Human Relations Press, 1964.

Wolfgang, M., and Cohen, B. *Crime and Race: Conceptions and Misconceptions*. New York: Institute of Human Relations Press, 1970.

Wright, E. O. *The Politics of Punishment*. New York: Harper & Row, 1973.

Wright, E. O. "Class Boundaries in Advanced Capitalist Societies." *New Left Review*, 1976, *98*, 3–41.

Wright, E. O., and Perrone, L. "Marxist Class Categories and Income Inequality." *American Sociological Review*, 1977, *42*, 32–55.

Yinger, J. M. "Social Discrimination." In D. Sills (Ed.), *International Encyclopedia of the Social Sciences*. New York: Macmillan, 1968.

Zeisel, H., deGrazia, J., and Freidman, L. *A Criminal Justice System Under Stress*. New York: Vera Institute of Justice, 1975.

Zuckerman, H. "Stratification in American Science." *Sociological Inquiry*, 1970, *40*, 235–257.

Zuckerman, H., and Cole, J. R. "Women in American Science." *Minerva*, 1975, *13*, 82–102.

Index

415